The Shaping of Modern America: 1877–1920

SECOND EDITION

Vincent P. DeSantis
General Editor

The Shaping of Modern America: 1877–1920

SECOND EDITION

Vincent P. DeSantis
University of Notre Dame

Forum Press, Inc.
Arlington Heights, Illinois 60004

Library of Congress Cataloging-in-Publication Data

De Santis, Vincent P.
    The shaping of modern America, 1877-1920.

    (Forum's American history series)
    Bibliography: p.
    Includes index.
    1. United States—History—1865-1921. I. Title.
II. Series.
E661.D35   1988   973.8   88-30971
ISBN 0-88273-136-X

Cover illustration: Chicago Historical Society. Detail from a chromolithograph, "Interior Views of a Modern First Class Pork Packing & Canning Establishment," 1880. ICHi-04064.

Manufactured in the United States of America
92 91 90 89 88 EB 1 2 3 4 5 6

For my sons
Vincent, Jr.,
Edmund,
Philip,
and John

Contents

Preface
to the Second Edition

Americans in the years between the Civil War and the First World War lived in a nation quite different from that of their parents. It became a nation where traditional ideas of democracy were modified by the values of a new industrial and urban society. The most important change was the rise of industrial capitalism and the burgeoning of corporations that controlled nationwide industries. But American life was fundamentally altered by other far-reaching developments: the passing of the physical frontier with the settlement of the last American West, the eclipsing of countryside and farm by city and factory, the tremendous urban growth with its accompanying problems, the substantial changes in communications and transportation through the telephone and the construction of the transcontinental railroads, the revolutionary innovations in agriculture, the new blood added to American life by a large influx of immigrants, the rise of large scale labor unions, and the emergence of the United States as a world power and its participation in affairs in the Western Hemisphere, Europe, and the Far East. These developments gave these years their dramatic character. They also established the foundations of modern America.

This new edition of *The Shaping of Modern America, 1877–1920*, while retaining the strengths and the essential character of the original, has been improved and expanded by additional material that reflects the evolving concerns of the historical profession and the interests of the students who will be reading this book. This second edition contains additional discussion of women and blacks, of the New South, and of the new political history of the end of the nineteenth century. Readers will find major additions in the chapters on the American entry into World War I, on the United States during the First World War, and on Wilson at the Paris Peace Conference and the defeat of the Versailles Peace Treaty. They will also find a new discussion of the American Peace Movement during the First World War era. And they will discover that all the bibliographies at the end of all the chapters have been updated, and that numerous changes have been made throughout the book.

A volume like this obviously rests upon the research and writings of many historians. Thus my greatest debt is to the large body of historians whose works I have drawn upon, and I have listed a number of them in the books for further reading. I am also indebted to friends, colleagues, and students.

However, I am responsible for the facts and interpretations used and for the errors made. And I shall be grateful to those readers who write to me about them at the Department of History, University of Notre Dame.

Vincent P. DeSantis
Notre Dame, Indiana

1

The Rise of Industrial America

In the post–Civil War generation there occurred in the United States a series of notable economic changes that resulted in what is commonly called the American Industrial Revolution. The most important feature of this phenomenon was a rapid and vast economic expansion. Between 1860 and 1900 the total railroad mileage increased from 30,000 to 193,000. Capital invested in manufacturing rose from $1 billion to almost $10 billion. The number of industrial workers grew from 1,300,000 to 5,300,000. The value of the annual industrial product mounted from less than $2 billion to more than $13 billion. By the end of the nineteenth century the United States was the leading industrial, as well as the richest, nation on earth. As Michael G. Mulhall, an eminent statistician, declared in 1895, the United States "possesses by far the greatest productive power in the world," and "this power has more than trebled since 1860."

This tremendous industrial growth not only made the United States materially the most powerful country in the world, but transformed it from a rural and agrarian nation into an urban and industrial one. By 1890 the value of this country's manufactured goods exceeded that of its agricultural products; ten years later manufactured products were worth twice as much as agricultural products. Americans now lived in a world far different from that of the pre–Civil War days. Big business had come to dominate the nation's economic life. The pre–Civil War factory and plant—where the relationship between owners and workers was close, where the workshop was small and the market was local, where ownership was controlled by an individual or a partnership—gave way to large impersonal corporations. Control over the country's hitherto scattered banking institutions now became concentrated in four or five financial centers. And east of the Mississippi River large, sprawling cities sprang up around industrial centers. Into these centers swarmed millions of immigrants from Europe, who were to alter the ethnic composition of the nation.

For more than a half-century prior to the Civil War, the forces responsible for the rapid postwar expansion of American industry had been developing. In the 1850s railroads revolutionized transportation, while at about the same time certain inventions transformed both industry and agriculture. The sewing machine paved the way for the ready-made clothing industry, and other machines did the same for the boot and shoe industry. The Hoe press changed the newspaper business. The reaper and other agricultural innovations not only introduced significant new methods of farming, but also enabled the North to meet the food demands of its military forces and yet have a surplus of wheat for shipment to Europe. By the time of the Civil War, Colt revolvers were the best in the world; vulcanized rubber was a commonplace; American iron manufacturers had experimented with the Bessemer process; and Boston was the world's leading boot and shoe center.

It has been customary to credit the Civil War with a major role in bringing about the Industrial Revolution. The war supposedly gave a powerful impetus to manufacturing in the North. But recent research shows that the Civil War may have retarded American industrial development, because growth rates slowed during the conflict. Statistics show that between 1839 and 1889 total output of commodities, including agricultural, increased elevenfold, or at an average rate per decade of slightly less than 50 percent. But growth rates varied widely from decade to decade. High growth rates occurred during the decades ending with 1854 and 1884; but a low growth rate occurred during the decade ending with 1869. Value added by manufacturing rose 157 percent from 1839 to 1849; 76 percent from 1849 to 1859; but only 25 percent from 1859 to 1869.

Nevertheless, the government did give strong encouragement to business entrepreneurs during the Civil War. The Republican party, seeking the businessmen's votes in the 1860 campaign, promised them favorable legislation. Once in power the Republicans carried out their pledges through tariff, railway, banking, and immigration legislation that created conditions suitable for industrial capitalism.

Just two days before Lincoln took office, President Buchanan signed the Morrill Tariff Act, marking the first increase in the tariff since 1842. Further increases pushed the average ad valorem duty up to 47 percent by 1864, the highest rate thus far in American history. The principal reason for the increases was the need for revenue, but they also protected American industry from foreign competition. Industrialists managed to keep the high tariff in effect after the war, although the federal government had much less need for the high revenue.

In the summer of 1862, President Lincoln signed the first of the bills for governmental assistance in building a transcontinental railroad. With the South out of the Union, there was no longer much controversy over the location of the route. The Union Pacific was to build westward from Nebraska, while the Central Pacific would build eastward from California. Each company was to receive public land on both sides of the track and a loan of federal money for each mile completed. There was little construction during the war, but the work went forward rapidly after 1865, and the two lines met at Promontory Point near Ogden, Utah, on 10 May 1869. With the railroads now spanning the continent, there was a national system of transportation.

By the National Currency Act of 1863 and the National Bank Act of 1864, Congress established the National Banking System, a measure also desired by some businessmen. Since the Jacksonian era, the regulation of the banking system had been left to the states, with chaotic results. At the time of the Civil War there were about 1,600 state banks, of which 1,500 were issuing circulating notes, many worth less than their par value. These banks were chartered under the laws of twenty-nine different states; they operated under varying privileges and restrictions; and their circulation was based on securities of diverse qualities and quantities. In addition there were independent banks, free banks, banks organized under general laws, and banks with special charters. This situation, combined with the circulation of all kinds of counterfeit notes, seriously handicapped the transaction of business.

A national banking system was a great improvement over the old state systems. Under the new law any banking association capitalized above a certain minimum ($50,000 for cities of less than 6,000 inhabitants, $100,000 for cities of from 6,000 to 50,000, and $200,000 for larger cities) could apply for a national charter of incorporation. The law required such banks to contribute at least one-third of their capital to the purchase of war bonds. In return the United States Treasury gave them national bank notes to the value of 90 percent of their bond holdings. The immediate aim of this legislation was to stimulate the sale of war bonds, but it served also to create a measure of financial stability.

Of further assistance to some business interests was the Contract Labor Law of 1864, which allowed the importation of labor under contracts similar to those which in the colonial period had brought so many indentured servants to America. The law permitted immigrant workers to enter into an agreement with prospective employers whereby they pledged a full year's wages to pay the expenses of their passage to the United States.

The new industrialism lost none of the momentum it had gathered during the war, and actually developed even more rapidly and extensively in the post–Civil War generation. A number of reasons account for this. The United States possessed bountiful raw materials and the government was willing to turn them over to industry for little or no money. The home market was steadily expanding as a result of immigration and a high birthrate. There was also an abundance of both capital and labor. The increase in trade and manufacturing in the Northeast in the years before the war had produced an accumulation of savings, while additional millions of dollars came from European investors. Unbroken waves of European immigration provided American industry with workers as well as customers. From 1860 to 1900 about 14 million immigrants came to the United States. Most of them settled in cities and became industrial workers and consumers.

An essential factor in the growth of industrialism was the continuation of the government's friendly attitude toward business. Protective tariffs, beginning with the Morrill Tariff, and expanded by the McKinley Tariff of 1890, the Wilson-Gorman Tariff of 1894, and the Dingley Tariff of 1897, allowed American manufacturers to charge high prices without fear of foreign competition. The National Banking System and the conservative financial policies pursued by the Treasury Department resulted in a currency deflation that benefited creditors at the expense of debtors. Additional favors to businessmen came in the form of grants of land and natural resources.

Equally helpful to the development of business was governmental inertia. There were no sweeping investigations of business practices, no legislation to protect workers and consumers, and no effective regulatory commissions or laws. Businessmen knew they could do virtually whatever they wished with impunity. This policy was consistent with the idea prevalent in post–Civil War America that government, beyond protecting property rights and maintaining law and order, should not meddle with the economic and social life of the country. American businessmen professed to believe in the laissez-faire economic theory set forth by Adam Smith in 1776 in his *Wealth of Nations.* The laissez-faire principle meant noninterference by government, either to regulate or foster, in the fields of commerce, industry, business, and labor. In practice, however, businessmen welcomed governmental intervention—high tariffs, land grants, and so forth—when such interference benefited them.

Just as tariffs and a hands-off attitude were beneficial to business, so also was the protection given by the Supreme Court in its interpretation of the Fourteenth Amendment. This amendment, added to the Constitution in 1868, was presumably designed to safeguard the newly emancipated blacks. But the original intent disappeared, and it became instead a refuge for private enterprise. The amendment declares in its first section that "No state shall make or enforce any law which shall abridge the privileges or immunities of citizens of the United States; nor shall any state deprive any person of life, liberty, or property, without due process of law." In the Slaughterhouse cases of 1873 the Supreme Court upheld a Louisiana law that granted a monopoly of the slaughterhouse business in New Orleans to one corporation on the ground that it was a legitimate exercise of the police powers of a state to protect its citizens. In *Munn* v. *Illinois,* 1877, the Court approved an Illinois law that fixed maximum storage rates for grain elevators on the ground that a state could regulate "a business that is public in nature though privately owned and managed."

These decisions so alarmed American businessmen that some predicted the end of private property. Others believed that a constitutional amendment was needed to protect business against state regulation. Then a change occurred in the makeup of the Court with the appointment of more conservative justices. The end of the depression years of the mid-eighties quieted radical demands, and a series of decisions, beginning with *Santa Clara County* v. *Southern Pacific Railroad* in 1886 and culminating with *Smyth* v. *Ames* in 1898, made the Fourteenth Amendment into something quite new. In these cases the Court greatly broadened the scope of the Fourteenth Amendment by holding that the word *person* in its first section included corporations as well as people. The Court widened the application of the "due process" clause, which had originally been intended only to prohibit confiscation of property or other arbitrary violations of individual rights. The new application invalidated any regulation that would prohibit a corporation from making a "reasonable" profit on its investment. The Court held that the courts, and not the states, should decide how much profit was reasonable. With these last cases the Fourteenth Amendment had been practically rewritten. Businessmen who denounced the rule laid down in *Munn* v. *Illinois* found protection in these later decisions. Lower courts handed down injunctions that tied the hands of regulatory commissions, and the Supreme Court became the bulwark of laissez faire.

It is impossible to conceive of the new industrialism without the tremendous expansion of the railroads. In fact, the railroads played such a dominant role that the period could well be called the railroad era. Between 1831 and 1861, a network of 30,000 miles of railroad connected the Atlantic seaboard with the Mississippi Valley. The war checked construction, but between 1867 and 1873 about 30,000 miles of railroad were added, and a record breaking 73,000 were added during the 1880s. In 1900 the American railroad system, reaching into every section of the country, measured 193,000 miles. This system represented 40 percent of the world's railroad mileage and was more than the mileage of all European countries combined. Railroad building increased more rapidly than the population. In 1865 there was one mile of track in operation for every 1,150 Americans; twenty years later there was one mile for every 450. Capital invested in railroads jumped in this period from $2 billion to nearly $10 billion.

After the war most of the short lines were consolidated into a few large systems. Cornelius Vanderbilt, who had already made a fortune in steamboats, led the way. Before his death in 1877 he had extended the New York Central Railroad to give through service between New York and Chicago with improved accommodations and reduced rates. The New York Central's chief competitor for the traffic between the East and the Middle West was the Pennsylvania Railroad, which under J. Edgar Thompson, Thomas A. Scott, and G. B. Roberts became the leading railroad and one of the foremost business enterprises in the country. At the end of the nineteenth century the Pennsylvania had lines tapping all major middle Atlantic and north central industrial centers. The Erie Railroad was a competitor for much of this traffic, but it suffered in the 1860s and 1870s in the hands of three of the most disreputable railroad manipulators of the era, Daniel Drew, Jay Gould, and Jim Fisk. Through bribery, chicanery, and fraud, they made the Erie synonymous with all the vices of the Industrial Revolution. Consolidation enabled the Baltimore and Ohio to push into the Middle West, and the New York, New Haven, and Hartford to fan into New England. By 1900 railroad consolidation had reached such vast proportions that more than two-thirds of the railroad mileage of the country was controlled by groups led by Cornelius Vanderbilt, James J. Hill, E. H. Harriman, Jay Gould, John D. Rockefeller, and J. Pierpont Morgan.

Along with expansion in railroads went improvements in service. Steel replaced iron in the construction of tracks as well as for the larger locomotives and the framework of freight and passenger cars. Inventions like the Westinghouse air brake, the automatic coupler, and the block and signal system increased safety and reduced the number of railroad accidents. The adoption of the standard-gauge track all over the country allowed the rolling stock of railroads to travel over each other's lines. The Pullman sleeping car, the dining car, and improved lighting added to the comfort and safety of travel.

More spectacular and more important than the railroad building that took place during these years in the older sections of the country was the construction of the transcontinentals authorized by Congress in 1862. As we shall see, they played an essential role in the opening up of the last frontier, and they also had an important role in the development of industrial America. No one has described their part better than Professor Thomas C. Cochran when he writes that they "really blazed the trail of American industry in the Gilded Age." They gave the nation its heroes as well as its villains. "These were the governments within governments, the owners of executives, legislators, and judges, the leviers of taxes, the arbiters of the destiny of cities, counties, industries, and farms. . . . in an age of corruption they knew best how to use their opportunities; that in a country of tremendous distances they were gaining a monopoly of long-haul transportation; that in regions where wealth was mainly land they were cornering the best of it." They "spent millions in Washington, state capitals, county seats, and city halls to get land grants, loans, and subsidies, and then spent millions more to maintain their land grants inviolate. The Union Pacific, for instance, between 1866 and 1872, handed out $400,000 in graft; the Central Pacific, as late as the decade between 1875 and 1885 distributed $500,000 annually."

The foregoing circumstances were not wholly responsible for the American Industrial Revolution. It required the superb talent found among those Americans who mobilized the nation's productive energies to build the railroads and factories. The new industrialists were ambitious, resourceful, and extremely able. At times they were ruthless and dishonest, but probably no more so than many other Americans of their day. They displayed the vigor, cleverness, and strength of will that have characterized the great entrepreneurs of all epochs of capitalistic expansion. They lived at a time when the highest goal was to acquire wealth, and one's position in society was determined by the amount amassed. In their day they were known as captains of industry and praised for the economic growth of modern America. But in time they were described, in many quarters, as robber barons who exploited the working class and exacted tribute from the public.

Few industrialists were guided by the morality and ethics that had seemed to prevail in business before the Civil War. To eliminate competitors and get around legal and political obstacles, the new industrialists did not hesitate to use trickery, bribery, and corruption. They brushed aside complaints about their methods with the "public-be-damned" attitude. Henry O. Havemeyer boasted that he did not know enough about ethics to apply them to business. Cornelius Vanderbilt exclaimed, "Law, what do I care about law? H'aint I got the power?" J. P. Morgan told a reporter that he "owed the public nothing."

The industrialists came mostly from lower- or middle-class families. The majority of them were native white and of Anglo-Saxon and New England descent. They had little or no formal education. Many had only bookkeeping training and experience. Usually they were Protestants, strict denominationalists, and outwardly pious. Scarcely any indulged in high living. Nearly all confessed to a strong craving for riches, a fact that should not set them apart from other Americans.

A number of the new industrialists were of military age during the Civil War, yet all but a handful took advantage of a law that allowed them to hire a substitute or to pay a certain amount of money in lieu of military service. Writing from Pittsburgh in 1863 Thomas Mellon, the founder of the aluminum fortune, declared that "such opportunities for making money had never existed before in all my former experience." When his son, James, asked permission to enlist, the elder Mellon wrote, "Don't do it. It is only greenhorns who enlist. Those who are able to pay for substitutes do so, and no discredit attaches." Then he added, "It is not so much the danger as disease and idleness and vicious habits. . . . I had hoped my boy was going to make a smart, intelligent businessman and was not such a goose to be seduced from his duty by the declamations of buncombed speeches."

Simon Cameron, Lincoln's first secretary of war, handed out military procurement contracts left and right and asked only for production in return. Frauds and large fortunes resulted from shoddy contracts and shady deals. Vanderbilt supplied the government with leaky ships. J. P. Morgan, who was twenty-four years old in 1861, furnished arms. Purchasing 5,000 discarded carbines for virtually nothing, he later sold them back to the army for $112,000. Both Morgan's and Vanderbilt's deals were exposed, but both went unpunished. Jim Fisk went South during the war to smuggle out cotton and sell it in the North at a considerable profit. Jay Gould's inside information enabled him to cash in on railroad deals and on speculation in gold. And so it went during the war years.

Invaluable to the rise of the new industrial order was the philosophy of Social Darwinism. Herbert Spencer, a leading English disciple of Charles Darwin, applied Darwin's law of evolution to social and economic life. Spencer held that evolution was leading inevitably to a society in which man would enjoy "the greatest perfection and the most complete happiness," and that competitive struggle was the means by which this millennium would come to pass. In this unremitting strife the weak fell by the wayside, and the strong pushed forward. Any governmental attempt to alter this situation impeded progress.

The Darwinian theory was attractive since it seemed to prove that those who survived were the fittest. This complacent assumption, translated into economic and social terms, seemed to give capitalism the backing of "science." Spencer's teachings were in great vogue in the United States from 1870 to 1890, and his theories considerably helped the new industrialism. John D. Rockefeller told his Sunday school class, "The growth of a large business is merely the survival of the fittest. . . . This is not an evil tendency in business. It is merely the working-out of a law of nature and a law of God." Andrew Carnegie exclaimed when he first read Spencer, "I remember that light came as in a flood and all was clear. Not only had I got rid of theology and the supernatural, but I had found the truth of evolution."

According to Spencerians the American economy was governed by a natural aristocracy that had risen to the top through a struggle for profits that rewarded the strong and eliminated the weak. The country could be served best by the economic independence of this natural aristocracy. The new doctrine crippled reform movements by justifying poverty and slums. Poverty and slums were natural for the unfit who had not survived the economic struggle; and any governmental effort to relieve poverty amounted to a perversion of the natural law, for as Spencer declared, "there shall not be a forcible burdening of the superior for the support of the inferior."

But philanthropy also played a part in the behavior of the businessmen. They were expected to be charitable. The businessman who failed to give did so by design and not by accident. Yet he was caught between the humanitarian sentiments and the status strivings of American society. On the one hand he was expected to relieve distress in whatever form it appeared; on the other, he was forbidden to do anything that might undermine self-reliance, initiative, and ambition.

Before the Civil War American business was highly competitive and consisted of small units—mostly individual enterprises or partnerships. After the war, however, businessmen sought ways to check increasing competition, which they had come to regard as inefficient, wasteful, and threatening to their profits. They thus established trade agreements, associations, and pools to limit competition. But none of these devices proved reliable or effective since they depended upon voluntary cooperation and were not enforceable in the courts. The answer seemed to lie in the formation of industrial trusts, which provided businessmen with more efficient control over the policies of all members within a single industry.

Under the trust system the stock of several competing companies was placed under the control of a group of trustees in exchange for trustee certificates. Ownership remained with the original companies, but management was consolidated into a single board of directors. John D. Rockefeller was by far the most important figure in this movement, and the formation of the Standard Oil Trust in 1879 established the trust pattern in the United States.

Rockefeller was a young merchant in Cleveland, Ohio, when he decided to enter the oil industry during the Civil War. In the industry he found violence, lawlessness, and waste; and, being no exponent of such free enterprise, he took steps to end this competitive spirit. Rockefeller adopted the most efficient methods of production, regularly saved a part of his profits, and surrounded himself with some of the ablest men in the industry. By 1867 he was the largest refiner of oil in Cleveland; in 1870 he organized the Standard Oil Company of Ohio with a capitalization of $1 million and eliminated his Ohio competitors. He then proceeded to take on the refiners in New York, Pittsburgh, and Philadelphia. Those who accepted Rockefeller's terms shared in the large profits, but those who continued to resist him were attacked with every weapon in cutthroat competitive warfare. He usually crushed his competitors with ruthless price cutting, but he also had an immense competitive advantage in the preferential treatment that he received through rebates from the railroads. By 1879, when the first trust was formed, Rockefeller controlled about 90 percent of America's refining industry.

Of all the trusts that appeared in the eighties and nineties, none aroused more alarm or pointed up more moral issues than Standard Oil. "I ascribe the success of the Standard Oil Company to its consistent policy of making the volume of its business large enough through the merit and cheapness of its products," declared Rockefeller. Senator James K. Jones of Arkansas offered another explanation on the floor of the United States Senate in 1889. "The iniquities of the Standard Oil Company have been enumerated and recounted until some of them are familiar to everyone," said Senator Jones, "and the colossal fortunes which have grown from it, which in all their vastness do not represent one dollar of honest toil or one trace of benefit to mankind, nor any addition to the product of human labor, are known everywhere." The controversy has continued to the present day. Some writers see in the rise of Standard Oil a dark record of unfair trade practices, railroad favors, bribery, and blackmail and an alliance between the corporation and politics in which legislators, officials, and judges closed their eyes to practices that violated the law. Others have argued that Standard Oil straightened out a disorderly industry and, by introducing efficiency and competency, lowered prices and created a great modern business enterprise. Both sides, however, agree that Standard Oil's methods frequently were ruthless and that they would not be tolerated today.

Rockefeller had a way of being ahead of the law most of the time, and William Vanderbilt, testifying about the leaders of Standard Oil before a congressional committee in 1879, expressed an opinion held widely in the country about the men of Standard Oil. "Yes, they are very shrewd men. I don't believe that by any legislative enactment or anything else, through any of the States or all of the States, you can keep such men down. You can't do it! They will be on top all the time. You see if they are not." Nevertheless, in 1892 the Ohio Supreme Court ordered the dissolution of the Standard Trust on the grounds it was designed to "establish a virtual monopoly," and was "contrary to the policy of our state." But this decision did not bring about the desired results, because the Standard Oil trustees, although they returned the stock to the stockholders, continued to manage the member concerns as "liquidating trustees" until they were forced by the court to abandon this strategy in 1897.

Prior to this, in 1889, New Jersey had changed its corporation laws in such a way to make legal the formation of a holding company —a company that owned a majority of the stock in a number of subsidiary corporations and was established for the purpose of maintaining unified control. In 1899 the various subsidiaries of Standard Oil were legally combined through the creation of a giant holding company, the Standard Oil Company of New Jersey, capitalized at $110 million (as compared to the first Standard Oil Company in Ohio at a capitalization of $1 million), and Standard Oil's control over the refining business was as complete as ever. In 1911, the United States Supreme Court held that Standard Oil had violated the Sherman Antitrust Act, but this decision, like earlier ones in the state courts, had little effect upon the management of Standard Oil's affairs.

Just as Rockefeller had cornered the refining market, so Andrew Carnegie captured much of the steel market from his rivals, although he never achieved a monopoly. He had made money in a variety of ways in the fifties and sixties and was already a millionaire when he turned to steel production in the early seventies. Like Rockefeller, Carnegie received rebates from the railroads and was also materially aided by the depression of the seventies. As he said about it afterward, "so many of my friends needed money, that they begged me to repay them. I did so and bought out five or six of them. That was what gave me my leading interest in this steel business."

From then on, Carnegie led the field in the steel industry. He bought out and took into his business Henry Clay Frick, who in the seventies had gained control of most of the coke ovens around Pittsburgh. Together they created a great vertical combine of coal fields, coke ovens, limestone deposits, iron mines, ore ships, and railroads. In 1892, when the Carnegie Steel Company was formed at a capitalization of $25 million, the Carnegie group controlled all their sources of supply, and it was soon making one-fourth of all unfinished steel in the United States. Between 1875 and 1900 the Carnegie Company made profits totaling $133 million; in 1900 alone the profits of the company were $40 million. At the turn of the century it became a New Jersey corporation with a capitalization of $160 million.

Carnegie was essentially an industrial capitalist in that he acquired his money from industry and not from bankers. He put a large part of his profits back into his business and did not allow his corporation's stock to be sold to persons outside his organization. Thus he eluded financiers and was free from the demands of stockholders. He was successful because of his efficient business methods and driving energy and because of his skill in choosing partners of almost equal ability, such as Frick and Charles Schwab. Like most of the corporation leaders of this era, his labor policy was one of long hours, low wages, and hostility to trade unions. He was a daring man in business, ready to discard equipment when better came along, and he made his improvements in times of depression so that when prosperity returned he was ready to produce. Carnegie was a skeptic and something of an intellectual. He had many friends in the political and literary world and contributed pieces to serious magazines. He advocated that great holders of wealth should distribute it, and after he retired he contributed large sums to founding public libraries, improving education, and promoting world peace.

After Standard Oil Company set the trust pattern in 1879 other business enterprises of this form soon appeared. Before long most Americans were referring to all large corporations as trusts, a word that soon became loosely synonymous in the public mind with monopoly. Many important industries ceased to be competitive and in addition to steel, oil, and railroads similar combinations were built by equally forceful and ambitious entrepreneurs in other fields. The McCormick Harvester Company of Chicago secured almost a monopoly of mechanical farm equipment. James B. Duke's American Tobacco Company established in 1890 and Henry O. Havemeyer's American Sugar Refining Company founded in 1891 gained almost complete monopolies in their industries, while Philip D. Armour and Gustavus Swift dominated the meat-packing business. Other consumer goods controlled by trusts were salt, whisky, matches, crackers, wire, and nails. Eventually, prosecution by states or the passage of state legislation declaring trusts illegal put an end to this type of organization. Although the original form of trust disappeared the term *trust* continued in use and was applied to any type of monopoly. Many of the former trusts organized themselves into pools under the friendly incorporation laws of New Jersey. Others became actual corporate combinations formed by mergers of separate industrial firms. New combinations were slowed down by the depression of 1893–1897, but after these years combinations, especially in the form of holding companies, increased at an extraordinary rate.

As the American people watched the proliferation of trusts and millionaires, many became convinced that something had to be done to restore effective competition. There arose a popular outcry against monopolies and by the eighties a movement against them was under way as public speakers and writers began to condemn them. In 1881 Henry Demarest Lloyd attacked the Standard Oil Trust in "The Story of a Great Monopoly" that appeared in the *Atlantic Monthly,* and similar articles against big business soon were being published. Edward Bellamy in his novel, *Looking Backward* (1887), assailed the economic conditions of the time and pictured a socialist Utopian state of the future where the necessities and luxuries of life would be produced through a cooperative society for the benefit of all. William W. Cook, an eminent corporation lawyer from New York, made a very sharp attack on monopolies in a volume on *Trusts* (1888) when he wrote:

It is currently reported and believed that the "Trust" monopolies have drawn within their grasp not only kerosene oil and cotton-seed oil, but sugar, oatmeal, starch, white corn meal, straw paper,...whisky, rubber, steel,... wrought iron, pipes, iron nuts, stoves, lead, copper, envelopes, paper bags, paving pitch, cordage, coke, reaping and binding and mowing machines, plows, glass, and water works. And the list is growing day by day. Millions of dollars, in cash or property, are being drawn into the vortex.

During the eighties a number of states passed laws prohibiting trusts and other forms of combinations, but these failed to check the development of industrial concentration. Some trusts appeared to be more powerful than the states that attempted to regulate them, and when one device for creating monopoly ran afoul of the law, businessmen and their lawyers simply used another technique. Such legislation was also ineffective so long as states like New Jersey, Delaware, and West Virginia placed few restrictions on the issuance of corporation charters and modified their laws to permit holding companies.

These frustrations aroused the opponents of monopoly to demand federal action. Between 1874 and 1885 more than thirty measures were introduced in the House of Representatives providing for the regulation of interstate railroads. Some of them were passed only to fail in the Senate. Finally, under pressure from easterners as well as westerners the Senate yielded and appointed the Cullom Committee to investigate the matter. In 1886 this committee made its report, concluding, "It is the deliberate judgment of the Committee that upon no public question are the people so nearly unanimous as upon the proposition that Congress should undertake in some way the regulation of interstate Commerce." This recommendation, together with the Wabash decision of 1886 forbidding the states to continue their regulation of interstate railroads, led to the Interstate Commerce Act of 1887.

The Interstate Commerce Act provided that all railway rates should be "reasonable and just." It prohibited such discriminatory practices as rebates and drawbacks and made illegal some of the long- and short-haul abuses. It forbade pooling agreements and required that all rates and fares be printed and publicly posted. The act established a five-man federal Interstate Commerce Commission (ICC), with power to investigate the railroads and to require reports from them. The commission could hear complaints regarding alleged violations of the law, but it had to depend upon the federal courts to enforce its rulings; thus the commission did not really receive the powers necessary to regulate adequately the transportation system. Furthermore, the commissioners were virtually required by the act to be inexperienced in railway practices; as a result they had difficulty in fully understanding and acting upon the complaints of the shippers. The chief weakness of the law, however, was its vagueness. What, for example, were "reasonable and just" rates? Such grave defects in the act were recognized even by such a staunch opponent of federal regulation as Senator Nelson W. Aldrich of Rhode Island, who described the new law as a "delusion and a sham, an empty menace to great interests, made to answer the clamor of the ignorant and unreasoning."

The commission soon discovered that it could not compel witnesses to testify, and that appeals to the courts produced endless delays. Even in those cases that reached the Supreme Court, the decisions generally favored the railroads over the commission. Between 1887 and 1905 the Court heard sixteen cases appealed by the ICC, and in fifteen it upheld the railroads.

When the states proved unable to curb the industrial trusts it was clear that the federal government would have to step in. In 1890 Congress passed the Sherman Antitrust Act by an almost unanimous vote. Introduced by Senator John Sherman of Ohio, this act was written mainly by Senators George F. Edmunds of Vermont and George F. Hoar of Massachusetts. It declared that "every contract, combination in the form of trust or otherwise, or conspiracy in restraint of trade or commerce" was illegal. Again, however, Congress left it to the federal courts to determine the meaning of the terms and phrases of the law, and the law could not be enforced without the cooperation of the attorney general. Consequently, it was not vigorously enforced. Between 1890 and 1901 the Justice Department instituted only 18 antitrust suits; and the Supreme Court, in *United States* v. *E. C. Knight Co.* (1895), vitiated the law by holding that manufacturing, being an activity wholly intrastate in character even though ultimately affecting interstate commerce, was not subject to federal regulation. This narrow definition of the scope of the commerce clause in the Constitution put trusts beyond effective federal control, at least until President Theodore Roosevelt reactivated the Sherman Act and the Supreme Court changed its mind on the applicability of the Sherman Act to manufacturing corporations.

During the 1890s industrial capitalism began to give away to finance capitalism as the influence of investment bankers substantially increased in the development of American industry. The industrial capitalists like Rockefeller and Carnegie were producers who had come up with their own industries. The finance capitalists such as J. P. Morgan and August Belmont were owners who had come to power not because they were skilled industrial organizers, but because they controlled enormous sums of capital by means of which they could virtually purchase control of an industry. Thus influence of the bankers resulted from their control of the investment market. A corporation in need of capital would ask a banking house to sell the industry's securities, and in turn the investment banker insisted that he have a share in the management of the concerns in which his customers had invested their money. Hard-pressed industrialists could not refuse such a request and gradually the bankers began to assume supervisory powers over corporation management. By the turn of the century a number of corporations had passed from the control of industrialists to that of bankers.

The leading American finance capitalist was J. P. Morgan, who was also the dominant figure in the entire national economy, but other important banking houses were August Belmont and Kuhn, Loeb of New York, and Lee, Higginson and Kidder, Peabody of Boston. Morgan worked to bring about order and stability in one industry after another, and he wanted to make sure that dividends would be paid regularly to stockholders, so that they would continue to purchase securities and thus contribute to further economic expansion. He opposed the idea of competition because he felt it would lead to cutthroat price cutting which would be bad for business. Instead he favored the plan of having corporations make agreements with each other about prices and markets. Morgan's policies, while giving more protection to stockholders, also often resulted in higher prices for consumers.

Probably the biggest of Morgan's promotions was his launching of the United States Steel Corporation in 1901. He bought out the Carnegie Steel Corporation (Carnegie received close to $250,000,000 for his personal holdings) and combined it with ten other steel companies into one vast corporation capitalized at the then unprecedented figure of $1,018,000,000 plus a bonded debt of $303,450,000. The Bureau of Corporations later estimated that the total value of the combined assets of all the merged companies was only $676 million, so that there was nearly 50 percent "water" in the company's stock plus the bonded indebtedness and the sum of $75 million which Morgan received for his services. In this symbolic sale of Carnegie to Morgan an old era of industrial capitalism came to a close and was replaced by finance capitalism.

Finance capitalism brought even greater economic consolidation. In 1893 there were twelve great companies with an aggregate capital of about $1 billion. By 1904, there were 318 industrial combinations—one of them being Morgan's United States Steel Corporation—with an aggregate capital in excess of $7.25 billion. Together these 318 companies controlled more than 5,000 separate plants.

The most important result of the Industrial Revolution was the making of modern technological America. But the Industrial Revolution created a number of problems for Americans in the twentieth century. A major one was a lack of social control over businessmen. Ruthless economic warfare, destruction of competition, and monopolistic control resulted. In a number of basic industries by 1900 it was difficult for new enterprises to enter the field. Even more serious was the rise of finance capitalism. Large bankers began to buy up railroads and industries and to organize financial combinations. This innovation further shifted control over American economic life to a very few men.

Then, too, under the impact of an expanding industrialism many cities grew too fast. Millions of Americans, especially women and children, lived in misery and squalor and were ruthlessly exploited. Additional social problems associated with old age, unemployment, illness, industrial accidents, and the like emerged. All this was a high price to pay for unrestrained industry and unregulated capitalism, and even for rapid growth to economic power and greatness.

Further Reading

Bruchey, Stuart. *The Growth of the Modern Economy.* 1975.
Cawelti, J. G. *Apostles of the Self-Made Man: Changing Concepts of Success in America.* 1965.
Chandler, Alfred D. *The Visible Hand: The Managerial Revolution in American Business.* 1977.
Cochran, Thomas C. *The Railroad Leaders.* 1953.
Cochran, Thomas C., and William Miller. *The Age of Enterprise.* 1942, 1968.
Diamond, Sigmund, ed. *The Nation Transformed: The Creation of Industrial Society.* 1963.
Fels, Rendig. *American Business Cycles, 1865–1897.* 1959.
Fine, Sidney. *Laissez-Faire and the General Welfare State: A Study of Conflict in American Thought, 1865–1901.* 1956.
Fogel, Robert. *Railroads and American Economic Growth.* 1964.
Hays, Samuel P. *The Response to Industrialism, 1885–1914.* 1957.
Hofstadter, Richard. *Social Darwinism in American Thought.* Rev. ed., 1959.
Josephson, Matthew. *The Robber Barons.* 1934.
Kirkland, Edward C. *Dream and Thought in the Business Community. 1860–1900.*
_____. *Industry Comes of Age.* 1961.
Kolko, Gabriel. *Railroads and Regulation, 1877–1916.* 1965.
Livesay, Harold. *Andrew Carnegie and the Rise of Big Business.* 1975.
Morison, Elting E. *From Know-How to Nowhere: The Development of American Technology.* 1974.
Nevins, Allan. *John D. Rockefeller.* 2 vols., 1953.
Porter, Glenn. *The Rise of Big Business, 1860–1910.* 1973.
Sinclair, Andrew. *Corsair: The Life of J. Pierpont Morgan.* 1981.
Stover, John F. *The Life and Decline of the American Railroad.* 1970.
Taylor, G. R., and I. D. Neu. *The American Railroad Network, 1861–1890.* 1956.
Temin, Peter. *Iron and Steel in Nineteenth Century America: An Economic Inquiry.* 1964.
Wall, Joseph F. *Andrew Carnegie.* 1970.
Wells, David A. *Recent Economic Changes.* 1889.
Williamson, Harold F., and Arnold R. Daum. *The American Petroleum Industry.* 2 vols., 1959–1963.
Wyllie, Irwin G. *The Self-Made Man in America.* 1964.

2

The Last West and the New South

At the same time industrial expansion was transforming post–Civil War America, another event of momentous consequence was occurring: the settlement of the western half of the country. It was a migratory movement probably unparalleled in the history of the world. In a single generation Americans established more than a million farms on this last frontier. They settled more new land than earlier Americans had settled in two and a half centuries.

Americans had always been accustomed to an advancing frontier. By the end of the Civil War, one American frontier was pushing westward beyond a line running roughly north and south through central Texas and parts of Kansas and Nebraska. Another frontier on the Pacific Coast, created in part by the gold rush to California, was moving eastward toward the Rocky Mountains. Between these two frontiers lay a stretch of fifteen hundred miles uninhabited except for the Indian population, the Spanish settlements in New Mexico, and the Mormon colony in Utah, which had been settled in 1847 around the Great Salt Lake. By 1890, however, the director of the census reported that the country's "unsettled area had been so broken into by isolated bodies of settlements that there can hardly be said to be a frontier line." Between 1864 and 1896 ten new states had been carved out of the western country. The end of the frontier, which from the days of the very first colonial settlement had played such a vital role in American history, was now in sight. From 1607 to 1870, Americans had occupied an area of 407 million acres and had put 89 million of them under cultivation. In the last three decades of the nineteenth century they occupied an area of 430 million acres and brought 225 million of them under cultivation.

Many forces contributed toward the settlement of the West during the decades following the Civil War. A favorable land policy, the extension of the railroad network, an attempted solution of the Indian problem, the discovery of gold in the Black Hills of the Dakotas, and the cattle boom on the Great Plains were among the most important. The thousands of settlers who came had little capital and few household possessions, so that their new homes contained few of the simple comforts of life. With a scarcity of timber, they lived in dugouts or sod houses. They suffered from Indian attacks, prairie fires, blizzards, insects, and droughts. Even after they organized communities and built better homes, they faced the depredations of railroads, financiers, and mortgage companies. The population was heterogeneous, coming as it did from different countries, speaking numerous languages, and worshiping God in a variety of ways.

The opportunities for obtaining cheap or free land induced many a settler to go west. He could buy a farm outright from the national government under the terms of the Preemption Act of 1841, which allowed him to obtain a quarter section or 160 acres at the nominal price of $1.25 an acre. Or he could purchase his quarter section from one of the land-grant railroads or from any one of the states whose holdings of public domain were greatly increased by the passage of the Morrill Act of 1862. (This Act had given every state establishing a public agricultural college 30,000 acres for each senator and representative then in Congress.) Finally, the western settler could secure his quarter section free of charge under the Homestead Act of 1862. This law made it possible for any American citizen, or any alien who had declared his intention of becoming a citizen, to acquire 160 acres of unoccupied government land by living on it or by cultivating it for five years. If the homesteader wished to gain ownership sooner, he could, after six months of residence, buy his quarter section at the prevailing minimum price, usually $1.25 an acre, though the residence requirement went up to fourteen months in 1891.

The Homestead Act has been called "the greatest democratic measure of all history," but its critics pointed out that under its terms the government bet a man a stake of 160 acres that "he couldn't live on it for five years without starving to death." The law had a number of faults. It was not adaptable to the area to which it applied. The best farm lands east of the one hundredth meridian (the line approximately bisecting the Dakotas and Nebraska east and west) was largely taken by 1862, and the law applied chiefly to the region from the Great Plains to the Pacific, where small homesteads were inadequate. Moreover, the Homestead Act did not end land speculation. In fact, larger purchases than ever were made by individuals. For example, William S. Chapman bought one million acres in California and Nevada, while Francis Palms and Frederick E. Driggs together procured 486,000 acres of timberland in Michigan and Wisconsin. There was also fraudulent administration of the law. False claims were made; claims were turned over to speculators and to land, mining, and timber companies; and perjury and bribery of land officials were common. In practice the act was a perversion of land reform ideas. The land-grant railroads received four times more land than the homesteaders; and when the homesteaders did get land, it was usually of poor quality and far removed from railroad facilities.

A generous Congress passed other measures during this period to dispose of the public domain. The Timber Culture Act of 1873 provided free grants of 160 acres in certain regions on condition that the settler plant forty acres (later reduced to ten acres) in trees and keep them growing for ten years. Under the terms of the Desert Act of 1877 the government offered semiarid lands in 640 acre tracts to those who would irrigate them. But since irrigation projects usually required more capital than most settlers had, the law primarily benefited large-scale grazing companies. The Timber and Stone Act of 1878 permitted the sale of quarter sections of land not suited for agriculture but valuable for timber, and large corporations and speculators managed to get possession of more than 13 million acres of such government lands.

The completion of the transcontinental railroads was another important element in the settlement of the West. When the Civil War checked expansion, a railroad network connected the Atlantic seaboard and the Mississippi Valley. With the return of peace the time seemed right for further railroad construction. Through a policy of generous subsidies the federal government helped to stimulate this railroad boom. In 1862 Congress chartered the Union Pacific and the Central Pacific Railroads. The Union Pacific was to build a line from Omaha, Nebraska, to the eastern boundary of California; the Central Pacific, across California to meet the Union Pacific. Each company, after the completion of the first forty miles of track, was eligible to receive from the government, for each mile of track laid, ten alternate sections of free land, checkerboard fashion, along the right of way. Each road would also receive in government bonds a loan of $16,000 per mile over level areas, $32,000 per mile over hilly country, and $48,000 per mile in mountainous regions. Although these terms seemed generous, the work progressed so slowly that in 1863 Congress modified the original terms. The government now doubled the land grants, took a second mortgage for the loans it had made, and allowed the railroads to obtain private loans on first mortgage bonds up to the amount of the government loans. At first the eastern boundary of California was to be the boundary between the two lines, but eventually they were permitted to build until they met each other. In 1869, when they met near Ogden, Utah, the Union Pacific had laid 1,086 miles of track, and the Central Pacific 689. Altogether, the two railroads received 54 million acres of land and loans amounting to about $60 million. In addition to government loans, the Union Pacific issued 1,000,000 shares of stock at $100 a share.

The Union Pacific was built chiefly by Irish "paddies" and Civil War veterans; the Central Pacific was constructed mainly by Chinese coolies in their basket hats, pigtails, blue blouses, and flapping pantaloons. Indian hostility forced much of the work to be done under protection of armed scouts. The *Overland Monthly* for May 1869 presents a colorful picture of the building of railroads in the Far West:

All the vigor, vice, and lawlessness of border life characterized the railroad population, but it was made subservient to one of the grandest instruments of refined civilization. The woods of the Sierra and Rocky Mountains rang with the strokes of axemen and the click of steel in the quarries. The streams were bordered with camps of lumbermen and checked with floating logs. . .Lumber, iron, and material of every description lined the road, and the wake of advancing workmen was marked by odd debris of deserted camps.

Unfortunately, the building of both roads was accompanied by much unsavory profiteering. The railroad builders used the device of a dummy construction company owned by the same persons who possessed the charters for the railroads. A large portion of the Union Pacific, for example, was built by the Crédit Mobilier, a Pennsylvania corporation organized in 1867. It was owned chiefly by the officials of the Union Pacific, who awarded themselves construction contracts at high prices. A congressional committee in 1888 estimated that the Union Pacific actually cost $50 million; but by the time the Crédit Mobilier had completed its work, the costs approximated $94 million. The Crocker Company, builder of the Central Pacific, amassed a profit of $64 million on an investment of $121 million. Most of this profit went to the four leading officials of the Central Pacific—Leland Stanford, Collis P. Huntington, Charles Crocker, and Mark Hopkins, each of whom left a fortune of $40 million or more at his death.

Finally, in May 1869 the Union Pacific engine "No. 119" touched heads with the Central Pacific's "Jupiter" at Promontory Point five miles east of Ogden, Utah. The two locomotives "kissed amid a shower of champagne"; crowds in other parts of the country listened to the news sent by telegraph; the last spike—one of gold—was driven into a laurel tie. A great engineering feat affecting the entire country had been accomplished.

While individual initiative and enterprise played a large part in the building of America's great railroad empire, it is doubtful whether American railroads would have become so highly developed had it not been for the generosity of the federal, state, and local governments. Between 1850 and 1871, the railroads received from the federal government alone more than 130 million acres of land—an area as large as the New England states, Pennsylvania, and New York combined—and from the states about 49 million additional acres of land. It is nearly impossible to assess the value of this land, but a conservative estimate (based on $2 an acre) would place the value at $360 million. Some estimates have been as high as $2.5 billion.

Because they failed to meet all the conditions under which this land was granted, the railroads were able to retain only about 116 million acres. Even so, at the end of the land-grant era it was discovered that railroads had been granted one-fourth of the entire area of Minnesota and Washington; one-fifth of Wisconsin, Iowa, Kansas, North Dakota, and Montana; one-seventh of Nebraska; one-eighth of California; and one-ninth of Louisiana. At one point in 1882 Texas learned that her donation of land to railroads exceeded by 8 million acres the actual amount remaining in the state's public domain.

To such grants of land were added loans and subsidies. Towns, cities, and counties gave the railroads about $300 million, and the states, at a conservative estimate, furnished an additional $228 million. The federal government made loans of approximately $65 million, most of it going to the Union and Central Pacific. A town was at the mercy of a railroad, which could bypass it and thereby cause it to dry up. By this threat the railroads were able to secure cash grants, loans, exemptions from taxation, and subscription to their stocks. Yet many loans were made voluntarily and enthusiastically to get local railroad advantages. For, as the governor of Maine asked in 1867, "Why should private individuals be called upon to make a useless sacrifice of their means when railroads can be constructed by the unity of public with private interests, and made profitable to all?" By 1870, according to one estimate, public subsidies plus land grants contributed 60 percent of the cost of all railroad construction.

The miners were the first to reveal to the nation the untapped resources of the territory between the Missouri River and the Pacific. In 1848 the discovery of gold had lured many miners to California. Time and again during the 1860s, in Colorado, Arizona, Idaho, Montana, and Wyoming, gold attracted the first wave of settlers, the miners. Then, when the pay dirt was exhausted, the ranchers and the farmers, aided by the railroads and the government, laid the permanent foundations of the territory.

In 1858, gold was discovered in the foothills of the Rocky Mountains near Pike's Peak. Within a year one hundred thousand people set out for Colorado. Denver became full-grown almost overnight, and within a few weeks other mining camps grew to sizable proportions. Horace Greeley, of the New York *Tribune,* who went out to see what a gold rush was like, has left a graphic picture of one of these camps: "As yet the entire population of the valley sleeps in tents or under booths of pine boughs, cooking and eating in the open air," he wrote, "I doubt that there is . . . a table or chair in these diggings, eating being done on a cloth spread on the ground, while each one sits or reclines on mother earth."

The mining boom soon spent itself, however, and the development of Colorado was retarded by the Civil War and by Indian uprisings. Covered wagons that had gone west with the sign, "Pike's Peak or Bust," returned eastward by the same route with the placard, "Busted, by gosh." Yet many people stayed on to farm or to engage in more scientific types of mining. In 1861 Congress made Colorado a territory, and in 1876 admitted her to the Union as a state.

In 1859 gold was discovered also near Lake Tahoe on the eastern slopes of the Sierra Nevadas. This strike was the famous Comstock Lode, one of the richest veins in the world. In 1861 Nevada became a territory, and three years later gained statehood. Probably nowhere else in history is there an example of a society such as that found in Nevada, so completely dependent upon mineral wealth. The history of Nevada for the first decade is largely that of the Comstock Lode. Within twenty years the Lode yielded $306 million in gold and silver, though little of this remained in Nevada. Most of it went to California mining companies or to eastern gamblers and speculators.

The story of Idaho and Montana parallels that of Colorado and Nevada. Gold was discovered in 1860 on the reservation of the Nez Perce Indians in the eastern part of the Washington territory. This discovery soon brought some 15,000 miners who had been described by one historian as being "like quicksilver. A mass of them dropped in any locality, broke up into individual globules, and ran off after any atom of gold in their vicinity. They stayed nowhere longer than the gold that attracted them." In 1863 the Territory of Idaho was carved out of Washington and Montana.

By this time the miners had crossed the Bitter Root Mountains and discovered gold in Montana in Last Chance Gulch. Within six years, Last Chance Gulch (now Helena) had 20,000 inhabitants, and more than $100 million in gold was taken from the mines in the neighborhood. N. P. Langford, one of the residents, described (*Vigilante Days and Ways,* Vol. I, 1893) this typical mining town in 1864, after several months of its existence:

This human hive, numbering at least ten thousand people, was the product of ninety days. Into it were crowded all the elements of a rough and active civilization. Thousands of cabins and tents and brush wikiups...were seen on every hand. Every foot of the gulch was undergoing displacement, and it was already disfigured by huge heaps of gravel, which had been passed through the sluices and rifled by their glittering contents....Gold was abundant, and every possible device was employed by the gamblers, the traders, the vile men and women that had come in with the miners...to obtain it. Nearly every third cabin in the town was a saloon where vile whiskey was peddled out for fifty cents in gold dust. Many of these places were filled with gambling tables and gamblers....Hurdy-gurdy dance houses were numerous....Not a day or night passed which did not yield its full fruition of fights, quarrels, wounds, or murders. The crack of the revolver was often heard above the merry notes of the violin. Street fights were frequent, and as no one knew when or where they would occur, every one was on his guard against a random shot....Sunday was always a gala day....The stores were all open....Horseracing was among the most favored amusements. Prize rings were formed, and brawny men engaged in fisticuffs until their sight was lost and their bodies pommelled to a jelly....Pistols flashed, bowie knives flourished, and braggart oaths filled the air, as often as men's passions triumphed over their reason....All classes of society were represented at this general exhibition. Judges, lawyers, doctors, even clergymen, could not claim exemption.

The last gold rush came in 1875 on the reservations of the Sioux Indians in the Black Hills region of the Dakota Territory. Here the town of Deadwood, consisting mainly of two long rows of saloons, had its day of glory. Calamity Jane earned dubious fame in Deadwood, and it was here that Wild Bill Hickok was curbed by vigilantes. It was probably the most lawless place in the country, although in it a stage company played Gilbert and Sullivan's *The Mikado* for a record run of 130 nights.

The story of the mining towns has become a familiar one through books and motion pictures. Their lawlessness has attracted much attention in history and fiction alike. To be sure, it existed. But it would be a mistake to picture the mining communities as mere nests of desperadoes or to argue, as most easterners did, that mining camps had abandoned the institutions of civilized society. Mining camps had few churches, schools, newspapers, or theaters, but these services were quickly established. Miners did not conform to usual standards of society or of law; instead they set up their own. Each mining camp was an administrative and judicial district. It had its own governing officials; it passed and enforced its own laws. The legal codes and practices of these mining camps were eventually recognized in American courts, many of them being incorporated into constitutions and laws of the western states.

The miners' frontier came to an end in the 1880s. No other important gold mines were discovered, and the individual prospector was gradually replaced by large corporations, usually run by eastern financiers. Between 1860 and 1890, $1,242 million in gold and $901 million in silver were taken out of the mines in the West. This bullion enabled the federal government to resume specie payment. It also helped to precipitate the money question, one of the major political issues of the last quarter of the nineteenth century.

The Indians of the Great Plains and the Rocky Mountains, about 250,000 in number, were opposed to white settlement in their areas. The land had been theirs for centuries and they were determined to fight, if necessary, to keep it. The strongest and most warlike of the tribes were the Sioux, Blackfeet, Crow, Cheyenne, Comanche, and Apache. They clung tenaciously to their land and fought doggedly for it. For the most part, the Indians of the eastern United States had been easily overwhelmed. The density of settlement in the East helped the whites, and Indians there were less stubborn fighters than those of the Great Plains. But the old instruments of defense for the whites were useless on the Plains. Mounted on swift horses and superbly armed with bows and arrows, the Indians of the Great Plains were more than a match for the white man until he perfected the repeater rifle. The Plains Indians were nomadic and were not inclined toward agriculture as were their eastern counterparts. Though doomed to end in defeat, they taxed the resources of the white men to the limit.

The advance of miners into the mountains, the building of the transcontinental railroads, and the invasion of the grasslands by cattlemen threatened to exterminate the Indians. The wanton destruction of the buffalo herds was most serious, as these animals were indispensable for food, fuel, hides, lariats, and bowstrings, among other Indian needs. Then, too, came the perfection of the Colt repeating revolver, so efficient in warfare on the Plains, as well as the spread of the white man's diseases among the Indians.

Until 1861 the Indians of the Plains had been relatively peaceful. Beginning that year miners invaded their hunting grounds, white settlement advanced, and dissatisfaction set in over treaties with the federal government. During the Civil War savage fighting occurred with the Apaches and the Navahos in the Southwest and with the Arapaho and Cheyenne tribes on the Great Plains. For the next twenty-five years, Indian warfare was prevalent and continual in the West. Most tribes in the mountain areas were eventually persuaded to give up their lands and move to reservations, but those on the Great Plains were unwilling to abandon their hunting grounds to encroaching whites.

In 1867 Congress passed a law providing for the removal of all Indians to reservations. This legislation broke the promises given to the Plains tribes in the 1820s and 1830s that they could keep their lands forever. The government decided to create two reservations for the Plains Indians—one in the Black Hills of Dakota, the other in present-day Oklahoma. By 1868 treaties to this effect had been forced upon the Indians. Then difficulties arose. While the tribal chieftains signed the treaties, individual Indian warriors often refused to be bound by them. "We have now provided reservations for all, off the great roads," General Sherman observed. "All who cling to their old hunting grounds are hostile and will remain so till killed off. We will have a sort of predatory war for years . . . but the country is so large and the advantage of the Indians so great, that we cannot make a single war end it."

Sherman was correct in his prediction. Between 1869 and 1875 more than two hundred battles took place between the army and the Indians. A few years earlier General S. R. Curtis, United States Army commander in the West, had notified his subordinate officers: "I want no peace till the Indians suffer more." And the Indians did suffer, for a white trader reported that Cheyenne "were scalped, their brains knocked out; the men used their knives, ripped open women, clubbed little children, knocked them in the head with their guns, beat their brains out, mutilated their bodies in every sense of the word." What took place in the conflicts after the 1868 treaties can be understood, to some extent, in light of a statement by General Francis A. Walker, commissioner of Indian affairs, in 1871: "When dealing with savage men, as with savage beasts, no question of national honor can arise. Whether to fight, to run away, or to employ a ruse, is solely a question of expediency."

Probably the most publicized of the Indian conflicts of this period took place in 1876 at the Battle of the Little Big Horn. The Sioux in Dakota bitterly resented the encroachment on their reservation protected by the Treaty of Fort Laramie (1868). Their indignation was aroused not only by the Northern Pacific railroad crews but by the opening of the Black Hills area when the gold rush began in 1874. When the Sioux refused to accept the terms offered for their rights, the government ended its protection. In 1876 war broke out again, and troops were sent into the area under the command of General George A. Custer. On a June day, Custer and his men ran into a large group of Indians at the Little Big Horn River in Montana. What Custer mistook for a small band turned out to be the main Sioux force of several thousand men under Chief Sitting Bull. The Sioux annihilated Custer and his 264 men, but the Indians gained little by their victory. Shortages of ammunition and food forced them to scatter, and by October of the same year the largest group had been captured. Sitting Bull escaped to Canada, but, facing starvation, he returned in 1881. The Nez Perce Indians in Oregon continued to give trouble until they succumbed to disease and starvation. When their leader Chief Joseph surrendered, he said, "I am tired of fighting. My heart is sick and sad. From where the sun now stands I will fight no more forever." In the 1880s the Apaches in New Mexico took to the warpath until their chief, Geronimo, was captured in 1886. In 1890 another Sioux uprising was easily suppressed. Indian resistance to the white man's conquest of the last frontier was at an end.

The Indian wars after 1865 cost the government millions of dollars and hundreds of lives, and yet nowhere did a solution to the problem seem to be at hand. Blame for the failure rested upon the federal government, which regarded each tribe as a sovereign, yet dependent, nation. Indians frequently misunderstood the terms of the treaties, and many individual Indians did not feel bound by them. Moreover, authority over Indian affairs was divided between the Interior and War departments, and each department pursued different policies and objectives. Then, too, the majority of frontiersmen believed that the only good Indian was a dead one, and soldiers agreed. Easterners, far removed from the scene of strife, had a different attitude. Here churchmen and reformers united to urge a policy of humanitarianism toward the Indians.

Gradually new ideas about the problem began to have some influence in Washington. A new Board of Indian Commissioners, comprised of civilians, was created in 1869 to advise the Bureau of Indian Affairs, which since 1849 had been in the Department of the Interior. This new board tried to convert the Plains Indians on the reservations to agriculture and to convince the government that it should break down tribal autonomy. This latter change was accomplished in 1871 when Congress abolished the policy of dealing with tribes by means of treaties, as though they were independent nations. In the seventies, too, the government began to establish Indian boarding schools removed from the reservations. Year after year the Indian commissioners recommended individual land holdings for Indians and the elimination of reservations. Books were written on behalf of the Indian, among which Helen Hunt Jackson's *A Century of Dishonor* (1881) had the greatest influence in arousing public opinion toward efforts to improve the lot of the Indians. Finally, in 1887, in the Dawes Act, the government adopted a new Indian policy that reversed the old one of extermination conducted by the army.

The Dawes Act was the first serious attempt to "civilize" the Indian, teach him the practice of agriculture and social life, and merge him into the American body politic. It provided for the dissolution of tribal autonomy and the division of the tribal lands among individual members on the basis of 160 acres to heads of families, 80 acres to single adults or orphans, and 40 acres to dependent children. To protect the Indian in his property, the right of disposal was withheld for twenty-five years. At the end of this probationary period, the Indian received both full rights of ownership and full citizenship in the United States. In 1906 the Burke Act gave the Secretary of the Interior discretionary authority to reduce the probationary period and correct other defects in the law. In 1924 the United States granted full citizenship to all Indians born in the country.

The new policy did not work well. The Indian was too easily persuaded to sell his land; often he became a victim of liquor. Some tribes, especially in Arizona and New Mexico, continued to hold their land in tribal fashion and to retain their tribal organizations. Perhaps even more disheartening was the lack of incentive for the Indians to cultivate their land. Many of them became paupers, and the feeling began to spread that it had been a mistake to compel the Indians to abandon their traditional way of life. In 1934, in the Indian Reorganization Act, the government again reversed its Indian policy when it allowed the tribes to hold their land as communal property. But this did not end Indian problems, which have persisted to our own day.

Flourishing on the Great Plains for about two decades after the Civil War was an open-range cattle industry originating in Texas and Spanish Mexico. Several centuries earlier, the Spaniards had established ranches in Mexico, and in the eighteenth century they had brought cattle into Texas. Here the animals had been allowed to run wild and to multiply until, at the end of the Civil War, they totaled about five million. For a number of years the cattle industry was thwarted, not because it was unable to raise cattle, but because it lacked a market. With the Civil War over, Texas ranchers learned that steers, which sold for no more than $3 or $4 a head in Texas, would bring $35 to $40 a head in northern markets. They decided to make the "long drive" north to a railroad town, from which the railroad would haul the cattle to the large cities.

The first long drive from Texas got under way in the spring of 1866, when 260,000 head of cattle set out on a thousand-mile journey over what was called the Chisholm Trail to Sedalia, Missouri, a station on the Missouri Pacific Railroad. Most of the herd perished en route, but the few Texas steers to make it brought $35 a head. This price encouraged a number of the ranchers to try again. In the following year a more accessible meeting place for ranchers and packers was found at Abilene, Kansas, on the Kansas Pacific line. Here Joseph G. McCoy, an enterprising meat dealer from Illinois, built a hotel, and erected barns, stables, pens, and loading chutes. In 1868 Abilene received 75,000 head of cattle, and in 1871, a record year, 700,000 head. Over the next dozen years a total of four million cattle were driven over the Chisholm Trail to Abilene, Dodge City, and other Kansas cow towns. The cowboys moved the cattle slowly in herds of two or three thousand head. This required the services of sixteen or eighteen cowboys, a cook with a chuck wagon, and a "wrangler" with extra cow ponies.

It was on the long drive that the cowboy came into his own as a unique character of the frontier. He was a romantic figure who had borrowed much from the Mexican *vaquero,* for his saddle, bridle, bit, lariat, and spurs were adaptations of equipment used by Mexicans. The cowboy was picturesquely dressed in a "broad felt hat, a flannel shirt, with a bright silk handkerchief loosely knotted around his neck, trousers tucked into high heel boots, and a pair of leather 'chaps' or heavy riding overall with great spurs and a large revolver." But his outfit was utilitarian as well as ornamental. High heels on the boots gave him a better grip on the stirrup; fringed chaps protected his legs and trousers; the large handkerchief around his neck had obvious uses on the Great Plains; his broad-brimmed hat protected him from the sun and held water. His saddle also served as a pillow.

While the cowboy's life had a romantic and glamorous side, it was also hazardous. With only a cow pony, a lasso, and a six-shooter, he and his group tried to keep under safe control several thousand head of steer during two months of continuous travel. There were many risks along the trail—the danger of stampedes, of sudden noises and lights, of thefts by rustlers, and of raids by Indians. "It was tiresome grimy business for the attendant punchers," wrote one of the veterans of the long drive, "who travelled over in a cloud of dust, and heard little but the constant chorus from the crackling of hoofs and of ankle joints, from the bellows, lows, and bleats of the trudging animals." The cowboy's life was also a lonely one. He sang sentimental words to soothe the restless cattle and to cheer himself as he whiled away the lonely hours on the Chisholm Trail and its counterparts.

The cattle business reached its peak in the early 1880s when annual profits of from 40 to 50 percent were common. But such returns quickly attracted so many prospective ranchers that they overstocked the range. The unfenced Plains of the public domain were bountiful and free, and the ranchers made use of this public land. Between 1882 and 1884 they sent as many young steers north to the ranges as they shipped east to the markets. But two disastrous winters of 1885–1886 and 1886–1887 and the blistering summer of 1886 destroyed most of the feed and the cattle. What steers eventually reached market were so inferior in quality that the bottom fell out of the beef prices despite the great shortage. Also at this time large numbers of sheep herders began to cross the Plains, and both herders and flocks were especially obnoxious to cattlemen. The sheep stripped the range of grass, so when the sheepmen came to stay, the cattlemen had to fight or leave. Farmers were also homesteading the Plains and fencing the open range. Soon they were able to produce beef of higher quality than that found on the open range. With the increase of railroad facilities, long drives became unnecessary. Gradually the colorful cattle country of the Plains changed, and with the change came an end to the last frontier.

The passing of the frontier seemed to herald the end of the long period of virtually unbounded economic opportunity that began with the first English settlements in America in the seventeenth century. And no doubt many Americans in the 1890s believed that this development also meant the end of an old way of life that had brought prog ress and prosperity to the nation.

True, a frontier line beyond which practically no one lived was gone, but there were still large areas of free or cheap land to be opened up. For instance, four times as many homesteads were taken up after 1890 as had been taken up during the period 1862 to 1890. Thus, the announcement of the end of the frontier by the director of the census in 1890 was premature in a number of ways, as future developments would show.

While the frontier seemed to be passing in the Last West, it appeared to be making a comeback in the New South—the South that emerged from the Civil War and the South of the post–Civil War generation. Probably the major prophet and mythmaker for the New South was Henry W. Grady, youthful editor of the *Atlanta Constitution,* who in late December 1886, in an address to the New England Society of New York in New York City, set forth the vision and creed of "The New South," the topic of his talk. "The Old South rested everything on slavery and agriculture," he said. "The New South presents a perfect democracy, the oligarchs leading in the popular movement—a social system compact and closely knitted, less splendid on the surface, but stronger at the core—a hundred farms for every plantation, fifty homes for every palace—and a diversified industry that meets the complex need of this complex age."

As historian Paul Gaston has pointed out, the New South creed responded to a deep-seated intellectual concern in this section. Essential was a need to believe that wealth and fundamental changes were nearby. The New South program, as envisaged and prophesized by Grady and by other champions of the New South such as Walter Hines Page, Henry Watterson, and Daniel Thompkins, was a call for industrial progress, diversified agriculture, and cooperation with the North. In racial matters the proponents of a New South talked about a benevolent version of white supremacy that by the end of the nineteenth century developed into the "separate but equal" formula.

This post-Reconstruction image of the South began as an optimistic prophecy and as a program for action aimed at bringing pride, prosperity, and racial harmony to a section devastated and humiliated by the Civil War. But the promises of economic development and friendly race relations were not realized. While the New South creed had some worthy qualities, it did not have a successful outcome. According to Gaston this was because the New South concept was "manipulated through most of its history by men who served the region poorly, and the hold it gained over the American mind had obstructed more frequently than it had promoted achievement of its ideal." This can be ascribed to the destructive force of the paradoxes of the New South creed. Though it sought to shove into the background the defects in the pre–Civil War southern social, economic, and political life, it also attempted to retain loyalty to the Old South. It professed a desire for immigration though it displayed a personal hostility toward such newcomers. And it pursued interdependence with the North as part of an effort for regional independence.

However, the most destructive of the ambiguities of the New South's creed was its praise for Negro freedom while it maintained a politics of white supremacy. The creed tried to talk of equal treatment of whites and blacks, but the New South, like the Old South, regarded the two races as unequal. Unable either to face this situation squarely or to take the action to remedy it, the New South's preaching about progress and success was remote from reality. Southern spokesmen for the New South creed, therefore, by the end of the nineteenth century took refuge in a "mythic view" of their society. Thus a program for change became a widely accepted myth that would sustain a conservative, racist society well into the twentieth century.

When the Civil War was over, the South quickly resumed production of large quantities of cotton. But poverty remained and even became worse. Though the promoters of the New South preached local industrialization, and cotton textile factories did come and stay, the southern economy generally did not improve. Recent studies of this development ascribe the South's postwar economic miseries to the region's peculiar labor market. It was separate from the larger national labor market, and southern wages resisted following national trends. As late as World War II, the New South remained a low wage regional market in the midst of a high wage national economy. Industrialization failed to remove the isolation of the southern labor market, because the large supply of unskilled agricultural workers kept industrial wages low.

These new studies, especially that of Gavin Wright, show that the reluctance of the New South leaders to mitigate racism and to invest much in education helped keep the entire section isolated and backward. Northern capital did not make the New South a colonial economy, argues Wright. The South's colonial status came instead from its late start toward industrialization, its separate labor market, and its failure to develop the necessary technology for a low wage economy that made intensive use of labor.

The Civil War and Reconstruction destroyed the old plantation system in the South and brought about a redistribution of land and changes of land tenure. Under the impact of a military defeat there was a large transfer of land ownership from planters to yeoman farmers, small businessmen, and to northerners such as carpetbaggers and Union soldiers. This appeared to be a breakup of plantations into small farms as the number of farms in most of the former Confederate states in the postwar years increased many fold.

But in actuality the change came mainly in the nature of farm labor and not in land ownership. There was about the same number of plantations, but these were now split into small holdings and were cultivated no longer by slaves but by tenant farmers and sharecroppers. As the leading historian of the New South, C. Vann Woodward, wrote, "The evils of land monopoly, absentee ownership, soil mining, and the one-crop system, once associated with and blamed upon slavery, did not disappear, but were instead, aggravated, intensified, and multiplied."

During the antebellum years the chief asset of the planters was slave labor. Emancipation changed the plantation owners into landlords and turned them away from slave labor to cheap labor to make gains from the planters' new chief asset, land. Freed blacks during Reconstruction negotiated labor contracts with landlords. But by the 1870s the contracts had developed into the sharecropping and crop lien system. Sharecropping was an arrangement by which planters could have labor without paying wages and landless farmers could have land without paying rent. The planter provided his tenant with land, shelter, seed, fertilizer, and implements and received at the end of the season one half of the crop raised by the tenant. The tenant supplied labor and acquired the rest of the crop and anything else that he raised on a small plot for vegetables. At the end of the Civil War, most black freedmen and many poor white farmers agreed to such an arrangement. But working out such a contract was very difficult for blacks, because neither they nor southern whites had done this before. In the process, many freedmen were defrauded. Many times they discovered that instead of receiving their share when the crop was in, they were fired without getting anything.

Recent studies of southern agriculture in the post–Civil War period, however, maintain that sharecropping was not a labor coercion system. The sharecroppers participated in a labor market, frequently moving from one landlord to another every few years. But this labor market was very localized.

The crop lien system kept the southern agricultural labor market localized. Under this system sharecroppers had to obtain credit from their landlords or local merchants to acquire supplies for growing crops and for their personal use. Rates of interest were high, and sharecroppers had to pay a price of from 10 to 25 percent above the normal retail price. The sharecroppers' need for credit, and their need to be known locally to obtain it, kept them within a labor market limited by rural neighborhoods.

The crop lien system was an especially vicious one because farmers had to mortgage their ungrown crops. By the end of the nineteenth century about two-thirds of the farmers of the southern cotton belt had done this. The crop lien system kept the poorer southern farmers in continual debt to their creditors—planters, country storekeepers, and bankers—because when the sharecropper's portion of the crop did not pay for his charges at the country store, he had to renew the lien on next year's crop to the same merchant.

Black sharecroppers had two ways to escape this trap. They could become either a landowner or an industrial worker. After Reconstruction only a few managed to move up the agricultural ladder from a sharecropper to a fixed rent tenant to a landowner. But even these few successful blacks could not escape exploitation and subordination by southern whites.

Outside the lumber and timber industry, the largest industrial employer in the New South, and the tobacco industry, there were few industrial opportunities for blacks in the New South. Because of the large supply of unskilled agricultural labor, industrial labor wages remained low for blacks as they were for whites in the cotton textile mills, the second largest industry employer, which hired whites almost exclusively. It was only in the iron and steel industry around Birmingham that blacks gained industrial opportunities. Here many blacks were able to get skilled and semiskilled jobs and were paid better wages than unskilled workers, but the wages were still below what was paid for similar jobs in the North.

As for southern agriculture as a whole in these years, Gilbert Fite, a leading historian of American agriculture, has recently contended that tens of thousands of southern farmers in the late nineteenth and early twentieth centuries "were caught in the trap of low productivity, poverty, and despair with no apparent way out." According to Fite, the trap that southern farmers found themselves in was that the farming operations of most farmers were too small and unproductive to provide an adequate standard of living in a commercial, capitalistic economy. With many more people going into farming there was a surplus of agricultural labor and too many farms, which kept farm income depressed. Most farmers could not break out of the trap, because they could not accumulate the capital, either from earnings or loans at high interest rates, they needed for larger and more profitable operations. Finally, most of the suggestions for agricultural reform—self-sufficiency, diversification, cheaper credit, and improved efficiency— "did not get at the basic problem of surplus workers in agriculture. There were too many people trying to get a piece of the southern agricultural pie, and the pie was too small."

There were other reasons why so many southern farmers in the post–Civil War years were so poor, but not having enough capital in an expanding capitalistic society put them in a trap from which they could not escape. There was no solution to their income problem. Things did not begin to change until government action and opportunities in the 1930s and 1940s for off-farm employment and migration brought Southerners and their resources into better economic balance.

Further Reading

Adams, Andy. *Log of a Cowboy.* 1964.
Andrist, Ralph K. *The Long Death: The Last Days of the Plains Indians.* 1969.
Athearn, Robert G. *High Country Empire: The High Plains and Rockies.* 1956.
Atherton, Lewis. *The Cattle Kings.* 1961.
Billington, Ray A. *Westward Expansion.* 4th. ed., 1974.
Bogue, Allan G., Thomas P. Phillips, and James E. Wright, eds. *The West of the American People.* 1970.
Brown, Dee. *Bury My Heart At Wounded Knee: An Indian History of The American West.* 1970.
Clark, Thomas D. *Frontier America, The Story of the Westward Movement.* 1969.
Day, David. *Cowboy Culture: A Saga of Five Centuries.* 1981.
DeVoto, Bernard. *Across the Wide Missouri.* 1947.
Durham, Philip, and Everett L. Jones. *The Negro Cowboys.* 1965.
Dykstra, Robert. *The Cattle Towns.* 1968.
Fogel, Robert. *The Union Pacific Railroad.* 1960.
Frantz, Joe B., and Julian E. Choate. *The American Cowboy: The Myth and the Reality.* 1955.
Gaston, Paul M. *The New South Creed: A Study in Southern Mythmaking.* 1970.
Greever, William S. *The Bonanza West: The Story of Western Mining Rushes, 1848–1900.* 1963.
Grodinsky, Julius. *Transcontinental Railway Strategy, 1869–1893.* 1962.
Jackson, Helen Hunt. *A Century of Dishonor.* 1881.
Lewis, Oscar. *The Big Four.* 1951.
Molane, Michael P. *The Battle for Butte: Mining and Politics on the Northern Frontier, 1884–1906.* 1981.
Paul, Rodman W. *Mining Frontiers of the Far West, 1848–1880.* 1963.
Priest, Loring G. *Uncle Sam's Stepchildren: The Reformation of United States Indian Policy, 1865–1887.* 1942, 1975.
Prucha, Francis Paul. *American Indian Policy in Crisis: Christian Reformers and the Indians, 1865–1900.* 1976.
Rollins, Philip Ashton. *The Cowboy.* 1922.
Shagg, J. M. *The Cattle Trading Industry.* 1973.
Smith, Duane A. *Rocky Mountain Mining Camps.* 1967.

Smith, Henry Nash. *Virgin Land: The American West as Symbol and Myth.* 1950.

Spence, Clark C., ed. *The American West: A Source Book.* 1966.

Stratton, Joanna L. *Pioneer Women: Voices from the Kansas Frontier.* 1981.

Taft, Robert. *Artists and Illustrators of the Old West, 1850–1900.* 1953.

Twain, Mark. *Roughing It.* 1872.

Utley, Robert M. *Frontier Regulars: The United States Army and the Indian, 1866–1891.* 1973.

Washburn, Wilcomb E. *The Indian in North America.* 1975.

Webb, Walter P. *The Great Plains.* 1931.

3

The Politics of Dead Center

American political activity in the last quarter of the nineteenth century seemed to lack the vitality and productivity of earlier periods in American history. The presidents often had executive ability and high principles, but they, like most of the important men in Congress, proved to be mediocre and uninspiring leaders. "No period so thoroughly ordinary has been known in American politics since Christopher Columbus first disturbed the balance of power in American society," wrote Henry Adams, that mordant commentator on the Gilded Age. "One might search the whole list of Congress, Judiciary, and Executive during the twenty-five years 1870 to 1895 and find little but damaged reputation. The period was poor in purpose and barren in results."

The most serious charge leveled against the major parties of the Gilded Age was that they failed to deal with the problems created by the Industrial Revolution. Far-reaching economic changes had come to America and extensive social adjustments were necessary to meet these alterations. Yet politics seemed to develop into the fine art of evading issues. Not that there was any lack of important issues, for problems arising out of the recurrent industrial crises and depressions of the period demanded vigorous government action. But both parties preferred to ignore these new problems and to revive the ones of a bygone age. For the most part politicians did not recognize the issues, or, if they were aware of them, they closed their eyes to them. Thus the problems of the new economic order seldom got a hearing in the political arena except through the third parties. The chief concern of most political leaders was to gain office, and they seemed to have little concern for the public interest.

The usual explanation for this shortcoming is that there were no important differences on major issues between Democrats and Republicans. Neither one wished to disturb the status quo, and neither one believed that there was anything fundamentally wrong with American life. The two major parties in this period, wrote James Bryce, a contemporary observer of the party system, "were like two bottles. Each bore a label denoting the kind of liquor it contained, but each was empty." This is why some historians have called this period the "age of negation," characterized by "the politics of dead center." But it is important to remember that the government in this generation rarely concerned itself with economic and social matters, as it has become used to doing now, and the prevalent feeling among Americans was that it should not do so.

But there are other reasons for this political inactivity. Probably the most important was the sharp contest for power between the major parties and the failure of either one to dominate the national government for any appreciable length of time. Contrary to popular belief these were not years of one-party supremacy. Rather it was a period of party stalemate and equilibrium. In the five presidential elections from 1876 to 1892 the Republicans, while winning three, failed to gain a majority of the popular vote in any one election and secured a plurality only once (1880), and even that plurality was less than one-tenth of 1 percent. In three of these elections the difference between the popular vote for the two major party candidates was less than 1 percent, although electoral vote majorities ranged from 1 in 1876 to 132 in 1892. For much of this period the Republicans depended for victory upon the small majorities they received in such key states as Indiana and New York, and they never once obtained a plurality of the counties of the nation as a whole. The Democrats, while electing a president only twice (1884 and 1892), won a majority of the popular vote one time (1876) and a plurality in 1880, 1884, and 1892. Added to the struggle to win the presidency was that to have charge of Congress. Each party managed to control the presidency and Congress at the same time for only two years—the Republicans from 1889 to 1891 and the Democrats from 1893 to 1895.

National political power was then vested in Congress and not in the presidency. A group of arrogant Republican politicians had dominated the federal government for about a decade during Reconstruction and ran the country much to suit themselves. They had overthrown President Johnson, had gained nearly complete possession of Grant, and set out to put the succeeding presidents at their mercy. The bitter fight between the executive and legislative branches that had begun with Johnson and Congress, instead of dying down, continued to harass most of the presidents in this period. In addition, the office of president was at low ebb in power and prestige. Senator John Sherman, Republican leader of Ohio, himself a perpetual aspirant to the office, wrote that "The executive department of a republic like ours should be subordinate to the legislative department. The President should [merely] obey and enforce the laws." Congressional leaders acted on these principles. "The most eminent Senators," observed George F. Hoar, Republican from Massachusetts, about his colleagues in the Senate, "would have received as a personal affront a private message from the White House expressing a desire that they should adopt any course in the discharge of their legislative duties that they did not approve. If they visited the White House, it was to give, not to receive advice." Henry Adams agreed with this observation when he commented that "so far as the President's initiative was concerned, the President and his Cabinet might equally well have departed separately or together to distant lands."

Sectionalism also accounted for legislative inactivity. The sectionalism of the seventies and eighties resulted from two developments: expansion of the West, particularly the trans-Mississippi West, and the growth of industrialism in the Northeast. Political personalities played a role subordinate to an adjustment between the interests of sections and party allegiances in determining the outcome of the vote on national policies. The leading issues of the country as indicated by party platforms and congressional action were currency and banking, tariffs, public lands, internal improvements, railroad and trust regulation, and immigration. While all these produced strong sectional feeling, they manifested one common feature—opposition of the agricultural regions to the industrial centers of the country.

More sectional voting occurred during depressions and more party voting took place during times of prosperity. Those sections hardest hit during a depression broke party ranks and combined with other distressed areas to attempt to redress their grievances. The vagueness of party platforms in this period until 1888 also stimulated sectional divisions, since it allowed discontented sections to interpret the planks to suit their own interests without being accused of party disloyalty. Sectional voting was also more pronounced in Congress when the houses were divided between the two parties than in those instances when one party was in control. This was equally true for depression and prosperity years in the seventies and eighties. Thus, not only did the presidents have to deal with divided Congresses, but with Congresses in which their own party members did more sectional than party voting.

The considerable power that business wielded also contravened governmental action. It is a commonplace to emphasize the alliance between politics and business in this period and the dominant role of the latter in both major parties. The usual explanation for this development is that the politicians were the hirelings of the business community. "Business ran politics, and politics was a branch of business," writes one leading historian. Business had a pre-eminent position in the councils of government on all levels, and businessmen could usually obtain what they wanted regardless of which party was in power. This was because rival political machines could either be purchased or were so amenable that they did not need to be bought.

The important thing to remember about the combination between politics and business is not so much that there was one, but that it lasted so long without effective restraint by the voters. E. L. Godkin, editor of the influential New York *Nation,* went to the heart of the matter when he wrote: "All being corrupt together what is the use of investigating each other."

It should also be remembered that the bulk of Americans in the Gilded Age were sympathetic to business. They fervently believed that laissez faire and free competition reduced prices and provided a higher rate of employment. Therefore, they considered government regulation unnecessary, unjust, and even immoral. Even the reformers crusaded for only the most urgent reforms and then only after a careful study had confirmed the need.

Despite its favorable position, business did not control American politics. Nor did politicians merely act for the benefit of big business. Businessmen had to pay heavily for political favors, and many times they were blackmailed by threats of regulation or withdrawal of government assistance. Many businessmen complained that politicians treated them simply as customers, compelling them to pay money for protection, selling political benefits to the highest bidder, and refusing to do the proper thing without pay. These facts alone furnish proof that the independence of the politician was so complete that it was necessary for the businessman to bribe him. Politicians were eager to deal with businessmen because they were better organized and had more money to spend than any other group in the country. Farmers and workers were also able to secure political favors once they were organized and began to put pressure on politicians.

The political rulers of the day were not the titular leaders but the party bosses, many of them United States senators, who headed powerful state machines and rewarded followers with public offices. The two most important Republican bosses were Senator James G. Blaine of Maine, who led the Half-Breed faction in the party, and Senator Roscoe Conkling of New York, who led the Stalwarts. Both in Congress and the party these two men clashed and were bitter opponents. Both waved the bloody shirt,* supported sound money and the protective tariff, championed the spoils system, and fought civil service reform.

In addition to Blaine and Conkling there were Senators Zachariah Chandler of Michigan, chief lord of the pork barrel; James Donald Cameron of Pennsylvania, quiet, judicious, unemotional, and a despiser of the methods so commonly used by the bosses to gain popularity with the masses; Oliver P., Morton of Indiana, who ran his machine like a despot; and John A. ("Black Jack") Logan of Illinois, who was a great supporter of the Grand Army of the Republic. Their source of power came from having at their disposal, before 1883, the entire public service, an enormous amount of spoils in federal, state, and local offices. They controlled a hierarchy of workers down to the ward heelers to whom they distributed offices for faithful service rendered. Other sources of power for the spoilsmen came from the funds they obtained from businessmen—a process described as "frying the fat," the use of city or state treasuries, the assessment of officeholders, and the indirect sale of nominations and offices.

When the Civil Service Reform Act of 1883 began to limit patronage as a source of revenue, politicians turned increasingly to businessmen for money and support. A new type of political boss began to replace the swashbuckling one of before: a business type who resem-

---

*This strategy exploited the themes that Democrats were either disloyal or untrustworthy and that the party of patriotism was the Republican party.

bled and worked closely with the corporation executive, made few speeches, and conducted his activities in the anterooms, caucuses, and committees. Matthew S. Quay of Pennsylvania, Leland Stanford of California, Philetus Sawyer of Wisconsin, Arthur P. Gorman of Maryland, Thomas Platt of New York, and Nelson W. Aldrich of Rhode Island were bosses of the new type. They were no rabble-rousers or demagogues, but men of affairs and practical. Some of them had been prosperous bankers and businessmen who had entered the Senate to protect their interests. In 1889 William Allen White could say that "a United States Senator... represented something more than a state, more even than a region. He represented principalities and powers in business." According to White, one senator "represented the Union Pacific Railway System, another the New York Central, still another the insurance interests of New York and New Jersey....Coal and iron owned a coterie from the Middle and Eastern seaport states. Cotton had half a dozen senators. And so it went." Many labeled this imposing body the "Millionaire's Club." Senator George Hearst of California, one of the group, stated what these men thought of themselves: "I do not know much about books; I have not read very much; but I have traveled a good deal and have observed men and things and I have made up my mind after my experiences that the members of the Senate are the survivors of the fittest."

The principal effect of the spoils system was to transfer party control from publicly elected leaders to "inside" rulers or bosses. The most flagrant examples of "invisible government" occurred in the cities, many of them run by corrupt political machines. Whether they were Democratic, like Tammany Hall in New York, or Republican, like the Gas Ring in Philadelphia, their methods were much the same.

It was nearly impossible for reformers to overthrow the urban machines and bosses, for they seemed to have an unbeatable system. The nature of city government itself—the dispersal of power and responsibility among many agencies—allowed an extra-legal organization to grab control. Machines secured most of their votes from the poorer classes, especially recent immigrants, by finding them jobs, protecting them when they were in trouble with the law, seeing that they were naturalized as quickly as possible, and by contributing food and fuel at Christmas and during periods of emergency. Machines obtained further support, as well as money, by selling franchises and privileges to businessmen. Contractors and politicians seemed always to be seeking some kind of a deal. The press was nearly always bought to insure secrecy. In 1896 a speaker told the Ohio Gas and Light Association, "Keep the newspapers on your staff as well as the city officials."

New York City furnished the country its most notorious example of a municipal machine. There Tammany Hall, an organization dating back to the eighteenth century, controlled the Democratic party and the local government. William Marcy Tweed, or "Boss" Tweed, president of the Board of Supervisors of New York County (coterminous with New York City) and "Grand Sachem" of Tammany Hall, and his followers, A. Oakey Hall, the mayor, Peter B. Sweeney, the county and city treasurer, and Richard B. Connolly, the city controller, ran Tammany Hall and plundered the city. In 1869 this ring secured control of the city councils and soon afterward the police, district attorney, the courts, and most of the newspapers were under its thumb. Tweed managed to have one of his henchmen, John T. Hoffman, elected governor of the state and had plans for his winning the Democratic nomination for president.

By every type of peculation this repulsive crew robbed the city treasury year after year until at the height of their power they were splitting among themselves 85 percent of the total expenditures made by the city and county. Their technique was simple. Everyone who had a bill against the city was told to pad his bill—at first by 10 percent, later 66 percent, finally 85 percent. Tweed's gang received the padding. For example, the actual cost of maintaining the city's armories totaled for a given period $250,000, but the amount paid out allegedly for that purpose was $3,200,000. The courthouse, originally estimated at $3,000,000, cost the taxpayers $11,000,000 before it was completed. The plastering bill alone amounted to $2,870,000, and the carpeting to $350,000, "enough to cover the whole City Park three times." The loot taken by the Tweed Ring has been variously estimated from $45 million to as high as $100 million.

Although respectable citizens protested, they were powerless for several years to move against Tweed because he controlled every arm of the government. Finally, courageous editorials in the New York *Times* and the cartoons of Thomas Nast in *Harper's Weekly* exposed the corruption of the Tweed Ring and aroused the general public. His own followers, Tweed said, could not read, but they could "look at the damn pictures." Tweed offered George Jones, owner of the *Times,* a million dollars to quiet his paper and Nast a half million to go to Europe to study art, but they refused. A citizens' committee headed by

Samuel J. Tilden and Charles O'Connor launched an investigation that was able by the end of 1872 to drive every member of the Tweed Ring out of office. Tweed himself died in jail.

Nevertheless, the traditional view of the boss as nothing but a corrupting force in American politics needs to be modified. Recent studies of Boss Tweed and of the Cox and Pendergast machines in Cincinnati and Kansas City show that these political organizations furnished some element of order and stability in a rapidly expanding and disordered society. They point out that the boss provided a valuable service in giving services to many people who had no other institutional or social order to which to appeal.

Moreover, not all bosses used politics to advance their material interests. Common as the various forms of graft and corruption were in the Gilded Age, not all bosses sought material profit. Boies Penrose, Republican boss of Pennsylvania, apparently never made a dollar out of politics. And according to Theodore Roosevelt, "Senator Platt [Republican boss of New York] did not use his political position to advance his private fortunes—therein differing from many other political bosses. He lived in hotels and had few extravagant tastes. Indeed, I could not find that he had any tastes at all except for politics and on rare occasions for a dry theology wholly divorced from moral implications."

In this age of cynicism and corruption voices such as those of the "single tax" advocate Henry George and the socialist Edward Bellamy called for reform. Probably the most respectable of all the reformers were the "Mugwumps," as they were called by their opponents. Mugwumps generally were newspapermen, scholars, intellectuals—earnest and high-minded men of high social position and conservative economic views and usually of Republican background. Foremost among them were George William Curtis, editor of *Harper's Weekly,* E. L. Godkin, editor of *The Nation;* Carl Schurz; William Cullen Bryant; Whitelaw Reid; and Samuel Bowles. They lashed out against the spoils system and worked to purify politics through civil service reform. Since they believed in laissez faire they restricted their economic program to tariff reform and sound money.

The Mugwumps spoke in moralistic rather than economic terms. They appealed primarily to the educated upper classes, and they seldom identified themselves with the interests of the masses, whom they viewed with an aristocratic disdain. They regarded the reform movements of labor and farmers as radical and dangerous and had little use for the other reform movements of the period. But this was characteristic of most contemporary reform movements. They had little in common and had great difficulty in understanding one another. Divided and mutually suspicious, the reformers thus exerted little influence.

The Mugwumps have long been praised by historians who accepted their censure of Gilded Age society. But recent studies of these reformers challenged both the indictment of that society and Mugwump beliefs. It will be difficult in the future for scholars to extol the "independents" who condemned alleged corruption, without recognizing that they also abhorred coalition party government in a pluralistic society and that they were elitists who opposed the democratizing directions of their time. According to historian Geoffrey Blodgett, they found close communion with the lower classes a hard adjustment to make; "they seemed to dislike thinking about the working man as such"; "they had no solution for the poor," doubting that there was a solution, because poverty "resulted from poor people spending too much money"; and unlike the Progressives of the succeeding generation they "made no real effort to break the control of the elective process enjoyed by party professionals."

These liberal reformers of the Gilded Age believed political independence helped to purify politics. But, as historian John G. Sproat demonstrated, they also had a price for their reforms. They wanted a small efficient government run by themselves or by men like themselves, reducing property taxes, encouraging individualism, and cutting back public services. "Unable to come to terms with his age, the liberal reformer exaggerated its defects and overrated the past." "Everything considered, his campaign to reform postwar society was a pathetic failure," wrote Sproat. Liberal reformers are now found wanting almost as much as the Gilded Age was found wanting by them.

The new political histories by Paul Kleppner, Richard Jensen, and Samuel McSeveney have significantly altered our old assumptions about voter behavior and party alignment in the late nineteenth century, at least in the Middle West and the Northeast. They showed that voters were more sharply divided on issues than historians later gave them credit for and more interested in local questions such as prohibition and the public school than in national questions such as the currency, the tariff, governmental corruption, and civil service reform. Local issues affected voters more than national issues. Voter behavior and party alignment revolved primarily around ethno-cultural issues and responses, mostly religious and sectarian in nature. Although the new studies did not reject economic or class antagonisms as a basis of political behavior out of hand and in some cases confirm that they played a substantial role during the depression of the 1890s, they did indicate that in general these matters were of lesser importance. These new studies also contended that party loyalty was stronger and voter turnout higher in the last third of the nineteenth century than has been true since. Furthermore, they pointed to a shift in campaigning during the early 1890s from an "army" style, featuring colorful rallies and other forms of hoopla usually associated with election campaigns in those years, toward a more intellectual appeal to the needs and wants of the voters or, as Jensen put it, "a fresh approach to elections based on advertising, the 'merchandising' style."

The major conclusions of Kleppner, Jensen, and McSeveney, therefore, challenged the conventional view that class-consciousness and economic radicalism were major characteristics of the American voter in the late nineteenth century. They also buttressed the new notion of decentralization and localism in the major parties. If the findings of these new studies are correct, particularly the argument that local issues were more important than national issues in voter behavior and party alignment, then there will have to be some major reconsideration of the importance and play of the national issues usually identified with the Gilded Age. Yet, as Blodgett pointed out, the new scholarship, by its very nature, "renders generalizations about the operations of national politics more hazardous than ever." And he raised a most thoughtful point when he observed, "How the discoveries of Kleppner, Jensen, and McSeveney relate for instance to the perpetual congressional dance around the protective tariff is a puzzle which neither they nor anyone else has entirely solved."

Historians have portrayed Republican President Rutherford B. Hayes as a respectable mediocrity with an average capacity and an impeccable public and private life. True, there was no dramatic flair to his personality and he lacked brilliance, but he was a man of high integrity and honest intentions and had such a determination and steadfastness of purpose about his plans that he eventually frustrated even his bitterest foes. But his presidency is an excellent illustration of how party stalemate and equilibrium hampered effective executive leadership. Hayes worked under severe handicaps that have not been fully appreciated. His right to office in 1877 was disputed and Republicans and Democrats alike referred to him as "the de facto president," "His

Fraudulency," and "Old Eight to Seven." His programs for the South and civil service reform plus his show of independence caused such a deep split within his own party that he was nearly read out of it. At one time he had but three supporters in the United States Senate, one of them a lifelong friend and relative. Moreover, the Democrats controlled the House of Representatives throughout his administration and the Senate during the last two years of his term. Under these circumstances it is amazing that he could accomplish anything.

Hayes endeavored to reestablish presidential power and prestige and to redress the balance between the executive and legislative branches. He first challenged congressional dominance in the makeup of his cabinet when he picked men who were most unwelcome to the bosses, particularly the reformer Carl Schurz for secretary of the interior and the southern Democrat and former confederate, David M. Key, for the important patronage-dispensing position of postmaster general. At first the Senate balked and refused to confirm the entire cabinet list, but under much pressure from the public it finally gave in to the president.

Hayes gained another victory over congressional encroachment by refusing to yield the right given him by the Force Acts of 1870–1871 to intervene in federal elections in the states. Democratic majorities in Congress sought to nullify these Reconstruction laws by attaching to army appropriation bills riders aimed at removing federal supervision of elections. Hayes fought these attempts because they would have placed him under the "coercive dictation" of a "bare" majority in Congress, and because he wanted to make the executive "an equal and independent branch of the government." He vetoed eight such bills, and Congress lacked enough votes to override him.

Hayes struck daring and spectacular blows for reform against the spoils system and its greatest champion, Senator Conkling. The president had already vexed the bosses with his inaugural statement that "he serves his party best who serves his country best," and he really angered them with his declaration that "Party leaders should have no more influence in appointments than other equally respectable citizens. No assessments for political purposes, on officers or subordinates, should be allowed. No useless officer or employee should be retained. No officer should be required to take part in the management of political organizations, caucuses, conventions, or election campaigns." He appointed a commission headed by John Jay of New York, grandson of the first Chief Justice, to investigate the largest patronage office in the federal service, the New York customhouse—long an example of the spoils system at its worst. The commission found that most of the employees had been appointed in the interest of the Conkling machine, that 20 percent of them were superfluous, and that the place was ridden with "ignorance, inefficiency, and corruption." When Conkling's lieutenants, Collector of the Port, Chester A. Arthur and naval officer Alonzo B. Cornell, refused to clean up the corruption or to resign, Hayes boldly removed them and named two others for the posts. On Conkling's insistence the Senate refused to confirm the nominations, but Hayes persisted and within a year his choices were approved. He had won a battle, but he had not routed the spoilsmen.

In addition to regaining for the presidency some of the powers that Congress had preempted, Hayes removed the last of the federal troops from the South and ended military Reconstruction. While his recall of the troops was primarily political—a move to rejuvenate the Republican party in the South, he was influenced by other reasons. He acted to restore harmony and good feeling between the North and South and between whites and blacks. He knew of the overwhelming demand of Republicans throughout the country and of the business community for a change from military Reconstruction. He concluded that Republican state governments in the South had lost so much support they had become completely unable to sustain themselves even with the use of force.

Hayes also dreamed of building in the South a strong Republican party that would no longer depend upon the blacks for its main strength and that could command the esteem and support of southern whites. He became the first Republican president to experiment with the plan of appointing regular Democrats to important posts in the South in the hope of gaining Republican success there. He seldom was credited with any honest motives, for the public in 1877—and many years later—believed this was part of the bargain that had made him president. His experiment was a sharp departure from the strategy of the Radicals during Reconstruction; had it worked the "solid South" as a Democratic stronghold might not have come into being.

When Hayes entered the presidency the country was experiencing the worst years of a depression that had begun in 1873, and he was caught without a policy and without much understanding of what was happening. Almost immediately he was confronted with the first great industrial conflict in our history—a railroad strike that began on the

Baltimore and Ohio and spread through fourteen states, affecting two-thirds of the railroad mileage in the country outside of New England and the South. At the request of four state governors, Hayes sent federal troops to intervene in the strike and restore order.

Hayes ran further afoul of labor, especially on the West Coast, when he vetoed a bill passed in 1879 to restrict Chinese immigration. He believed the measure violated the Burlingame Treaty of 1868, which had given the Chinese the right of unlimited immigration to the United States. However, Hayes sent a mission to China to negotiate a new treaty, and the resultant Treaty of 1880 gave the United States the right to regulate or suspend Chinese immigration. The Exclusion Act, passed by Congress in 1882, suspended such immigration for ten years.

The president also took an unpopular stand on the currency question. Discontented agrarians wanted "cheap money" and the repeal or modification of the Resumption Act of 1875, which obligated the Treasury to redeem greenbacks in specie at full face value on 1 January 1879. Many predicted that such redemption would wreck the monetary system, for everyone would want gold rather than paper notes. But Hayes resisted the pressure and aided Secretary of the Treasury John Sherman in accumulating a gold reserve to redeem the currency. Greenback dollars which were worth only sixty-seven cents in 1865 rose to one hundred cents before the deadline of resumption, and people, realizing this, preferred the notes, which were easier to handle; thus no run on the gold reserve developed.

Inflationists now pushed their demands in the form of free coinage of silver, and once again Hayes took the unpopular side. The old ratio between gold and silver had been 16 to 1; there was sixteen times as much silver in a silver dollar as there was gold in a gold dollar. But when the Gold Rush of 1849 lowered the price of gold, an ounce of silver became worth more than one-sixteenth of an ounce of gold, and Americans sold their silver on the open market rather than have it coined at a loss. Silver dollars nearly disappeared from circulation, and in 1873 Congress abolished their coinage. Then silver mines in Nevada, Arizona, and Colorado produced such large quantities of silver that the price of silver fell, and miners and agrarians called for a return to the coinage of silver at the old ratio.

Congress responded by passing over Hayes's veto in 1878 the Bland-Allison Act authorizing the Treasury to purchase not less than $2 million and not more than $4 million worth of silver each month and to coin it into dollars at the former ratio of 16 to 1. The act, however, did not fully meet the demands of the silverites who wanted the "free and unlimited coinage of silver"; moreover, the Treasury consistently purchased only the minimum amount of silver required by the act.

Hayes did not seek reelection, and the Republican convention of 1880 was deeply divided: the Stalwarts sought a third term for Grant, the Half Breeds backed Blaine, and the Independents favored John Sherman. When it became clear that none of the three could secure a majority, the delegates nominated Congressman James A. Garfield of Ohio on the thirty-sixth ballot. To appease the Stalwarts, second place on the ticket went to one of Conkling's closest associates, Chester A. Arthur, whom Hayes had dismissed as head of the New York customhouse. When Samuel J. Tilden declined to run, the Democrats picked General Winfield Scott Hancock, a Pennsylvanian and a Union hero in the Battle of Gettysburg. His running mate was William H. English of Indiana.

The platforms of the two parties revealed few basic differences on policy and no real understanding of the country's problems. The campaign turned largely on personalities and irrelevant issues that produced a great deal of sound and fury but nothing of any importance. Five-sixths of the voters turned out, and Garfield won by a margin of fewer than 10,000 popular votes, although his electoral vote was 214 to 155 for Hancock. Despite the failure of the two major parties to discuss the vital issues of the day, less than 4 percent of the electorate voted for a protest party candidate (General James B. Weaver of Iowa of the Greenback party), who advocated inflationary policies and stricter federal regulation of interstate commerce.

Garfield was a handsome, massive figure of a man, who had been an effective speaker and an able party leader in the House, but his friends found him timid and vacillating. Overwhelmed with the demands of office seekers he exclaimed, "My God! What is there in this place that a man should ever want to get into it?" After accepting the aid of the Stalwarts during the campaign and apparently reaching some understanding with them on patronage matters, Garfield antagonized Conkling by making his great rival, Blaine, secretary of state, and by appointing a Conkling opponent in New York collector of the port. In the ensuing fight between the president and the Stalwarts, Conkling and his colleague from New York, Thomas "Me Too" Platt, resigned their seats in the Senate and were not reelected by the New York legislature. At the height of this conflict, on 2 July 1881 Charles

J. Guiteau, a madman and disappointed office seeker, shot Garfield and shouted, "I am a Stalwart and Arthur is President now." Garfield died of the wound on 19 September, and Arthur became president.

To many Americans the succession of Arthur seemed a calamity, for he had the reputation of a New York machine politician. Reformers shuddered at the thought of a spoilsman in the presidency, and there was widespread feeling that the Stalwarts would take over. But, in spite of his unsavory past, Arthur was personally honest and did have ability. The responsibilities and dignity of the high office caused him to rise to the occasion and to give the country a good administration. He did not turn over the patronage to Conkling, as many thought he would. He supported civil service reform, prosecuted frauds in the Post Office, cleared the way for the construction of our modern navy, and had the Chinese immigration question settled. He also tried to check federal spending on unnecessary public works by vetoing an $18 million rivers and harbors bill and to bring about a reduction in the tariff, but both efforts were defeated by Congress.

The most important legislation during Arthur's presidency was the Pendleton Civil Service Act of 1883. Since the end of the Civil War reformers had been denouncing the spoils system and advocating the establishment of a permanent civil service based on merit. Garfield's murder dramatically advanced their cause. The Pendleton Act authorized the president to appoint a Civil Service Commission of three members to provide "open competitive examinations for testing the fitness of applicants for the public service now classified or to be classified." In addition, the act forbade the levying of political campaign assessments against federal employees and protected them against ouster for failure to make such contributions. At first the act affected only the lowest offices—about 14,000 or 12 percent of the total number of federal employees, leaving the remainder under the spoils system—but the president had the authority to extend the classified list at his discretion. Arthur demonstrated good faith by making excellent appointments to the commission. Every subsequent president extended the classified list, and by the end of the century it included 40 percent of all federal positions.

In 1884 the Republicans turned their backs on Arthur and nominated Blaine for president and John A. Logan of Illinois for vice-president. The Democrats named Grover Cleveland of New York and Thomas A. Hendricks of Indiana. Viewing Blaine as an old guard politician inimical to good government, George William Curtis, Schurz, and other reformist Mugwumps bolted the Republican party and supported Cleveland. As in 1880 there were few real issues, and the campaign degenerated into one of personal abuse and vilification. "The public is angry and abusive," observed Henry Adams. "Every one takes part. We are all doing our best, and swearing like demons. But the amusing thing is that no one talks about real issues." The Democrats publicized the "Mulligan letters" to prove that Blaine, as Speaker of the House, had been guilty of unethical conduct in connection with land-grant railroads, and the Republicans retaliated with the charge that Cleveland was the father of an illegitimate child, the responsibility for whom he had accepted. Since Blaine seemed to have led an impeccable private life but a culpable public one, and Cleveland just the reverse, one Mugwump suggested that "we should elect Mr. Cleveland to the public office he is so admirably qualified to fill and to remand Mr. Blaine to the private life which he is so eminently fitted to adorn." Overall, the decision in 1884 was nearly as close as in 1880. Cleveland's plurality in popular votes was only 23,000 and his electoral vote was 219 to 182 for Blaine. So narrow was the margin of victory for Cleveland that he carried the pivotal state of New York by a mere 1,149 votes.

Cleveland, a strapping figure of well over 200 pounds, came to the White House in 1885 with the reputation of a reformer and a man of courage, integrity, and prodigious work habits. Actually he was unimaginative, stolid, obdurate, brutally forthright and candid, and he lacked a sense of timing. He was also a thoroughgoing conservative, a believer in sound money, and a defender of property rights. In his inaugural he promised to adhere to "business principles," and his cabinet included conservatives and business-minded Democrats from the East and South. His administration signified no break with his Republican predecessors on fundamental issues.

Cleveland faced the task of pleasing both the Mugwumps and the hungry spoilsmen of his own party who had been cut off from the federal patronage for twenty-four years. At first he refused to yield to the bosses on appointments and thereby won the acclaim of the reformers. But, faced with a revolt within his own party, Cleveland gave in to the spoilsmen and replaced Republicans with "honest Democrats." Carl Shurz wrote, "Your attempt to please both reformers and spoilsmen has failed," and Cleveland broke with the Mugwumps. At the end of his presidency he had replaced about two-thirds of the 120,000 federal officeholders. On the credit side he increased the classified list to 27,380, almost double the number when he took office.

Cleveland was more successful as a watchdog of the Treasury than he was as a civil service reformer. He halted the scandalous pension racket by vetoing hundreds of private pension bills that congressmen had pushed through for constituents whose claims had been rejected by the Pension Office. Cleveland signed more of these bills than had all his predecessors since Johnson put together, but he was the first president to veto any. The Grand Army of the Republic (GAR), the powerful Union veterans association, screamed at these vetoes, and in January 1887 Congress responded by passing a Dependent Pension bill that provided a pension for all honorably discharged disabled veterans who had served as little as three months in the Union Army if they could not work, irrespective of how they had become disabled. Cleveland vetoed it and angered the GAR. Congress upheld his veto, however.

Cleveland's unpopularity with the GAR increased by his "rebel flag order" of 30 April 1887. This instructed the adjutant general to return to the southern states a number of flags which had been captured from Confederate forces and had been in storage in the War Office Building. The storm of protest that arose over this decision amazed Cleveland. Reconsidering, he concluded that the disposal of the flags belonged to Congress, not to the president. Thus he revoked the order. More than twenty years later a Republican Congress under Theodore Roosevelt voted unanimously to return the flags.

Cleveland accepted the prevalent idea that the president should obey and enforce the laws and that he had little obligation to provide initiative and leadership. Aside from the Interstate Commerce Act, for which he deserves no credit, and which he signed with reluctance and "with reservations," little significant legislation was enacted during his term. He did compel railroad, lumber, and cattle companies to give up 81 million acres of public land that they had fraudulently occupied. In 1886 Congress passed the Presidential Succession Act which provided that after the vice-president, the succession should pass to the members of the cabinet, beginning with the secretary of state, in the order of the creation of their departments. In 1887 the Dawes Act inaugurated a new Indian policy.

For the first time in this era both major parties were forced to take a position on the tariff issue. Cleveland devoted his entire annual message of December 1887 to the tariff question and presented a well-reasoned argument against the existing high rates. He maintained that a high tariff raised prices and that protective schedules were not needed to keep wages up since only 15 percent of workers were employed in protected industries. Pointing to the annual surplus of about $100 million brought in each year by the Tariff of 1883, he declared, "It is a condition that confronts us, not a theory." Cleveland's foes branded his message a "free trade" document, but all he advocated was a drastic reduction of duties.

During the ensuing congressional session the Democrat-controlled House passed a low tariff bill sponsored by Roger Q. Mills of Texas, chairman of the Ways and Means Committee. This reduced the tariff from an average level of about 47 percent to an average level of about 40 percent, and put such items as lumber, wool, flax, hemp, salt, and tinplate on the free list. The Republican-dominated Senate turned down the Mills bill and passed a highly protective measure that the Democratic House would not accept. This led to a deadlock and the injection of the tariff question into the 1888 election.

The Democrats renominated Cleveland and chose the elderly ex-Senator Allen G. Thurman of Ohio as his running mate. The Republicans selected Senator Benjamin Harrison of Indiana whose main qualifications were a distinguished ancestry (he was a grandson of former President William Henry Harrison) and residence in a doubtful state. Second place on the ticket went to Levi P. Morton, a wealthy New York banker. Two labor parties, reflecting the industrial unrest of the period, entered the campaign. The Union Labor and the United Labor parties condemned the two major parties for being under the control of monopolies and for being indifferent to the welfare of workers.

The campaign was waged largely on the tariff issue, with Republicans defending protection and Democrats advocating a reduction in duties. The Republicans appealed to the manufacturing interests, who would profit by a high tariff, and to veterans who were promised generous pension legislation. Both parties used money freely, and throughout the country voters were bribed in probably the most corrupt presidential election in American history. Although Cleveland had a plurality of nearly 100,000 popular votes, Harrison carried the crucial doubtful states of Indiana, New York, and Ohio, and gained 233 electoral votes to Cleveland's 168. Despite all the campaign talk about the tariff, the vote did not indicate a national decision against Cleveland on that issue. Cleveland carried the manufacturing states of New Jersey and Connecticut and increased his strength of 1884 in such pro-tariff states as Ohio, Michigan, and California. The decisive factors were probably the efficiency of the Republican organization with

Senator Quay at its head and the purchase of the floating vote in the doubtful states.

Harrison possessed intellectual gifts and was an eloquent orator, but he was very cold in his personal relationships. "Harrison sweats ice water" became a popular phrase, and one of his close associates remarked that "Harrison can make a speech to ten thousand men and every man of them will go away his friend. Let him meet the same ten thousand in private, and every one will go away his enemy." Although Harrison had ability he lacked forcefulness and the leadership passed largely to the Republican kingpins in Congress, especially to Senator Nelson W. Aldrich of Rhode Island and Speaker Thomas B. Reed of Maine. Reed pushed through the House a revision of the rules that gave him almost dictatorial powers over proceedings and earned for him the title of "czar."

For the first time since 1875 the Republicans had the presidency and a majority in both houses of Congress, and they began to pay off their political debts. The McKinley Tariff of 1890 raised rates to a higher level and protected more products than any previous tariff in American history. In the same year the Dependent Pension Act, substantially the same measure vetoed by Cleveland, granted pensions to all GAR veterans suffering from any disability, acquired in war service or not, and to their widows and children. By 1893 this measure had increased the number of pensioners to 966,000 and the annual cost to $157 million. Also in 1890, to meet the demands of the silverites, the Sherman Silver Purchase Act increased the amount of silver to be purchased by the Treasury to 4,500,000 ounces a month. To appease the popular clamor against monopolies, the Sherman Antitrust Act was also passed in 1890. However, this Congress acquired the unsavory label of the "Billion Dollar Congress." By distributing subsidies to steamship lines, passing extravagant rivers and harbors bills, offering large premiums to government bondholders, and returning federal taxes paid by northern states during the Civil War, Congress handed out so much money that by 1894 the Treasury surplus was gone, and the United States has never had a surplus since.

Instead of the widespread support that such policies were expected to bring, the public reaction was one of hostility, and in the congressional elections of 1890 the Republicans were severely rebuked. They retained only 88 of the 332 seats in the House and had their majority in the Senate reduced from 14 to 6. The appearance of 9 new congressmen representing farm interests and not associated with either of the major parties indicated that a third-party revolt was shaping up and that a new phase in American politics was under way. These developments would dominate and alter the course of American parties and politics during the ensuing decade.

Further Reading

Adams, Henry. *The Education of Henry Adams.* 1918.

Blodgett, Geoffrey. *The Gentle Reformers: Massachusetts Democrats in the Cleveland Era.* 1966.

Bryce, James. *The American Commonwealth.* 2 vols., 1888.

Davison, Kenneth E. *The Presidency of Rutherford B. Hayes.* 1972.

DeSantis, Vincent P. *Republicans Face the Southern Question: The New Departure Years, 1877–1897.* 1959.

Dobson, John A. *Politics in the Gilded Age: A New Perspective on Reform.* 1972.

Doenecke, Justus. *The Presidencies of James A. Garfield and Chester A. Arthur.* 1981.

Garraty, John A. *The New Commonwealth, 1877–1890.* 1968.

Gould, Lewis L. *The Presidency of William McKinley.* 1980.

Hirshon, Stanley P. *Farewell to the Bloody Shirt: Northern Republicans and the Southern Negro, 1877–1893.* 1962.

Hoogenboom, Ari A. *Outlawing the Spoils.* 1961.

Jensen, Richard J. *The Winning of the Midwest: Social and Political Conflict, 1888–1896.* 1971.

Josephson, Matthew. *The Politicos.* 1938.

Keller, Morton. *Affairs of State: Public Life in Nineteenth Century America.* 1977.

Kleppner, Paul. *The Cross of Culture: A Social Analysis of Midwestern Politics, 1850–1900.* 1970.

Kousser, J. Morgan. *The Shaping of Southern Politics.* 1974.

Logan, Rayford W. *The Negro in American Life and Thought: The Nadir, 1877–1901.* 1954.

Marcus, Robert D. *Grand Old Party, Political Structure in the Gilded Age 1880–1896.* 1971.

McFeeley, William S. *Grant: A Biography.* 1981.

McSeveney, Samuel. *The Politics of Depression: Political Behavior in the Northeast, 1893–1896.* 1972.

Merrill, H. S. *Bourbon Democracy in the Middle West, 1865–1898.* 1953.

Morgan, H. Wayne. *From Hayes to McKinley: National Party Politics, 1877–1896.* 1969.

Ostrogorski, Moisei. *Democracy and the Organization of American Parties.* 2 vols., 1902.

Peskin, Allan. *Garfield: A Biography.* 1978.

Polakoff, Keith Ian. *The Politics of Inertia: The Election of 1876 and the End of Reconstruction.* 1973.

Reeves, Thomas C. *Gentleman Boss, The Life of Chester Alan Arthur.* 1975.

Rothman, David J. *Politics and Power: The United States Senate, 1869-1901.* 1966.

Sievers, Harry. *Benjamin Harrison: Hoosier President.* 1968.

Sproat, John G. *"The Best Men": Liberal Reformers in the Gilded Age.* 1971.

White, Leonard D. *The Republican Era, 1869-1901.* 1958.

Wiebe, Robert H. *The Search for Order, 1877-1920.* 1967.

Woodward, C. Vann. *Origins of the New South, 1877-1913.* 1951.

_____. *Reunion and Reaction.* 1966.

4

The Agrarian Revolt

The most important result of the off-year elections of 1890 was the appearance of a number of new congressmen representing farm interests independent of either one of the major parties. This revolt against "the politics of dead center" took the form of agrarian insurgency in the West and South that had been building up after the Civil War and reached its culmination in the 1890s. There were several reasons why the farmer was discontented. The conversion of American agriculture to a commercial basis during and after the war had made the farmer a specialist and integrated him into a capitalistic system of mass production for a world market. He had the special role of producing a surplus by which the United States could adjust any unfavorable balance of trade created by a large volume of imports. But whereas the industrialist had some control over his market and prices, the farmer had none. He worked in an unorganized individualistic manner and competed in both the American and the world farm markets. Instead of benefiting from the new order of things, he was a victim of it. Leonidas L. Polk, a North Carolina farm editor, expressed the view of almost every farmer in the country when he wrote in 1887:

There is something radically wrong in our industrial system. There is a screw loose. The wheels have dropped out of balance. The railroads have never been so prosperous, and yet agriculture languishes. The banks have never done a better or more profitable business, and yet agriculture languishes. Manufacturing enterprises have never made more money or were in a more flourishing condition, and yet agriculture languishes. Towns and cities flourish and "boom,". . . and yet agriculture languishes. Salaries and fees were never so temptingly high and desirable, and yet agriculture languishes.

Another hardship for the farmer was the decline in the prices that he received for his crops. Between 1870 and 1897 wheat prices dropped from $1.06 to 63.3 cents a bushel, corn from 43.1 to 29.7 cents a bushel, and cotton from 15.1 to 5.8 cents a pound. These figures were market prices, after warehouse and transportation charges had been paid, not the lower prices that the farmer received. In Kansas in 1889 corn sold for 10 cents a bushel and was commonly used in place of coal as a fuel; in 1890, a farmer in Nebraska stated that he had shot his hogs since he could neither sell nor give them away.

Another grievance of the farmer was the increased debtor and tenancy status under which he lived. By 1900 nearly one-third of the country's farms had mortgages, with the highest percentage in the Middle West—45 percent in Wisconsin, 48 percent in Michigan, and 53 percent in Iowa. Southern farmers had fewer mortgages, because they could not easily secure them. The number of tenant farmers increased from 25.8 percent of all the farms in 1880, to 29.4 percent in 1890, and to 35.3 percent in 1900.

The basic cause of the farmers' misfortune was an overexpansion in agricultural production that caused supply to outrun demand from the 1870s down to about 1900. Not understanding the complicated reasons for his plight, the farmer naturally blamed others. He regarded the railroads as the chief villain. He resented discrimination and rate differentials and felt that he was a helpless victim of the rail monopoly. On through routes and long hauls the rates were comparatively low, because there was competition for this freight; but on local and short hauls, where competition was either scanty or nonexistent, the rates were disproportionately high. Sometimes the western local rate was four times that charged for the same distance and commodity in the East. It cost Minnesota farmers more to ship their grain to St. Paul or Minneapolis than to New York. The railroads also favored the big shipper over the small shipper; they dominated politics and bought up legislatures. The middleman was also the farmer's foe. The farmer found himself at the mercy of local merchants, grain dealers, brokers, and speculators in his crops. He also attacked the national banks because they refused to lend money on real estate and farm property and because they seemed indifferent to his seasonal needs for money.

The farmer complained, too, that he bore the brunt of the tax burden. Tax dodging, especially on the part of corporations, was notorious. The merchant could underestimate the value of his stock; the householder might exclude some of his property; and the owner of securities could conceal them. However, the farmer could not hide his land. Finally, the farmer opposed the high tariffs, because he had to purchase his consumer goods in a highly protected market while he sold his own crops in an unprotected market. He shared none of the benefits of protection, but instead contributed heavily to the subsidization of business. This injustice was all the more difficult to bear in view of his belief that the tariff was "the mother of trusts."

The farmers not only felt they were ignored; they suspected the government of indifference and even hostility. They decided to organize and protest against their condition. In 1867 Oliver Hudson Kelley, a government clerk, founded the Patrons of Husbandry, which became better known as the Grange, for the purpose of promoting agricultural education and creating social fellowship among farmers. The Grange, as the local unit was called, was a club where farmers met with their families to enjoy games and a picnic supper. Or they might listen to a lecture on scientific agriculture or discuss the cooperative purchase of a new reaper for general use.

At first the Grangers took no part in politics. They welcomed the new railroads, which increased the value of their land and furnished transportation for their products. By 1875 there were some 30,000 Granges in all parts of the country. In the upper Mississippi Valley—in Illinois, Wisconsin, Minnesota, and Iowa—where more than one-third of the wheat was grown, they boasted a membership of over half a million. They were equally strong in the South, and South Carolina ranked second only to Iowa in the number of Granges.

The Grangers, in their campaign for self-improvement, soon began to aim at higher goals than education and fellowship. They also tried to increase farmers' income by establishing cooperative stores, banks, factories, and insurance companies. But these ventures were often unsoundly financed and operated and could not weather the competition of businessmen and the Panic of 1873. They left a burden of discredit and indebtedness and were the prime cause of the disintegration of the Grange movement in the mid-1870s.

It was impossible for so many farmers, with their long background of participation in politics, to get together without eventually going into the political arena. They had too many grievances, as we have noted, which they thought they could remedy by political action. Consequently, new protest parties were formed under various names in about a dozen midwestern and southern states in the 1870s. They were never powerful enough to control a national party or to directly dictate national legislation. But they were an influential pressure group within both major parties, and they were able indirectly to affect important national legislation.

Beginning with Illinois in 1870, moreover, the Grangers won control of the legislatures of several midwestern and southern states. They worked in state capitals mainly for the regulation of railroads and grain elevators. The midwestern Granger legislatures tried to impose reasonable rates by direct legislation, by simply decreeing what rates should be charged. The railroads quite generally refused to obey these laws and either persuaded the legislatures to repeal them or won cases in the state courts. On the other hand, the beginning of railroad regulation was more promising in the South. Georgia, for example, established a railroad commission in 1879 that pioneered in the field of scientific regulation of rates and services.

The farmers, for a while, then turned to the Greenback movement, which grew out of demands to increase the amount of currency in circulation or to halt the withdrawal of greenbacks and to prevent government bonds from being redeemed in gold. The movement fell into two periods. The first lasted from 1867 to 1872 and was known as the social reform or wage earners' period. Eastern labor dominated it in these years, when its primary objects were to lower the interest rates on money and to reduce taxation by changing the war debt into interconvertible war bonds. After 1873 the movement entered the inflationists' or farmers' period. The farmers were interested in the expansion of the currency in the hope that inflation would result in higher prices for their products. It was not until the Panic of 1873 had intensified the agricultural depression and the Granger movement had failed to relieve the situation that the farmers took over the Greenback movement. Then it developed into the Greenback Labor party, which reached its high-water mark in the election of 1878, when its candidates polled about one million votes and it elected fifteen congressmen. The party's main strength was in the Middle West, but even in the East the movement was largely agrarian. But with the failure in 1879 to prevent resumption of specie payment and with the price of corn further reduced in 1880, the farmers lost interest in greenbackism, and its support rapidly declined. In the presidential election of 1880 the Greenback candidate, James B. Weaver of Iowa, received only 300,000 votes, about 4 percent of the total; by 1888 the party was dead.

With the decline of the Grange and the disappearance of greenbackism, a new crop of farm associations appeared. By far the most important was the Farmers' Alliance, which was really two organizations of different origins. In the old Granger states of the Midwest the organization was known as the Northwestern Farmers' Alliance, and in the South, as the Southern Farmers' Alliance. The Southern Alliance originated in 1875 in a frontier county of Texas for protection against horse thieves and land sharks. It remained small until 1886, when it began to expand throughout the South under the vigorous leadership of C. W. Macune and absorbed rival farmers' organizations. The Northwestern Alliance was organized by Milton George in Chicago in 1880. There was also the National Colored Farmers' Alliance and Cooperative Union.

The Alliances, especially the Southern, experimented more extensively with cooperatives than the Grange, but with no greater success. An attempted merger of the two Alliances in a meeting at St. Louis in 1889 also failed. The Southern Alliance insisted upon the retention of its secret rituals and the exclusion of blacks, at least from the national body. The Northwestern Alliance wanted a federation in which each organization would keep its identity. Then, the Southern Alliance changed its name to the National Farmers' Alliance and Industrial Union and induced the three strongest state alliances of the Northwestern Alliance—those of Kansas and of North and South Dakota—to join it. In the same year it gained the endorsement of the Knights of Labor.

Alliance leaders, realizing that most of the farmer's needs were beyond the power of the state governments to solve, developed a national program between 1890 and 1892. Its chief plank was inflation, mainly through the free coinage of silver at the ratio of 16 to 1. This, farm leaders reasoned, would raise farm prices and relieve farmers of an intolerable debt burden. The leaders also wanted to repeal the National Banking Act and abolish national bank notes tied to United States bonds. They believed that the federal government alone should control the money supply and issue currency according to the needs of the country, not according to the bonded indebtedness or the supply of gold.

The farmers also demanded more stringent regulation of railroad rates. In fact, the Northwestern Alliance leaders generally favored governmental ownership and operation of railroads.

Another agrarian demand was for greater democratization of politics through the direct primary, secret ballot, and popular election of United States senators. Finally, the Alliancemen, hoping to attract large labor support, advocated the eight-hour day for workers, governmental support of labor unions in their struggle for collective bargaining, and an end to the employment of contract labor.

These developments gave the appearance that a new party was underway. Most of the Alliance leaders in the West believed so. Between 1890 and 1892, therefore, they made vigorous efforts to persuade the southern agrarians to join them in forming a new national party. It would unite all forces of discontent—farmers, workers, and various reform groups.

In May 1891 the Northwestern Alliance held a convention of over 1,400 delegates in Cincinnati. It included representatives from the Knights of Labor, Free-Silverites, and Greenbackers, as well as leaders of both the Southern and Northwestern Alliances. This gathering issued a call for a national convention of a new People's (soon to be called Populist) party. It would meet the following year in Omaha to write a platform and nominate a presidential ticket.

Populism originated within and grew out of the Alliance. The constitution of the Alliance proclaimed it to be a nonpolitical organization, as was the Grange. Yet there was a certain ambiguity about this. Each year the Alliance put forth a series of demands that could only be realized by political means. For example, the Ocala, Florida, platform of 1890 called for the abolition of national banks, establishment of a subtreasury system, a graduated income tax, the direct election of United States senators, and government control of communication and transportation facilities. By 1890 the Northwestern Alliance concluded that nonpartisan activities were a failure and decided to enter politics. Kansas led the way by organizing a People's (Populist) party in June 1890, and Alliancemen in other western states set up independent parties under other names. The West was in the throes of a mighty upheaval; a later commentator called it "a pentecost of politics in which a tongue of flame sat upon every man and each spoke as the spirit gave him utterance."

"Sockless" Jerry Simpson, Ignatius Donnelly, Mary Elizabeth Lease, Anna L. Diggs, and General Weaver were among the leaders of

western populism. The party, though hastily constructed, was successful in Kansas where it elected five congressmen and one senator in the
1890 elections; in Nebraska, where it gained control of both houses of
the legislature and elected two congressmen; and in South Dakota
where it elected a senator.

In the South the Alliance, fearing that the establishment of a third
party might bring the blacks into power, first tried to gain control of
the Democratic party machine. It attacked the industrial and urban
leadership of the Democratic party and endorsed candidates who
pledged themselves to the Ocala platform. The Alliance appeared to
have captured the Democratic party in the elections of 1890 when four
governors, eight state legislatures, forty-four congressmen, and three
senators promised to support Alliance demands, but nearly all these
elected officials reverted to Democratic orthodoxy once in office. This
disillusioning experience, plus the prospect of Cleveland's renomina-
tion by the Democratic party, stimulated Southern Alliancemen to become Populists. In July 1892, the national People's party was formally
organized in Omaha, Nebraska.

When the Populists met in national convention at Omaha in 1892
they adopted a far-reaching progressive platform, which is one of the
most important documents in American political history. In a long
preamble the Omaha platform condemned national conditions and
the major parties.

We meet in the midst of a nation brought to the very verge of moral, political
and material ruin. Corruption dominates the ballot-box, the legislature, the
Congress, and touches even the ermine of the bench...Business prostrated,
homes are covered with mortgages, labor is impoverished, and the land is con-
centrating in the hands of capitalists....The fruits of the toil of millions are
boldly stolen to build up colossal fortunes for a few....We have witnessed for
more than a quarter of a century the struggles of the two great parties for
power and plunder....Neither do they now promise us any substantial reform....They propose to sacrifice our homes, lives and children on the altar
of mammon.

More important were the specific planks of the Populist platform.
They demanded: (1) free coinage of silver at the ratio of 16 to 1, (2) the
subtreasury system, (3) abolition of national bank notes and the issuance by the federal Treasury of abundant legal tender currency, (4) a

graduated income tax, (5) governmental ownership of railroads, telegraphs, and telephones, (6) return to the government of unused lands granted to the railroads, (7) restriction of immigration, (8) an eight-hour day for labor, (9) postal savings banks, and (10) election of United States senators by popular vote. General James B. Weaver of Iowa, the candidate of the Greenback-Labor party of 1880, was nominated for the presidency. Thus a new third party entered the national political arena.

The two major parties had already held their conventions in June. The Republicans renominated Harrison, in spite of a feeble attempt to stampede the convention to Blaine. The Democrats named Cleveland for the third successive time. Machine politicians, under the leadership of Governor David B. Hill of New York, tried to prevent Cleveland's nomination, but he was so strong with the rank and file of the party that he easily won on the first ballot.

The campaign of 1892 would have been a totally dull affair had it not been for the effort by the Populists to build their party and to make a good showing. Still, as Henry Adams observed, "the two candidates were singular persons, of whom it was the common saying that one of them had no friends; the other only enemies."* Cleveland came out for sound money but made his fight mainly against the McKinley Tariff Act. Harrison straddled the money question and defended protection as a boon to labor. His claims that workers were prosperous and happy were undercut by a violent and bloody strike against Carnegie's Homestead plant in the middle of the campaign. However, the main issue seems to have been the personalities of the candidates. Cleveland was not glamorous, but he was more appealing than Harrison. Voters eager for a change not only elected Cleveland by a large plurality but also returned Democratic majorities to both houses of Congress.

Weaver polled slightly more than a million popular votes and carried Colorado, Kansas, Nevada, and Idaho, with twenty-two electoral votes. But the Populist showing was an exaggeration of the party's actual strength. In several western states the Democrats either had put no ticket in the field or else had supported Populist nominees. Furthermore, three states were carried by the silver interests rather than by the Alliance itself. No state east of the Mississippi and north of the

---

*Henry Adams, *The Education of Henry Adams*. Modern Library Edition, 1931, p. 320.

Ohio rivers gave Weaver as much as 5 percent of its vote. Cleveland would have won the election by a large margin even if all the Weaver states had gone for Harrison.

Yet the campaign showed how much populism had spread throughout the West. The new party elected three United States senators and eleven members of the House. Moreover, it more than held its own in the mid-term elections of 1894, when the Republicans once more regained control of the House.

Like Martin Van Buren and Herbert Hoover, Grover Cleveland had the bad luck to be in the White House when a major depression struck the country. The storm broke in the summer of 1893, causing more than five hundred banks to close and sixteen thousand business firms and railway systems to go into bankruptcy by the end of the year. With the closing of factories and mines, thousands of workers were unemployed. And within a year there were four million unemployed out of a population of about sixty-five million Americans. In the West the suffering was increased by the failure of the corn crop and by the continued decline in the price of agricultural products. But worst still were the hard times of the next four years, marked by acute personal hardships and a deterioration in the government's financial position.

Like all earlier presidents, Cleveland did not believe it was his duty to use the arm of the federal government to combat a depression, and he complacently stated in his second inaugural address that "while the people should patriotically and cheerfully support their Government, its functions do not include the support of the people." Cleveland believed that the Sherman Silver Purchase Act and the McKinley Tariff had caused the panic and subsequent depression. Whatever else was wrong in the national economy resulted from the folly or misfortune of individuals, and thus was not the concern of the federal government.

In the face of the all pervading social unrest, Cleveland concentrated his first efforts on repealing the Silver Purchase Act so as to maintain the gold standard and to prevent the Treasury's gold reserve from falling below the established minimum of $100 million. On the other hand the silverites believed that the law of 1873 demonetizing silver had caused the economic disaster. They thought that the cure lay in the free and unlimited coinage of silver at a ratio of 16 to 1 of gold, and that the Sherman Act had provided them with inadequate relief. Many debtor agrarians agreed with them.

But Cleveland was convinced that the silver certificates issued under the Sherman Act and redeemed in gold were responsible for the drain on the gold reserve that was reducing it to the $100 million minimum, which had been used since 1882 as a metallic basis for the $350 million in greenbacks still in circulation. Thus he summoned Congress into special session in August 1893, and asked for the immediate repeal of the Sherman Silver Purchase Act. The House voted for the repeal a few weeks later by a large majority, but the contest in the Senate was long and bitter. Cleveland withheld patronage from some senators and purchased the support of others such as Senator Daniel Vorhees of Indiana, a lifelong inflationist, by giving him control of all the patronage in his state. The silver senators, supported by the Populists and southerners, fought against the repeal of the Sherman Act until the end of October when the Senate finally approved repeal by a close vote. Most Republicans voted for it; most western and southern Democrats voted against it, widening the split within the Democratic party on the currency issue.

Cleveland's leadership, however, fell short of the accomplishment of positive legislation to meet the Treasury crisis. Though he had said that "the administration must be ready with some excellent substitute for the Sherman Law," he failed to offer any constructive alternative. Many business leaders, as well as Democrats who favored repeal, had advocated the enactment of a substitute measure to provide for currency expansion and flexibility. Most of the Democrats, being practical politicians, feared that unconditional repeal might destroy their party, which was already sharply divided on the currency matter. But Cleveland insisted on unconditional repeal. At a cabinet meeting on the matter, he smote the table with his fist and asserted he would not yield an inch, and the compromise movement collapsed.

Unfortunately, the repeal of the Sherman Act did not restore prosperity or have any noticeable effect on the depression. The Treasury's gold reserve continued to fall, and, to maintain an amount sufficient to remain on the gold standard, Cleveland had the Treasury sell United States government bonds for gold. A group of bankers headed by J. P. Morgan absorbed three bond issues in 1894 and 1895, but it was not until 1897, when the depression had run its course, that the Treasury crisis ended. The gold purchases had enabled the Treasury to meet its obligations, but the decision to sell bonds to New York bankers was one of the most unpopular ones Cleveland ever made. The silverites grew more resentful of the president, and many Americans became alarmed over the dependence of the government upon a syndicate of Wall Street bankers.

Cleveland also failed to bring about any substantial reduction of the tariff. The Democrats, fulfilling their campaign promises, had passed a tariff bill in the House drawn up by William L. Wilson of West Virginia, which provided for a reduction in rates. But when the measure reached the Senate a group of protectionists from both parties, led by Senator Arthur Gorman, an influential Democrat from Maryland, attacked the bill with more than 600 amendments and restored most of the cuts that had been made in the House. The bill, now known as the Wilson-Gorman Tariff, was a far cry from genuine reform. Disappointed by this result, Cleveland allowed the measure to become law without his signature.

But Cleveland had contributed to this failure. He had played no effective part in framing the tariff. Then, too, the bitterness within the Democratic party that had been aroused during the fight over repeal of the silver act made agreement nearly impossible. Discipline and party loyalty no longer existed, and Cleveland had already used his political ace—patronage—in getting the Senate to repeal the Sherman Act. It was only when the Senate had mutilated the Wilson Tariff that Cleveland took some kind of action. Through a letter read on the floor of the House, he declared, "Every true Democrat knows that this bill in its present form... falls far short of the consummation for which we have long labored.... Our abandonment of the cause or the principle upon which it rests means party perfidy and party dishonor."

While the blast relieved the president of his anger, it further antagonized the Senate and failed to accomplish the ends sought. Democratic senators savagely attacked Cleveland and defied him. While he refused to sign the Wilson-Gorman bill, he also declined to veto it. Cleveland's crusade for a lower tariff, which he had launched in 1881, had come to a sad conclusion. The reform phase of his public career had also ended. For the remainder of his presidency, Cleveland reduced his role to that of a protector of the status quo. In this he was more successful than he had been as a crusader for change, for he could play his usual, and many times more effective, role of righteous chief executive. He vetoed a bill that would have increased the supply of the currency. Through subordinate officials, he rudely rejected the petitions of angry wage earners, such as those who marched with Coxey's Army in 1894, to support a measure in Congress providing for the issuance of $500 million in legal tender notes to be spent on road construction by the unemployed. And in 1894 he sent federal troops to crush the Pullman strike.

As a result of the Panic of 1893, the Pullman Palace Car Company laid off a large number of its workers and in 1894 reduced wages as much as 25 percent without lowering the rents in the town of Pullman, Illinois, completely owned by the company. When their requests for lower rents or higher wages were refused and their spokesmen discharged, the Pullman employees went on strike in May 1894. In June the American Railway Union, founded by Eugene V. Debs in 1893, came to the assistance of the Pullman workers by voting to boycott all Pullman cars. The General Managers' Association, made up of officials from twenty-four railroads, joined forces with the Pullman Company. The strike spread rapidly and resulted in delaying the mail and tying up railroad traffic in the Chicago area. The president received numerous appeals to intervene from railroad officials, shippers, and business leaders.

Under pressure from the business community and urgings from Attorney General Richard Olney, a former railroad lawyer who was a foe of labor unions, Cleveland decided to end the boycott. Olney had the federal circuit court in Chicago serve an injunction, under the provisions of the Sherman Antitrust Law, on officers of the American Railway Union against obstructing the railroads or interfering with the mails. When the union ignored the injunction, Cleveland exploded. "If it takes the entire army and navy to deliver a postcard in Chicago, that card will be delivered," he vowed. He dispatched some 2,000 troops from nearby Fort Sheridan to Chicago to "restore law and order," and soon the strike collapsed. At the same time Debs and other union leaders were arrested for violating the injunction and were sent to jail.

Cleveland was severely criticized for his actions in the Pullman strike. He sent the troops to Chicago over the strong protests of John P. Altgeld, the Democratic governor of Illinois, and there was an angry exchange between the two men. Altgeld challenged the right of the president to order soldiers to the scene, and he gave detailed information to show that local and state officials had the situation completely under control. "To absolutely ignore a local government," the governor charged, "not only insults the people. . . but is in violation of a basic principle of our institutions." Cleveland answered that the troops had been sent "in strict accordance with the Constitution and laws of the United States" and that there was no intention on the part of the federal government of "interfering with the plain duty of the local authorities to preserve the peace of the city."

Cleveland's solution of this labor dispute was costly. The imprisonment of Debs by a court order, without jury trial or conviction, and the use of a blanket injunction in the strike gave serious concern to many Americans, even to the conservatives. All over the country advocates of organized labor and of states' rights as well launched a heavy attack on Cleveland, whose popularity was now definitely on the wane. Yet Cleveland's unpopularity was temporarily offset by his actions in the Venezuelan boundary dispute. This arose out of a controversy between Venezuela and Great Britain over the boundary line of British Guiana. At stake were some 23,000 square miles of rich mineral country in an area claimed by both Venezuela and British Guiana. The British in 1887 turned down the good offices of the United States in settling the dispute. Then Cleveland in his annual message to Congress in 1894 offered to renew his attempt to have the matter arbitrated, but Britain refused to arbitrate. In February 1895 Congress passed a joint resolution urging arbitration. When no conciliatory word came from Britain, Richard Olney, now Secretary of State, with Cleveland's approval, in July 1895 sent a strong note to London which said, "Today the United States is practically sovereign on this continent, and its fiat is law upon the subjects to which it confines its interpretation. . . . Its infinite resources combined with its isolated position render it master of the situation and practically invulnerable as against any or all other powers." Under the Monroe Doctrine, the United States could not permit a European power to seize the territory of an American republic. Thus the United States wanted a definite answer as to whether Great Britain would submit the dispute to arbitration. Cleveland called the note "Olney's twenty-inch gun." After a four-month delay, Lord Salisbury, British prime minister and foreign secretary, replied politely but firmly on 26 November to the effect that the Monroe Doctrine could not be applied to the dispute and was not part of international law and that Great Britain and Venezuela alone were concerned with the matter.

Cleveland then sent a special message to Congress in December, making public the correspondence between Olney and Salisbury and recommending that the United States take the decision of the boundary line between British Guiana and Venezuela into its own hands. "In making these recommendations," Cleveland said, "I am fully alive to the responsibility incurred and keenly realize all the consequences that may follow." While a few prominent Americans such as Carl Schurz and President Charles W. Eliot of Harvard criticized the president's words, his message was widely approved in the country. Congress responded at once by unanimously authorizing the president to appoint a boundary commission and appropriating $100,000 for its expenses.

This action caused influential citizens in both the United States and Great Britain to work to maintain the peace. Also by this time the British government had become involved in difficulties with the Boers in South Africa and was concerned about its international position in general. Thus Great Britain agreed to submit its entire claim to arbitration. The tribunal, meeting in Paris in 1899, made a series of decisions that largely supported the original British position. The Venezuelan controversy came to an amicable conclusion and in the end led to closer relations between the United States and Great Britain.

Although the nation had supported Cleveland in the Venezuelan affair, the continuance of the depression and the president's failure to do much about it caused a steady decline of his popularity with many voters and politicians in his own party. Cleveland had many opponents. Silver Democrats, Populists, and other agrarians were alienated by the repeal of the Sherman Silver Purchase Act and by Cleveland's defense of the gold standard. He had lost the support of organized labor by the use of troops to break the Pullman strike. Businessmen blamed him for the Panic of 1893, and industrialists were irritated by his attack on the protective tariff. Democratic party leaders charged him with splitting his party in the tariff and currency fights and of allowing the Republicans to win the midterm election of 1894. And his negotiation of bond issues with Wall Street financiers to maintain the gold reserve laid him open to the charge that he was "a tool of Wall Street."

Three Supreme Court decisions in 1895 added to the general discontent on the part of farmers, workers, and the lower middle class. The Court in a five to four decision in *Pollock* v. *Farmers' Loan and Trust Company* invalidated the income tax clause of the Wilson-Gorman Tariff on the ground it was a direct tax. Therefore, according to the Constitution, it had to be apportioned among the states on the basis of population. Moreover, the Court, through Justice Stephen J. Field, had earlier called the income tax "an assault upon capital" and a "stepping stone to others, larger and more sweeping, till our political contests...became a war of the poor and against the rich." About a week after this decision the Court, in the case of *in re Debs,* unanimously upheld the injunction under which Debs had been imprisoned at the time of the Pullman strike. And at the same time the Court, in *United States* v. *E. C. Knight Company,* distinguished manufacturing from commerce and held that the Sherman Antitrust Act did not apply to manufacturing combinations within states, thus sanctioning the use of the holding company device and for some time hampering the prosecution of monopolies.

There was a widespread feeling in the country in the mid-1890s that there was a war on between the rich and the poor, and that Cleveland, the Supreme Court, and Congress were on the side of the rich. The agrarians looked upon Cleveland as an enemy, and he became the personification of the northeastern conservatism against which they were in revolt. Within the Democratic party, insurgent Democrats prepared to denounce Cleveland and advocate free silver. They hoped both to win the Populists and take over the Democratic party. Their work was so effective that by the summer of 1896, after the state conventions had met, they had gained control of every Democratic state organization south of the Potomac and west of the Alleghenies, except in South Dakota, Minnesota, and Wisconsin.

The Republicans met in St. Louis in June and nominated William McKinley of Ohio for president and Garret A. Hobart, a corporation lawyer from New Jersey, for vice-president. Marcus Alonzo Hanna, a wealthy Ohio industrialist, had been largely responsible for McKinley's nomination. On the monetary question, McKinley's record was not consistent. He had voted for both the Bland-Allison Act and the Sherman Silver Purchase Act; and yet in 1891 in running for governor he had condemned the free coinage of silver and had advocated international bimetalism. McKinley hoped that the tariff would be the chief issue of the campaign. Hanna had already decided upon a gold standard plank, but at the convention he gave the impression that he had to be "persuaded." Upon the adoption of the gold plank a small group of silver advocates led by Senator Henry M. Teller of Colorado dramatically left the hall and organized the National Silver Republican party.

The Democrats were torn by bitter strife when they met in Chicago in July. The convention was dominated by the silverites who denounced Cleveland in resolutions and speeches. The platform repudiated the Cleveland program and attached the protective tariff, the national banks, trusts, and the Supreme Court. It called for an income tax and the free coinage of silver at the ratio of 16 to 1. The leading contender for the nomination was Congressman Richard P.

("Silver-Dick") Bland of Missouri, who since the seventies had fought for free silver. But he was passed over, and on the fifth ballot the convention nominated William Jennings Bryan of Nebraska, who had captivated the silver delegates with a speech that rose to a stirring peroration: "You shall not crucify mankind upon a cross of gold." Bryan's nomination has the appearance of being won by the accident of a spontaneous speech. Yet Bryan, only thirty-six at the time, had been rounding up support for several years before 1896 and had already presented his ideas many times to other audiences. His convention speech was simply the last step, a step that became inevitable when the silverites gained control of the convention. Bryan's running mate was Arthur Sewall of Maine, a wealthy shipbuilder, banker, and protectionist, and an advocate of free silver.

The silver issue split the Democratic party as well as the Republican. The Democratic platform and the repudiation of Cleveland at the convention caused conservative Democrats to organize a gold, or National Democratic party, which put candidates in the campaign. This party had the support of President Cleveland and all members of his cabinet but one. But probably more conservative Democrats supported the Republican party than the gold Democratic ticket.

The Populists were in a dilemma. They had anticipated that both old parties would adopt conservative platforms and nominate conservative candidates. The Populists would then have a clear field to win the support of all the advocates of reform. But the capture of the Democratic party by the silverites and reform elements posed a problem for the Populists. If they nominated a Populist candidate, they feared that they would split the reform vote and permit McKinley to win. Yet if they sought to unite the reform vote by endorsing Bryan, they would surrender their identity to the Democrats and sacrifice their broad program of reform for a Democratic program that placed a disproportionate emphasis on the silver question.

When the Populists met at St. Louis in July, the fusionist faction (urging fusion with the Democrats) was organized with the aim of nominating Bryan. Southern Populists, who regarded fusion with the Democrats as anathema, agreed to support Bryan only after Senator William V. Allen of Nebraska, chairman of the convention, told the southerners that the Democrats had promised to withdraw Sewall and accept Thomas E. Watson of Georgia as their vice-presidential nominee. This arrangement would have created a true Democratic-Populist partnership, but these promises were later broken. The Populists nominated Bryan for president and the Georgia Populist, Watson, for vice-president. But the Democrats persisted in running their original choices, Bryan and Sewall. Henry Demarest Lloyd watched the convention with profound disgust and concluded, "The People's party has been betrayed...but after all it is its own fault."

The campaign was highly emotional and dramatic. Campaigning in an unprecedented fashion, Bryan spoke in 21 states, traveled 18,000 miles, made more than 600 speeches, and reached an audience of some 5,000,000 persons. McKinley remained at his home in Canton and read well-prepared speeches from his front porch to carefully coached delegations that visited him. The real work of McKinley's campaign was done by Hanna. The powerful response to Bryan's appeal frightened eastern conservatives, and Hanna took advantage of their panic to collect campaign funds. From trusts, banks, railroads, and tycoons he raised an estimated $3.5 million as against a bare $300,000 raised by Bryan. Hanna used the money lavishly but wisely, and he received great assistance from the press, which heaped all kinds of abuse upon Bryan. The *Louisville Courier Journal* called Bryan "a dishonest dodger...a daring adventurer...a political faker," and the New York *Tribune* referred to him as a "wretched, rattle-pated boy." The Philadelphia *Press* described the "Jacobins" of the Democratic convention as "hideous and repulsive vipers," and Theodore Roosevelt was reported as saying that the silver men should "be stood up against the wall and shot." Writing to Henry Adams in London, John Hay said of Bryan, "The Boy Orator makes only one speech—but he makes it twice a day. There is no fun in it. He simply reiterates the unquestionable truths that every man who has a clean shirt is a thief and should be hanged, and there is no goodness or wisdom except among the illiterates and criminal classes." Added to these tactics were those of threats. The idea was spread that Bryan's victory would bring disaster. Farmers were told that mortgages would not be renewed. Workmen were informed that factories would be closed or wages cut if Bryan won.

In the election the popular vote was unusually large, with each of the candidates receiving a larger total than any previous candidate of his party. Out of almost 14 million popular votes, McKinley won with a margin of just over a half million and with 271 electoral votes to 176 for Bryan. The Republicans also gained a majority in both houses of Congress. Bryan failed to carry a single industrial and urban state; nor could he carry a single state north of the Potomac and east of the Mississippi. In spite of the widespread unrest among labor, Bryan did not win labor's support and this failure was one of the principal reasons for his defeat. But he had nowhere the resources that backed McKinley, and he represented the party blamed for the depression.

The new work by Kleppner, Jensen, McSeveney, and others threw fresh light on the conventional narratives of the "crisis of the nineties" and the origins of the Progressive era. These writers contended that the ethno-cultural issues and responses previously mentioned were important well after the depression began in 1893, evidenced by shifts away from the Democratic party in areas little affected by the economic downturn. The Republicans' success in 1894 resulted in part from their ability to play down the cultural issues dividing them earlier, in part from their advocacy of plausible solutions to the depression (particularly the protective tariff), and in part from the deep divisions within the Democratic party. In spite of some Democratic regrouping in 1895, the Bryan campaign confirmed the Republican strengths and Democratic weaknesses of 1894. Meanwhile Republican party professionals refused to commit their party to a single issue, like prohibition, strongly advocated at the local level by the party's pietistic rural wing. Instead McKinley in 1896 led a new coalition of business-backed pragmatists who favored a pluralistic approach to interest groups and national issues.

Bryan, on the other hand, turned his campaign into a moral crusade aimed at rural, pietistic, old stock voters in the Midwest. This shift in appeal, along with the continuing depression, confirmed the voter realignment that began in 1894, insuring Republican dominance in the Midwest for nearly a third of a century. In the urban Northeast, Bryan failed not so much because he did not address himself to ethnic and religious differences among the voters "as because northeastern workers regardless of background, rejected the economic arguments he did advance—just as they had those of the Cleveland Democrats earlier in the depression" and instead "favored Republican arguments" on the tariff, currency, and the return of prosperity.

Thus the new literature, while emphasizing ethno-cultural forces, also recognized the importance of economic pressures on voters during a depression. The political realignment taking place during the depression of the 1890's therefore did not rest solely on ethno-cultural matters. In fact they subsided as issues, to be replaced by the economic ones of depression and the Republicans' positive responses to it. Consequently, "its depression victories enabled the Republican party to resolve a number of [ethno-cultural] disputes to the satisfaction of groups that supported the G.O.P." wrote McSeveney. This view of the political realignment of the 1890s is consistent with that in some of the most recent studies of the two major parties.

In establishing its position as the majority party after 1894, the Republican party obviously benefited from the depression and Democratic mistakes. "But the Republicans prevailed because they more nearly met the needs and desires of the mass of American voters than any other party," and they provided "plausible solutions to the dilemmas of economic expansion." The Democrats, awarded national power in 1892, failed to meet this challenge satisfactorily, or to strengthen their party organization and thereby insure continued Democratic election victories. If the voters turned after 1894 to "the party of progress, prosperity, and national authority" (the Republican), wrote historian Lewis L. Gould, they "also turned against the party and principles of Grover Cleveland. This was Cleveland's main legacy to his party and the nation."

The election of 1896 was the most important one since 1860, and it marked a decisive triumph for conservative Republicanism. In a negative sense the election represented the last bid of the farmers for leadership of a national reform movement. In a positive sense it ushered in a new era of political leadership and a new set of issues.

The McKinley Administration came in under highly favorable circumstances. Businessmen knew that their interests would be safeguarded for four years. There was a return to prosperity which was to continue for several years. Farmers largely dropped politics and were busy raising crops. Politicians were happy and looked forward to a long period of abundance. McKinley, well aware of the economic distress that had affected Americans, promised in his first inaugural that this would be his chief concern. To maintain recovery he advocated two principal measures—a higher tariff and a gold standard act. Congress responded with the Dingley Tariff of 1897, which raised duties to an average of 52 percent, the highest in American history, and with the Gold Standard Act of 1900, which declared the gold dollar from that time on would be the sole standard of currency.

With these two laws the McKinley administration made good its campaign promises. Beyond this neither the president nor Congress intended to interfere with the country. They planned to let it alone and to allow business to create prosperity. McKinley's inauguration marked the beginning of one of the great consolidation movements in American industry (1897–1904). This, coupled with the Spanish-American War, probably produced the golden years of prosperity under McKinley and Hanna.

McKinley's presidency also marked the beginning of a new era not only in national politics but in the running of the national government; as Professor Wilfred Binkley, a leading authority on the president and the Congress, wrote: "Not since the presidency of Thomas Jefferson had there been achieved such an integration of the political branches of the federal government and such consequent coherence and sense of direction in its functioning." The equilibrium and stalemate of the preceding two decades had given way to Republican supremacy.

Further Reading

Bogue, Allan G. *From Prairie to Corn Belt: Farming on the Illinois and Iowa Prairies in the Nineteenth Century.* 1963.
_____. *Money at Interest: The Farm Mortgage on the Middle Border.* 1955.
Coletta, Paolo E. *William Jennings Bryan.* 3 vols., 1964–1969.
Durden, Robert F. *The Climax of Populism: The Election of 1896.* 1965.
Fite, Gilbert C. *The Farmer's Frontier, 1865–1900.* 1966.
Glad, Paul W. *McKinley, Bryan, and the People.* 1964.
Goodwyn, Lawrence. *Democratic Promise, The Populist Movement in America.* 1976.
Hackney, Sheldon. *From Populism to Progressivism in Alabama.* 1969.
Hicks, John D. *The Populist Revolt.* 1931.
Hofstadter, Richard. *The Age of Reform.* 1954.
McMath, Robert C. *Populist Vanguard: A History of the Southern Farmers Alliance.* 1975.
Morgan, H. Wayne. *William McKinley and His America.* 1963.
Noblin, Stuart. *Leonidas Lafayette Polk: Agrarian Crusader.* 1949.
Nugent, Walter T. K. *Money and American Society, 1865–1880.* 1968.
_____. *The Tolerant Populists: Kansas Populism and Nativism.* 1963.
Palmer, Bruce. *Man over Money: The Southern Populist Critique of American Capitalism.* 1980.
Pollack, Norman. *The Populist Response to Industrial America.* 1966.
Ridge, Martin. *Ignatius Donnelly.* 1962.
Shannon, Fred A. *The Farmer's Last Frontier, 1860–1897.* 1945.
Tindall, George B. *A Populist Reader, Selections from the Works of American Populist Leaders.* 1961.
Unger, Irwin. *The Greenback Era: A Social and Political History of American Finance, 1865–1879.* 1964.

Weinstein, Allen. *Prelude to Populism: Origins of the Silver Issue, 1867–1878.* 1970.
Woodward, C. Vann. *Tom Watson, Agrarian Rebel.* 1938, 1975.

5

American Culture in the Gilded Age

The term most commonly used by historians to describe the decades that followed the Civil War is *the Gilded Age,* taken from the title of a novel by Mark Twain and Charles Dudley Warner published in 1873. It seemed a fitting epithet for the tawdry gilt that characterized many features of American life in this period. It reflected the cynical spirit and crudeness of the new age and the graft, corruption, and praise of material values that accompanied it. The United States, wrote E. L. Godkin in *The Nation* in 1866, is a "gaudy stream of bespangled, belaced, and beruffled barbarians...Who knows how to be rich in America? Plenty of people know how to get money; but...to be rich properly is, indeed, a fine art. It requires culture, imagination, and character." Godkin spoke for a number of perceptive Americans who were appalled by what they called the materialism, crassness, and immorality that accompanied the new industrialism. They were alarmed especially that the men of new wealth—the new plutocracy—lacked the "restraints of culture, experience, the pride, or even the inherited caution of class or rank." The ideals, character, and moral values of a rural and agrarian America seemed outmoded in industrial America.

But even though perceptive social critics of the Gilded Age, as well as some modern historians, assailed the captains of industry as robber barons who undermined the country's moral fiber and imposed their coarse tastes upon the nation, the ordinary American saw these industrialists only in their role as respected members of society, pillars of the churches, and philanthropists who occupied positions of prestige and power both here and abroad. As a consequence, millions of Americans admired and emulated the successful businessmen. This favorable view of industrialists was given further support by the prevailing economic and social theories of the period—laissez faire and Social Darwinism—both of which extolled the rugged individualism practiced by the captains of industry.

The dominant economic philosophy of the times was laissez faire. Beyond what was necessary to maintain law and order and to protect life and property, the government was not to interfere in the conduct of business or in personal matters. According to this view, men pursuing their business interests free of government meddling would achieve the best possible use of resources, would promote steady economic progress, and would be rewarded each according to his deserts. Acquisition of wealth was considered evidence of merit, for did not wealth come as a result of frugality, industriousness, and sagacity? Conversely, poverty carried with it the stigma of worthlessness, for did it not result from idleness and wastefulness? During most of the late nineteenth century these attitudes prevailed in America and were upheld by prominent educators, editors, clergymen, and economists.

Free competition and government nonintervention were sanctioned not only by the laissez-faire economic theories of Adam Smith and the English classical school; rugged individualism also found "scientific" support in Social Darwinism. Spencer's idea proved especially attractive to American businessmen since they justified free competition and made successful businessmen feel that they themselves were the finest flower of evolution. Many industrialists cited Spencer's views to defend their business activities and to resist government regulation. The new doctrine opposed poor relief, housing regulations, and public education and justified poverty and slums. Spencer believed that these conditions were the proper lot of the unfit who had been bested in the economic struggle and that any governmental effort to relieve poverty was an interference with the operation of the natural law.

Spencer's ideas had an enormous vogue in the United States in the last quarter of the nineteenth century. By the time of his death in 1903 Americans had bought nearly 400,000 copies of his books, an incredibly high figure for a sociological or philosophical work. Numbered among his many devoted followers in America were Edward Livingston Youmans and John Fiske, who spread the gospel of Social Darwinism all over the country through magazine articles, popular books, and lectures. Such leading universities as Harvard, Johns Hopkins, and Yale included the Spencerian philosophy in courses on religion, biology, and social science.

Spencer's most influential American disciple was William Graham Sumner, who taught sociology and political economy at Yale from 1872 until his death in 1910. Sumner vigorously supported economic individualism and hailed the millionaires as products of natural selection. He scornfully derided reformers and their programs to protect the weak; he ridiculed democracy as the "pet superstition of the age" and he repudiated the idea of equality among mankind. Sumner was interested in the welfare of the "forgotten man," who to him was the middle-class citizen who worked hard, minded his own business, paid his taxes, and never asked the government for help. Sumner remained true to his individualism and incurred the hostility of Social Darwinists who were businessmen when he attacked the protective tariff for violating genuine individualism.

The Social Darwinists took the position that since society was the outcome of natural processes, man could not hope to control it. Hence, they considered the efforts of reformers both mischievous and futile. In the 1880s, however, a number of sociologists and economists began revolting against the individualism and fatalism of Social Darwinism. The "reform Darwinists" maintained that societies could command their own destinies and that human intelligence could improve the existing system.

A leader among the dissenters was Lester Frank Ward, a largely self-educated sociologist. He came from a poor family in Illinois, endured privation in his early life, worked in factories, fought in the Civil War, and for many years was a government official. When he was sixty-five, Ward became professor of sociology at Brown University, where he taught "A Survey of All Knowledge." His ideas were first presented in his *Dynamic Sociology* (1883) but were more readably set forth in *The Psychic Factors of Civilization* (1893). Ward opposed the prevailing theory that "neither physical nor social phenomena are capable of human control," asserting "that all the practical benefits of science are the result of man's control of natural forces." Ward argued that man must use his intelligence to plan and direct his future. He distinguished between "telic" forces, those governed by human purpose, and "genetic" forces, those resulting from blind natural processes, and maintained that there was "no natural harmony between natural law and human advantage." Thus he believed that a laissez-faire economic system did not necessarily advance human progress, and he advocated state management and social planning. "Those who dismiss state interference," Ward said, "are the ones who most frequently and successfully invoke it."

Younger professors of sociology, such as Albion Small of Illinois, Charles Horton Cooley of Michigan, and Edward Allsworth Ross of Wisconsin, seconded Ward's assault on Social Darwinism. Contrary to Spencer's notion that society was composed of separate individuals operating independently of one another, they asserted that each individual personality was shaped by social institutions, which were themselves amenable to social control. In *Sin and Society* (1907) Ross argued that in the new industrial society morality required the impersonal corporation to accept full responsibility for its antisocial acts. Followers of Spencer and Sumner gradually declined in numbers and influence in the universities. In 1906 the American Sociological Society was founded, and Ward was its first president. His ideas on government social planning eventually came to influence much of American social thinking in the twentieth century.

Similarly, the viewpoint of economists also changed. Leading university economists in the Gilded Age—men such as Francis Amasa Walker of the Massachusetts Institute of Technology and J. Lawrence Laughlin of Harvard and Chicago—believed in the orthodox laissez-faire economics of Adam Smith and the classical school and taught that natural economic laws could function properly only in an unregulated society.

In the mid-1880s, however, a new group of scholars, many of whom had been trained in German universities, began to challenge these sentiments. In 1885 they founded the American Economic Association, which boldly declared that the state was "an agency whose positive assistance is one of the indispensable conditions of human progress" and that "the doctrine of laissez-faire is unsafe in politics and unsound in morals." Among the leaders of this revolt were Richard T. Ely of Johns Hopkins University and the University of Wisconsin, Simon Nelsen Patten of the University of Pennsylvania, John R. Commons of the University of Wisconsin, and Wesley C. Mitchell of Columbia University. Although they differed in their economic and political programs, they all dissented from the classical belief in absolute economic laws valid for all societies. They insisted that society, constantly changing, had to be examined in terms of process and growth. Using the historical approach to study economic realities, they discovered that there were great differences between what actually happened and what, according to classical economics, was supposed to happen.

The leading academic rebel was Thorstein Veblen. Born in Wisconsin of Norwegian immigrants and educated at Yale and Johns Hopkins, he taught at the Universities of Chicago, Stanford, and Missouri. Veblen bitterly assailed what he called the "kept classes" and their "pecuniary" society. He derided the idea that the wealthy leisure class was the most biologically fit and that millionaires were a product of natural selection. Veblen argued that the millionaire was not responsible for the creation of the industrial technology but rather had taken possession of the wealth produced by the skill and labor of other people.

In his most widely read book, *The Theory of the Leisure Class* (1899), and in a number of other volumes Veblen analyzed the role of the upper class in American society. Although Veblen had little popular appeal, he did wield a great deal of influence among intellectuals of the twentieth century, particularly after the Great Depression of 1929.

Outside academic circles, increasing numbers of "radicals" and reformers began to attack the existing social and economic system and to propose new plans of economic organization. They too rejected Spencer's fatalism and the idea that progress resulted from the struggle for existence and the consequent removal of the unfit.

The most important of these reformers was Henry George. Born in Philadelphia, he moved to San Francisco as a young man, where for twenty years he watched a frontier society become transformed into a wealthy and class-stratified society. What was the cause of this imbalance that deepened the poverty of the masses and increased the wealth of a few? George believed the explanation lay in the inequities of private land ownership that allowed landowners to enrich themselves solely through the rise of real estate values. Land took on value not because of anything the owner did but because people lived on it. George believed that the "unearned increment," instead of going to private individuals, ought to be taken by the government in the form of a "single tax" on land values. This would make other taxes and other forms of government intervention unnecessary, leave individual enterprise otherwise free, and promote "the Golden Age of which poets have sung and high-raised seers have told us in metaphor!"

George set forth his theories in *Progress and Poverty* (1879) and found a wide audience both in the United States and abroad. George spent the rest of his life working for the single tax program and continued to develop his theme in subsequent books. In addition, he edited a newspaper, gave many speeches, and came close to being elected mayor of New York City in 1886.

More radical than George's program was that of his contemporary, Edward Bellamy. Also rejecting the fatalism of the Social Darwinists, Bellamy concentrated his attack on the competitive system itself. He had long been troubled by the suffering and poverty seen in industrial America, and he turned to socialism as a cure for these ills. In his utopian novel, *Looking Backward* (1888), Bellamy portrayed an ideal socialist community in the year 2000 whose beauty and tranquility contrasted sharply with the ugly industrial towns of his day. Bellamy believed the Golden Age he depicted would come after the nationalization of great trusts and the "substitution of scientific methods of an organized and unified industrial system for the wasteful struggle of the present competitive plan with its countless warring and mutually destructive undertakings."

Bellamy's book reached a wide public; at least 500,000 copies were sold. He called his system "Nationalism," and "Nationalist" clubs sprang up to spread the new faith. "Nationalist" magazines advocated public ownership of railroads and utilities, civil service reform, and government aid to education. This served to renew interest in socialism and caused the American public to consider socialist ideas and programs. Bellamy, however, avoided the word "socialism" because he found it distasteful and because he realized that in the United States the term was often identified with "anarchism" and "communism," words that frightened most Americans.

Laissez faire and Social Darwinism were thus increasingly criticized as the nineteenth century came to a close. Similarly, formalism in social thought and orthodoxy in philosophy were being subjected to reexamination. The traditional philosophy prevalent in the United States was Scottish or commonsense realism. Its main purpose was to explain traditional Protestant theology, but it also justified the status quo and conservative thought. First introduced in the late eighteenth century, it still dominated academic circles in the late nineteenth century. Its leading exponents were the Reverend James McCosh of Princeton and the Reverend Noah Porter of Yale.

From the 1870s on, the most important new influence was German idealism, particularly as expressed by George Wilhelm Friedrich Hegel (1770–1831). Hegel viewed the whole course of history as the working out of divine purpose by certain general laws of nature and culminating in the achievement of perfect freedom. But Hegelianism, like the Scottish philosophy, rationalized existing conditions, and what Hegel meant by "freedom" was very different from the traditional American conception. Hegel's philosophy glorified the state and taught that the individual could be free only by subordinating himself to his national government and to his social institutions.

Thus in philosophy as in economics the initial stimulus toward a new outlook came from Germany. Most of the young men who founded new schools of philosophy in America had studied at German universities and had been influenced by Hegel, although they did not accept German idealism uncritically. The earliest centers of new philosophic thought were outside the colleges and universities. Very influential was the Philosophical Society of St. Louis, whose leading figure was William T. Harris, superintendent of the St. Louis public schools and then later United States commissioner of education. Other well-known institutions were the Fellowship of the New Life, founded in 1884 by Thomas Davidson; the Concord Summer School of Philosophy and Literature (1879–1888); and the Society for Ethical Culture, founded in 1876 by Felix Adler.

An idealist movement displaced the commonsense school in academic circles in the 1880s. It was strongest in New England, where its leaders were Josiah Royce of Harvard and C. E. Garman of Amherst, but it was not confined to any one part of the country. The idealist awakening was evident also at such universities as California, Columbia, Cornell, Johns Hopkins, Michigan, and Princeton. The idealists believed in the priority of mind over matter and in the fundamental unity of the universe, but they modified these concepts to support American individualism.

Probably the most influential American idealist was the California-born Josiah Royce, who taught at Harvard from 1882 until his death in 1916. Royce accepted the German belief that individuals were parts of a single absolute mind, but unlike the orthodox Hegelians he asserted that each separate individual was an essential part of this whole and made his own singular contribution to it. Thus he gave to the individual a more significant, active role in the universe.

Meanwhile, a school of philosophy more distinctively American and opposed to idealism was growing in popularity. Pragmatism, unlike most earlier philosophies, did not offer theories about God and the universe. It presented instead a way of evaluating acts and ideas in terms of their consequences in concrete experience. Pragmatism maintained that men should not reject *any* hypothesis if consequences useful to life flow from it. The pragmatist's decision regarding the truth or falsity of an idea, then, is based on experimental tests; "workability" is the correct method for finding truth. This concept was closely associated with two ideas that had gained wide currency in American thought—the idea of progress through evolution and the idea of truth obtained through scientific investigation. The forerunners of pragmatism were Chauncey Wright and Charles S. Pierce, but two other men, William James and John Dewey, developed it.

William James, philosopher and psychologist at Harvard, rejected Spencerian determinism, which afforded no place for chance or human will. He upheld the independence of the mind and "the right to believe at our own risk any hypothesis that is live enough to tempt our will." At times he was inclined to suggest that if a person felt happier or behaved better as a result of believing in a particular idea, that idea should be regarded as true. While James repudiated absolutes, he also spoke out against a skepticism that would inhibit impulsively generous commitment. He distrusted all general laws and abstractions that denied man's capacity for free action. James contended that man's decision could influence the course of events and that in spite of the existence of God, good or evil would result from human device and intelligence.

In his *Principles of Psychology* (1890), James made the first important American contribution to the scientific study of the mind. In later books he expounded his views on pragmatism. Theories to him were "instruments, not answers to enigmas." Pragmatism "has no dogmas, and no doctrines save its method," which was a method for reaching the truth. "The true is the name of whatever proves to be good in the way of belief," James said, "and good, too, for definite, assignable reasons." Such views were a sharp departure from nearly all the philosophies and religions of the past, and they captivated many Americans. Yet they also laid James open to the charge that pragmatism was simply another name for experience—anything is good that works.

James's chief disciple was John Dewey, who considered himself an "instrumentalist" rather than a pragmatist. Born in Vermont in 1859, Dewey taught at the Universities of Michigan, Chicago, and Columbia and remained an active force in American thought until his death in 1952. Originally an idealist, Dewey was converted to pragmatism in the 1890s after reading James. Though he lacked James's lucidity he developed his ideas in greater detail.

Dewey believed philosophy should become a tool for society to use in meeting its problems. To him no thinking was valid that did not spring from experience, for while ideas led to action it was only through action that men could acquire sound ideas. As he himself put it, his philosophy stemmed from the "growth of democracy—the development of the experimental methods in the sciences, evolutionary ideas in the biological sciences, and the industrial reorganization." Dewey put much faith in intelligence as a tool for social reform; he considered the mind "at least an organ of service for the control of environment." Like other social dissenters of this period, Dewey criticized laissez faire and Social Darwinism and argued that life need not be accepted passively but could be shaped by man. Since his instrumentalism meant using philosophy to advance democracy he urged philosophers to leave their ivory towers, stop speculating about what he felt were meaningless trifles, and occupy themselves with politics, education, and ethics.

There was also a revolt against formalism in law. The preceding generation regarded the law as fixed and unchanging and as a standard measure which the judge applied to the question at hand. But Oliver Wendell Holmes, son of the poet of the same name and friend of William James, declared in his book, *The Common Law* (1881): "The life of the law...has not been logic; it has been experience....The felt necessities of the time, the prevalent moral and political theories, intuitions of public policy, avowed or unconscious, even the prejudices which judges share with their fellowmen, have a good deal more to do than the syllogism in determining the rules by which men should be governed." Law, Holmes felt, should be based upon changing social needs or political policies rather than upon logic or precedent. "It is revolting," he said, "to have no better reason for a rule of law than that it was laid down in the time of Henry IV. It is still more revolting if the grounds upon which it was laid down have vanished long since, and the rule simply persists from blind imitation of the past." A new school of legal theorists arose who not only accepted Holmes's reasoning but went on to contend that the meaning of any general legal principle must always be judged by its practical effects.

The Gilded Age has often been characterized as one of the most sterile periods in the cultural history of the United States. Everywhere in this generation, according to some critics, materialism so abounded that it perverted tastes and debauched the intellectual life of the country. There is ample evidence to suggest this point of view. But the age has too often been measured by its political record, which frequently misfired, and this criterion alone is not sufficient. The age was roundly condemned by such contemporary critics as Walt Whitman, Mark Twain, and Henry George, but their reasons were mostly superficial.

It was an age of crassness and vulgarity, and its unhappy aspects must be recognized. But historian and socioliterary critic Vernon L. Parrington, though sharply critical of the period, was fascinated by it. He interpreted the Gilded Age as one in which the energies damned up by frontier life and the inhibitions of backwoods religion were suddenly released.

One of the better known aspects of the Gilded Age was society's freedom to revise its morals and manners. The new rich of the industrial age were unsure of themselves and employed gaudy display to impress outsiders. The conspicuous waste of money was the measure of social status; it prompted the American craze for antiques and European collections and launched perhaps the greatest plunder of the continent since the sack of Rome.

Nothing exhibits better the excesses of the Gilded Age than its architecture and interior decoration, which declined to a new low. Houses were copied from European styles, and it was an age of the jigsaw, the cupola, the mansard roof with its dormer windows and an orgy of decoration. "A stuffy and fussy riot of fancy," Parrington says of it, "restrained by no feeling for structural lines, supplied the lack of creative imagination, and architecture sank to the level of the jerry-builder. Bad taste could go no further." The same excess can be found in dress with its bustles, paddings, and corsets; in furniture; and even in machinery. In morals, low and broad standards commingled with Victorian morality.

Yet despite these obvious cultural excesses, intellectual and artistic developments of the Gilded Age were among the most fruitful this country has ever seen. We have already observed how the original and creative thinkers of the eighties and nineties made these two decades perhaps one of the most intellectually fertile periods in the whole of American history. Unfortunately, too many observers of the period have been preoccupied with the second-rate thinkers and artists and have neglected those who made contributions of the first order.

In the field of scholarship, the age saw the birth of two new social sciences: Lewis Henry Morgan founded anthropology and Lester Frank Ward fathered American sociology. The period also witnessed a revolution in higher education. Until this time institutions of higher education concentrated on training ministers and lawyers, but now learning began to shake off its fetters and to range freely in the physical, natural, and social sciences, the arts, and the humanities. The most important of the daring new university presidents were Charles W. Eliot of Harvard and Daniel Coit Gilman of Johns Hopkins. At Harvard, Eliot greatly expanded the curriculum and sponsored the elective system, which had originated at the University of Virginia at the time of its founding. He also drastically reformed Harvard's medical and law schools and gave them true professional status. At Johns Hopkins, Gilman built the first great graduate school in America. The graduate school and the seminar method were introduced from Germany in the 1870s, and some graduate work was done at Harvard and Yale in the 1870s. But Johns Hopkins, designed primarily as a center for graduate work at its founding in 1876, took the lead in this field and held it for the next quarter of a century. At this time also, professional schools got under way: the Columbia School of Mines (1864), the Massachusetts Institute of Technology (1865), Stevens Institute (1871), and the Johns Hopkins Medical School (1893).

During the two or three decades following the Civil War, the most popular form of American literature was the regional short story. Bret Harte and Hamlin Garland in the West, George Washington Cable and Joel Chandler Harris in the South, and Sarah Orne Jewett in New England gave readers a fresh and exciting view of regional America and contributed to the reunification of the country.

Mark Twain, whose works were written in this period, was in his own day considered a regional author, but his novels, essays, and sketches have made a lasting reputation for him as a humorist, moralist, and social critic. The materials for Twain's best narratives—*The Adventures of Tom Sawyer* (1876), *Life on the Mississippi* (1883), and *The Adventures of Huckleberry Finn* (1884)—were his boyhood home,

Hannibal, Missouri, and the great Mississippi River which rolled before it.

Twain, along with many other writers of the period, pointed out the evils of crass materialism and ridiculed the get-rich-quick schemes of his money-mad countrymen. In *The Gilded Age,* for example, Twain and Charles Dudley Warner maintained that sober industry and contentment with a modest income honestly earned were infinitely preferable to frantic money-making schemes.

Growing social ills during the Gilded Age called forth specific indictments that became increasingly prominent in the literature of the late nineteenth and early twentieth centuries. William Dean Howells, who by 1900 was considered by many young writers to be the dean of American letters, exhibited the grime and squalor of New York City in *A Hazard of New Fortunes* (1890); Stephen Crane's *Maggie: A Girl of the Streets* (1893) exposed the ugly life of New York's Bowery; and Hamlin Garland in *Main-Travelled Roads* (1891) described the hardships and injustices suffered by farmers in Iowa and Wisconsin. While they emphasized the injustices and abuses of the new industrial order, the treatment by writers of the captains of industry was for a good many years comparatively gentle. In Howells's *The Rise of Silas Lapham* (1884), for example, the author implied that the great majority of American financiers were honest—that robber barons were the exception, not the rule. The novelist and literary critic Henry James (brother of William James), who lived abroad most of his life, considered the ethics of the American financiers who vacationed in Europe to be fundamentally sound. The principal characters of James's *The American* (1877) and *The Golden Bowl* (1904) were businessmen of integrity and charm.

The literature of social criticism frequently contained proposals for specific utopias, the most influential being Edward Bellamy's *Looking Backward.* Bellamy, believing that economic inequality was the cause of all social ills, described a socialist utopia in which wealth was distributed equally among its members. Other writers of the period who proposed a socialist solution were Howells in *A Traveller from Altruria* (1893) and Upton Sinclair in *The Jungle* (1906). Most of the literature dealing with social problems, however, proposed reforms rather than a radical alteration of the American system of free enterprise.

Because many poets—Bryant, Longfellow, Holmes, Lowell, Emerson, and Whittier—whose careers had begun in an earlier period, continued to satisfy and to determine tastes after the war, much of American poetry showed remarkably few effects of the changing intellectual climate. By the end of the century, however, American poets and prose writers were feeling the full impact of the scientific movement. For example, much of Stephen Crane's poetry inferred from the biological struggle for survival and the astronomical immensity of the universe that man is unimportant:

A man said to the universe
"Sir, I exist!"
"However," replied the universe,
"The fact has not created in me
A sense of obligation."

The Gilded Age knew virtually nothing of Emily Dickinson, because only seven of her poems were published during her lifetime (1830–1886), but she is today considered one of the leading poets of the post–Civil War period. She began to write poetry in the mid-fifties and continued until her death in 1886, but she spent the last half of her life as a recluse in Amherst, Massachusetts. In striking contrast was Walt Whitman, whose revolutionary volume of poetry, *Leaves of Grass,* had been published in three editions before the Civil War and who continued to be an important figure in American poetry of the postwar period. Although many critics objected to Whitman's departures from the conventions of versification and to his frank treatment of sex, he became for many others the very voice of America—enthusiastic, optimistic, energetic, and free. Whitman's Quaker inheritance contributed to the independence, love of peace, and sense of brotherhood celebrated in so many of his works—among them *Drum Taps* (1866), a volume of poems recounting the experiences and suffering shared by both North and South and the richest account of the Civil War to be found in our poetry.

Increasing wealth and leisure after the Civil War contributed to a new awareness of art among Americans, and such high caliber painting was done by George Inness, Thomas Eakins, Winslow Homer, Albert Pinkham Ryder, and Eastman Johnson that perhaps the Gilded Age could be called the most important era in American painting. Inness pioneered a new landscape school. Homer and Eakins were the leading American representatives of the naturalistic movement in painting. Homer grounded his art in direct observation of nature, while Eakins depicted the ordinary middle-class city life of the United States in the late nineteenth century. Johnson's illustrations of contemporary domestic scenes were enormously popular. Ryder, haunted throughout his life by the sea, was the most original Romantic of his time. Two American expatriates, James McNeill Whistler and John Singer Sargent, both of whom lived for most of their lives in London, enjoyed international reputations—Whistler for his portrayals of contemporary life, Sargent as the most sought-after portraitist of the Anglo-Saxon world. A third expatriate artist, Mary Cassett settled in Paris and exhibited with the leading French Impressionists.

Although in architecture the Gilded Age has been said to mark the nadir in taste, there were fine and outstanding architects. Henry Hobsen Richardson and Louis H. Sullivan were the first major architects to meet the demands of industrialism upon their art. To these men, buildings had a sociological function as well as an artistic one. In his *Autobiography of an Idea,* Sullivan wrote that "masonry construction was a thing of the past...that the old ideas of superimposition must give way before a sense of vertical continuity."

Most of these first-rate writers and artists worked in obscurity and did not receive the recognition then deserved from their contemporaries. Americans of the post–Civil War generation regarded others we now consider second-rate to be the leading figures in their respective fields, and because of this the Gilded Age has often been characterized as one of the most sterile periods of American culture. But viewed from the perspective of history it proves to have been one of America's richest and most fruitful eras.

As in the pre–Civil War generation, an effort was made, through privately sponsored agencies, to keep Americans of limited schooling informed and to make culture popular in the country. There was a mass desire for knowledge, and some men, realizing this and being motivated by idealistic and monetary reasons, launched a program of having lecturers tour the country.

The most successful of these ventures in popular learning was the Chautauqua movement, founded in western New York in 1874 by Lewis Miller, an Ohio businessman, and John H. Vincent, a Methodist minister. They first organized at two-week summer course for a few Sunday school teachers at Lake Chautauqua in New York. But it was such an enjoyable experience for those who attended that the word spread and within a few years thousands from all parts of the country were coming to Lake Chautauqua. When this happened, the Chautauqua movement, like the earlier lyceum movement, expanded its activities. The founders broadened their range of instruction to include such subjects as economics, government, science, and literature. During the years of Chautauqua's greatest popularity, eminent authorities, including some of the presidents of the period, gave talks to open-air audiences on every subject conceivable. In addition, the Chautauqua Literary and Scientific Reading Circle was organized and became a national society. This organization provided correspondence courses leading to a diploma. Textbooks were written for the program, and a monthly magazine, the *Chautauquan,* was published to keep members informed about the program. According to Reverend Vincent, the program was formulated to give "the college outlook" to those who did not have a higher education.

Because the Chautauqua movement was so successful, various imitators appeared, until by 1900 there were about 200 Chautauqua-type organizations in the country. Most of these were of a more commercial character but were designed to satisfy the craving for self-culture. They furnished a varied fare of music, humor, and inspirational lectures and probably provided more entertainment than enlightenment.

The Chautauqua movement and its imitators helped popularize information that earlier had been the property of experts only. And, in addition, thousands of Americans who sought cultural and intellectual improvement probably felt rewarded by many of the programs and perhaps their interests were broadened by them.

Further Reading

Baker, Paul R. *Richard Morris Hunt.* 1980.

Bannister, Robert. *Social Darwinism: Science and Myth in Anglo-American Thought.* 1979.

Barker, Charles A. *Henry George.* 1955.

Barth, Gunther. *City People: The Rise of Modern City Culture in Nineteenth Century America.* 1980.

Berthoff, Walter. *The Ferment of Realism: American Literature, 1884–1919.* 1965.

Chugerman, Samuel. *Lester F. Ward: The American Aristotle.* 1965.

Clark, Michael D. *Worldly Theologians: The Persistence of Religion in Nineteenth Century American Thought.* 1981.

Commager, Henry S. *The American Mind.* 1950.

Curti, Merle E. *The Growth of American Thought.* 3d. ed. 1964.

Curtis, Bruce. *William Graham Sumner.* 1981.

Dykhuizen, George. *The Life and Mind of John Dewey.* 1973.

Geismer, Maxwell. *Rebels and Ancestors: The American Novel, 1890–1915.* 1953.

Gould, Joseph E. *The Chautauqua Movement: An Episode in the Continuing American Revolution.* 1961.

Hale, Nathan G., Jr. *Freud and America: The Beginnings of Psychoanalysis in America, 1876–1917.* 1971.

Hitchcock, Henry-Russell. *The Architecture of Henry H. Richardson and His Times.* 1966.

Hofstadter, Richard. *Social Darwinism in American Thought.* 1959.

Jones, Howard Mumford. *The Age of Energy: Varieties of American Experience.* 1970.

Kaplan, Justin. *Mr. Clemens and Mark Twain.* 1966.

Kulick, Bruce. *The Rise of American Philosophy.* 1977.

Larkin, Oliver W. *Art and Life in America.* 1960.

Lynn, Kenneth S. *William Dean Howells: An American Life.* 1970.

Martin, Jay. *Harvests of Change, American Literature, 1865–1914.* 1967.

Miller, Perry. *American Thought: Civil War to World War I.* 1954.

Nye, Russel. *The Unembarrassed Muse: The Popular Arts in America.* 1970.

Page, Charles. *Class and American Sociology: From Ward to Ross.* 1969.

Rossiter, Clinton. *Conservatism in America: The Thankless Persuasion.* 1962.

Thomas, John L. *Alternative America: Henry George, Edward Bellamy, Henry Demarest Lloyd, and the Anniversary Tradition.* 1983.

Trachtenberg, Alan. *The Incorporation of American Culture and Society in the Gilded Age.* 1982.

White, Morton G. *Social Thought in America.* 1957.

White, Morton, and Lucia White. *The Intellectuals vs. the City.* 1962.

Ziff, Larzer. *The American 1890's.* 1966.

6

American Society in the Industrial Age

The rapid and vast economic expansion of the post–Civil War years brought far-reaching social and cultural changes. Probably the most important was the transformation of the United States from a rural and agrarian nation to an urban and industrial one. "When we get piled upon one another in large cities," Jefferson had stated in 1787, "we shall become as corrupt as in Europe, and go to eating one another as they do there." More than a century later in 1899, one observer wondered why farm youth were so eager to "leave the country where homes are cheap, the air pure, all men equal, and extreme poverty unknown, and crowd into cities," where they seemed to find "in the noises, the crowds, the excitements, even in the sleepless anxieties of the daily struggle for life, a charm they are powerless to resist." Yet the growth of cities could not be checked, much less reversed, and Americans accepted the fact.

This urban growth can be strikingly seen in terms of statistics. In 1790 only 5.1 percent of the population lived in centers with more than 2,500 inhabitants. In 1860 this percentage had gone up to 19.8 and in 1900 to 39.7. A more significant feature of urbanization was the concentration of Americans in large metropolitan areas. The population of New York City and Brooklyn (which were consolidated in 1898) together grew from 1,200,000 in 1850 to over 3,000,000 in 1900. Chicago, which had only 30,000 inhabitants in 1850, shot up to 500,000 in 1880, and to 1,700,000 in 1900, to become the second largest city in the country. In the same period the population in Philadelphia increased from 560,000 to 1,300,000 and Pittsburgh from 67,000 to 450,000. Minneapolis rose from 2,500 in 1860 to 200,000 in 1900 and Los Angeles from 5,000 to 100,000.

This tremendous urban growth brought many problems. The poor lived in cold, cheerless tenements that often lacked sun and fresh air and running water. Tenements were built on the basis of crowding as many people as possible into the smallest possible space. For block upon block in the slum areas these ugly structures were to be found covering every inch of building space. The congestion was so great in some areas of New York, for example, that Jacob Riis, the housing reformer, estimated in 1890 that about 330,000 persons were living in one square mile in the Lower East Side. In the nineties, according to the federal commissioner of labor, one-tenth of the population of the sixteen largest cities in the country lived in these slums. Lack of adequate sanitation and public health services allowed contagious diseases—typhoid fever, scarlet fever, smallpox, diphtheria—to run rampant. As late as 1888, in a group of blocks in New York City's East Side, the death rate for children under five was 139.83 per 1,000, compared to 85 per 1,000 as the death rate for the same age group in the entire city. Fire hazards were numerous and flagrant. As the city grew there was a rapid increase in crime and general lawlessness.

Cities eventually provided some public services, although only those that were absolutely necessary. They did begin to dispose of sewage and to remove the garbage from the streets instead of leaving it to be eaten by pigs. They constructed gas mains and public waterworks, supplied some sort of transportation and lighting, and made police and fire protection available. Facilities for recreation and health, however, came only as afterthoughts, if at all. The first city board of health was established in New York in 1866, and the first state board in Massachusetts in 1870. The American Public Health Association was founded in 1872.

In an age of laissez faire there was very little planning in urban growth. City development lay largely in the hands of the real estate men, who did what they pleased. They usually cut up the land into rectangular lots, and cities usually followed the gridiron design of straight streets running at right angles to each other. Little was done to set aside desirable sections for public use. Businessmen built factories and offices wherever they wished, they polluted streams and rivers, and made ugly slag heaps out of residential areas. Only gradually and reluctantly, and generally after irreparable harm had been done, did city governments abandon laissez-faire attitudes and take action.

The poor administration of cities was a serious blight upon American life, and, according to James Bryce, the English observer, "the one conspicuous failure in the United States." Andrew D. White, a prominent educator, wrote in 1890 that "with few exceptions, the city governments of the United States are the worst in Christendom—the most expensive, the most inefficient, and the most corrupt." Bryce found that city mismanagement resulted from crooked and incompetent officials and the control of local affairs by state legislatures unfamiliar with the needs of city government. But he also added:

In large cities we find an ignorant multitude, largely composed of recent immigrants, untrained in self-government; we find a great proportion of the voters paying no direct taxes and therefore feeling no interest in moderate taxation and economical administration; we find able citizens absorbed in their private businesses, cultivated citizens unusually sensitive to the vulgarities of practical politics, and both sets therefore specially unwilling to sacrifice their time and tastes and comforts in the struggle with sordid wire-pullers and noisy demagogues.

Into cities poured hordes of immigrants to meet some of the demands in nonagricultural employment that rose 300 percent between 1860 and 1900. With a rapid expansion of the American economy and improved ocean transportation facilities, Europeans came to the United States in unprecedented numbers, and a large proportion of them found work in American cities. In 1900 three-fourths of the population of Chicago was foreign-born. In the 1890s the Italian population in New York City equaled that of Naples; its German population equaled that of Hamburg; its Irish population was twice that of Dublin. In 1910 it was estimated that one-third of the inhabitants of the nation's eight largest cities was foreign-born, while more than a third was second-generation Americans. There were larger concentrations of foreign-born persons in some of the smaller industrial areas: in the coal and iron towns of Pennsylvania, for example, and in places like Paterson and Passaic, New Jersey. This trend alarmed many native-born Americans who expressed concern, as one of them did in the 1890s, "at the prospect of adding enormously to the burden of municipal governments in the large cities, already almost breaking down through corruption and inefficiency."

From the very beginning of American history, the character of the nation's people has been determined by the tides of Europeans coming to its shores. The colonies were peopled mainly by immigrants from England and northern Ireland (the Scotch-Irish), along with substantial numbers from Scotland, Germany, the Netherlands, and France. The mixture of these peoples had gone so far before the Revolution that one French observer could write that a new national type—the American—had come into being. Between the end of the Revolution and the 1840s immigration continued, but at a fairly slow pace. Most newcomers during this period still came from England, Scotland, and northern Ireland.

A sudden shift in the tide of immigration occurred in the late 1840s. It began when a terrible famine swept over southern Ireland, and poor farmers by the hundreds of thousands began to flee to America to escape starvation. Once begun, this migration continued through the nineteenth century and into the twentieth, until by 1914 some four million Americans were of immediate Irish ancestry.

In far greater numbers came the Germans, beginning about 1848 and growing in volume during the 1850s and 1860s. Although the stream from Germany slowed down in the 1870s, it continued until the First World War. By 1914 there were between eight and ten million German-Americans in the United States. The last great tide of immigrants from northern Europe were the Norwegians and Swedes, around four million of them altogether, who came to the United States between 1860 and 1880.

These newcomers helped to build the country. Irish labor constructed the railroads and canals. Germans contributed farmers and professional people. Scandinavians opened up the frontier in Minnesota and the northern Plains states.

The immigrants also helped to change the social character of the nation. Sociologists describe the United States as a "pluralistic" nation, that is, as one with wide diversity in the racial, religious, and cultural backgrounds of its people. Actually the American people have always been "pluralistic," even from the earliest days of English settlement in North America. To cite an example, the presence of a significant minority of people of African descent made Americans pluralistic as early as the mid-seventeenth century. The coming of the Irish and to some extent the Germans had the result of transforming the United

States from an almost exclusively Protestant country into one in which the Roman Catholic Church would play a more significant role.

Between 1860 and 1900 almost fourteen million immigrants came to the United States. Another fourteen and a half million followed between 1900 and 1915. The most important thing about this huge movement of peoples was not its size but the immigrants' origins. It reflected the shift in the tide of migration from northern Europe to southern and eastern Europe that began very quietly in the 1880s and then gained startling speed in the late 1890s and early 1900s. Previously, nearly all immigrants came from northern and western Europe—from Germany, Ireland, England, and Scandinavia. Now their numbers began to decline, and there was a rapid increase in those from southern and eastern Europe—particularly from Italy, Austria-Hungary, Poland, and Russia. In the 1860s these latter immigrants constituted only 1.4 percent of the total number coming to the United States, but their percentage rose to 7.2 percent in the seventies, to 18.3 percent in the eighties, to 51 percent in the nineties, and to 70 percent in the first decade or so of the twentieth century. This heavy influx is called the "new immigration," in contrast with the "old," and it brought a variety of new ethnic groups that had never been here before in appreciable numbers.

There was a contrast between the "old" and the "new" immigrants. Most of the former came from countries that were economically and culturally advanced; most of them could read and write; except for the Irish and some of the Germans, they were Protestants; and most of them settled on farms. The new immigrants came from "backward" countries; most of them were illiterate; most of them were Roman Catholic, Greek Orthodox, or Jewish; and most of them turned to industry and settled in the cities.

The new immigrants, like so many of the colonists and the earlier immigrants, came primarily to improve their economic and social lot. Promoters of American industry recruiting cheap labor and agents of steamship companies seeking passengers spread the news that America was the land of opportunity and the haven of the oppressed. The glowing pictures they painted created an irresistible pull toward the United States. Their claims were amply substantiated in letters from immigrants already here and in stories told by immigrants who returned to their native lands. In addition, transportation was cheap, and wages by European standards were high; there was religious freedom and no compulsory military service. Moreover, there was the overpowering lure of freedom. "If it was a merit in 1620 to flee from religious persecution," said a woman who fled Russia in 1894, "and in 1776 to fight against political oppression then many of the Russian refugees of today after the uprising of 1905 are a little ahead of the Mayflower troops, because they have in their own lifetime sustained the double ordeal of fight and flights, with all the attendant risks and shocks....If it is the scum of Europe that we are getting in our present immigration it seems to be a scum rich in pearls."

Castle Garden, at the foot of Manhattan Island, became after 1855 the formal reception center for most of the immigrants reaching the United States, and in 1891 Ellis Island in New York harbor assumed this function. At both places the officials did little more than record the immigrant's arrival. A few immigrants were met by friends and relatives and some by representatives of welfare agencies and churches; but most were left to shift for themselves or were herded off to harsh employment by unscrupulous operators for industry. Strangers in a new world and ignorant of its language and customs, immigrants of the same nationality flocked together in the same areas, spoke the same language, and attempted to preserve their own customs and beliefs. This tendency resulted in a modification of American society. Crowding into large cities and often forming communities of their own, with their own institutions and traditions, and with newspapers and theatrical productions in their own languages, the new immigrants greatly complicated the process of assimilation.

While the immigrants peopled the American cities and furnished much of the manpower for the new industrialism, their coming in such large numbers gradually changed the attitude of the United States government and of native and older American stock from one of welcome to one of growing hostility. Because the new immigrants were so different in language, political background, and social customs, older Americans began to wonder whether they could ever be assimilated into the mainstream of national life. They also feared that the waves of new immigrants would annihilate the native American stock. The columnist Finley Peter Dunne's "Mr. Dooley" expressed one popular position of native Americans when he said: "As a pilgrim father that missed th' first boats, I must raise me claryon voice again' th' invasion in this fair land by th' paupers an' anychists in effete Europe. Ye bet I must—because I'm here first." Important, too, were the objections of labor leaders. They contended that the new workers from abroad were degrading American labor standards by accepting lower wages, working longer hours, living in slums, and allowing themselves to be used as strike breakers. Labor leaders also found it difficult to unionize people speaking so many different languages. And some of the older Americans resented the fact that so many of the new immigrants were Roman Catholics and Jews. Others were sure that the immigration of so many "foreigners" spelled dangers for the country. A few frightened Americans thought that the new immigrants were inferior "racially" and that their assimilation would weaken the dominant "Nordic" stock. Such hostilities and fears provoked anti-immigrant movements that were unworthy of American traditions. They bore various names—for example, the United Order of Deputies, the American League, the Minute Men of 1886, and the Red, White and Blue. But the most powerful group during this period was the American Protective Association, which was organized in 1887 to rally Americans for a fight against Catholicism. It grew with startling rapidity after the onset of the Panic of 1893 and stirred hostilities that would affect American society for decades to come.

True, the new immigration was of the lower classes, but this did not set it apart from earlier immigration. Irish and German immigrants of the mid-nineteenth century also were poor, so that poverty was not a trait peculiar to the new immigration. It is also true that the new immigration was hard to assimilate, but it is doubtful whether it was any more difficult than was German immigration of the mid-nineteenth century. Neither can the new immigration be held as a cause for unemployment, because this followed the business cycle and the demand for labor. Did the immigrants replace native workers? Statistics show that native labor increased in these years, especially in coal and steel where predictions were that native labor would be displaced. In fact, immigrants pushed up native labor to a new position of aristocracy. Nor did immigration reduce skilled labor, for this reduction was a consequence of new technical advances. In regard to the reduction of wages, the decline in the number of skilled workers proportionately affected the whole wage picture. The underpaid and unorganized laborers were Anglo-Saxon textile workers of the South where the new immigration had little effect. In respect to longer hours and dangerous work, American workers were used to these conditions before the arrival of the new immigrants. So also it was with sweatshops and poor living conditions. The new immigrants moved into those neighborhoods vacated by older immigrants. Neither sweatshops nor slums were new. Finally, the new immigration was not a deterrent to labor organization. On the contrary, the new immigration was often the backbone of labor unions.

For nearly a hundred years the federal government exercised no control over immigration. Then in 1875 it assumed its first responsibility in this area by excluding prostitutes and persons with prison records. In 1882 Congress forbade the immigration of Chinese laborers for a period of ten years, a prohibition which subsequent legislation extended and which an act of 1902 made permanent. The act of 1882 also barred paupers, the insane, and others likely to become public charges; and it imposed a head tax of 50 cents upon each immigrant. Under pressure from organized labor, Congress in 1885 ended the importation of contract laborers but exempted professional, skilled, and domestic labor. Then attempts were made to restrict immigration on the basis of a literacy test. Such tests, said Senator Henry Cabot Lodge of Massachusetts in 1896, would "bear most heavily upon the Italians, Russians, Poles, Hungarians, Greeks, and Asiatics, and very lightly, or not at all upon English-speaking immigrants or Germans, Scandinavians, and French."

Lodge maintained that "the mental and moral qualities which made what we call our race" could be protected only by preserving America from "the wholesale infusion of races whose traditions and inheritances, whose thoughts and beliefs are wholly alien to ours and with whom we have never assimilated or even been associated in the past."

President Cleveland in 1897, President Taft in 1913, and President Wilson in 1915 and 1917 each vetoed a bill imposing a literacy test as a condition of entry to the United States. But in 1917 Congress passed over Wilson's veto an act by which any alien who could not read English or his own language was denied admittance to this country. Still more restrictive measures lay in the future as nativists' fears of the "alien tide" were nurtured by developments during the First World War and the postwar decade.

The story of the growth of organized labor in the United State parallels almost exactly that of the development of economic enterprise. Industries and trades were local in character roughly down to the Civil War. So, too, were labor unions. Local unions of workers in the same crafts, such as carpenters, tailors, or shoemakers, had existed from the earliest days of the Republic. As early as 1799 the shoemakers of Philadelphia conducted a strike. An attempt was made in New York in 1834 to unite workers in various crafts into a general organization of "the productive classes of the country." The time was not yet ripe for such a movement however.

Nor was the time yet ripe for a labor movement such as we know today on any level. Class consciousness developed very slowly among American industrial workers. Most of them in the first half-century of the Industrial Revolution in the United States refused to regard factory work as a career, or themselves as a separate class apart from employers and consumers. Hence they concentrated in the 1820s, 1830s, and 1840s not upon organization for collective bargaining but upon various reform movements to achieve their goals. Even their goals—such as liberal land policies and abolition of imprisonment for debt—were those of other reform groups in society.

The beginning of what would be a momentous if slow change occurred in the 1850s. This decade saw the first important formation of trade unions primarily for the purpose of improving wages and conditions of employment. Among these trade unions were the National Typographical Union, the International Union of Machinists and Blacksmiths, and the Iron Molders International Union. They were the forerunners of a modern labor movement.

Laissez-faire principles almost invariably governed relations between capital and labor. While businessmen solicited government assistance in the form of tariff protection, they did not regard this aid as a form of government intervention in economic life. They bitterly opposed, however, any attempt to improve the condition of labor by legislation on the ground that such regulation represented "unwarranted" interference with the natural laws of the economic system. Most businessmen believed that wealth was a sign of favor from God and that there was some form of divine right upholding capital. For example, during the coal strike of 1902 George F. Baer, chief spokesman for the mine owners, declared, "The rights and interests of the laboring man will be protected and cared for—not by the labor agitators, but by the Christian man to whom God in His infinite wisdom has given control of the property interests of the country."

Nevertheless, as business formed combinations, so did labor. Only three national unions (hatters, printers, and stonecutters) remained at the end of the Civil War. About the only national labor leader was Ira Stewart, who advocated an eight-hour day. His proposal attracted wide support, and hundreds of eight-hour leagues, including farmer groups, were established in the country. Although the movement had little practical success, it did provide a stimulus for bringing about the national labor organization which emerged into the National Labor Union.

The National Labor Union was mainly a reform organization which sought redress for grievances that had been in agitation since the mid-nineteenth century. It demanded an eight-hour day, abolition of slums, and establishment of cooperatives. It favored arbitration of labor disputes and opposed independent political action. William Sylvis of the Molders' Union assumed the presidency of the National Labor Union in 1868 but died the next year. Had he lived longer, the union might have played a more important role. After his death the union engaged in political activity, and the trade union aims became secondary. In 1872 the organization formed the National Labor Reform party and nominated David Davis of Illinois for president. But Davis withdrew, causing the collapse of both party and federation.

The National Labor Union was a loose federation of autonomous societies. When the societies withdrew their support, the movement broke down. Its leadership came from the top down, and there were few prominent leaders. The successors of the National Labor Union were to profit by avoiding these weaknesses. Thus, though the National Labor Union was short-lived, it did have a certain significance in the history of labor. It prepared the way for other more successful labor organizations.

The Knights of Labor was organized in Philadelphia in 1869 under the leadership of Uriah Stephens. Believing in the solidarity of labor, the Knights admitted almost everybody to membership, excluding only lawyers, bankers, stockbrokers, liquor dealers, and professional gamblers. Their announced primary purpose was "to secure to the toilers a proper share of the wealth they create." They hoped to achieve their goals by secrecy, by the use of cooperatives, and by education and propaganda. Secrecy was of prime importance to the Knights. It was their means of defense against capital, which locked out workers belonging to unions. The Knights did not make public the name of their organization until 1881. Secrecy got the Knights into difficulty with the churches. Only the intercession of Cardinal Gibbons of Baltimore kept the pope from excommunicating Catholics in the federation.

The Knights were of national prominence from 1879 to 1893, while Terence V. Powderly was their Grand Master Workman. Powderly was denounced by some as a revolutionary and by others as a faker who sold out labor. He never gave full attention to the union, for he considered it only a part-time job. He engaged in a number of activities—mayor of Scranton, 1878–1884; leader of the Irish Land League; and member of the Socialist party. He was a capitalist as well, for he owned a store. His greatest strength with the workers was his oratorical power. He supported land reform, temperance, and public education; he made wild pronouncements against wage slavery, opposed strikes, and was willing to come to terms with capital at almost any price.

The Knights of Labor hoped to do nothing less than to organize all workers, skilled and unskilled, black and white, into one big union for mutual protection against "the aggression of employers." Early mottoes expressed their basic ideas: "Injury to one is the concern of all," and "Harmonize the interests of labor and capital." The Knights worked for the eight-hour day, abolition of child labor, settlement of industrial disputes by arbitration rather than by strikes, and encouragement of cooperative stores and factories. Officially the Knights opposed the use of strikes. Unions in the seventies generally opposed them, because most strikes had been unsuccessful. The depression of 1873 had dealt the unions some very severe blows. They lost strength and saw wages drop as much as 40 percent in textiles and on the railroads. They faced increasing unemployment, prosecution of strikers, and use of police and private detective agencies as strikebreakers. Employers resorted to lockouts (restricting employment to nonunion labor), to blacklisting (circularizing names of union leaders and members), and to yellow-dog contracts (pacts under which employees agreed not to join unions). Very few unions pulled through the depression. Out of 39 national unions, only 8 remained at the end of the depression in 1877.

The Knights took the position that, if employers did not recognize the union in a dispute, no effective solution was possible. Yet the Knights did engage in strikes and were so successful in winning them that by 1886, their peak year, their membership increased from 100,000 to 700,000 between July 1885 and June 1886, with local assemblies rising from 484 to 5,892 since 1882. Hard times of the mid-eighties led to railroad boycotts and strikes, notably on the Union Pacific Railroad in 1884 and Jay Gould's Wabash Railroad in 1885. These spontaneous strikes by shopmen and trainmen caught the companies off guard and compelled Powderly to support the strikers. They were labor's first major victories, and they forced Gould to negotiate with the Knights. An illusion of easy success arose, and a sudden flood of workers joined the Knights.

The Knights of Labor were weakened by the very same conflict over basic objectives that had earlier rent the National Labor Union. It was the division between a national leadership dedicated to general economic and political reform and the national trade unions that wanted to concentrate on the immediate economic betterment of workingmen. This controversy came to a head, ironically, during 1886, the year of the organization's most spectacular growth. But Powderly and other leaders of the union, instead of welcoming new members, reacted in alarm. They refused to support new strikes against the Missouri Pacific and Texas and Pacific railroads and certain Chicago meatpackers. These and other dissensions over immediate strategy and long-range goals led to the withdrawal of the national trade unions. From there on the Knights declined in numbers and influence, and by 1890 the membership had fallen to 100,000. Failure of their cooperatives and their identification with some of the labor violence of the eighties also contributed to the downfall of the Knights.

While the power and influence of the Knights of Labor were waning, a new labor organization was coming into its own under the leadership of Samuel Gompers. As an immigrant boy of 14, Gompers joined the Cigar Makers Union in Pittsburgh. In 1877, after his local had been all but ruined by a long strike, he and Adolph Strasser reorganized their unit. Gompers abandoned the ideal of labor solidarity. Pure trade unionism was his aim. His plan was to group laborers according to crafts. Appraising the vertical organization of the Knights of Labor as a structural weakness, Gompers adopted the horizontal approach of a separate union for each craft. His union pursued three practical objectives, higher wages, shorter hours, and better working conditions. Gompers fought labor agitators and radicals, and he opposed direct affiliation of labor organizations with political parties. He favored cooperation with employers and advocated mediation of labor disputes.

Gompers's concept of the labor movement caught on throughout the country. In 1881 at Pittsburgh, he was active in the foundation of the Federation of Organized Trades and Labor Unions. In 1886 he was chosen president when this national body was reorganized as the American Federation of Labor. At that date the AFL had nearly 550,000 members, or about 60 percent of the total membership of all labor organizations in the country. It was a decentralized organization with individual craft unions preserving local autonomy. The Knights of Labor and the AFL competed for supremacy in American labor, and by the end of the century the AFL had won.

It should be emphasized that all major labor organizations in these years rejected violence per se as a weapon in their struggle to improve the condition of labor. The AFL, the National Labor Union, and the Knights of Labor all worked through the democratic process.

There were some notable exceptions to this generalization, however. One was the Molly Maguires, an organization active among Pennsylvania coal miners from about 1865 to 1877. They resorted to violence, killing mine superintendents and destroying property until they were exposed by agents of the Pinkerton Detective Agency and destroyed. Another exception was the Anarchists, a small group that gave support to acts of terror aimed at destroying capitalism. The Haymarket Riot of 4 May 1886 was this period's worst instance of violence in the conflict between capital and labor involving the Anarchists. Strikers against International Harvester had assembled for a meeting in Haymarket Square in Chicago to protest the shooting of several strikers. When police attempted to disperse the gathering, someone threw a bomb at the police killing seven of them and injuring seventy others. Guilt for throwing the bomb has never been established. Eight alleged Anarchists were arrested, tried, and convicted of inciting to murder, and four were hanged. Governor John P. Altgeld pardoned the survivors in 1893 on the ground that they had not received a fair trial.

Occasionally, there was violence in some of the strikes. A bloody episode occurred in a strike of steelworkers against Carnegie's Homestead plant near Pittsburgh in 1892. Pinkerton men, hired by the Carnegie company, and strikers met in armed battle in which a number of men was killed or wounded. The strike was finally broken when the governor of Pennsylvania called out the national guard. Another bloody episode occurred during the strike against the Pullman company in 1894. This violence and bloodshed occurred primarily because the industrialists of the day were determined to use every means to prevent the effective organization of labor and not because the labor unions themselves favored the use of violence.

Organized religion also had to adapt itself to industrialism. This adjustment proved to be difficult for the Protestant churches. Most of them had always regarded the Bible as the supreme authority. But the

Darwinian theory of evolution had challenged belief in the authority of the Scriptures, and the rise of large corporations had weakened Protestant belief in the virtues of economic individualism.

In the eighties and nineties an increasing number of Protestant clergymen accepted the theory of evolution and sought to reconcile it with religious belief. The most notable convert was Henry Ward Beecher, one of the most celebrated preachers of the time, who declared that evolution was merely "the deciphering of God's thought as revealed in the structure of the world." A few clergymen went beyond his position to deny the supernatural character of miracles in Christianity, and this development alarmed the Fundamentalists who reasserted their belief in the supreme authority of the Bible as the only solid foundation for religious faith. A struggle developed in the Protestant churches between the Fundamentalists and their opponents, the Liberals, as they were called.

Throughout the Gilded Age most Protestant clergymen held conservative economic views and, believing that the existing economic system was just, they sanctified the cult of business success. Beecher, for instance, condemned the eight-hour day, insisted that poverty was a sign of sin, and advocated the use of force, if necessary, to put down strikes. The conservative views of some clergymen were influenced no doubt by wealthy businessmen in their congregations who made heavy contributions to church funds. Whatever the reason, the conservative attitude toward the workingman's demands for shorter hours and government regulation caused a falling off of working-class attendance at churches.

In the eighties a few socially conscious Protestant clergymen disagreed with Beecher's teachings on current economic questions and began to preach either the Social Gospel or Christian Socialism. Among the chief exponents of the Social Gospel were Josiah Strong and Washington Gladden. They declared that the problems of industrialism could only be solved by the universal application of the teachings of Christ. In many writings and sermons Gladden defended the rights of labor to organize and proposed that industrial disputes be eliminated by "an industrial partnership" that would allow workers to receive "a fixed share" of industry's profits. He espoused the idea of governmental ownership of public utilities although he rejected socialism as a system.

The Christian Socialists proposed a collective society, but they differed from the Marxists on how to achieve it. The Marxists sought their ideal through a class struggle; the Christian Socialists sought their ideal through a program based upon the law of God and the precepts of Christ. The leader and spokesman of Christian Socialism was Walter Rauschenbusch, professor of Church history at Rochester Theological Seminary. An ardent Socialist, he severely censured industrial capitalism as "a mammonistic organization with which Christianity can never be content."

The heavy flow of immigration caused the Catholic Church to expand in size and influence in the late nineteenth and early twentieth centuries. In 1860 there were 3,500,000 Catholics in the United States, representing 11 percent of the total population. In 1910 they numbered 16,000,000 or 16 percent of the total. As the Church grew, more schools and convents were built. The Irish dominated the leadership in the Church, a situation which rankled some of the new immigrants. A German Catholic, Peter Cahensly, in 1890 proposed that each national group should have its own priests and bishops, but Cahenslyism was condemned by the Pope and made little headway. The Roman Catholic Church's attitude toward social reform was mostly negative, or at most one of toleration. Only in part was the hierarchy moved by considerations of justice and charity. James Cardinal Gibbons, archbishop of Baltimore, insisted that Catholics cultivate a patriotic citizenship in keeping with the nation's civil institutions and customs. Gibbons asserted, "The accusation of being un-American—that is to say, alien to our national spirit—is the most powerful weapon which enemies of the Church can employ against her."

Archbishop John Ireland of St. Paul minimized the economic problems of the time and advocated only temperance and conservative trade unionism. In 1903 he said publicly, "I have no fear of great fortunes in the hands of individuals, nor of vast aggregations of capital in the hands of corporations." Ireland's friendship with James J. Hill, the railroad builder, and President McKinley brought him under the criticism of reformers. Yet he often expressed strong sympathy for organized labor, saying on one occasion, "Until their material condition is improved it is futile to speak to them of spiritual life and duties."

Through this indifference to social reform, the Church jeopardized its hold on the loyalty of its communicants. Catholics in large numbers lost interest in a Church which seemed indifferent, if not hostile, to movements for the promotion of their economic welfare. Many Catholics turned to socialism. As the Church began to lose its members to Protestantism and socialism, it developed a greater interest in social problems. Also helping to change the Church's attitude was Pope Leo XIII's famous encyclical *Rerum Novarum* (1891), which condemned the exploitation of labor and asserted that it was the duty of the state to foster social justice.

America's most tragic problem in the post–Civil War years was the plight of the blacks who comprised one-tenth of the American population. Though the Civil War had settled the question of human slavery, it did not settle the problem of securing for all Americans the inalienable rights set forth in the Declaration of Independence. Nor did it alter the fact that white supremacy in the country was generally taken for granted. During Reconstruction significant constitutional and legislative steps such as the Thirteenth, Fourteenth, and Fifteenth Amendments and the Civil Rights Acts of 1866 and 1875 were taken to insure the freedman's political and civil rights, but developments during the last quarter of the nineteenth century virtually destroyed these political gains.

When President Hayes removed the last of the federal troops and federal control from the South in April 1877, he left southern blacks to the custody of southern whites, such as Governor Wade Hampton of South Carolina, who promised to "secure to every citizen, the lowest as well as the highest, black as well as white, full and equal protection in the enjoyment of all his rights under the Constitution." Because of such promises Hayes believed that a new "era of good feeling" was developing in the South between the two races. Even before 1877 was over, he learned differently. "By state legislation, by frauds, by intimidation, and by violence of the most atrocious character, colored citizens have been deprived of the right of suffrage," he wrote in his diary. But he did practically nothing to correct the situation. And when these southern white pledges regarding the Negro were not kept, there was little protest from the blacks' former northern champions until well into the twentieth century.

The Republican party had emerged from the Civil War as the champion and protector of Southern blacks. It had emancipated and enfranchised them and had provided them with political and civil rights. In their campaign platforms in the last quarter of the nineteenth century the Republicans promised to enforce the Fourteenth and Fifteenth Amendments. But while they talked much about this, they did very little for the freedmen.

Actually, throughout most of this period the Republicans did not control Congress enough to enforce these amendments. But their abandonment of blacks was also part of a new political strategy they were using in the South. In an effort to develop a stronger party in the South and to compete with the Democrats in this section, the Republicans shifted their appeals in the South mainly from blacks to whites. While they wanted to maintain their black support their principal aim was to increase their ranks with southern whites. The Republicans of the post-Reconstruction years sought to conciliate Southern whites and to ingratiate the Republican party with them. This they attempted to do by removing the troops, by appointing southern whites to federal positions, by working with white Independent politicos in the South, and by subordinating blacks in the leadership of the Republican party in the South. While these moves failed to bring much Republican political success in the South they did result in the desertion of southern blacks whom the Republicans had publicly pledged themselves to protect.

The Republican abandonment of the blacks in these years was also part of a general abandonment of them by Northerners. By the end of Reconstruction most Northerners probably agreed with Southern whites that blacks were not prepared for equality and that the South should be allowed to deal with them in its own way. Northerners had also come to believe that the elimination of the issue of blacks from politics was necessary for a return to national reconciliation and a development of trade between the North and the South.

Blacks were also abandoned by the courts. After 1877 practically every Supreme Court decision affecting blacks nullified or curtailed their rights. The Court drastically limited the powers of the federal government to intervene in the states to protect the rights of blacks. To all intents and purposes, it invalidated the Fourteenth and Fifteenth Amendments as effective safeguards for black people. When in 1883 the Court set aside the Civil Rights Act of 1875 on the ground that the Fourteenth Amendment was binding on states but not on individuals, it ended federal attempts to protect blacks against discrimination by private persons. There would be no federal civil rights legislation thereafter until 1957. And in the 1870s, when the Court held that the Fifteenth Amendment did not confer the right to vote upon anyone and that Congress did not have the authority to protect the right to vote generally, sections of the Enforcement Act of 1870 were declared unconstitutional because they provided penalties for hindering a person in voting. In 1894 Congress repealed the entire law. Again, there was no further legislation on the subject until 1957.

Blacks had continued to vote after the return of white supremacy in the South though in reduced numbers. In some parts of the South they were prevented from voting by threats or intimidation, and in other parts their vote was nullified by artful means such as the use of tissue ballots and a complicated system of ballot boxes. In the 1890s, however, the southern states proceeded to disfranchise them with laws. Within two decades practically all black voters had been disfranchised by means of poll taxes, white primaries, and literacy or property qualifications that were enforced against blacks but not against whites. In the same years the southern states also passed numerous "Jim Crow" laws, segregating blacks in virtually every aspect of public life.

Most Northerners shared the Court's attitude toward blacks. They deplored agitation on behalf of blacks and were willing to accept the South's racial policies. Even educated, intelligent Northerners believed that black people were racially inferior, because most scientists at the time believed this. Most of the Northern press supported the decisions in the civil rights cases. And as Rayford W. Logan, a leading black historian, has shown, Northern newspapers usually described blacks in a derogatory manner, regardless of the actual circumstances, strengthening a stereotype of the "criminal Negro." The leading literary magazines of the North such as *Harper's, Scribner's,* and the *Atlantic Monthly,* mirroring the refined tastes of the upper classes, regularly used derisive terms when they referred to blacks.

Most Americans did not especially wish blacks ill, wrote John A. Garraty, a leading historian on the Gilded Age. "They simply refused to consider them quite human and consigned them complacently to oblivion, along with the Indians."

The position of black leader Booker T. Washington among his race from 1885 to his death in 1915 may have also contributed to the assault upon the rights of blacks. Washington, founder and principal of Tuskegee Institute in Alabama was, according to Louis R. Harlan, a recent biographer, a "white man's black man" and a "safe, sane Negro" to Southern whites. In the Northern white world, Washington was "deferential but dignified," drawing philanthropy from such men as Carnegie. Among Southern whites, says Harlan, Washington made a point of not crossing the color line and sought to reduce social friction. He believed that for the time being blacks should forgo agitation for the vote and social equality and should devote their efforts to achieving economic security and independence. "In all things that are purely social," Washington said in a speech at the Atlantic Cotton Exposition of 1895, "we can be as separate as the fingers, yet one as a hand in all things for mutual progress." This idea won the enthusiastic support of whites, and it had much to do with fixing the pattern of race relations in the country for the remainder of Washington's lifetime. While Washington accepted a subordinate position for southern Negroes he was convinced that it would have been folly at the time to ask for equal rights for blacks. While blacks then generally accepted Washington's view, a later generation would repudiate it as an "Uncle Tom's" attitude.

In view of the foregoing development it is no wonder that Logan could write, "At the beginning of the Twentieth Century what is now called second class citizenship for Negroes was accepted by presidents, the Supreme Court, Congress, organized labor, the General Federation of Women's Clubs—indeed the vast majority of Americans, North and South, and by the 'leader' of the Negro race." It was indeed the saddest aspect of American life. Congress had repudiated or abandoned the federal government's pledges on Negro rights. Civil rights for blacks were a dead letter; disfranchisement enjoyed federal approval and support; "separate but equal" was the law of the land; racism was not merely a regional but a national creed. In short, by 1900 there was a merging of the southern and national outlook and a general acceptance of the theory of white supremacy. This situation would persist without serious disturbance into the second half of the twentieth century.

While blacks were losing their rights women were struggling for more rights, opportunities, and privileges and for a more equal place with men in the participation in and conduct of American affairs. Much of this activity centered on the effort to win the vote.

There was considerable opposition to women's claims of equal political rights with men. Politicians insisted that the political arena was a male preserve, that politics itself was masculine, and that any attempt to change that situation was contrary to human nature. Politicians were not alone in holding this view. Francis Parkman, one of the era's most prominent historians, thought women's suffrage would leap over "Nature's limitations," disrupt the home and give women excitement and cares "too much for their strength." But a number of supporters of women's rights disagreed.

The two major political parties, Republican and Democratic, however, either ignored or opposed the demand for women's suffrage, and many women decided to take action themselves. They did several things. Under the leadership of Susan B. Anthony and Elizabeth Cady Stanton they worked for the suffrage from the 1870s on. Then some women's groups, such as the Equal Rights party, took direct political action by nominating women for president of the United States— Victoria Claflin Woodhull in 1872 and Belva Ann Lockwood in 1884 and 1888.

In the last part of the nineteenth century there was a battle for women's suffrage in the nation's magazines, public meetings, legislative assemblies, and state constitutional conventions. Prominent reformers such as Thomas Wentworth Higginson and George William Curtis and John Greenleaf Whittier, a leading poet, as well as the two most important labor organizations of the day, the Knights of Labor and the AFL, supported the women's suffrage movement.

Women tried unsuccessfully to win the vote through the Fifteenth Amendment. At first they failed in efforts in the states, as seven states turned down women's suffrage proposals between 1867 and 1877. They also had a serious legal setback when the United States Supreme Court in *Minor* v. *Happersett* (1875) refused to accept the argument that women could vote because they were citizens and unanimously ruled that the Fourteenth Amendment had not conferred the vote upon women. Also, when some states barred women from the legal profession, the Supreme Court upheld such laws, with one justice saying, "The natural and proper timidity and delicacy which belongs to the female sex, unfits it for many...occupations." Women, he said, should stay with "the noble and benign offices of wife and mother."

In 1878, Senator Aaron Augustus Sargent of California introduced into Congress an equal suffrage amendment. During the remaining years of the century, Senate committees reported five times and House committees twice in favor of the amendment, but Congress never took action on it. Despite considerable effort by the suffragettes, the increasing militancy of the women's suffrage movement, and a growing sympathy and backing for it generally, only four states at the close of the nineteenth century had given the vote to women— Wyoming (1869), Colorado (1893), Utah (1896), and Idaho (1896).

Women seemed to make more progress in other aspects of American life than they did politically. More women were working outside their homes and going to college than had been the case in earlier periods of American history. The old prejudice against self-support for women was beginning to weaken, and at the same time colleges and universities were preparing increasing numbers of women for positions previously held mainly by men. "We have reached a new era," asserted *Harper's Bazaar,* a leading women's magazine, in 1883. "Slowly as woman has come to her inheritance, it stretches before her now into illimitable distance, and the question of the hour is rather whether she is ready for her trust than whether that trust is hampered by conditions."

Though there had long been a large number of women who worked for a living outside the home, the great economic expansion of the late nineteenth century brought many more into the work force. From 1880 to 1900, the number of women workers went up from 2.5 million to 5.3 million. Unfortunately this was counterbalanced by women usually filling the lowest paid jobs and receiving unequal pay in virtually every position they held for work equal to that done by men.

Since unions did not pay much attention to working conditions for women, not much was done to correct the injustice of the unequal wage scale. One gain was made when Congress in 1872 enacted the Arnell Bill giving women government workers equal pay with men for equal work. Belva Ann Lockwood had much to do with this Act. She drafted the measure, and its passage was hastened by a petition she circulated at the meetings of the National and American Women's Suffrage Associations in New York in 1870. Another gain was that legislatures in the industrial states began in the 1880s to consider legislation regulating working conditions of women in factories.

Women also made progress in education in these years despite their being up against a generally held view, expressed by a clergyman in 1880, that women's emotional nature "painfully disqualifies" them from the effort to be educated. By this time women had been accepted in colleges for about twenty years, and by 1870 nearly one-third of American colleges were coeducational.

Most educational opportunities for women were in the Middle West and the South where new state universities began to admit them as well as men. President James B. Angell of the University of Michigan observed in the 1880s that "none of the ladies had found the curriculum too heavy for their physical endurance."

Angell's concern about women's physical stamina for the rigors of study was shared by other Americans, both women and men. M. Carey Thomas, a graduate of Cornell in 1877 and the first president of Bryn Mawr, expressed this concern when she said, "The passionate desire of the women of my generation for higher education was accompanied. . . by the awful doubt, felt by women themselves as well as by men, as to whether women as a sex were physically and mentally fit for it."

Women clearly demonstrated their fitness for college, and coeducation grew rapidly in these years. Between 1880 and 1898 the proportion of coeducational colleges increased from 51 percent to 70 percent and the number of women students from 2,750 to more than 25,000. At the same time some women's colleges, on a level with the top ones for men, were established—Vassar (1861), Wellesley (1870), Smith (1871), and Bryn Mawr (1885). Mount Holyoke, a girl's seminary since 1836, became a college in 1893. Also, two of the country's leading universities, Harvard and Columbia, added women's colleges—Radcliffe in 1879 and Barnard in 1889. By the end of the nineteenth century, four out of every five colleges, universities, and professional schools in the country admitted women.

Women, especially of the upper middle class, also turned their attention to club activities and joined in large numbers the women's organizations springing up all over the country. These various associations provided a good way for women to find out more about the world in which they were now playing a larger role. In one decade, 1888-1897, three important groups were formed placing more women in public affairs—the National Council of Women, the General Federation of Women's Clubs, and the National Congress of Parents and Teachers. By the close of the nineteenth century, the General Federation of Women's Clubs claimed a membership of 150,000 and was supporting such reforms as child welfare, education, and sanitation.

Of course the participation of women in reforms was not new. Women had taken an active role in reform movements before the Civil War, and this momentum continued. Probably the strongest women's reform group of these years was the Women's Christian Temperance Union (WCTU) established in Cleveland in 1874 to fight the saloon and to promote prohibition. The prohibition movement had begun in the first half of the nineteenth century. By the time of the Gilded Age four states—Maine, New Hampshire, Vermont, and Kansas—had prohibition laws. The United States Supreme Court upheld such laws in 1847 but reversed itself in 1888 on the grounds that the interstate control of liquor belonged to Congress.

Frances E. Willard became the head of the WCTU in 1879 and began to work through schools and churches to arouse public opinion against liquor. With pressure from the WCTU, virtually every state added the requirement of "scientific temperance instruction" to the school curriculum between 1882 and 1898.

Many women who saw the saloon as an implacable foe were also aware of other social problems such as child labor, unsanitary housing, lack of public health measures, and penal conditions that needed their support for reform. Not all women, however, agreed that increased activities of women meant progress for them. "What is this curious product of today, the American girl or woman?" asked one woman writer in 1880 in the *Atlantic Monthly.* "Is it possible for any novel, within the next fifty years, truly to depict her as a finality, when she is still emerging from new conditions. . . , when she does not yet understand herself. . . .?"

Thus, by the end of the nineteenth century, increasing economic independence and more educational opportunities for women had enlarged their social freedom and widened their range of activity. They had gone far, but they had much farther to go.

Further Reading

Abell, Aaron. *American Catholic Thought on Social Questions.* 1968.
_____. *The Urban Impact Upon American Protestantism, 1865-1900.* 1943.
Berthoff, Rowland. *British Immigrants in Industrial America.* 1953.
Carter, Paul A. *The Spiritual Crisis of the Gilded Age.* 1971.
Chudakoff, Howard. *The Evolution of American Urban Society.* 1975.
Dinnerstein, Leonard and David Reimers. *Ethnic Americans: A History of Immigration and Assimilation.* 1975.
Dubofsky, Melvyn. *Industrialism and the American Worker, 1865-1920.* 2d. ed., 1985.
Duff, John B. *The Irish in the United States.* 1971.
Garraty, John A. *The New Commonwealth, 1877-1890.* 1968.
Grob, Gerald N. *Workers and Utopia.* 1961.
Gutman, Herbert G. *Work, Culture, and Society in Industrializing America.* 1976.
Handlin, Oscar. *The Uprooted.* 1951.
Harlan, Louis R. *Booker T. Washington: The Making of a Black Leader, 1865-1901.* 1972.
Higham, John. *Strangers in the Land: Patterns of American Nativism, 1860-1925.* 1955.
Huthmacher, J. Joseph. *A Nation of Newcomers.* 1967.
Jones, Maldwyn A. *American Immigration.* 1960.
Kousser, J. Morgan. *The Shaping of Southern Politics: Suffrage Restriction and the Establishment of the One-Party South, 1880-1910.* 1974.

Livesay, Harold C. *Samuel Gompers and Organized Labor in America.* 1978.

Logan, Rayford W. *Betrayal of the Negro from Rutherford B. Hayes to Woodrow Wilson.* 1965.

Lyman, Stanford M. *Chinese Americans.* 1974.

May, Henry F. *Protestant Churches and Industrial America.* 1949.

McKelvey, Blake. *The Urbanization of America, 1860-1915.* 1973.

Meier, August. *Negro Thought in America: Racial Ideologies in the Age of Booker T. Washington, 1880-1915.* 1963.

Miller, Zane. *The Urbanization of America.* 1973.

Nelli, Humbert. *Italians in Chicago, 1880-1930.* 1970.

Philpott, Thomas L. *The Slum and the Ghetto.* 1978.

Powderly, Terence V. *Thirty Years of Life and Labor, 1859-1889.* 1890.

Rabinowitz, Howard N. *Race Relations in the Urban South, 1865-1900.* 1978.

Rayback, Joseph G. *A History of American Labor.* 1959.

Renshaw, Patrick. *The Wobblies: The Story of Syndicalism in the United States.* 1967.

Rischin, Moses. *The Promised City: New York Jews, 1870-1914.* 1962.

Rudiwick, Elliot M. *W. E. B. DuBois: Propagandist of Negro Protest.* 1969.

Salivatore, Nick. *Eugene V. Debs: Citizen and Socialist.* 1983.

Schlesinger, Arthur M. *The Rise of the City, 1878-1898.* 1933.

Sowell, Thomas. *Ethnic America: A History.* 1981.

Ware, Norman J. *The Labor Movement in the United States, 1860-1895.* 1929.

Woodward, C. Vann. *The Strange Career of Jim Crow.* Rev. ed., 1974.

7

America's New Manifest Destiny

Foreign affairs from the end of Reconstruction to the Spanish-American War played a subordinate role to domestic matters. Americans in these years were preoccupied with internal developments such as Reconstruction, the Industrial Revolution, and the settlement of the last frontier. Controversies over the national debt, taxation, the currency, and the new South precluded a vigorous foreign policy. With the possible exception of James G. Blaine there were no outstanding secretaries of state between Hamilton Fish (Grant's secretary of state) and John Hay (McKinley's secretary), and American foreign policy seemed to be conducted without much plan or purpose. Diplomatic historians until recently have not attached much significance to these postbellum years and have generally regarded them as an interlude before the great expansion of the late 1890s and the acquisition of an overseas empire. This was also generally the view of contemporaries of the era for as Henry Cabot Lodge wrote in 1889, foreign affairs filled "but a slight place in American politics and excite generally only a languid interest." But in the 1890s American foreign policy became more expansionist and more belligerent as the United States began to assume the role of a great power. Until that time, however, American foreign relations were of little importance and generated little public interest.

During the 1880s some Americans became interested in Latin America in the hope of finding new markets for American industry and of creating a sphere of influence for the United States in the Caribbean. Blaine, who served as secretary of state in 1881 under Garfield and again from 1889 to 1892 under Harrison, favored an aggressive and spirited diplomacy in Latin America. An ardent admirer of an earlier Pan-Americanist, Henry Clay, Blaine in 1881 sent invitations to the Latin American countries for a Pan-American conference in Washington. But Garfield's assassination caused the meeting to be cancelled, and Blaine's successor, Frederick T. Frelinghuysen, set aside the project.

Back in the office in 1889, Blaine revived his plan and issued invitations for another conference. That year eighteen American republics sent delegates to Washington. At the conference they discussed such subjects as the promotion of peace by arbitration and the formation of an American customs union. More important they established an International Bureau of American Republics, which in 1910 became the Pan-American Union. Though the concrete results of this first conference were meager, it is significant as the beginning of a long and important series of inter-American gatherings.

Blaine also fell heir to the dispute with Great Britain over the capture of seals in the Bering Sea. The United States had acquired with Alaska the two small Pribilof Islands, the breeding place of fur seals. In 1870 the United States government had given to the Alaska Commercial Company the exclusive monopoly to kill seals on their breeding grounds. But since sealskin coats were then fashionable, other countries and hunters claimed the right to hunt the seal off American islands outside the international three-mile limit. The activities of these hunters and the Alaska Commercial Company resulted in the slaughter of enormous herds of fur seals. To protect the American monopoly and to save the seals from the fate of the buffalo, American ships began to seize vessels on the high seas encroaching on American rights in the Bering Sea.

Attempts made in the mid-1880s to decide the question by an international convention fell through because of Canada's opposition. Blaine carried on a long diplomatic correspondence with the British government in which he contended that deep sea sealing was contrary to "good public morals" and the United States had the right to protect the seals in the entire region. Great Britain did not accept Blaine's position, and the dispute was finally referred to an arbitration tribunal in

Paris in 1893. The board decided every major legal point against the United States. The tribunal ruled that the Bering Sea was not a closed sea but a high sea and thus was beyond American jurisdiction. The United States had to pay $473,150 in damages for the British vessels it had seized during the dispute. It was not until 1911 in an agreement signed by four nations—the United States, Great Britain, Japan, and Russia—that America's North Pacific seal herd was saved from extermination.

Blaine was also interested in expansion in Pacific Ocean areas. He regarded the Hawaiian Islands as "part of the American system" and when he was Arthur's secretary of state he had worked to keep Great Britain from controlling them. Then in 1889 Blaine became involved in Samoan matters. In 1878 the United States had obtained rights to a naval base in Samoa, at the harbor of Pago Pago. Britain and Germany also became interested in Samoa, and Britons, Germans, and Americans manuevered for commercial and strategic control of this archipelago. In 1889 the Germans, dissatisfied with the lack of Samoan cooperation, replaced the reigning chieftain with a friendlier one under their armed protection. The United States supported the deposed ruler and, together with Britain, sent warships to the harbor of Apia. A battle seemed imminent, but on 16 March 1889 a tropical hurricane wrecked all the ships except a British cruiser. This effectively put off hostilities.

In the meantime the United States and Britain had agreed to attend a Berlin Conference in the spring of 1889 and there, in the summer of the same year, the three powers established a tripartite protectorate over Samoa. This checked German expansion in the area, but friction continued until 1899 when, in a new agreement, Samoa was formally divided between the United States and Germany. The United States received Pago Pago harbor and surrounding territory, and Germany acquired the rest of the land. In return for withdrawing, Britain got the Gilbert and Solomon Islands in the southern Pacific.

The United States also had disputes with Italy and Chile in these years. In 1891 a mob took eleven men, thought to be Italians, from the city jail in New Orleans and lynched them for the murder of the chief of police who had been able to bring to justice some members of a secret society of Italians known as the Mafia. The Italian government wanted United States authorities to punish those responsible for the killings. Secretary of State Blaine expressed regrets and pointed out that the federal government could not do anything in this instance. Italy then recalled its minister, and diplomatic relations between the two countries were severed. A short time afterward the United States, in a friendly gesture, agreed to pay $25,000 to the families of the victims. Learning that only three of the murdered men were actually Italians, the Italian government accepted the American offer, and diplomatic relations were resumed.

A more serious and uglier dispute occurred with Chile in 1892 that almost led to war. In a civil war in Chile in 1891 the United States had sought to prevent shipment of arms to some Chilean revolutionists and had supported the losing side in the struggle. These American actions naturally aroused the hostility of the revolutionists, who now controlled the government of Chile. When a number of American sailors on shore leave at Valparaiso on 16 October 1891 from the cruiser *Baltimore* visited the True Blue Saloon, they were attacked by a Chilean mob on their return through the streets to their vessel. Two Americans were killed and nearly a score severely wounded, and some of the sailors were thrown into the local jail. The Chilean government not only refused to apologize but even blamed the American sailors for the fracas.

President Harrison was incensed by the affair, and, when Secretary Blaine attempted to defend the Chileans in a cabinet meeting, the president emphatically said, "Mr. Secretary, that insult was to the uniform of the United States sailors." On 21 January 1892 Blaine sent an ultimatum, written by the president, to Chile, and four days later Harrison sent a special message to Congress virtually asking for war. The country was greatly aroused by the Chilean affair.

Fortunately war was averted. The Chilean government, bowing to superior American force, finally apologized for the attack on the American sailors and paid an indemnity of $75,000. Harrison referred to the settlement in his annual message of December 1892 and said he accepted the reparation not only as an indemnity for a wrong done, but as evidence that the Chilean government appreciated the willingness of the United States to act in a fair and friendly manner toward the people of Chile.

Hardly had the Chilean affair died down when the United States became involved in a revolution in the Hawaiian Islands. These islands had had a special relation to the United States for a number of years. American missionaries, merchants, and planters had been making their homes and fortunes in the islands since the early part of the nineteenth century. As early as the 1840s the American State Department had warned other powers to keep their hands off the Hawaiian Islands. The United States gained a tighter grip on Hawaii with a commercial reciprocity agreement in 1875 and with a guarantee of naval base rights at Pearl Harbor in a treaty of 1887. And as early as the 1850s there had been talk of the annexation of Hawaii to the United States. But before annexation could take place there was violence. White planters in the islands became alarmed by two developments. In 1890 Hawaii's single-staple economy, sugar, received a serious blow when the McKinley Tariff removed the duty from other foreign sugar sellers and thus made the Hawaiians compete with everyone else in the American sugar market. To protect the higher-cost American domestic sugar producers, the 1890 act gave domestic sugar a bounty of two cents a pound. The two-cent bounty and the removal of the sugar tariff broke Hawaiian sugar prices, which fell from $100 to $60 a ton with an estimated loss to Hawaiian producers of $12 million. In 1890, the year of the McKinley Tariff, 99 percent of Hawaiian exports consisted of sugar for the United States. Thus, the tariff was a severe body blow to the Hawaiian sugar economy.

In addition to economic troubles there were political problems. In 1891 King Kalakaua died and was succeeded by his sister, Queen Liliuokalani, who opposed the American naval base at Pearl Harbor and American annexation of the islands and who insisted that native Hawaiians, and not whites, should control Hawaii. On 14 January 1893 the queen repudiated the constitution of 1887, which gave Hawaiian-born whites control of the legislature and which extended the vote to white foreigners, and proclaimed a new constitution by royal edict. Three days later the white group in the island, though only a small minority, managed to overthrow the queen's rule. In this they were openly assisted by American marines, who were landed from the cruiser *Boston* in Honolulu harbor under the unauthorized orders of the expansionist American minister to Hawaii, John L. Stevens.

Stevens promptly recognized the new government set up by the American settlers who quickly sent a commission to Washington to negotiate a treaty of annexation. In the meantime the islands were declared a "protectorate" of the United States, and the American flag was raised over the government building. On 14 February 1893 the Hawaiian delegation signed a treaty of annexation with the American secretary of state, John W. Foster, who had replaced Blaine in 1892. President Harrison, who favored the treaty, sent it to the Senate the next day.

In the Senate the Democrats held up the treaty until Cleveland was inaugurated in March. Suspicious of Stevens's activities in Hawaii, Cleveland withdrew the treaty from the Senate only five days after his inauguration. Then he sent James H. Blount, a former Democratic congressman from Georgia, as a special commissioner to the islands to investigate the situation there. Blount submitted his report to the president in the summer of 1893, and it was harshly critical of Stevens's actions in the revolution. Cleveland's secretary of state, Walter Q. Gresham, charged Stevens with doing a great wrong to a "feeble but independent state."

Cleveland concluded that the revolution could not have succeeded without the support of Stevens and that the majority of the natives were against annexation. The president refused to send the treaty back to the Senate. Instead he sent a new minister to Hawaii. The minister called upon president Sanford B. Dole of the provisional government and suggested that he resign. In a reply several days later Dole invited the minister to go to hell. Dole said the United States had recognized the provisional government and that Cleveland had no right to interfere in Hawaii's internal affairs. Cleveland was prepared to restore the queen to her throne on the condition that she pardon the revolutionists. But when she replied, "My decision would be, as the law directs, that such persons should be beheaded . . .," the president abandoned his plan to restore the old government.

The whites in Hawaii would never allow Queen Liliuokalani to sit on the throne again, and President Cleveland was not willing to go ahead with annexation. But the president realized that he would have to use force to unseat the new government. Thus, when in 1894 it wrote another constitution, proclaiming a Hawaiian republic, and confirming Sanford B. Dole as president, Cleveland recognized it in August of that year. But he refused to comply with Dole's urgent request for annexation. This would have to wait until 1898.

In the United States many supporters of Hawaiian annexation were embittered by Cleveland's actions, and the New York *Commercial Advertiser* in a sharp editorial reflected some of their anger:

In ordering Old Glory pulled down at Honolulu, President Cleveland turned back the hands on the dial of civilization. Native rule, ignorant, naked, heathen is reestablished; and the dream of an American republic at the crossroads of the Pacific—a dream which Seward, Marcy and Blaine indulged, and the fulfillment of which the more enlightened of our 65,000,000 people awaited with glad anticipation—has been shattered by Grover Cleveland, the Buffalo lilliputian [Buffalo was Cleveland's home]. . . . He has declared. . . that the Hawaiian islands shall be tossed a prize into the arena of international strife, for which the Japanese, the English, and heaven knows who else may scramble and quarrel.

These predictions of course were never realized. Hawaii remained tranquil and quiet until it was annexed by the United States during the Spanish-American War.

If foreign affairs had played only a subordinate role in American life for much of the post–Civil War years, the situation changed drastically during the 1890s culminating in the Spanish-American War, the acquisition of an overseas empire, and the declaration of an Open Door Policy in the Far East. As we have seen, the United States became more expansionist, more quarrelsome, and more jingoistic in the early 1890s. American diplomacy became more aggressive in these years as evidenced by the disputes with Italy and Chile and by the Venezuelan boundary quarrel of 1895. It is noteworthy that in all three instances neither the national security nor the national interests of the United States were vitally involved. Yet in all three the United States government conducted aggressive diplomacy and considered the possibility of war, and the American press and public displayed a good deal of nationalism.

In addition to this change there was a reappearance of the spirit of "Manifest Destiny" in the 1890s. In the 1840s and 1850s the term had been used to rationalize the conquest of Texas and California. In the 1890s it was used to rationalize American policy in the Far East and the Caribbean.

Between the Civil War and the Spanish-American War the United States had become a great power with interests in two oceans. Although the Mexican War and the Oregon Treaty of 1846 had extended American territory to the Pacific Ocean, it was not until after 1865 that the Far West was linked with the East by railroad, and it was not until 1890 that the major portion of the last frontier was settled by Americans. Expansion to the Pacific Coast compelled those Americans who made foreign policy to pay attention to developments in the Pacific as well as in the Atlantic. A policy in the Pacific involved an enlarged navy, an isthmian canal, and the acquisition of Caribbean bases to protect its approaches.

Economic developments in the United States were also affecting American foreign affairs. As the economy changed from agriculture to industry, there were increased demands for overseas bases to protect and stimulate American commerce. These expansionist views became known as the "large policy," and increasingly Americans began to debate its merits.

In 1886 Theodore Roosevelt stated that he looked forward to the "day when not a foot of American soil will be held by any European power," and around the same time Henry Lodge declared, "From the Rio Grande to the Arctic Ocean there should be but one flag and one country." Lodge believed the United States should control the Hawaiian Islands, Samoa, an isthmian canal, and Cuba. Reinforcing this position were those writers who contended that Darwin's theory of evolution applied to nations as well as to animal beings. According to these writers no nation could be static, and the stronger nations were destined by a higher law to assimilate weaker and less fortunate peoples. Among these writers was Alfred Thayer Mahan, a naval captain, whose seminal book, *The Influence of Sea Power upon History,* was published in 1890. Mahan argued that sea power was the most powerful force in the making or breaking of nations. Sea power and commercial supremacy went hand in hand, and both could be promoted by a powerful navy, a large merchant marine, and overseas colonies. Specifically, Mahan advocated for the United States the building of a canal across the Isthmus and the seizing of commercial and naval outposts in the islands of the Pacific and the Caribbean.

Other followers of Darwin maintained that the "racial superiority" of Americans made for their inevitable expansion over large areas of the world. John Fiske, in a magazine article in 1885, asserted that the English race was destined to take over the entire world. Josiah Strong, a Congressional minister, wrote in a book published in 1885 that the Anglo-Saxon was "divinely commissioned to be in a peculiar sense his brother's keeper," and that the United States was to "become the home of this race, the principal seat of his power, the great center of his influence." Strong contended that the racial superiority of the American people ordained that there could be no limit to the territorial expansion of the United States. In a similar vein Senator Albert J. Beveridge of Indiana pointed out that overseas conquests were inevitable, for the "American Republic is part of the movement of a race—the most masterful race in history—and the race movements are not to be stayed by the hand of man."

No one can doubt that these ideas of expansionism gradually had some effect upon the thought of Americans. The advocates of expansionism published articles in popular magazines, lectured in major cities and many small towns, and had numerous and varied avenues of access to those in power. In the last two decades of the nineteenth century the United States developed an intense nationalism, and the advocates of expansion both promoted and reflected its growth.

The first sign of the change in American attitudes about foreign affairs was the building of a new navy. During the administrations of Grant and Hayes the naval strength of the United States declined almost to the vanishing point. But beginning in 1881 Congress appropriated growing sums for new construction, and the navy was rapidly enlarged and modernized so that at the end of the century the American navy was surpassed only by those of Britain and Germany.

The United States had also embarked upon a program of overseas expansion during the Johnson administration, when in 1867 Secretary of State Seward negotiated the purchase of Alaska and the annexation of the Midway Islands. Such moves had little public support then, for the country was preoccupied with the problems of Reconstruction. Later on, the increasing emphasis on sea power led to the acquisition of naval bases in the Pacific. In 1898, as we have seen, the United States received the right from Samoa to establish a naval base at Pago Pago. And, as we have also seen, a more important Pacific possibility was Hawaii, a natural strategic outpost guarding the approach to the American coastline.

The Spanish-American War resulted in the admission of the United States to the circle of great powers. Yet by most essential tests the United States had already been a great power for nearly a generation. At the close of the Civil War she possessed the greatest military force in the world. In 1880 the nation's population of over fifty million exceeded that of Great Britain, Germany, and France, and by the mid-1890s the United States had become the greatest industrial nation in the world. Thus, the victory over Spain did not really make the United States a world power. It simply confirmed the fact that the United States was one already, and it ratified the country's right to be so considered. It required the European powers to concede a new status to the United States, and it led the nation to think of itself and to conduct itself as a great power.

The Spanish-American War grew out of the Cuban revolt against Spain in 1895. While the harsh Spanish rule in itself contributed fundamentally to Cuban restiveness, the United States also had a hand in Cuba's misfortunes after 1890. A large part of Cuba's sugar crop, which made up about 80 percent of the island's wealth, had been sold in the United States through a preferential tariff agreement. Then the Wilson-Gorman Tariff of 1894 deprived the Cubans of this free market and imposed a duty on sugar. The high duty dealt a nearly fatal blow to Cuban exports to the United States. The resulting economic slowdown caused business failures and widespread unemployment, and the ensuing distress intensified Cuban discontent and set off open rebellion against Spanish rule.

Yet to explain the Spanish-American War only in terms of the Cuban revolt would be an oversimplification of what happened. It should not be forgotten that much of the territory the United States had acquired before the Civil War had been parts of Spain's crumbling empire in America. Louisiana, Florida, Texas, New Mexico, and California had all at one time or another belonged to Spain. But while the United States had acted as the receiver of Spain's North American empire, the American government had not been able to extend its power over Cuba, which was Spain's most valuable possession in the Caribbean. This American failure did not result from a lack of trying, because for a long time Cuba had been an object of much interest to the United States. The potential value of Cuba was widely recognized. Its location made it the strategic key to the Caribbean. From 1820 to 1860 American trade with Cuba was exceeded only by our trade with Great Britain and France. On a number of occasions before the Civil War, American presidents and expansionists had displayed an interest in Cuba. Both Jefferson and John Quincy Adams had predicted that the island was destined to become a part of the United States. And Presidents Polk and Pierce, under pressure from southern expansionists, had sought unsuccessfully to obtain Cuba.

The Cuban uprising began in February 1895. The insurgents established a government in Cuba, formed a junta in New York to seek support for their cause and to issue anti-Spanish propaganda, and sent a spokesman to Washington. In Cuba the insurgents waged a cruel and ruthless war and were determined to make the island valueless to Spain. Bands of guerillas roamed the countryside destroying plantations, setting fire to fields of sugar cane, terrorizing those of the local population who hesitated to support the rebellion, and resorting to ambush and assassination. The insurgents tried to work Americans both ways. By destroying American property they hoped to force the

United States to intervene. By not destroying American property when Americans paid bribes or protection money they could obtain funds to help finance their revolt.

To put down the uprising Spain's governor general in the island, General Valeriano Weyler, inaugurated the "reconcentration" policy whose cruelties caused Americans to label him "the Butcher." What Weyler did was to set up large concentration camps in and about the larger cities and towns. The purpose was to get all subjects loyal to Spain into these camps. Those who remained outside were hunted down as enemies. But what happened was that large numbers of women, children, and old men were herded into camps without adequate shelter, clothing, food, or sanitation, and thousands of them died from starvation and disease.

Americans who traditionally had been sympathetic to any colonial people engaged in a struggle for independence were naturally aroused by the tragic events of the Cuban revolution. And they were particularly upset and even shocked by the vivid newspaper disclosures of the alleged Spanish atrocities in Cuba. Lurid and highly exaggerated, if not false, accounts were enthusiastically publicized by the yellow press, led by two New York dailies: William Randolph Hearst's *Journal* and Joseph Pulitzer's *World*. Both papers colored the news in favor of the insurgents and even fabricated stories, for as Hearst told his correspondent in Havana, "You furnish the pictures and I'll furnish the war." The chief motive of Hearst and Pulitzer was profits as they were engaged in a fierce contest for circulation. Their sensational accounts playing up Spanish atrocities provided one of the chief causes of the growth of a war fever in the United States. A wave of sympathy for the Cuban insurgents swept the country, accompanied by a growing demand that the United States intervene to end the struggle and to secure independence for Cuba.

There were other reasons besides humanitarian sympathy for the insurgents that made Americans concerned over the war in Cuba. American citizens, usually naturalized Cubans, were arrested by Spanish authorities and asked the State Department for assistance. There was the increased costs of the patrolling operations of the navy and Coast Guard to prevent the Cuban junta and its American sympathizers from running guns and ammunition to the insurgents. American business interests, too, suffered from the war. Approximately $50 million of American capital was invested in Cuban plantations, railroads, mines, and utilities, and these were exposed to the same dangers as those owned by the Spaniards. Moreover, American trade with Cuba, which in good years amounted to as much as $100 million, nearly disappeared.

As popular sentiment in favor of intervention increased, President Cleveland grew more determined to prevent the United States from being drawn into the conflict. In the face of a steady stream of atrocity stories and frequent demands for a firmer attitude toward Spain, the Cleveland administration refused to intervene. When the House of Representatives and Senate adopted a concurrent resolution in February and April 1896 favoring recognition of Cuban belligerency, Cleveland treated it as nothing more than an expression of congressional opinion. Under Cleveland the American navy and revenue service attempted to intercept filibustering expeditions to Cuba. Cleveland did offer American mediation in the spring of 1896, only to be rebuffed by Spain. Secretary of State Richard Olney urged Spain to promise liberal reforms in Cuba which the United States could use in an effort to get the insurgents to stop fighting and to resume their allegiance to Spain.

Spain's minister in Washington, Dupuy de Lôme, rejected the offer of mediation and contended that if the United States could prevent illegal aid from reaching the insurgents and would publicly recognize the justice of Spain's position, the insurgency would collapse. Though Cleveland strongly opposed American intervention, he came to realize that the inflexible position of both Spain and the insurgents, and the dragging on of the war, might make intervention unavoidable. In his last annual message to Congress in December 1896 President Cleveland warned that the American people and government would not remain idle if the slaughter in Cuba continued. When it became clear that Spain was unable to put down the insurrection, the President continued, then the United States would face a situation "in which our obligations to the sovereignty of Spain will be superseded by higher obligations, which we can hardly hesitate to recognize and to discharge."

This was the situation President William McKinley inherited when he entered the White House on 4 March 1897. McKinley was aware of the nationalist enthusiasm of the 1890s because he told Senator Henry Cabot Lodge a few months before assuming office that he might be "obliged" to go to war as soon as he entered the presidency. McKinley expressed a preference for having the Cuban matter settled one way or the other between his election and inauguration. Yet for all this there was little immediate change in American policy when McKinley succeeded Cleveland. The earlier attempts to prevent filibustering expeditions from going to Cuba and to protect American lives and property there were continued. And McKinley's offer of mediation in the fall of 1897 was turned down just as Cleveland's had been in the spring of 1896.

In 1897 a ministry from the Liberal party came to power in Spain. It promptly recalled General Weyler, promised abandonment of the reconcentration policy, and granted limited autonomy to the Cubans. But the autonomy program had little support in Cuba. The insurgent leaders rejected it and now demanded full independence. The island Spaniards opposed such a move because they could not accept the prospect of rule by the native Cuban majority.

In the United States, also, the autonomy program aroused little enthusiasm. Earlier the American minister to Spain, Stewart L. Woodford, had expressed skepticism about it. "I doubt," he had written, "whether the Spanish official mind comprehends real autonomy as Englishmen and Americans would understand autonomy. I doubt whether Spain would give in theory or enforce in fact such autonomy as Canada has." President McKinley in his annual message to Congress of 6 December 1897 treated Spain's new program in a hopeful manner. He talked about the possible courses of action that the United States might be able to follow: recognition of Cuban belligerency or Cuban independence; intervention to impose a compromise solution; intervention in behalf of one side or the other. "I speak not of forcible annexation," said McKinley, "for that can not be thought of. That, by our code of morality, would be criminal aggression."

In spite of the friction between the United States and Spain, relations improved somewhat by the beginning of 1898. Then two incidents occurred within one week in February inflaming American passions and seeming to justify intervention. One event was the publication on 9 February in the New York *Journal,* with screaming headlines and other fanfare, of a private letter written by Dupuy de Lôme, the Spanish minister to the United States, to a journalist friend in Havana criticizing McKinley. The letter described the president as "weak and a bidder for the admiration of the crowd . . . a would-be-politician who tries to leave a door open behind himself while keeping on good terms with the jingoes of his party." The letter had been stolen from the correspondent's luggage by an insurgent sympathizer and in time appeared in all leading American newspapers, renewing hostile sentiment against Spain. The unlucky minister cabled his immediate resignation to Madrid, and the Spanish government accepted it. The Madrid authorities also sent a formal expression of regret and disavowal of the indiscretion to the American government.

The Spanish minister had said of McKinley what a number of Americans believed and published in their newspapers, but a foreign diplomat has to be discreet and tactful. For example, Theodore Roosevelt believed McKinley "had no more backbone than a chocolate eclair." And a current joke about the president went like this: "Why is McKinley's mind like a bed?" Answer: "Because it has to be made up for him every time he wants to use it."

Before feeling had calmed down on the de Lôme faux pax, however, Americans were stunned by the news of the sinking of the battleship *Maine* in Havana harbor on 15 February, with the loss of 2 officers and 264 enlisted men. The *Maine* had been sent to Havana as a show of force and to protect American citizens there, although Spain had been assured that the ship's visit was a mark of friendship and in the form of a friendly naval visit. American popular opinion held Spain responsible for the tragedy. Washington officials were at first incredulous and then angered. McKinley was described as walking the floor of the White House and murmuring "The *Maine* blown up! The *Maine* blown up!" Yet the president told Senator Charles Warren Fairbanks of Indiana that he was not going to be swept off his feet by the catastrophe; that his duty was to "learn the truth and endeavor, if possible, to fix the responsibility."

American and Spanish authorities made separate investigations of the sinking and reached different conclusions. The Americans maintained that the disaster had been caused by an external explosion setting off the forward magazine of the vessel; the Spaniards reported that an internal explosion had been responsible. In 1911 the vessel was raised, and a second board of inquiry confirmed the earlier American finding that "the injuries to the bottom of the *Maine*. . . were caused by the explosion of a low form of explosive exterior to the ship." But European experts continued to support the Spanish conclusion pointing to an internal explosion.

Though the cause of the sinking of the *Maine* has never been determined, the American public in 1890 overwhelmingly decided that Spain was responsible. Most Americans agreed with Theodore Roosevelt's pronouncement that "The *Maine* was sunk by an act of dirty treachery on the part of the Spaniards." Pulitzer's and Hearst's newspapers flooded the country with war propaganda claiming that Spain had sunk the *Maine* and that now "Intervention is a plain and imperative duty." A front page headline on 18 February 1898 in Hearst's New York *Journal* announced; "The Whole Country Thrills with War Fever." To the exhortations of the press were added the cries of the jingoes. Mass meetings called for a declaration of war, and at Lehigh University students held daily drills. The slogan "Remember the *Maine*! To Hell with Spain!" swept the country:

> Ye who made war that your ships
> Should lay to at the beck of no nation,
> Make war now on murder, that slips
> The leash of her hounds of damnation;
> Ye who remembered the Alamo,
> Remember the *Maine*!

President McKinley said little and wrote little during this period of intense excitement over the sinking of the *Maine*. But apparently he had reached a decision that the war in Cuba must stop before the start of the rainy season in May. And apparently he hoped to bring this about peacefully by using the excitement to bring Spain to terms. In March the president asked Congress for an appropriation of $50 million for national defense, to be used at his discretion. Congress unanimously approved this without delay. Along with other military and naval activities this action had a twofold effect; it encouraged the Cubans to continue resistance and it caused Spain to doubt the sincerity of American professions of peace. General Stewart L. Woodford, the American minister to Spain, reported that this appropriation "has not excited the Spaniards—it has stunned them."

As historian Julius Pratt has shown, the only significant check upon the demands of the interventionists came from the business community. American trade with Cuba and American capital invested in the island represented only a small segment of total American economic activity, and the large majority of American businessmen, who had no financial stake in Cuba, opposed a war with Spain. After suffering from the depression of the mid-1890s they were convinced that the signs of returning prosperity would quickly be dispersed by a war. Throughout the winter of 1897–1898, every threat of war was accompanied by antiwar editorials in the financial press and sharp declines in the stock market. Theodore Roosevelt became so angry with the attitude of businessmen that he exclaimed, "We will have this war for the freedom of Cuba in spite of the timidity of the commercial interests."

About the only business interests to agitate for intervention to Cuba were the eastern seaboard firms that normally engaged in trade with Cuba, and these firms did not advocate Cuban independence nor armed intervention. All they wanted was a restoration of peace in Cuba so that trade might again flourish. Nor is there much evidence that Americans with investments in Cuba wanted military intervention in the island's troubles. On the contrary a number of these people warned the State Department that they would suffer more from a war between the United States and Spain than from the existing civil war.

There was pressure, however, for intervention from others than the yellow press. Many Protestant clergymen argued that the United States had a moral and religious duty to aid the Cubans. Nearly all Prostestant groups, with the exception of the Quakers and the Unitarians, favored intervention. On the other hand, few Catholics saw any religious justification for a war to free Catholic Cuba. Pressure for war came also from politicians looking for a popular issue. It could possibly divert the attention of their constituents from the money question and other issues that were a part of the agrarian discontent. In addition to these kinds of politicians there were key political figures such as Theodore Roosevelt and Henry Cabot Lodge who favored overseas expansion on principle and who welcomed the growing spirit of nationalism.

Following the sinking of the *Maine* both the United States and Spain faced a dilemma. Both hoped to maintain peace. But if Spain tried to sell Cuba or gave in too easily to American demands, popular pride and indignation in Spain might overthrow the government. McKinley, too, was aware of the political implications. If he stood against public pressure too long, he might lose his popularity and endanger his reelection in 1900. Between the sinking of the *Maine* in February 1898 and the declaration of a state of war with Spain in April of the same year, nine weeks elapsed. These were nine tense weeks, and historian George Kennan pointed out two important things about them: (1) the United States never really considered any peaceful solution to the problem with Spain in these nine weeks, and (2) this was unfortunate because in the same period Spain made a number of concessions and moved far in the direction of meeting American demands and desires.

Under pressure from the public, the press, nearly all Democrats, and a large number of his own party, President McKinley on 27 March 1898 sent his final proposals for ending the war to Spain: (1) an armistice until 1 October with negotiations in the meantime to be conducted through the good offices of the president, (2) immediate abandonment of the reconcentration policy, (3) if peace terms were not agreed upon by 1 October the president was "to be the final arbiter between Spain and the insurgents." If Spain agreed to these terms McKinley would try to get the consent of the insurgents.

Spain confronted now a grave choice. If she refused the president's demands she faced war with the United States. If she met the demands in full, angry Spaniards might overturn the government and even the crown. Spain's only hope was to have European powers support her against any intervention by the United States. Spain had already sought such aid from every major European power and knew in advance of the 27 March American note the outcome of her plea. Every country, except Great Britain, expressed a willingness to join in a combined demonstration against the United States if someone else would take the lead, but no one was willing to do that.

Thus Spain, without substantial assistance from her European neighbors, slowly and reluctantly met most of the American demands. On 5 April she agreed to abolish the reconcentration policy, and on 9 April she yielded to the demand for an armistice. The American minister Woodford was optimistic and he cabled the following to the president on 10 April:

I hope you can obtain full authority from Congress to do whatever you shall deem necessary to secure immediate and permanent peace in Cuba by negotiations, including the full power to employ the army and navy according to your own judgment to aid and enforce your action. If this be secured I believe you will get final settlement before August 1 on one of the following bases: either such autonomy as the insurgents may agree to accept, or recognition by Spain of the independence of the island, or cession of the island to the United States.

I hope that nothing now will be done to humiliate Spain, as I am satisfied that the present government is going, and is loyally ready to go, as fast and as far as it can. With your power of action sufficiently free you will win the fight on your own lines.

It seemed that diplomacy had been successful, but the question of peace or war lay in McKinley's hands. He was under intense pressure for war from Congress and within his administration. Theodore Roosevelt wrote near the end of March: "Shilly-shallying and half measures at this time merely render us contemptible in the eyes of the world; and what is infinitely more important in our own eyes too...." Secretary of War Russell A. Alger approached a leading senator and urged him to advise the president "to declare war." According to Alger the president was making a great mistake and endangering himself and the Republican party "by standing in the way of the people's wishes. Congress will declare war in spite of him. He'll get run over and the party with him." It was a period of great stress for the president and on one occasion, while talking with a friend about the Cuban matter, McKinley broke down and cried. He said he had not slept for more than a few hours a night during the previous two weeks.

Unwilling to run the risk of defying public opinion any longer, resenting the slurs of the jingoes, fearing the possibility of Congress declaring war over his head, and worrying about reelection in 1900. McKinley prepared a war message on 4 April but delayed it to allow Americans to evacuate Cuba. Despite his awareness of Spain's surrender to his demands and Woodford's optimistic cable, McKinley sent his war message to Congress on 11 April. The only change he made in his original message was to add a last paragraph stating that Spain had made concessions to which he hoped Congress would give "just and careful attention."

McKinley has been severely criticized for not emphasizing Spain's concessions and for brushing them off in such a light manner. Yet in all fairness it should be noted that the press knew about Spain's offer of an armistice and spurned it. It should also be added that continued negotiations might not have prevented war. Spain had shown few signs of willingness to go beyond autonomy. And autonomy no longer seemed sufficient. The insurgents wanted nothing less than independence, and this seemed to be the position of the United States. In fact the insurgents had not even accepted the armistice. McKinley and many Americans had concluded that American armed intervention was necessary to make Cuba independent and to put the island back on its feet.

In his message to Congress the president asked for authorization to use the armed forces to end hostilities in Cuba, and he justified intervention on four grounds: (1) "humanity...to put an end to the barbarities, bloodshed, starvation, and horrible miseries" in Cuba, (2) to afford American citizens in Cuba "that protection and indemnity for life and property which no government there can or will afford . . .," (3) to redress "the very serious injury to the commerce, trade, and business of our people . . . and the wanton destruction of property and devastation of the island," and (4) "the present condition of affairs in Cuba is a constant menace to our peace and entails upon this Government an enormous expense."

Congress regarded McKinley's message as a demand for war. After the House and the Senate adopted different resolutions, both houses approved the congressional joint resolution of 19 April—the House by a vote of 311 to 6 and the Senate by a vote of 42 to 35—that demanded the independence of Cuba, the withdrawal of Spanish forces, empowered the president to force Spain's withdrawal, and disclaimed any intention by the United States of exercising "sovereignty, jurisdiction, or control" over Cuba. This last part, embodied in the Teller Amendment, passed Congress without a dissenting vote.

When Spain learned of the resolutions she broke off diplomatic relations with the United States. On 22 April, President McKinley proclaimed a blockade of portions of the Cuban coast. Two days later the Spanish government declared war upon the United States. On 25 April, upon recommendation of the president, Congress declared war, making the declaration retroactive to 21 April to cover the blockade of 22 April. Thus the "splendid little war," as it was called, had begun.

Although the official reason for going to war was to liberate Cuba, the first battle was fought in the distant Philippines, also a possession of Spain. Two months before Congress declared war, Assistant Secretary of the Navy Theodore Roosevelt had directed Commodore George Dewey, commander of the Asiatic Squadron, that in the event of hostilities he was to take offensive action in the Philippines. McKinley confirmed these instructions in a cable to Dewey on 24 April 1898. On 1 May Dewey destroyed the small and decrepit Spanish fleet in Manila Bay. Most Americans had never heard of the Philippine Islands, but the expansionists of 1898 knew their location and wanted them badly. Dewey's victory stirred wild enthusiasm, and in July about 11,000 American troops under General Wesley Merritt were landed in the Philippines. Aided by Filipino insurrectionists under Emilio Aguinaldo, with whom Dewey had established contact, Merritt captured Manila on 13 August. In this fashion the United States ousted Spanish authority and assumed a major new responsibility in the Far East.

On the other side of the world the war was likewise being quickly won. In June a poorly equipped expeditionary force under General William R. Shafter landed on the Cuban coast near Santiago. After some engagements along the coast the Americans stormed the heights of El Caney and San Juan Hill overlooking Santiago on 1 July. But as the American land attack petered out, Admiral William T. Sampson and Commodore Winfield Scott Schley destroyed the main Spanish fleet under Admiral Cervera as it attempted to escape from Santiago. On 16 July, Santiago surrendered. On 28 July a second expeditionary force, under General Nelson A. Miles, occupied Puerto Rico. Within three months Spain had lost two fleets and one army. By the middle of July Spain sought a peace treaty, and on 12 August hostilities were declared to be over and a preliminary peace treaty was signed at Washington. The following day the Americans took Manila.

While the war did not have any worthy military campaigns it did have some picturesque units, notably the First Volunteer Cavalry Regiment, popularly known as the "Rough Riders." It was comprised of cowboys, ranchers, hunters, Indians, and some Harvard and Yale graduates. Colonel Leonard Wood commanded this unit, and Theodore Roosevelt resigned his post as assistant secretary of the navy to become second in command as a lieutenant colonel. The "Rough Riders" gained their fame in the attack on San Juan Hill, and Roosevelt his military reputation for helping to lead them.

But on some occasions the military operations were so ludicrous that "Mr. Dooley," the character created by Finley Peter Dunne, remarked in regard to General Miles' Puerto Rican campaign, that it was "Gin'ral Miles' gran picnic an' moonlight excursion... "Tis no comfort in being' a cow'rd," he added, "whin ye think iv them br-rave la-ads facin' death be suffication in bokays an' dyin iv waltzin' with th' pretty girls iv Porther Ricky."

At the start of the war it appeared that the United States had no territorial ambitions. The war resolution had declared that Cuba should be free and independent, and the Teller Amendment had disclaimed any intention on the part of the United States to annex Cuba. As the war progressed, however, the American attitude changed. The annexation of Hawaii on 6 July 1898 by a joint congressional resolution was the first evidence of change. Then later in the month, in setting forth terms for an armistice in the war, McKinley demanded the cession of Puerto Rico and Guam. In addition he stipulated that the United States was to occupy the "city, bay, and harbor of Manila pending the conclusion of a treaty of peace." The president had said earlier that annexation "By our code of morality would be criminal aggression." But by July 1898 he had a different view. "We must keep all we get," he then said; "when the war is over, we must keep what we want."

By the armistice of 12 August Spain agreed to give up all claim to Cuba and to cede Puerto Rico and Guam to the United States. No difficulty arose over these matters when formal peace negotiations began in Paris on 1 October 1898. The question of the responsibility for the Cuban debt of $400 million divided the conference for some time. Spain argued that the assumption of the debt went along with sovereignty, but the Americans remained firm in the conviction that the debt was Spain's responsibility. In the end Spain was compelled to yield.

The disposition of the Philippines was a more serious matter. Manila did not capitulate until a day after the peace preliminaries were signed. The terms of the peace protocol dealing with the Philippines were ambiguous, for neither the president nor his advisers had made up their minds on the problem. At first McKinley asked only for the cession of the main island of Luzon. But various considerations caused him to change his mind and demand the cession of all the Philippine Islands to the United States. There was the fear that Germany might seize the Philippines. Then, too, it was hoped the Philippines would give the United States a strategic and economic base in the Far East. Businessmen who had opposed intervention in Cuba were now convinced that the Philippines would give them access to the Oriental market. Humanitarians insisted that the United States had an obligation to uplift the benighted but obstinate Filipinos. Finally, many Americans wanted the Philippines because their acquisition seemed to be a fitting climax to the glorious adventure of war. As McKinley later told a group of Methodists visiting at the White House on 21 November 1899:

When I realized that the Philippines had dropped into our laps I confess I did not know what to do with them. I sought counsel from all sides—Democrats as well as Republicans—but got little help. I first thought we would take only Manila; then Luzon; then other islands, perhaps, also. I walked the floor of the White House night after night until midnight; and I am not ashamed to tell you, gentlemen, that I went down on my knees and prayed to Almighty God for light and guidance more than one night. And one night late it came to me this way— I don't know how it was, but it came: (1) That we could not give them back to Spain—that would be cowardly and dishonorable; (2) that we could not turn them over to France or Germany—our commercial rivals in the Orient—that would be bad business and discreditable; (3) that we could not leave them to themselves—they were unfit for self-government—and they would soon have anarchy and misrule over there worse than Spain's was; and (4) there was nothing left for us to do but to take them all, and to educate the Filipinos, and uplift and civilize and Christianize them, and by God's grace do the very best we could by them, as our fellow-men for whom Christ also died. And then I went to bed, and went to sleep, and slept soundly, and the next morning I sent for the chief engineer of the War Department (our mapmaker), and I told him to put the Philippines on the map of the United States, and there they are, and there they will stay while I am President!

Spain's peace commissioners stubbornly resisted American demands for the Philippines but ultimately accepted $20 million for the islands. When the treaty arrived in the Senate, the main issue was the annexation of the Philippines. Many Americans had opposed the talk of annexation from the outset. In November 1898 they organized the Anti-Imperialist League and sought to prevent annexation even if it meant defeating the treaty. Opposed to them were the expansionists who wanted the fruits of war. The debate lasted several months, and on 6 February 1899 the Senate narrowly approved the treaty 57 to 27— only two more votes than the required two-thirds.

The acquisition of the Philippines and Hawaii heightened American interest in the Far East. Before the end of the century the United States was further involved in this part of the world through enunciation of the Open Door doctrine in China, which was to become one of the cornerstones in American foreign policy.

China had been badly beaten by Japan in a war in 1894-1895, and the great powers began to divide the Chinese empire into spheres of influence. Great Britain, France, Germany, Japan, and Russia forced China to grant them large areas of land. Political authority nominally remained in China's hands, but the great powers had the right to invest capital and to exercise economic control. They seemed to be setting up protectorates within China. The United States acquired the Philippines just at the time the powers were cutting up the ancient empire.

Since the Treaty of Wanghia of 1844 (also known as the Cushing Treaty), with its "most favored nation" clause, the United States had enjoyed equal opportunity of trade in China. But now the spheres of influence of the great powers threatened this American parity. The prospect of new markets in the Far East made Americans anxious to preserve their equal opportunities for trade in China. Besides, Americans had extensive educational and missionary activities in China, possessed a sentimental sympathy for her, and wished to see her fairly treated. Moreover, Great Britain, who had the biggest economic stake in China, was urging the United States to make a joint effort to maintain equal opportunity in China.

On 6 September 1899 Secretary of State John Hay sent what is known as the first Open Door Note to the powers then engaged in dividing up China, asking them to agree: (1) not to interfere with freedom of trade in any of the treaty ports in China or with vested interests within any sphere of influence; (2) not to interfere with the regular collection of the Chinese custom duties; and (3) not to discriminate against other nations in their spheres of influence in levying port dues and railroad rates.

With the exception of Italy (who had no sphere of influence) and Russia, the governments addressed by Hay replied they would accept the terms of the note on condition that all the other governments would. Italy concurred without qualification, and Russia declined to give any pledge. China herself was not consulted or asked to participate in keeping her doors open. Hay ignored the evasive and contingent replies of the powers and instead announced that all of them had agreed to respect the Open Door in China.

It should be noted that the Open Door was a narrow concept in 1899—even narrower than equal commercial opportunity as so many Americans conceived of it then. Hay did not insist upon the territorial integrity of China, or the independence of China, as Britain had suggested in 1898. Hay went on believing that spheres of influence would persist—he used and accepted the term "sphere of interest" in his note, and he made no reference to mining and railroad concessions and investments of capital.

In its own day and for years to come the Open Door concept was lauded and acclaimed a great diplomatic achievement. The London *Times* predicted it would keep the door open for American trade and hailed it as "a signal public service that Mr. Hay has performed." Hay himself claimed he had "accomplished a good deal in the East, but thus far without the expense of a single commitment or promise." A myth developed that in the Open Door Note "a tremendous blow had been struck for the triumph of American principles in international society."

Later on Hay's policy was severely criticized as being ineffectual and even detrimental to the true interests of the United States by getting her needlessly involved in the Far East. The Open Door policy was workable so long as diplomatic equipoise continued in the Far East— so long as one power did not become dominant in that part of the world, as was to be the case first with the ascendancy of Russia and then of Japan. But as a permanent policy to stick to and to defend, the Open door was a futile effort. The Open Door would not stay open if the territory or government of China fell under the control of one power. And in an effort to try to keep the door open in China, the United States was drawn ever more deeply into the politics of Asia, especially when she expanded the doctrine to include the territorial and administrative integrity of China.

In 1900 Chinese nationalist resentment at the exploitation of their country led to the Boxer Rebellion. The Boxers, a secret patriotic society called the "Righteous Fists of Harmony" with an emblem of the clenched fist, spearheaded the drive to expel foreigners from China. When the dowager empress seized the government in a contest with the emperor, the Boxers launched a campaign of violence to oust all foreigners. In the summer of 1900 the Boxers seized Peking, the imperial capital, murdered the German minister in the street, and laid siege to all foreign legations. For weeks foreigners, including the diplomatic colony, were cut off from the outside world. Finally the leading powers, including the United States, sent a joint military expedition to protect their citizens. This army captured Peking, and the imperial court fled.

Secretary Hay feared that the powers might use this occasion to broaden their spheres of influence in China. Thus on 3 July 1900 he circulated a second Open Door Note among the powers stating that it was the policy of the United States to seek a solution which would "preserve Chinese territorial and administrative entity" (the word integrity rather than entity generally came to be used). This second note went further than the first and was much more important because the United States was taking a stand against the further partitioning of China. It even expanded the commercial activity phase of the first note from spheres of influence to "all parts of China." Americans believed that Hay had achieved a major diplomatic victory in preventing further partition, and the Chinese government was "profoundly impressed with the justice and great friendliness of the United States."

Hay never dreamed that the Open Door policy would be more than a temporary solution to China's problems and troubles. Surely he did not envision that in time it would become the underlying basis of American policy in the Far East in the twentieth century. But as time went on and as Japan became the dominant power in the Orient and threatened the integrity of China in many ways and on different occasions, the idea of preserving Chinese territorial and administrative entity gave way to the idea of a guarantee of Chinese territory. The United States never actually agreed to a guarantee of Chinese territory, but by the time of Pearl Harbor many Americans believed this was so.

Time and again between 1900 and 1941 the United States would ask the other powers to pledge adherence to the principles of the Open Door, and time and again the United States would fail to receive from the other powers straightforward replies or actual adherence to these principles. For the most part no power denied the principles, but everything depended on how they were interpreted. Despite the evasiveness of replies the United States government indicated to Americans that they represented diplomatic achievements and an acknowledgement of the United States' position in the Far East.

Throughout the years 1900 to 1941, moreover, the United States never admitted that the Open Door policy gave it any specific responsibility, or placed it under any obligation to anyone or anything save its own conscience. And in no instance during this period was the United States prepared to use force to compel other powers to comply with the principles of the Open Door. Despite American reiteration of these principles, the Open Door did not prevent happening much of that what was bound to happen in the Far East, and the United States recognized this in a number of ways. As early as 1901 when Japan asked the United States about using force against Russia, then on the move in the Far East, Secretary Hay replied that the United States was "not at present prepared to attempt singly, or in concert with other Powers, to enforce these views in the east by any demonstration which could present a character of hostility toward any other power." And as Theodore Roosevelt wrote to Taft in 1910. "The Open Door Policy in China was an excellent thing, and I hope it will be a good thing in the future, so far as it can be maintained by general diplomatic agreement; but-... the 'Open Door' policy, as a matter of fact, completely disappears as soon as a powerful nation determines to disregard it, and is willing to run the risk of war rather than forego its intentions."

Because of her own immense power—and the decline of the once mighty Spanish empire—the United States enjoyed a relatively easy time making her debut on the world scene in the closing years of the nineteenth century. In the twentieth century, however, she would encounter stronger challenges and challengers. Then the Open Door policy and other policies and positions established in this early period of America's new status would become more difficult to sustain—and more susceptible to debate.

Further Reading

Beisner, Robert L. *From the Old Diplomacy to the New, 1865–1900*. 2d. ed., 1986.

_____. *Twelve Against Empire: The Anti-Imperialists, 1898–1900*. 1968.

Brown, Charles H. *The Correspondents' War: Journalists in the Spanish-American War*. 1967.

Campbell, Charles S. *The Transformation of American Foreign Relations, 1865–1900*. 1976.

Challener, Richard. *Admirals, Generals, and American Foreign Policy, 1889–1914*. 1973.

Cohen, Warren. *America's Response to China*. 1971.

Freidel, Frank. *The Splendid Little War*. 1958.

Griswold, A. W. *The Far Eastern Policy of the United States*. 1938.

Gould, Lewis L. *The Presidency of William McKinley*. 1980.

Healy, David A. *United States Expansion: The Imperialist Urge in the 1890's*. 1970.

_____. *The United States in Cuba, 1898–1902*. 1963.

Israel, Jerry. *Progressivism and the Open Door: America and China, 1905–1921*. 1971.

Karster, Peter. *The Naval Aristocracy*. 1972.

La Feber, Walter. *The New Empire*. 1963.

May, Ernest R. *Imperial Democracy: The Emergence of America as a Great Power*. 1961.

McCormick, Thomas. *The China Market*. 1967.

Miller, Stuart C. *"Benevolent Assimulation": American Conquest of the Philippines, 1899–1903*. 1982.

Millis, Walter. *The Martial Spirit*. 1931.

Morgan, H. Wayne. *America's Road to Empire*. 1965.

Plesur, Milton. *America's Outward Thrust: Approaches to Foreign Affairs, 1865–1900*. 1971.

Pratt, Julius W. *America's Colonial Experiment*. 1950.

_____. *Expansionists of 1898*. 1936.

Rickover, Herman G. *How the Battleship Maine Was Destroyed.* 1976.

Roosevelt, Theodore. *The Rough Riders.* 1899.

Russ, William A. *The Hawaiian Republic. . . 1894–1898.* 1961.

_____. *The Hawaiian Revolution.* 1959.

Thomson, James, Jr., Peter Stanley, and John C. Perry. *Sentimental Imperialists: The American Experience in East Asia.* 1981.

Tompkins, E. Berkeley. *Anti-Imperialism in the United States: The Great Debate, 1890–1920.* 1970.

Trask, David F. *The War with Spain.* 1981.

Varg, Paul A. *The Making of the Myth: The United States and China, 1899–1922.* 1968.

Williams, William Appleman. *The Tragedy of American Diplomacy.* 1972.

Young, Marilyn B. *The Rhetoric for Empire: America's China Policy, 1893–1901.* 1968.

Young, Marilyn B., ed. *American Expansion: The Critical Issues.* 1973.

8

The Great Reform Era

For most of the first two decades of the twentieth century a comprehensive reform movement affecting nearly every aspect of American life swept the country. It is what historians call the Progressive movement. It aroused a large number of Americans, especially the middle class, who were deeply concerned about the country's rapid industrial and urban growth. They feared that the United States as an industrial giant would forget some of the democratic ideals of the past. And they believed that conditions in the United States seemed to guarantee perpetual political and economic control to a privileged few.

The Progressive movement is a major period in the history of American reform because it was such a broad response of the American people to the many problems created by the industrialization and urbanization of the country in the post–Civil War years. These problems involved the breakdown of responsible representative government in cities and states, the spread of slums, crime, and poverty in the large cities, the exploitation of women and children, the growth of industrial and financial concentration, and the emergence of trusts and monopolies in railroads, industries, and banking interests that vitally affected the lives of the people and yet were beyond their control.

It is not easy to define a movement which, according to one of the leading scholars of American progressivism was nothing less than "a social quest . . . [that] attempted to find solutions for the amazing number of domestic and foreign problems spawned by the great industrial, urban, and population changes of the late nineteenth century." For in reality the Progressive movement was not one nationally organized campaign but rather an aggregation of many movements for social, economic, and political reform. The reformers were as varied as the faults they attacked, and sometimes the reform movements were mutually antagonistic, a fact that sometimes causes confusion in understanding progressivism. There was never much sentiment to support an integrated reform campaign, because often the reformers worked independently of one another. Thus the movement manifested itself in no single political party, geographical section, or social class. As a historian of American social reform movements since the Civil War has pointed out: "Here was a social reform movement with no set leadership, no single platform, no disciplined organization, and no planned means of action." The only cohesive force was the desire and enthusiasm for reform.

Neither did the Progressive movement have any single leader as such with a reform program that appealed to all reformers. It did produce four nationally known political leaders—Robert M. La Follette, William Jennings Bryan, Theodore Roosevelt, and Woodrow Wilson. But none of these men could be called the national leader of progressivism. Of the four, La Follette was probably most identified with the whole sweep of the movement, but he cannot be regarded as the single leader.

Though the movement appeared to begin in the cities and then to spread to the states and to the national arena, it actually occurred on all three levels at about the same time. And in national as well as state politics the Progressive movement cut across party lines. There were progressives in both major parties. Popular sentiment so strongly favored reform that most responsible political leaders recognized that it was necessary, although some of them wished to move faster and farther than others.

The broad political aim of the progressives was to renew the vigor of democratic institutions by overthrowing bosses and machines and by making public officials more directly responsible to the voters. Their economic goal was to subject big business to public control to protect the interests of the farmer, the workingman, the small businessman, and the consumer. There was nothing revolutionary about these ends. The progressives believed in the traditional ideas of democracy, individual liberty, and the rule of law, but they thought new political techniques were necessary to maintain them in an industrial age. They also favored the free enterprise system but were of the opinion that it could not continue unless it was reformed. The progressives really wanted to go back to a time in American history when the individual counted for more than the group in our political and economic life. In a sense progressives were conservatives, because they wished to conserve traditional American values now under attack in the new order of things.

To achieve their ends progressives came to rely more and more on governmental action. They championed an expansion of governmental power and resorted to politics and to legislative and administrative solutions. In fact, legislation became so important as a means that it appeared as an end in itself, encouraging many Americans to believe that the enactment of a law would automatically cure any social evil. Henry Cabot Lodge in a speech in the Senate in 1910 warned against the sentiment so widespread in the Progressive period "to bring in laws for everything, for everything that happens, to try and find a remedy by passing a statute, and to overlook the fact that laws are made by men and that laws do not make men."

While progressivism was grounded in economic matters and in a desire for political success it also possessed a strong moral appeal. Most political reformers of this era subscribed to the doctrine of progress which for a long time had been a part of the American creed. This belief made progressives optimistic, and at the same time it tied the reform movement to a long cherished folk tradition. Thus progressives fought with determination. They assumed the future was on their side, and they believed that an aroused opinion and sustained effort would surely bring victory.

In some ways progressivism stemmed from the same sources and worked toward the same objectives as populism, but there are important differences between the two. Progressivism, as already noted, was a very broad movement embracing dozens of varied reforms and appealing to the American people at large rather than to any special group such as the farmers. As a political force it did not operate primarily through a third party as did populism (though it did produce a third party in 1912) but instead worked within the major parties. Populism was largely a rural, agrarian, and sectional movement. Progressivism was mainly an urban, middle class, and nationwide movement. It received much of its support and leadership from the urban middle class who hitherto had opposed Bryan and his followers. The Populist leadership had been almost entirely agrarian, but after the turn of the century farmers enjoyed the renewed prosperity and their discontent diminished. Leadership in the reform movement now largely passed to the cities and the small towns, and the reform impulse ceased to be mainly agrarian in outlook. Furthermore, as the reform movement spread from the Populist party to the two major parties, and from a leader such as Bryan to men such as Theodore Roosevelt and Woodrow Wilson, it became stronger and more respectable.

While populism and progressivism coalesced after the turn of the twentieth century there remained two principal strains of thought in progressivism—one influenced chiefly by the Populist inheritance, the other largely a product of urban life. Thus while progressivism was concerned with urban problems—labor and social welfare, city government reforms, consumer problems—it also had to deal with national issues such as the tariff and financial legislation and railroad and trust regulation. These measures depended on the votes of congressmen and senators from agricultural regions and had to be written in such a way as to meet their demands and command their support.

Historians agree that progressivism had its roots in the reform movements of the Gilded Age. Many groups and individuals in this earlier period envisioned changes that would improve society. Reformers then sought civil service reform, the eight-hour day, scientific agriculture, woman suffrage, enforcement of vice laws, factory inspection, nonpartisan local elections, trust-busting, conservation, tax reforms, abolition of child labor, businesslike local government, regulation of railroad rates, and scores of other causes that would subsequently be identified with progressivism. And as we have already seen, a number of young social scientists were attacking formalism and conservatism in their fields, advocating ideas that would undergird progressivism, and attempting to win government support for them. For example, the work of the economist Richard T. Ely on the Maryland Tax Commission in the mid-1880s led the way in the application of the new economics to government and brought about a number of the programs that later reformers and politicians adopted.

Despite this fertility of reform in the Gilded Age, Americans still remained largely unorganized in their efforts to improve society. There was no common program that could rally all the reform groups, and the general prosperity until the Panic of 1893 reassured people that industrialism might cure its own ills. As late as 1892 the Milwaukee *Sentinel* could optimistically say, "the rich are growing richer, some of them, and the poor are growing richer, all of them."

But the depression of 1893–1897, the worst the country had experienced up to that time, fundamentally changed all of this. It dramatically underscored the failures of industrialism. The chasm between rich and poor became wider and could no longer be ignored. The severe economic distress that followed, and the inability of national political leaders to alleviate it, produced a widespread atmosphere of restlessness and hard questioning of the nation's economic and political system. "On every corner stands a man whose fortune in these dull times has made him an ugly critic of everything and everybody," observed a newspaper editor in the spring of 1896. A state university president told his graduates in 1894 that "you will see everywhere in the country symptoms of social and political discontent. You will observe that these disquietudes do not result from the questions that arise in the ordinary course of political discussion. . . but that they spring out of questions that are connected with the very foundation of society and have to do with some of the most elemental principles of human liberty and modern civilization."

The depression of the 1890s broke down the fragmentation of reform sentiment prevalent during the Gilded Age. The depression created a number of issues on which just about all classes could unite. And from these issues progressivism began to develop its momentum. This was especially true in regard to large corporation. The more corporations sought or managed to secure legislative favors from city and state governments, the more communities attempted to regulate them or to displace them with municipal or consumer-owned utilities and to fight to destroy the political machines that protected the corporations. This is why political reform such as the initiative, direct primary, and home rule were so important in the early stages of progressivism. But the failure of the political system to deal with the depression convinced many Americans that more radical measures were needed.

While historians agree that progressivism had its immediate origins in the reform movements of the Gilded Age they disagree over why it began and ended, what it stood for, and whether it changed American life for the better. Some historians look upon progressive values and accomplishments as an unmixed good; others regard them as reforms that reformed nothing. Most historians until recently accepted the thesis of John D. Hicks that progressivism issued from populism and that radical farmers were the most important originators of the progressivism program. But this view has been challenged, and new interpretations contend that the progressive thrust came from other groups such as the urban elite, the big-city masses, the new middle class, or the businessmen.

One of the most difficult problems for historians in dealing with progressivism is to explain why it had its greatest momentum and gained its most important victories between 1897 and 1917, a time which was almost entirely a period of sustained and general prosperity. Why did middle-class Americans, most of whom had accepted the conservative leadership of Hanna and McKinley during the crisis of the mid-nineties, now rally to the support of progressive leaders in both parties in the period of expanding prosperity that followed? Two prominent historians of the Progressive movement, Richard Hofstadter and George Mowry, have explained this development with their stimulating and influential theory of the "status revolution." The older aristocracy and middle-class Americans—victims of an upheaval in status during the closing decades of the nineteenth and the early years of the twentieth century as a result of being thrust aside by the upsurge of the new industrialists—generated movements for social justice, clean government, and regulated capitalism to restore their social position and to cure the injustices in American society.

Recent studies, however, have questioned the validity of the "status revolution" interpretation of progressivism. In fact this theory seems to break down wherever it has been tested. For example, in Des Moines and Pittsburgh the middle class opposed the municipal reform movement. In Ohio a number of the progressive leaders were laborers, and the two most prominent figures in this state, Samuel M. Jones of Toledo and Tom L. Johnson of Cleveland, were nouveau riche businessmen lacking a college education. While composite biographies of progressive leaders in Massachusetts, Iowa, Washington, and Wisconsin have generally confirmed the Mowry-Hofstadter thesis, they have found almost identical features to be characteristic of nonprogressives and conservatives. That is, the progressives were similar to their opponents in terms of class, occupation, age, education, religion, political experience, and geographical origin. One can hardly explain the Progressive movement as a middle-class response to an upheaval in status, because nonprogressives also shared that status. Conversely, a number of businessmen in the towns and smaller cities of the South and the Midwest had the anxieties of status decline, but they generally opposed change more often than they favored it. Thus, any attempt to interpret the Progressive movement in terms of the status revolution is confronted with the perplexing fact that the progressive leaders generally were indistinguishable from their nonprogressive contemporaries.

To understand progressivism it is necessary to realize that diverse forces brought it about. A most important influence was that of populism, already referred to. Though defeated in the national arena, populism had a lasting effect in the states. Farmers still feared corporate wealth and monopoly, and this apprehension was one of the main ingredients of progressivism. Populism and Bryanism revived the idea of positive government working to promote economic well-being and emphasized greater popular participation in and control of the political machinery, and this helped prepare the way for the important institutional reforms of the Progressive era.

Another element was growing familiarity with the doctrines of socialism and the progress that socialism was making in Europe. In continental Europe various forms of "Social Democracy" appeared. England had its "New Liberalism"—Lloyd George's Liberal party and the new Labour party—with health acts, and laws for housing, social security, accident compensation, minimum wages, old-age pensions, and the like. When socialism first appeared in the United States in the post–Civil War years it had little appeal to native-born and old-stock Americans. But at the turn of the century there appeared new Socialist leaders such as Eugene V. Debs of Indiana and Victor Berger of Wisconsin. These men demonstrated that it was possible to put socialism into an American idiom and to attract a number of followers. Many Americans, however, were disturbed by the rise of socialism. Socialist demands for public ownership of the means of production repelled both conservatives and progressives. Faced with a similar problem, European conservatives had backed reforms to please the workers and to keep them from turning radical. Thus a number of thoughtful Americans joined the Progressive movement to oppose radicalism.

Americans were also agitated by the steady rise in the cost of living. Between 1897 and 1913, the cost of living went up 35 percent. The generation experiencing this, especially those whose incomes remained fairly stable, did not accept the price rise complacently. "Just as falling prices of the period 1865–96 had spurred agrarian discontent," writes historian Richard Hofstadter, "so the rising prices of this era added to the strength of the Progressive discontent." While rising prices were bad enough, they were connected in the public mind with two developments—a small but vigorous labor movement and an increase in the number of "trusts," as they were popularly called. Both of these occurred with suddenness within a few years around the turn of the century. For example, of the 318 trusts listed by John Moody in 1904, 82 with a capitalization of about $1.2 billion had been organized before 1898, while 234 with a capitalization of more than $6 billion had been created between 1898 and 1904. In the course of only six years nearly three-fourths of the trusts and nearly six-sevenths of their capital had come into being.

The ordinary American seemed helpless in the face of such a development. He connected the increase in the trusts and the growth in the labor movement with the rise in prices. Woodrow Wilson's words, "The high cost of living is arranged by private understanding," meant something to most Americans. There were numerous magazine articles protesting the high cost of living and denouncing the protective tariff, middlemen, and "trust executives." While there was very little organization of consumers, and while consumer consciousness was vague, it became an important element in the reform movement because it was the lowest common political denominator among groups who had little or nothing else to unite them on concrete issues.

Millions of Americans were also distressed by their personal poverty and misery under the country's vaunted economic system. There was an almost incredible disparity between the incomes of the wealthy few and the poor masses. One percent of American families owned nearly seven-eighths of the wealth in the country; seven-eighths of the families owned only one-eighth. While a fifth of the nation's families were comfortable or rich, four-fifths just subsisted. In contrast with a year's wages of $500 for the average working man was the estimated $23 million Carnegie earned from his steel company alone in the one year, 1900, and the average of $10 million a year it had paid him during the previous five years. And on none of this did he have to pay a cent of income tax. The new industrialists and new millionaires amassed their fortunes largely as a result of the low cost of labor in their factories. The exploitation of working girls was almost beyond belief. One out of every five women worked and frequently for wages as low as $6 and $8 a week.

The human distress of millions of Americans under the economic system was intensified during the depression of the 1890s. And it made a deep impression on the clergymen and social workers who were working in the slums of the great cities. The Reverend Dr. Walter Rauschenbusch, one of the leaders of the Christian Socialist movement, described the poor he saw in a New York settlement house during the depression of the 1890s: "They wore down our threshold, and they wore away our hearts. . . . One could hear human virtue cracking and crumbling all about." The effect of the depression was a stimulus for two movements that provided much of the moral zeal for progressivism—the Social Gospel and the movement for social justice.

Protestant church leaders challenged by the new immigrants, the slums, labor problems, and Social Darwinism launched the Social Justice movement aimed at revitalizing and proclaiming the message of Christianity to an industrial society. The increasing wealth of the Protestant churches had alienated many workers who had previously been church members. Workers found themselves in rich surroundings in some of the elaborate churches where there were many well-dressed and wealthy families. This made workers uncomfortable. In addition they discovered that Protestant clergy were siding with employers during the strikes of the last quarter of the nineteenth century. Henry Ward Beecher, a Congregational minister and one of the great speakers of his time, spoke for many fellow ministers when he said, "God has intended the great to be great and the little to be little. . . . I do not say that a dollar a day is enough to support a workingman. But it is enough to support a man! Not enough to support a man and five children if a man insists on smoking and drinking beer. . . . But the man who cannot live on bread and water is not fit to live."

But, as we have seen, some Protestant clergy disagreed with Beecher and began to preach either the Social Gospel or Christian Socialism. As one Social Gospel leader put it, "Man is called in the providence of God to build on earth the city of God. There are no necessary evils. There are no insoluble problems. Whatever is wrong cannot be eternal, and whatever is right cannot be impossible." As for the Christian Socialists they gained little support outside their circle, for as Walter Rauschenbusch, their most prominent leader, later wrote, "We were few and we shouted in the wilderness."

In the Roman Catholic Church, the hierarchy's attitude toward social reform in the last quarter of the nineteenth century was, according to historian Aaron Abell, "more negative than positive, more tolerating than approving. Only in part," continues Abell, "it must be confessed was the Hierarchy motivated by considerations of justice and charity. . . ." And only as an aspect of Americanization did the leaders of the Catholic Church display any marked interest in social reform before the second decade of the twentieth century.

Still another influence supporting progressivism was the appearance of the writings of innovative political and social thinkers and the exposures of the muckrakers in the new popular magazines. The Progressive movement owed much to these people. There had been a number of precursors of the Progressive movement in the last quarter of the nineteenth century who had spoken out against the deplorable conditions resulting from the rise of industrialism and urbanism. Two very important forerunners were Henry George and Henry Demarest Lloyd. As we have seen, when George lived in California in the 1860s he had been impressed by how a movement of population into an area sent up property values and gave land speculators an unearned income. On a visit to New York City in 1869, the contrast between the great material progress of the city on the one hand and the poverty in the slum sections on the other further impressed him. After much reading and research he concluded that the land system explained this paradox. In 1879 he published his theories in *Progress and Poverty,* and the book soon reached a wide audience. His theories on rent were similar to those of the classical economist Ricardo.

But the book also contained an able analysis of the American economy. George argued that the expropriation of land by a few individuals and groups had caused the great inequities of nineteenth-century America. His solution was a single tax—a tax upon the unearned profits secured from land through the rise of its value, which he believed was caused, not by its improvement, but by the increased demand for it as the population increased. George thought such a tax would produce enough income to pay all the costs of government, would cause land speculators to sell their land at reasonable prices, and would eliminate land monopoly and with it the main obstacles to individual progress. He was persuaded all this could be accomplished without eliminating the essential features of capitalism. While few progressives supported the single tax as a solution, many of them were influenced by George's analysis of why wealth was not distributed equally in the United States.

Henry Demarest Lloyd also influenced progressives. His book *Wealth Against Common Wealth* (1894) disseminated a mass of facts about the growth and effect of monopoly in the United States. He had gathered his information from court records and legislative reports.

He provided names, dates, statistics, and examples, and his book became the model for most of the muckraking exposes of the Progressive era.

George and Lloyd were probably the most important and most influential precursors of the progressives, but while progressives relied heavily upon them they did not merely imitate them; they differed from their forerunners in several respects. Progressives, for example, put forth their reform program at a time when Americans were both willing and able to listen to their protests. The great depression of 1893–1897 had caused many Americans to question the blessings of unrestricted industrial capitalism. The progressives had a wider audience than their precursors because of the great expansion in schools and the existence of popular magazines and newspapers that allowed reformers to reach many Americans. Also assisting the progressives was a group of able writers who dramatized the protest against the status quo.

The latter were called muckrakers—a term used by Theodore Roosevelt to compare them to the character in *Pilgrims Progress* "who could look no way but downward with the muckrake in his hands." The term *muckraker* was intended to convey a rebuke, and some of the more irresponsible writers who placed sensationalism ahead of facts may have deserved condemnation. In time, however, the term became almost a title of nobility. Many muckrakers were careful in their research. Writing in cheap and popular magazines and thereby reaching a wide audience, they exposed all kinds of scandals and corruption: fraudulent letting of contracts, payroll padding, alliance of the police with vice, bribing of legislators, and the workings of political machines and bosses. They painted a dark picture of American life only because they had discovered the unpleasant truth.

Muckraking enjoyed only a short life—from about 1902 to about 1906. But in those few years there were some notable exposes. Ida Tarbell's history of the Standard Oil Company began publication of *McClure's Magazine* in 1903. Lincoln Steffens's series "The Shame of the Cities," an exposure of corruption in a number of cities, was printed in *McClure's* in 1904. Ray Stannard Baker wrote "Railroads on Trial" for the same magazine in 1905 and 1906. Thomas Lawson exposed the workings of high finance, and Charles Edward Russell did the same for the beef trust in *Everybody's Magazine* in 1905. Samuel Hopkins Adams in 1905 began a series of articles in *Collier's* on patent medicines, and David Graham Phillips in *Cosmopolitan* in 1906 wrote a series on business affiliations of Untied States senators.

The research of the muckrakers cost thousands of dollars. At first it was largely paid for by one man, S. S. McClure, whose motive was to secure timely articles for *McClure's Magazine*. When the venture was successful and the circulation of *McClure's Magazine* increased, other magazines such as *Everybody's, Cosmopolitan, Collier's,* and *American Magazine* followed the lead of McClure. At first muckraking was more concerned with general economic and social problems and less with specific grievances. The difference may be explained in part by the fact that later muckraking was to some extent a journalistic stunt. It was the sensationalism of the later period that led Theodore Roosevelt to denounce muckraking in 1906.

Why did the revelations of the muckrakers fascinate many Americans for some years? According to a contemporary writer in the British *Fortnightly Review,* there was nothing like the muckraking movement outside the United States. This being so, Richard Brown contends that the answer "must lie in a juxtaposition of American history and American character." That is to say the muckrakers articulated the nation's conscience. They dwelt on the greed of the immediate past, deplored departures from traditional ways, and cried out "Repent, repent!" They fascinated the American people, writes Brown, "for much the same reason that an occasional drinker, recovering from an unaccustomed debauch, is fascinated by tales of what he did while under the influence. And, to their everlasting credit, after listening to the Muckrakers the American people guarded against getting drunk again on the same brew by enacting the reforms of the Progressive era."

The most important book of the time for intellectual progressivism was Herbert Croly's *The Promise of American Life,* published in 1909. Croly noted that America had been a land of opportunity and a haven for the oppressed for 300 years, but he questioned whether this could go on forever without further control and direction by the government. Croly maintained that a large measure of government regulation was needed to keep the promise of American life intact. Reformers spoke of a moral awakening, but Croly maintained that the results would be illusory unless the principle of noninterference by the government in economic life was abandoned. The government could not be negative, wrote Croly. He did not call for the breakup of big industries, but he did advocate the regulation of the distribution of their benefits. And according to him the government had a duty to foster a higher standard of living for the masses of the people. Croly's book had a great impact. His ideas played an important part in the Bull Moose campaign in 1912, and some of them reappeared in the New Deal. Croly founded a magazine, *The New Republic,* in 1914 to provide a continuing forum for his views.

Other writers also influenced the course of progressivism. Walter Weyl in his *The New Democracy* (1912) argued that economic democracy was a prerequisite for an effective political democracy. Walter Lippmann in his *Preface to Politics* (1913) had much the same viewpoint in emphasizing the intimate connection between economics and government and the necessity of greater collectivism. Gustavus Myers in his *History of Great American Fortunes* (1909–1910) showed how great fortunes were made through the clever use of governmental machinery and even through the plundering of the government. Myers exploded the idea of the divine gift of property—property as a gift for virtuous living. Van Wyck Brooks in *The Wine of the Puritans* (1909) used a similar approach to social and intellectual history in an effort to demonstrate his thesis that the Puritan tradition was largely responsible for the defects in contemporary American society. J. Allen Smith in *The Spirit of American Government* (1907) shocked conservatives by calling the Constitution a reactionary and antidemocratic document. In 1913, Charles Beard in his *An Economic Interpretation of the Constitution* undertook to explode the myth of the disinterestedness of early Americans. Beard contended that the Constitution owed its character to those who, with money or public securities in their hands, as manufacturers and traders, or as spokesmen for the shipping interests, were gravely threatened by the chaotic insecurity that existed under the Articles of Confederation. Beard argued that the Constitutional Convention produced an "economic document based upon the concept that the functional private rights of property are anterior to government, and morally beyond the reach of popular majority." And Thorstein Veblen in his *Theory of the Leisure Class* maintained that "pecuniary emulation" was the key to American life, and money the test of American civilization.

Novels were also influential in the Progressive movement. Writers such as David Graham Phillips in *The Plum Tree,* Booth Tarkington in *The Gentleman from Indiana,* and William Allen White in *A Certain Rich Man* stressed that the system itself was not evil, and that it would work if good men were elected. Another view was reflected by Upton Sinclair in *The Jungle,* Frank Norris in *The Pit* and *The Octopus,* and Theodore Dreiser in *The Titan* and *The Financier.* They contended that a fundamental change in the system was necessary. But the effect of most of these writings was to convert readers to the reform movement, rather than to the Socialist party.

Politics to a considerable extent reflects the civilization of a people, and under the impact of an expanded industrialism and urbanism there was a decline in the tone and character of American life in the Gilded Age. There was also a decline in the tone and character of American politics in the same period. The great wealth and influence of the world of business took most of the best talent away from politics. Because politicians and businessmen had something to offer to each other, their ethics suffered as they worked together to concentrate control of the American economy and American politics in fewer and fewer hands. All this was made easier by the indifference of the public, who took the alliance between business and politics for granted.

This decline in politics was most evident in the cities and the states, but it could also be found on the national level. Lincoln Steffens's *Shame of the Cities* revealed that conditions in American cities by the turn of the century had not materially improved since the gloomy observations of James Bryce and Andrew D. White in the eighties. Steffens discovered in the cities that he visited the same conditions—a political machine headed by a boss (who seldom held office) in league with the underworld on the one hand and with the franchise-grabbing public utilities on the other. The primary objective of these machines appeared to be perpetual power and the fleecing of citizens rather than maintaining honest and efficient government. The exposures of the muckrakers drove home the shocking fact that representative government had very nearly broke down on the municipal level. Cities were not run by representatives fairly and impartially chosen, but by political machines resembling corporations in their hierarchical structure.

There had been municipal reformers in the seventies and eighties, but there was no real concerted effort until the Progressive era. By 1900, there was at least one reform group in every major city attempting to destroy the machine and the boss and the alliance between wealth and politics. But as we have seen it was a difficult task for the reformers, because the machines seemed to have an unbeatable system. The nature of city government itself allowed extraconstitutional organizations to grab power. City charters, granted or rewritten during the Jacksonian period, dispersed power and responsibility among many agencies. This created a power vacuum for the machine to occupy. The machine held the loyalty of many voters through patronage and favors. Machines obtained their money and also some of their support from selling street railroad and lighting franchises, building contracts, police protection, and many other privileges to businessmen who were able and willing to pay the price. The schools, roads, and public health services also provided great temptations. Contractors and politicians were nearly always entwined in some sort of a deal.

Reformers realized that unless machines and bosses were broken and corrupt alliances between wealth and politics destroyed there could be no lasting reform. What the progressives hoped to do was to restore government to what they imagined it had been in an earlier and purer age by rejuvenating the morale of the voter and by using his rejuvenated zeal to put through political reforms. The progressives further hoped that these measures would deprive the machines of their advantages and would make government more accessible to the honest, disinterested, and intelligent American. This in turn would break the power of the machines and restore more honest and efficient government.

Wilson described this as an effort "to bring government back to the people and to protect it from control of the representatives of selfish and special interest." This attempt took various forms—election of reform candidates, introduction of more efficient methods of government, laws for better control of vested interests, and new techniques in democracy. More specifically the progressives wanted honest government, city planning, housing codes, the enforcement of safety and health regulations in slums, and larger appropriations for schools, parks, playgrounds, and the like. Many times during these battles for city reform progressives found wealthy and powerful streetcar and other public utility corporations a greater obstacle than political machines. As a result of this many progressives advocated public ownership of streetcars and utilities, although they usually found state laws prohibiting this goal.

The crusade for municipal reform marked the chronological beginning of progressivism as a political movement. It got under way in the 1890s when Tammany Hall was temporarily overthrown by organized reform forces in 1894 and by the establishment of civic leagues in various cities. The most spectacular and important reform movement in the 1890s occurred in Chicago against the sale of valuable city rights by the city council to Charles T. Yerkes, a wealthy utilities magnate. Yerkes had come to Chicago in 1882 and had secured control of the street railway in the city. In 1895 he bribed the Illinois legislature to pass bills renewing his franchise for 100 years without paying a cent to Chicago. Governor John P. Altgeld vetoed this legislation, and Yerkes used his money to discredit and defeat Altgeld for reelection in 1897. Then the Illinois legislature and a new governor pushed through a law authorizing the Chicago city council to do what the vetoed bills would have done.

This led to a serious protest movement in Chicago. In 1895 the Municipal Voters League was established. It won control of the council by 1897 and helped elect a progressive mayor, Carter Harrison, in the same year. The League played such a vigilant role that when Lincoln Steffens came to Chicago in 1903 he could find no evidence of a machine or large-scale graft. The Chicago reform movement demonstrated that aroused citizens even without a leader could secure reform. This pattern developed in other cities. A number of good government leagues joined hands in New York City in 1913 to oust Tammany rule and elect the young independent Democrat, John Purroy Mitchel, as mayor. In Minneapolis the citizens' commission and a grand jury exposed the system of police graft run by Mayor A. A. Ames and sent him and his lieutenants to jail.

But the usual pattern of municipal reform centered around reform mayors and their reform city administrations. Some were Republicans, some were Democrats, and some were Independents. Nearly all of them were men of better than average incomes. Their aim was to cleanse politics and establish good government. Some stressed municipal home rule to break the stranglehold of state bosses. Others pushed civil service reform. Still others concentrated on destroying the corrupt alliances between private interest and city officials. Some of the better known reform mayors were Hazen S. Pingree of Detroit, Samuel M. ("Golden Rule") Jones of Toledo, and Tom L. Johnson of Cleveland.

Perhaps the most famous and influential of reform mayors was Johnson of Cleveland. He had had a typical business career during the 1880s and had amassed a fortune as a trolley magnate and iron manufacturer. He was a monopolist, but after reading Henry George he joined in the crusade against monopoly. In 1901 he was elected mayor of Cleveland where he gave the people an administration so energetic and efficient that Steffens described him as the "best mayor of the best-governed city in America." Johnson held tent meetings to educate the voters in municipal affairs, brought the street railways under municipal control, reduced the fare to 3 cents and attacked tax assessment abuses. In 1909, after four terms, Johnson was defeated, but in 1911 Newton D. Baker was elected to continue the struggle for Johnson's ideals.

Samuel M. Jones, a successful factory owner, was elected mayor of Toledo, Ohio, in 1897, through the efforts of the local Republican boss and certain business interests. Jones soon discovered he was supposed to grant a favorable franchise to a railway company in gratitude. He rebelled against becoming a party to such a deal and thereby provoked a bitter fight with the Republican organization. Jones ran for mayor on an independent ticket and remained in office until his death in 1904. He gained favor as "Golden Rule" Jones because of his attempt to apply that Christian principle in his business dealings. He carried the same spirit into his administration of the city government. He took away night sticks from the police, introduced free kindergartens into the public schools, and established public playgrounds for children. He led an unsuccessful fight for the public ownership of Toledo's utilities. Good evidence of the fear Jones instilled in the hearts of his opponents is the fact that the stock of the Toledo Street Railway Company jumped 24 points the morning after his death. The Toledo reform movement did not die with Jones. In 1905 his disciple and former secretary, Brand Whitlock, became mayor. During his four terms Whitlock continued the battle against machine politics. His most notable achievement was a new city charter providing for the initiative, referendum, recall, and direct nominations.

Jones and Johnson were the most spectacular and picturesque of the municipal reformers, but there were others. In Detroit Hazen S. Pingree, a prosperous shoe manufacturer, was elected mayor in 1889. He used his office to insure competition among private interests bidding for public favors and franchises. He tried to regulate utilities rates and establish a city-owned electric plant. He helped the poor by providing vacant lots for potato patches. Seth Low, a wealthy tea importer and president of Columbia University, was elected mayor of New York in 1901 winning over Tammany Hall. Low checked the excesses of patronage by extending the merit system of appointment. In Minneapolis a grand jury uncovered a graft ring and forced prosecution of the culprits. In Jersey City Mark Fagin led a movement to free the city from the influence of utilities, railroads, and spoilsmen politicians. In St. Louis Joseph W. Folk, while circuit attorney, exposed corruption and prosecuted many bribery cases. It was much the same in many other cities.

Municipal reformers also worked to secure home rule to destroy state interference in city administration. A reform mayor soon realized that city machines were always a part of the state machine. Even though a local machine was destroyed the state ring, acting through the legislature, could nullify the gain. Thus, it became necessary to free the cities from legislative interference. But here the reformers had little success. Rural and small town legislators were reluctant to give up control over large cities. By 1900 Missouri, California, Washington, and Minnesota had given home rule to cities. Between 1900 and 1914 eight other states did this but only two of them, Ohio and Michigan, had any large cities. Hence progressives in the cities joined hands with other groups to obtain new machinery to assure popular control of political processes. These new devices included the direct primary for nominating candidates, the short ballot, and the initiative, referendum, and recall. These battles were fought on the state-wide level.

The movement for municipal reform was also aided by the National Municipal League, by municipal research bureaus, and by the commission form of government. The National Municipal League, founded in 1894, fought for improvements in city governments, simplification of governmental machinery, full publicity of accounts, protection against franchise grabbers, administration by experts, and municipal home rule. The research bureaus, modeled after one established in New York City in 1906, trained administrators and studied ways and means of improving city governments. The commission form of government came into being by accident in Galveston, Texas, after the great flood of 1900. This tidal wave and hurricane took the lives of one-sixth of the population and destroyed one-third of the property of Galveston. To meet the emergency, extraordinary powers were placed in the hands of a commission of five. The experiment was so successful that a new city charter was drafted to make the commission form of government permanent. Interest in the Galveston venture led to the inauguration of similar plans in other cities. Des Moines, Iowa, worked out a plan combining the efficiency of commission government with certain democratic checks that served as a model for many other cities.

Another widely copied plan was devised by Dayton, Ohio. Here the commission acted as a board of directors for the city while the actual administration was entrusted to a city manager, a nonpolitical executive hired to run the government along lines of business efficiency. The city manager plan helped to overcome the inherent weakness in the commission form of government—failure to concentrate responsibility for administration—since there was no guarantee commissioners would be expert managers. By 1923 more than 300 cities had adopted the city manager plan, and by the mid-1950s it had spread to more than 1,300 cities.

In a further effort to purify municipal government the reformers secured such changes as the public letting of contracts, central purchasing of supplies, city planning, and the municipal ownership of subways, water supply systems, and gas and electric utilities. In some ways the most impressive achievements of the Progressive movement were on the local level. Local problems were simpler than federal problems, corruption more open and obvious, and issues more easily dramatized and understood. But the local government had limited powers. They were in many ways the creatures of the states, restricted by state laws and state interference, and the states themselves had to conform to the federal Constitution. Moreover, progressivism had little effect in the country's larger cities. Despite occasional reform administrations, New York, Chicago, and Philadelphia continued to be governed, most of the time, by corrupt political machines.

The fight against political machines, bosses, corruption, and special privilege had to be waged also on the state level. There were state machines just like city machines that governed behind the facade of publicly elected officials. What was called "the System" worked with great efficiency.

Missouri and New Jersey offer graphic examples of the System in operation. In the former the bribery or boodle system was used to run the state in the interest of railroads and other corporations. A lobby at the state capital representing the leading railroads and other business interests in the state secured control of the party caucus through bribery and favors and in this fashion governed the state. In New Jersey the System worked through a corporation-machine alliance, in which corporations, railroads, and financial institutions provided the leadership in the dominant Republican party. The railroad lobby, for example, in 1903 furnished the chief justice of the state, the attorney general, the state comptroller, the commissioner of banking and insurance, and one of the members of the state board of taxation. At the same time both United States senators from New Jersey were interested in public utilities, and the retiring attorney general sat on the board of three public service corporations. It was probably no accident that railroads in New Jersey paid only one-third of their share of the tax burden, and that public utility companies were free from equitable taxation and public regulation.

Hence progressives were active in state as well as city politics. Because of their strong antipathy toward monopoly and their distrust of the economic and political power used by large corporations, they worked to have the state regulate railroads, insurance companies and the like. The progressives fought to establish public utility commissions which regulated, with varying degrees of effectiveness, the rates and practices of railroad and utility corporations. Believing that this regulation was possible only by making politics more representative and more responsible, progressives worked to strengthen popular control over elected officials by adopting a variety of new political devices. And aware of the need for public action to insure greater social justice, especially for workers, progressives supported workmen's compensation laws, safety and health codes, maximum hour statutes, old-age pension plans, and mothers' assistance programs. These proposals frequently encountered strong opposition from the courts, both state and federal, which regarded some of these reforms as violations of property rights.

There had been sporadic state reform movements in the 1890s led by such men as John Peter Altgeld of Illinois and Hazen Pingree of Michigan. But it was not until the first decade of the twentieth century that progressivism on the state level began to be felt in American politics. One of the first progressive leaders in state politics and surely one of the most outstanding of these reformers was Robert M. La Follette of Wisconsin. A Republican, like many other midwestern reform leaders, he led a successful insurgency against the conservatives in his party and the railroad and lumber interests with whom they were allied. He finally won the governorship in 1900, was twice reelected, and from 1906 until his death in 1925 he represented Wisconsin in the United States Senate.

Supported by small farmers, urban workers, and middle-class groups, La Follette developed a strong political organization and a reform program known as the "Wisconsin Idea" that became a leading example of state progressivism. His program included a workmen's compensation law and others limiting the hours of labor for women and children. Railroads, insurance companies, and banks were regulated more effectively; conservation was promoted by creation of a state forest reserve; lobbyists were restricted; and a civil service program and direct primary system were established. To pay for these and other reforms corporate taxes were increased and, for the first time in the United States, a state income and inheritance tax was adopted.

The essence of La Follette's progressivism was an effort to uphold representative government. He maintained that the people had never failed in a democracy, and that the danger came from the people not being allowed to have representative government. The railroads and other corporations were the threat to representative government, and the remedy for this was more democracy. One of La Follette's major contributions to progressivism was his insistence upon effective regulation of business being based on detailed and accurate information. Thus he used experts from the University of Wisconsin in implementing these reforms. Charles McCarthy, who has written about the Wisconsin Idea and who was one of La Follette's chief allies at the state university, maintained that the main purpose of the program in Wisconsin was "a new individualism" which would "give the individual a better chance to possess property."

Though the influence of the Wisconsin Idea was felt more strongly in other midwestern farm states, it had a nationwide impact. In the Middle West governors Albert B. Cummins of Iowa and John A. Johnson of Minnesota put through reform programs similar to La Follette's. Joseph W. Folk, a former corporation lawyer who had gained a reputation fighting corruption in St. Louis, was elected governor of Missouri in 1904 and inaugurated a reform program.

There were also reform administrations in the South. Governors Jeff Davis of Alabama, James K. Vardaman of Mississippi, and Hoke Smith of Georgia led fights against discriminatory railroad rates, control of the Democratic party in the South by Bourbon interests, and the "foreign" corporations of the Northeast that they charged with exploiting the citizens of their states. In Texas, Governor James S. Hogg secured legislation prohibiting railroads from issuing watered stock and increased the regulation of their rate-making practices.

State progressive movements in the East were often built upon the efforts of earlier reformers and the support of progressives in both parties. New Hampshire had a governor who curbed the power of the Boston and Maine Railroad and the political bosses allied with it. New

York progressives were led by Charles Evans Hughes who was governor from 1907 to 1911. Hughes, a young corporation lawyer, had gained fame because of his role in exposing scandals and favoritism in the operation of the country's largest insurance companies. As governor, Hughes was able to obtain several important changes in New York's insurance laws, as well as a strong public utilities commission and other reforms. Under Woodrow Wilson's leadership in 1911–1912, New Jersey enacted progressive laws such as direct primaries, workmen's compensation, the regulation of railroad and public utilities companies as well as others aimed at checking the power of corporations and purifying politics. On the West Coast progressivism scored victories under the leadership of reformers such as Hiram Johnson in California and William S. U'Ren in Oregon.

The reformers curbed or destroyed the System, as Steffens called it, on the state level in a variety of ways. They did it by strong aggressive leadership. In every state where progressives were successful there was an aggressive leader who carried the fight. They also did it with a series of devices for giving government back to the people. All state reformers supported measures to give voters more direct power over government and to restore democracy in its purity. The first and most important victory scored before 1900 was the adoption of the secret Australian official ballot. Previously, parties had printed and distributed at the polls their own lists of candidates. This allowed voters little opportunity to express their preference with any privacy. In 1888 Massachusetts required secret, uniform, and officially printed ballots. By 1898 all but four states had accepted this reform.

Another reform was the direct primary, which allowed the people themselves, rather than the bosses in convention, to nominate party candidates. Mississippi led the way with the first direct primary in 1902, to be followed by Wisconsin the following year. After this date the direct primary was widely adopted. By 1915 the direct primary was being used in thirty-seven states. In 1910 Oregon utilized the direct primary for instructing delegates to national nominating conventions, and, within two years, thirteen states were doing this.

Beyond the direct primary reformers obtained (1) the short ballot to enable voters to make more intelligent decisions, (2) the Seventeenth Amendment for the direct election of United States senators, (3) the initiative to allow voters to secure consideration of a proposal in the event the legislature refused to act, (4) the referendum to permit voters to review laws already enacted by the legislature, (5) the recall to let voters unseat a public official before his term was over, and (6) a corrupt practices act that generally prohibited contributions from corporations to political parties. Reformers sought to eliminate special privileges with antilobbying laws, measures regulating the granting of franchises, and the establishment of public utilities companies. Other innovations included a reduction in the number of state-elected officials, the creation of an executive budget, and the expansion of the civil service.

Another important extension of democracy was woman suffrage. This required a constitutional amendment. As early as 1869 the territory of Wyoming permitted women to vote, but before 1900 only four states—Colorado, Idaho, Wyoming, and Utah—allowed women to vote. The movement, like most other reform causes, gained momentum during the first decade of the twentieth century, largely as a result of agitation by the suffragettes and their leaders, Susan B. Anthony and Carrie Chapman Catt. By 1914 eight more states, all west of the Mississippi River, had given the vote to women. In 1916 a woman, Jeanette Rankin of Montana, was elected to Congress. Led by New York in 1917, the large eastern states began to come around. The movement for national action was now very strong, and Congress, in 1919, sent the Nineteenth Amendment to the states. It forbade the United States, or any state, to deny the vote to any citizen on the basis of sex. Enough states approved the amendment in time for women to vote in the presidential election of 1920.

The achievements of progressives in modernizing and democratizing city and state governments were impressive, and so too were their accomplishments in social and economic reform. By 1920 most of the states had instituted some kind of workmen's compensation, and legislation regulating the labor of women and children, wages and hours, and safety and health standards had been widely adopted despite adverse court decisions. Also appearing were some beginning programs in such areas as aid to dependent children and old-age pensions. In addition there were measures providing agricultural aid, conservation, educational reforms, and prohibition. "So successful were the progressive leaders in the several states by 1912," writes historian Arthur Link, "that all observers agreed that a thoroughgoing revolution had been accomplished since 1900. In most states the power of the bipartisan machines had been shattered or else curtailed. State governments were more representative of the rank and file and more responsive to their economic and social needs." "Even more important, moreover," continues Link, "was the fact that by 1912 progressivism had spread into the arena of national politics, subverted ancient party loyalties, and caused such a party commotion as the country had not seen since 1896."

However, progressives, despite their concern for improving American life, largely ignored the nation's most tragic problem, the plight of the blacks. Americans boasted of democracy and equal opportunities, and yet they denied necessary rights to one-tenth of the population. This was a paradox to most foreign observers and thoughtful Americans and it was not resolved during the Progressive era. While progressivism came to the United States in these years, it did not come to blacks. "Americans failed, somehow, to get very excited about muckraking materials on the Negro," writes historian Dewey W. Grantham, "and the Negro question proved a poor second to such topics as corporation evil and political corruption."*

The progressive belief that all were capable of more participation in politics and worthy of a fuller share of the economic life of the country did not extend to blacks. While progressives strove to purify politics and to renew and modernize the structures of government, they allowed negroes to be eliminated from politics and to be denied the right to vote. They regarded them as "a permanent clot in the social bloodstream" of the country. And instead of attempting to elevate them, progressives pushed them farther downward. They maintained that the blacks had been given their chance and had failed. Hence they must be left to the devices of the dominant race in the South.

Further Reading

Abell, Aaron. *American Catholic Thought on Social Questions.* 1968.

Abrams, Richard N. *Conservatism in a Progressive Era: Massachusetts Politics, 1900–1912.* 1964.

Buenker, John D. *Urban Liberalism and Progressive Reform.* 1973.

Chalmers, David M. *The Social and Political Ideas of the Muckrakers.* 1964.

Croly, Herbert. *The Promise of American Life.* 1909.

Davis, Allen. *Spearheads for Reforms: The Social Settlements and the Progressive Movement, 1890–1919.* 1967.

Ekirch, Arthur. *Progressivism in America,* 1974.

---

*Dewey W. Grantham, "The Progressive Movement and the Negro." *South Atlantic Quarterly* LIV (October 1955), 467.

Faulkner, H. U. *The Quest for Social Justice, 1898-1914*. 1931.

Goldman, Eric F. *Rendezvous with Destiny*. 1952.

Gould, Lewis L., ed. *The Progressive Era*. 1973.

Gould, Lewis L. *Reform and Regulation: American Politics, 1900-1916*. 1978.

Graham, Otis L. *The Great Campaigns: Reform and War in America, 1900-1928*. 1971.

Haber, Samuel. *Efficiency and Uplift: Scientific Management in the Progressive Era*. 1964.

Hackney, Sheldon. *Populism to Progressivism in Alabama*. 1969.

Hall, Jack. *Juvenile Reform in the Progressive Era*. 1971.

Hays, Samuel P. *The Response to Industrialism, 1885-1914*. 1957.

_____. *Conservation and the Gospel of Efficiency*. 1959.

Hofstadter, Richard. *The Age of Reform*. 1955.

Hofstadter, Richard, ed. *The Progressive Movement, 1900-1915*. 1963.

Josephson, Matthew. *The President Makers, 1896-1916*. 1964.

Kennedy, David M., ed. *Progressivism: The Critical Issues*. 1971.

Kirby, Jack T. *Darkness at the Dawning: Race and Reform in the Progressive South*. 1972.

Lasch, Christopher. *The New Radicalism in America, 1889-1963*. 1965.

Link, Arthur S. *Woodrow Wilson and the Progressive Era. 1910-1917*. 1954.

Lubove, Roy. *The Progressives and the Slums*. 1962.

Kolko, Gabriel. *The Triumphs of Conservatism*. 1963.

Mowry, George E. *The California Progressives*. 1951.

_____. *The Era of Theodore Roosevelt, 1900-1912*. 1958.

O'Neill, William L. *The Progressive Years: America Comes of Age*. 1975.

Quandt, Jean. *From the Small Town to the Great Community: The Social Thought of Progressive Intellectuals*. 1970.

Penick, James L. *Progressive Politics and Conservation*. 1968.

Resek, Carl, ed. *The Progressives*. 1967.

Rothman, David J. *Conscience and Convenience: The Asylum and Its Alternatives in Progressive America*. 1980.

Shergold, Peter R. *Working Class Life: The "American Standard" in Comparative Perspective, 1899-1913*. 1982.

Southern, David W. *The Malignant Heritage: Yankee Progressives and the Negro Question, 1901-1914*. 1968.

Steffens, Lincoln. *The Autobiography of Lincoln Steffens*. 2 vols., 1931.

_____. *The Shame of the Cities*. 1904.

Swados, Harvey, ed. *Years of Conscience, the Muckrakers*. 1962.

Thelen, David P. *The New Citizenship: Origins of Progressivism in Wisconsin, 1885-1900*. 1972.

Timberlake, James H. *Prohibition and the Progressive Movement, 1900-1920*. 1963.

White, William Allen. *The Autobiography of William Allen White.* 1946.
Wiebe, Robert H. *Businessmen and Reform.* 1962.
_____. *The Search for Order, 1877–1920.* 1967.
Wilson, Harold S. *McClure's Magazine and the Muckrakers.* 1970.

9

Theodore Roosevelt and Progressivism

Theodore Roosevelt (1858–1919) was not quite 43 years old when he assumed the presidency on McKinley's death—the youngest man to hold this high office to date. Possessing remarkable energy and drive he preached and carried out the strenuous life, which fitted in well with the national sentiment of the day. Americans, roused by their victory over Spain in 1898 and the acquisition of an overseas empire, wanted not only action, but action with a noise; Roosevelt gave them both.

Roosevelt is one of the most controversial figures in American history. Americans have considered him either as a great president and champion of reform or as a psuedoprogressive and a Johnny-come-lately to the reform movement. In his own day, a large personal following idolized him and looked upon him as the personification, and even creator, of the reform movement. Foes and admirers alike considered him something unique, and Lord John Morley was moved to say that there were two great natural phenomena in the United States: Niagara Falls and Theodore Roosevelt.

Clearly Roosevelt was not of the type that had largely occupied the presidency since the days of John Quincy Adams. He was not a folk hero, did not hail from the countryside of the West, was not self-educated or self-made, and was not born in a log cabin. Rather he came from an old and moderately wealthy mercantile and banking family of New York City. He was educated by private tutors and at

Harvard, had traveled in Europe, was interested in literature and art, and wrote a number of creditable books on history. After leaving Harvard in 1880 he entered politics, something well-bred young men such as Roosevelt did not ordinarily choose as their life work in his day, and subsequently served as New York state legislator, civil service commissioner, New York City police commissioner, assistant secretary of the navy, governor of New York, and vice-president before coming to the White House.

It is not easy to characterize or evaluate Roosevelt. He could not make up his own mind whether he was a "progressive Conservative" or conservative Progressive." While he made wonderful speeches in the progressive vein, he frequently took paths to reassure the conservatives, especially the men of property. Until he entered the White House there were few reform movements or reformers whom he had not at some time criticized, calling the latter "extremists," "radical fanatics," and the "lunatic fringe." While Roosevelt loved people and asserted that he placed human rights over property rights, he really loved stability most of all.

Roosevelt conceived the presidency as a "stewardship," and he called himself "the steward of the people." He believed it was not only his right but his duty to do anything that needs of the nation demanded unless such action was specifically prohibited by the Constitution or by the laws of the land. He also acted on the principle that it was his prerogative to determine the needs of the country, and according to Roosevelt he "did and caused to be done many things not previously done by the President...."

When Roosevelt became president, the Republicans had heavy majorities in both houses of Congress. But the party and congressional leadership was dominated by conservative politicians who represented big business and finance. The Senate was controlled by four regular conservative Republicans—Nelson W. Aldrich of Rhode Island, William B. Allison of Iowa, Orville H. Platt of Connecticut, and John C. Spooner of Wisconsin. By 1901 their power was practically unchallenged in the Senate, and other senators had to cultivate them to gain coveted committee assignments and other favors. From 1903 to 1911 Joseph G. Cannon of Illinois was Speaker of the House. He was very popular with the Democrats as well as the Republicans and wielded greater power than any Speaker before or since. Probably more conservative than the four Senate leaders, Cannon symbolized "standpat" Republicanism. Opposed to "class and local legislation," Cannon's committee assignments in the House placed "standpatters" in strategic posts, and this system was not broken until the congressional insurgency during the Taft administration.

At the outset, Roosevelt moved slowly and cautiously so as not to upset or challenge the Old Guard leadership of his party. He retained McKinley's cabinet and surrounded himself with advisers from the world of finance and big business. His first message to Congress in December 1901 was called by contemporaries a safe and conservative document. In this message, Roosevelt labeled the growth of large corporations a "natural" phenomenon, emphasized the need for expanding foreign markets, supported the current tariff schedules, and called for a subsidized merchant marine. He also recommended a reciprocity tariff measure with Cuba and the Philippines, a ship subsidy bill, construction of the Panama Canal, major additions to the navy, plans for reorganizing the army, new immigration restrictions, and the establishment of a permanent census bureau. He gave prominence to the trust question by putting it in first place in his list of recommendations.

Roosevelt thought the old laws regulating the accumulation and distribution of wealth were "no longer sufficient," and he spoke of the "real and grave evils" of big business. He asked for "practical efforts" to correct these evils, requesting the establishment of a new Department of Commerce with a Bureau of Corporations to collect and make public information about interstate industry, an act to expedite antitrust prosecutions, and a railroad bill prohibiting the giving of rebates on freight shipments. Thus the origins of much of his future legislative program can be found in this first message to Congress.

Probably the most important domestic problem facing Roosevelt was the concentration of capital in business and financial enterprises. Between 1900 and 1908 the number of large industrial combinations—or "trusts"—increased from 185 to 440, and their capitalization from $3 billion to $20.5 billion. By this time the trusts had few supporters. The muckraking disclosures, together with some state and federal investigations, had convinced most Americans that trusts had used illegal business methods, raised prices to artificial levels, and crushed small businessmen. The question was not whether monopoly should be curbed, but how the curbing should be done. Roosevelt, who seldom ignored a public demand and who was aware of the widespread opposition to trusts, placed himself at the head of the antitrust movement and developed the reputation of trust buster. He did not oppose bigness in business but the abuses arising from it. He believed the problem of monopoly could be handled only by distinguishing between "good" and "bad" trusts, because he was of the opinion that large corporations were inevitable and had come to stay and that therefore it was futile to prohibit them. He made this point clear in his annual message to Congress in 1902. "Our aim is not to do away with corporations," Roosevelt said. "On the contrary, these big aggregations are an inevitable development of modern industrialism, and the effort to destroy them would be futile unless accompanied in ways that would work the utmost mischief to the entire body politic. . . . We draw the line against misconduct," added Roosevelt, "not against wealth." Thus Roosevelt's remedy was regulation, not destruction of the trusts. Since the federal government had done little to curb the trusts before Roosevelt's presidency, his moves were a significant departure from previous policy.

Roosevelt dramatically invoked the Sherman Act when Attorney General Philander C. Knox on 18 February 1902 announced the government would file suit against the Northern Securities Company, a giant holding company organized by J. P. Morgan, James J. Hill, and Edward H. Harriman to control the Northern Pacific, the Great Northern, and the Chicago, Burlington, and Quincy railroads. These three lines comprised the main railway systems running from the upper Mississippi Valley to the Pacific Northwest. Roosevelt regarded the merger as a violation of the Sherman Act and therefore ordered the prosecution of the combination. The announcement of the suit was a staggering shock to financial leaders who were taken by surprise. The New York stock market was described as "temporarily demoralized," and Wall Street as "paralyzed." Roosevelt's "thunderbolt out of a clear sky" was depicted as "unreasonable" and "beyond comprehension."

Having started the Northern Securities suit, Roosevelt, in the summer and fall of 1902, took trips to New England and the Middle West to explain his trust policy and to seek popular support for it. Throughout he emphasized the distinction between good and bad trusts, maintaining that the bad ones must be regulated. And always he joined his determination to enforce the law together with assurances of his wish to preserve the economic good there might be in large units of business. At Cincinnati he expressed one of his favorite themes about the trusts when he said, "The biggest corporation, like the humblest private citizen must be held to a strict compliance with the will of the people."

In 1903 the federal circuit court of St. Paul, Minnesota, found the Northern Securities Company illegal and ordered its dissolution, a decision upheld by the Supreme Court by a vote of 5 to 4 in 1904. In the majority decision Justice John M. Harlan pointed out that "If the Anti-Trust Act is held not to embrace such a case such as is now before us, the plain intention of the legislative branch of the Government will be defeated." Justice Oliver Wendell Holmes, only recently appointed to the Court by Roosevelt, dissented on the ground that the organization of a holding company in itself was not illegal even though the purpose of the incorporation was to stop competition between competing railroads. When Roosevelt heard of the decision, he proclaimed it "one of the great achievements of my administration. . . . The most powerful men in this country were held to accountability before the law." But as Justice Holmes had predicted in his minority opinion, this did not happen, for the Sherman Act logically required criminal prosecution of Morgan, Harriman, Hill, and others involved in the company. While the prosecution was technically successful, it did not restore competition, although Roosevelt believed that the Knight case of 1895, upholding the device of a holding company, was dead. "This decision," he later wrote, "I caused to be annulled by the court that had rendered it."

Roosevelt moved against other trusts. In the seven years after 1902 his administration started antitrust suits against forty-four corporations, including some of the biggest industrial combinations in the country, and obtained twenty-five indictments. In addition to the Northern Securities Company the Supreme Court, in 1905, ordered the dissolution of the so-called beef trust, but the meat packers continued to defy the government and it was not until 1920 and 1921 that competition was effectively restored to the meat industry. The climax of Roosevelt's antitrust prosecutions came in 1906 and 1907, when suits were started against the Standard Oil Company, the American Tobacco Company, the New Haven Railroad, and the DuPont Corporation. Indictments were handed down against Standard Oil in 1907 and the American Tobacco Company in 1908, but they did not reach final settlement until the Taft administration. In 1911 the Supreme Court adopted the Roosevelt doctrine about good and bad trusts in the Standard Oil case when it formulated the "rule of reason"— holding that only "unreasonable" combinations in restraint of trade violated the Sherman Antitrust Act.

Roosevelt attacked the industrial problem in other ways too. He wanted a federal incorporation law and federal regulation of all concerns doing interstate business, but his ideas never received sufficient support to be enacted into law. To implement some of his views on the industrial problem, Roosevelt in his first term obtained additional legislation—all in February 1903—to aid in the enforcement of the antitrust laws. The Expedition Act gave precedence in the federal courts to cases brought under the Sherman Antitrust Act and Interstate Commerce Act. Then Congress added the Department of Commerce and Labor to the cabinet. The department's Bureau of Corporations was created to achieve the purpose set forth by Roosevelt in his first message to Congress. "The first essential in determining how to deal with the great industrial combinations is knowledge of the facts—publicity." While the bureau had no regulatory authority, its first head, James R. Garfield, so capably launched a program of fact finding as to cause businessmen to condemn it as a "vexatious interference with the industrial life of the country." Congress also enacted the Elkins Anti-Rebate Act to prevent railroads from limiting competition by granting special rates to favored persons. The new law prohibited any changes from the published rate schedules, strengthened the Interstate Commerce Act by providing punishment for the receiving as well as the giving of rebates, and made both railroad companies and their individual officials liable to prosecution.

Roosevelt's popularity rose with a good portion of the population as a result of his trust policies. He won further applause when he intervened in the coal strike of 1902. The United Mine Workers of America, led by John Mitchell, sought a 20 percent wage increase, a nine-hour day, payment on the basis of gross weight of coal mined rather than the net amount weighed in after the impurities were removed, and union recognition. When the coal operators refused even to meet Mitchell to discuss outstanding problems, the anthracite miners in May 1902 went on strike and succeeded in suspending the operations of the mines for five months. With fall approaching and with coal prices going up, there were appeals from all parts of the country for Roosevelt to do something.

Convinced the strike was a national problem, Roosevelt called representatives of both sides of the dispute to a White House conference early in October, where he urged them to conciliate their differences before the approaching winter brought widespread suffering.

When the White House conference broke down, because the operators scorned the offer of mediation, Roosevelt moved to force a settlement. He appointed a commission to investigate the dispute and made plans to have federal troops seize and work the mines. At the same time he sent Secretary of War Elihu Root to talk with J. P. Morgan. Under this pressure the operators agreed to submit the dispute to arbitration, and the miners returned to work pending the commission's report, which they had agreed to accept.

In March 1903 the commission made public its report granting only some of the miners' demands. They received a 10 percent wage increase, a nine-hour day, the right to check on the weighing of coal, and the right to submit future grievances to a conciliation board, comprised of both owners and miners. But the union was not accorded formal recognition as a bargaining agent. Not until 1916 did the union gain official recognition from the operators. The commission also recommended a 10 percent increase in the price of coal, and the operators put this into effect.

Roosevelt's actions in the coal strike are important. He reversed the role presidents like Andrew Jackson and Grover Cleveland had played in the Chesapeake and Ohio Canal strike in 1837 and in the Pullman strike of 1894 by exerting pressure on employers rather than on employees. Roosevelt was the first president to use his office impartially in a major labor dispute. He was the first president not to intervene in a major labor dispute on the side of capital or to use troops or an injunction to break a strike. His actions in the coal strike established a historic precedent for presidential intervention in an area hitherto reserved to private business and for the settlement of strikes by arbitration.

Roosevelt's intervention in the coal strike could be regarded as obtaining a "square deal" for labor. But Roosevelt did more. In 1905 he recommended to Congress an investigation of child labor and the adoption of an employers' liability law. In 1906 he warned against the "grave abuses" caused by the use of injunctions in strikes. In 1908 he restated his earlier points and also urged Congress to pass a workmen's compensation law for government employees and an employer's liability law for workers on interstate railroads. Yet his achievements in the field of labor legislation are not impressive when one considers the large Republican majorities Roosevelt had in Congress and the fact that he was regarded as a strong president. Roosevelt's Congresses failed to enact such important measures as federal control of child labor and limitations on the powers of federal courts in injunction proceedings in labor disputes. However, Congress appropriated $150,000 in 1907 to investigate causes of accidents and loss of life in the mines. And in 1906 it approved an employers' liability law for workers on interstate railroads. When the Supreme Court set aside this act, Congress in 1908 passed a new one overcoming the Court's objections. In the same year Congress also passed a law regulating the hours worked by trainmen and telegraph operators on interstate railroads.

Roosevelt wanted very much to be president in his own right. "I had rather be elected to that high office," he told someone in 1903, "than to have anything tangible of which I know." While his trust-busting activities and his intervention in the coal strike of 1902 had increased his popularity, they confirmed the fears of big business. Some conservatives supported a movement to replace Roosevelt with Mark Hanna in the 1904 presidential election, but when Hanna died in February 1904 the "dump-Roosevelt" movement ended, and the Republican national convention at Chicago unanimously nominated Theodore Roosevelt. His running mate was Senator Charles W. Fairbanks of Indiana. The Republican platform was unexceptional and simply stressed the Republican achievements since the party's victory in 1896.

The Democrats passed over Bryan, who had been defeated twice already, and picked a conservative, Judge Alton B. Parker of New York for president and Henry G. Davis of West Virginia for vice-president. Bryan attempted to have the convention include a free silver plank in the platform, which he hoped would compel Parker to decline the nomination. But this strategy was beaten. The Democratic platform denounced Roosevelt's administration as "spasmodic, erratic, sensational, spectacular, and arbitrary." It promised independence for the Philippines at the proper time and under proper circumstances, a gradual reduction in the tariff, and popular election of United States senators; it opposed trusts restricting competition, controlling production, and fixing prices and wages.

The only exciting incident in an otherwise dull campaign occurred in the closing days when Parker accused Roosevelt of securing campaign funds by blackmail. Parker charged George B. Cortelyou, who was both secretary of commerce and labor and Republican national chairman, with using information about the practices of trusts obtained from the Bureau of Corporations to extort campaign contributions from the corporations in return for a promise of immunity from antitrust prosecutions. Later investigations revealed the very large contributions made by the Standard Oil Company, J. P. Morgan and Associates, Harriman, and The Equitable, The Mutual, and New York Life Insurance Companies. In all, corporations donated about three-fourths of the $2,195,000 raised by the Republican National Committee. Roosevelt heatedly denied the charges of blackmail as being "monstrous" and "atrociously false." He said he was "unhampered by any pledge, promise, or understanding of any kind, save my promise, made openly to the American people, that so far as my power lies I shall see to it that every man has a square deal, no less and no more."

Roosevelt won decisively with 7,628,834 popular votes and 336 electoral votes to 5,084,401 popular votes and 140 electoral votes for Parker. The Democrats did not carry any states north of the Mason-Dixon line; Missouri, south of the line, went Republican. It was the most disastrous defeat for any major party since the Democrats lost with Horace Greeley in 1872. Immediately following his election, Roosevelt issued the following statement, "On the 4th of March next I shall have served three and a half years and this... constitutes my first term. The wise custom which limits the President to two terms regards the substance and not the form; and under no circumstances will I be a candidate for or accept another nomination."

In his message to Congress in December 1904, following his election, Roosevelt outlined much of his program for his second term. For labor he recommended an employers' liability act for federal employees and federal contractors, a limitation of working hours for railroad labor, and a requirement for safety devices on the country's railroads. On the trust problem Roosevelt listed a number of the well-known corporate abuses and to correct these he asked Congress to give the Interstate Commerce Commission power to establish railroad rates, to allow the Bureau of Corporations to license all interstate business, and to place the insurance business under the investigative authority of the bureau. Since Congress governed the District of Columbia, Roosevelt wanted to make it a model of social reform with child labor laws, compulsory school attendance, factory inspection, slum clearance, and juvenile court laws. A short time later in an address in February 1905 to the Union League of Philadelphia, a gathering place for wealthy easterners, Roosevelt stated bluntly the goal of his second term: "an increase in supervision exercised by government over business enterprise."

In his second term Roosevelt continued his reforms, signaling out railroads, a major target for reformers since the Granger movement, as his main objective. While the Elkins Act was aimed at preventing competitive lines from destroying one another, the problem of protecting shippers against excessive rate changes still remained, because the railroads still had the power to fix rates. And despite the vigorous efforts of the Roosevelt administration to enforce the antirebate part of the measure, rebates continued. Moreover, by 1905 the Supreme Court had so impaired the authority of the Interstate Commerce Commission that it was little more than a statistical bureau. In that same year Roosevelt asked for legislation to "prevent the imposition of unjust or unreasonable rates" and supported a stronger bill introduced in the House by Congressman Peter Hepburn of Iowa. The House quickly passed the Hepburn Bill in February 1906, but it did not become law until 29 June 1906, after a long struggle in the Senate and despite heavy pressure against it by a powerful railroad lobby.

The Hepburn Act increased the membership of the Interstate Commerce Commission from five to seven and extended its authority over express companies, sleeping car companies, oil pipelines, bridges, ferries, and terminals. It prohibited free passes for all except railroad employees. It required advance notice of any change in schedule rates and provided for the inspection of the books of the railroad companies by the commission. It required a uniform cost accounting system by the railroads and directed them to get rid of all outside properties after 1908. The most important new power the commission received was that of reducing unreasonable rates, on the complaint of a shipper, until the courts reviewed them. An order now issued by the commission went into effect immediately, a significant change from the former requirement of having to ask the courts to enforce its orders. The Hepburn Act was the strongest measure yet passed in the area of government regulation of private business, and it made the Interstate Commerce Commission an effective agent for the first time since it was established in 1887.

Another reform came in the field of food-processing industries. Dr. Harvey W. Wiley, chief chemist of the Department of Agriculture, had been warning the public of abuses in the food and drug industries for years and urging remedial legislation. Several hard-hitting muckraking articles also drew attention to the matter. But pure food bills passed in the House never came to a vote in the Senate. The National

Wholesale Liquors Dealers' Association and the Proprietary Medicine Association applied enough pressure to kill all such proposals. Then in 1906 Upton Sinclair's novel, *The Jungle*, painted a convincing picture of the filthy conditions in meat-packing plants.

Somewhat skeptical of what he had read in Sinclair's book, Roosevelt had the Department of Agriculture investigate the meat-packing business. When federal investigators largely confirmed Sinclair's charges, Roosevelt was convinced and vigorously supported a bill introduced by Senator Albert J. Beveridge of Indiana requiring federal inspection of the meat-packing business. The Senate quickly passed the bill, but the packing industry had enough influence in the House to hold up the measure for a while. To rally public support for the bill, Roosevelt published the Department of Agriculture report on the packing houses. This disclosed that meat was shoveled from filthy, wooden floors, along with splinters, dirt, "floor filth and the expectoration of tuberculous and other diseased workers," and carried from room to room in "rotten box cars." These revelations and the threat of others caused the meat packers to relent in their opposition, and on 1 July 1906 the Meat Inspection Act was passed. This law gave federal authorities the power to inspect all meat shipped across state lines and to condemn products found to be "unsound, unhealthful, unwholesome, or otherwise unfit for human food." The Pure Food and Drug Act passed on 23 June 1906 prohibited the sale of impure or adulterated foods or drugs, prohibited the sale of drugs containing narcotics or alcohol unless the label denoted the exact proportions of these ingredients, and forbade the sale of foods and drugs whose ingredients were misrepresented. The prohibition applied only to interstate and foreign commerce, but a number of the states had similar prohibitions. Both the Meat Inspection Act and the Pure Food and Drug Act were amended from time to time to correct loopholes and weaknesses.

Of all his domestic achievments, Roosevelt regarded his conservation program as the most important; it is probably his most enduring contribution. Deeply concerned about the preservation of the nation's natural resources, he regarded the problem as more than merely conserving coal, oil, and timber. This could be done by executive action, and Roosevelt used his authority to withdraw land from private exploitation and to increase the number and scope of national parks. More important was his insistence on the coordination of the question of natural resources with the economic and social problems of the country. Thus, he urged extensive river valley developments to include navigation, reclamation, irrigation, flood control, and water power production.

The nation's natural resources had been squandered ever since colonial days. Of the estimated original 800 million acres of timber, only about one-fourth was left in 1900, and three-fourths of this was in private hands. The once beautiful, navigable streams were badly silted and filled with sandbars, and much of the natural mineral resources such as coal, iron, copper, lead, oil, and gas were controlled and being exploited by the industrial trusts and railroads. In 1891 Congress had given the president authority to reserve forest land by executive order. When Roosevelt came to office, only 46 million acres of public land had been set aside under the law of 1891 as national reserves; when he left office almost 200 million acres—an area equal in size to Great Britain and France combined—had been placed under the control of the government. Roosevelt also withdrew from sale 70 million acres of public land containing coal, oil, and phosphates. In 1905 he had the forest lands transferred from the Public Land Office in the Department of the Interior to the newly formed United States Forest Service in the Department of Agriculture. Gifford Pinchot headed the Forest Service and contributed much to arousing the public to the need for governmental action and the creation of an enlightened conservation program.

In his first message to Congress in December 1901 Roosevelt maintained that "forest and water problems are perhaps the most vital internal problems of the United States." With his strong support, Congress in June 1902 passed the National Reclamation Act, usually called the Newlands Act. This measure, opposed by eastern Republicans and many eastern Democrats on the ground it was socialistic, allocated the income from the sale of public land in sixteen western states for the construction of irrigation works such as dams, canals, and ditches. The fund for this purpose was renewed by the proceeds of the sale of irrigated land, at moderate prices, to settlers. Within four years the Department of the Interior undertook twenty-six reclamation projects among them the Shoshone Dam in Wyoming and the Roosevelt Dam on the Salt River in Arizona. By 1915 about 1.5 million acres of semi-arid or desert land had been brought into use.

The need for a nationwide conservation program became obvious. In 1907 Roosevelt appointed an Inland Waterways Commission "to consider the relations of the streams to the use of all the great permanent natural resources," and to prepare "a comprehensive plan for the improvement and control of the river systems of the country." After making its study, the commission advised the president to call a national conference to discuss conservation. Roosevelt invited the governors of the states and territories to such a meeting at the White House in May 1908. Attending were the governors from thirty-four states and five territories, the members of the Supreme Court and the cabinet, congressmen, and delegates of labor and industry. The Governor's Conference emphasized the national character of the conservation problem and encouraged cooperation between the states and the federal government. Within a year and a half of this meeting, forty-one states had created conservation commissions and Roosevelt appointed a National Conservation Commission headed by Pinchot.

As already noted while progressivism came to the United States in these years, it did not come to blacks. In their platforms in this period the Republicans expressed concern about the plight of blacks. They condemned state action that had gotten around the Fifteenth Amendment and advocated the enforcement of that section in the Fourteenth Amendment proportionately reducing representation in Congress and in the electoral college when any state limited the franchise. The Republicans also called upon Congress to find some way to end lynching. The Democrats only came to life on the Negro issue—and in a negative way—when they denounced Republican demands for enforcing the Fourteenth Amendment as an attempt to revive sectional and racial agitation.

Roosevelt occasionally showed deep concern over the blacks' plight; and the disfranchisement, segregation, and lynching of blacks sometimes caused the president to moralize on racial discrimination. Just a few weeks after Roosevelt became president in 1901 he invited the prominent black leader and educator, Booker T. Washington, to have dinner with him and his family at the White House. The two men discussed southern patronage, however, rather than southern sociology. Washington had advised Roosevelt on southern patronage before he became president and continued to do so for years after this. But when Washington's visit to the White House became known, the South was furious. A "most damnable outrage," said one southern newspaper; "little less than a studied insult," commented another.

Roosevelt was surprised by the southern furor over the incident, and he wrote, "It never entered my head that any human being would so much as comment upon it...." But he did not apologize nor did he believe the southern viewpoint would have made him alter his policy. Instead he declared it was his policy to "insist upon good men and [to] take the best man white or black." As for Washington, Roosevelt maintained, "I shall have him to dine just as often as I please. . . ." But he never again invited Washington to a meal at the White House, and he even privately admitted there was some question about the prudence of his action in the first place.

Roosevelt did appoint some blacks to federal offices in the South. The most important of these was his selection of Dr. William D. Crum, prominent black physician, as collector of customs at Charleston, South Carolina. When the Senate failed to confirm Crum's appointment, Roosevelt kept him in office on an interim basis. And the president closed the Indianola, Mississippi, post office when the whites compelled the black postmistress to resign by threatening her life and refused to appoint another postmaster until it became clear no black would accept the position.

The White House invitation, the black appointments in the South, and the closing of the Indianola post office created the impression that Roosevelt was the champion of blacks. "As far as I can learn of him," said Booker T. Washington, "he makes no distinction as to the color of a man's cuticle when he wants to get at facts." And many other blacks probably regarded Roosevelt as their friend and ally. Yet Roosevelt believed that blacks were inferior to whites. "I entirely agree with you," he wrote to Owen Wister "that as a race and in the mass [blacks] are altogether inferior to the whites." He thought blacks would have to make their own future as the Germans and Irish had. Roosevelt also opposed Negro suffrage, stating in 1908 that he had always "felt that the passage of the Fifteenth Amendment at the time it was passed was a mistake." "I believe that the great majority of the Negroes in the south are wholly unfit for suffrage," he wrote to Henry Cabot Lodge, "and that if we were able to succeed in giving them an unbought, uncoerced, and undefrauded suffrage we would reduce parts of the south to the level of Haiti." Roosevelt could hardly be classified as either pro-black or anti-black. For although he regarded the black as inferior, he had no intention of blocking his advance; but neither did he feel deeply obligated to improve his condition. Roosevelt respected and rewarded the "occasionally good" black, and hoped he would someday "earn" social respect and economic security.

Though Roosevelt appointed some blacks in the South, he soon realized he "was faced with the detrimental political consequences of a policy that too many people condemned." So he abandoned it. After 1902 he adopted the policy of wooing the "lily-white Republicans" rather than the "black and tan" in the South, and he supported the idea of having a Republican white man's party in this section of the country. In 1904 Roosevelt explained his new policy to Booker T. Washington. "It seems to me," he wrote, "the safety for the colored man in Louisiana is to have a white man's party which shall be responsible and honest, in which the colored man shall have representation but in which he shall not be the dominant force...."

While Roosevelt adhered to his lily-white policy for the remainder of his presidency, he did not forsake blacks entirely. For example, in 1908 he directed the Department of Justice to take legal action, if necessary, to assure blacks equal accommodations on the Nashville Chattanooga, and St. Louis Railroad. And he occasionally asked Congress "to do everything in their power, officially and unofficially, directly and indirectly, to free the United States from the menace and reproach of lynch law." But Roosevelt did little more. Despite the Republican platforms of 1900 and 1904 condemning the violations of the Fourteenth and Fifteenth Amendments and the fact the Republicans controlled both houses of Congress from 1900 until the 1910 elections, Roosevelt and his party did nothing to fulfill their promises to blacks. The convict lease system in the South* was allowed to stand in virtual violation of the Thirteenth Amendment, and Congress refused to pass legislation to enforce the Fourteenth and Fifteenth Amendments despite increasing disfranchisement of blacks. Not only did Roosevelt make no effort to enforce these amendments, but in 1908 he opposed the insertion of a plank in his party's platform calling for the enforcement of the Fifteenth Amendment.

Blacks were further disappointed in Roosevelt when, in a tour he made of the South in 1905, he urged them to stay out of the professions and to look to southern whites as their best friends. And blacks openly condemned the president when he dishonorably discharged an entire battalion of black soldiers accused of provoking a racial riot in Brownsville, Texas, in August 1906. The New York *Age,* an important black newspaper, censured Roosevelt's order as "an outrage upon the rights of citizens who are entitled in civil life to trial by jury and in military life to trial by court-martial," accused him of being anti-black,

---

*This system, made legal by southern states, authorized the employment of imprisoned blacks by private individuals and corporations for the length of their sentence.

and called the affair "another sacrifice offered by the President upon the altar of southern race prejudice." Roosevelt defended his decision on the ground that his action was precisely the same "I should have taken had the soldiers guilty of the misconduct been white instead of colored men."

Roosevelt's presidency changed the tone of American life and American politics. He was the first president since the rise of industrial capitalism to insist on placing the public welfare above private interests. His principal contribution to the Progressive movement was probably educative rather than legislative. Throughout his presidency he tirelessly called for honesty in government and restraint in public affairs. In part he restored to the voters the political control which ever since the Civil War had been moving into the hands of political machines and wealthy businessmen. He aroused the American public and prepared the way for the later and more spectacular legislative victories of progressivism.

Further Reading

A number of readings for chapter 8 will also be useful for this chapter.

Blum, John M. *The Republican Roosevelt.* 1954.

Braeman, John. *Alfred J. Beveridge.* 1971.

Case, Belle, and Fola La Follette. *Robert M. La Follette, 1855–1925.* 2 vols., 1953.

Chessman, G. Wallace. *Theodore Roosevelt and the Politics of Power.* 1968.

Coletta, Paolo E. *William Jennings Bryan: Political Evangelist, 1860–1908.* 1960.

Cooper, John Milton, Jr. *The Warrior and the Priest: Woodrow Wilson and Theodore Roosevelt.* 1983.

Cutright, Paul Russell. *Theodore Roosevelt: the Making of a Conservationist.* 1985.

Garraty, John A. *Henry Cabot Lodge.* 1953.

Gatewood, Willard B., Jr. *Theodore Roosevelt and the Art of Controversy: Episodes of the White House Years.* 1970.

Harbaugh, William H. *Power and Responsibility: The Life and Times of Theodore Roosevelt.* 1961.

Koenig, Louis W. *Bryan: A Political Biography.* 1971.

Lowitt, Richard. *George W. Norris: The Making of a Progressive.* 1963.

Merrill, Horace S., and Marion G. Merrill. *The Republican Command, 1897–1913.* 1971.

Morison, Elting E., et al., eds. *The Letters of Theodore Roosevelt.* 8 vols., 1951–1954.
Morris, Edmund E. *The Rise of Theodore Roosevelt.* 1979.
Mowry, George E. *Theodore Roosevelt and the Progressive Movement.* 1946.
Pringle, Henry F. *Theodore Roosevelt.* 1956.
Pusey, Merlo J. *Charles Evans Hughes.* 2 vols., 1951.
Thelen, David P. *Robert M. La Follette and the Insurgent Spirit.* 1976.

10

Taft and Progressive Insurgency

Although in 1904 Roosevelt had declined consideration of another term of office pressure was put on him to change his mind. In fact, a movement to draft Roosevelt got under way until the White House issued a statement in December 1907 calling attention to what Roosevelt had said in 1904 about another term and pointing out that he had not changed his mind. Had Roosevelt decided to run again he could have won the nomination of his party in 1908 and likely have been elected. He was still a young man in 1908, only 50 years old, and still had his vigor and ambition. And he still very much wanted to be president, for as he said during the 1908 campaign, "I should like to have stayed on in the Presidency." But being devoted to democratic traditions, he stuck to his important and difficult decision not to run again.

Roosevelt, however, wanted a successor who would carry out his policies. He had strong preference for Elihu Root, his secretary of state, but Root was vulnerable because he had been a corporation lawyer, and Roosevelt realized this. So Roosevelt's friend and secretary of war, William Howard Taft of Ohio, became the leading candidate and was nominated on the first ballot at the Republican convention in Chicago. His running mate was James Sherman, a conservative from New York. The platform praised Roosevelt's "great achievements" and promised to continue his policies. It called for a strengthening of the Interstate Commerce and Sherman Antitrust Acts, conservation of natural resources and the reclamation of arid lands, good roads, and a postal savings system. It also advocated tariff revision. A number of western Republican delegates led by Robert La Follette tried to have the convention adopt more progressive planks advocating the direct election of United States senators, legislation requiring public reports of campaign expenditures, and a standard valuation of railroad properties, but they were unsuccessful.

At the Democratic convention in Denver, Bryan and his supporters were in control and, despite the opposition of the conservatives, he was easily nominated on the first ballot. John W. Kern, an Indiana lawyer, was nominated for vice-president. The platform denounced the Republican party as the organization of "privilege and private monopoly," and stated that the paramount issue was "Shall the people rule?" The platform called for a reduction in the tariff, new antitrust legislation, effective limitations on injunctions issued by federal courts in labor disputes, and laws prohibiting corporations from contributing to campaign funds. Five minor parties put candidates in the field.

The election failed to stir the voters. Stump speakers and political leaders were active, but the voters did not respond. Neither candidate aroused much inspiration. Taft was not the campaigner Roosevelt was, and the novelty of Bryan's campaign had worn off. Roosevelt plugged hard for Taft and advised him constantly on what to do. Taft won by more than a million votes and an electoral vote of 321 to 162 for Bryan. The outcome seemed to be a sweeping Republican victory, and on the surface there was little to cheer the Democratic party. Though Bryan was badly beaten, his party was not. While Taft's assurances of loyalty to Roosevelt's policies kept the western states in line, his pluralities in this part of the country were less than those of 1904, and his plurality in the country was far below that of Roosevelt's in 1904. Throughout the nation Democratic candidate for local and state offices gained victories. Republican majorities in Congress were smaller than those of 1906, and there was an increase in the strength of Republican insurgency in the Middle West. Roosevelt's name was still magic in politics, but there had been much independent thinking and voting. The future fate of the Republican party depended upon Taft's ability to reconcile its progressive and conservative wings.

Taft fell heir to a difficult situation when he entered the presidency. Roosevelt had entertained the country with his speeches, recommendations, and versatility. The nation expected Taft to carry

Roosevelt's policies to completion, and the new president had promised to do this in his inaugural address. To make Roosevelt's reforms permanent and at the same time to promote stability and security in business circles, new legislation was necessary. Therefore, Taft urged a reorganization of the Department of Justice, of the Bureau of Corporations, and of the Interstate Commerce Commission to establish a more definite policy concerning business. He also recommended changes in the monetary and banking laws to secure a more elastic currency and called for a new tariff law, expressing a hope for reduction in rates.

Taft regarded himself as a progressive. Like Roosevelt he believed in the supremacy of public over private interests. Had he held office at some other time he might have been a success. But he was president during a period of much agitation and unrest, both in the country and within his party. What was needed was bold, aggressive leadership, and Taft could not give this because of his judicial temperament. He had too many constitutional and judicial qualms about his role in the presidency from Roosevelt's. Roosevelt believed it was the president's duty "to do anything that the needs of the nation demanded, unless such action is forbidden by the Constitution or the laws." Thus, Roosevelt looked to the Constitution to see only what he could *not* do. Taft maintained the president could do only those things where he had specific authority under the Constitution, and thus he looked to the Constitution to see what he *could* do.

Taft's concept of the presidency is one of the reasons for the troubles and insurgency that emerged within the Republican party during his administration. Under Taft the national initiative, held firmly by Roosevelt, largely passed to Congress, and in this body to conservative leaders like Aldrich and Cannon. Their control of Congress was resented by the progressive Republicans. Aldrich and Cannon believed the reform program had gone far enough, if not too far already. Unfortunately, Taft appeared to be more conservative than he really was and seemed to be in the hands of the conservative leaders of his party. In theory he agreed with much of the program of the progressive Republicans, and in his own way he wished to promote progressivism. But he had no desire to fight the Old Guard who became his chief counsel and support. Besides, Taft had neither the great personal appeal nor dramatic quality of his predecessor.

Nonetheless, the achievements of Taft's administration are impressive. He did much in a quiet, untheatrical way to further reform, and during his presidency there was important progressive legislation. There are several reasons for this. The momentum given to reform legislation by Roosevelt carried over to the Taft administration. Many of the issues were nonpartisan in nature, and congressmen were responding to popular demands during a reform period. But in all fairness to Taft, he did support much of this legislation. Had he possessed Roosevelt's gift of showmanship he might have capitalized on these achievements for political advantage. While historians generally regard Taft as more of a progressive than did his contemporaries, they believe his effectiveness as a reformer was largely nullified by his ineptitude as a politician. Instead of attempting to mollify dissident groups within his party, he often gave the impression he was going out of his way to antagonize them.

Taft's first problem was the tariff. Roosevelt was aware of the popular discontent over the tariff and was tempted to take the leadership for tariff reform. But he failed to act, because the conservative Republican leaders warned him such action would disrupt the party, and because he placed railroad and trust regulation ahead of the tariff issue.

There had been no change in the tariff schedules since the Dingley Tariff of 1897, and many Americans believed these high rates were in part responsible for the increased cost of living and the rapid growth of trusts. During the campaign, Taft, against Roosevelt's advice, called for "a sizeable reduction" in the tariff rates. Taft realized the danger of this promise. He knew the progressives favored a reduction and the conservatives opposed it, and he also knew Cannon had told Roosevelt that any attempt to change the tariff would split the party.

Taft called Congress into special session in March 1909 for the sole purpose of considering revisions in the Dingley Tariff. The House passed the Payne bill which reduced many rates, but in the Senate Aldrich took charge of the tariff measure and practically rewrote it with the hundreds of changes the Finance Committee added to the bill, most of them increasing the rates. Aldrich wanted the Senate to adopt the amended version as a party measure and without discussing its details. But a group of progressive Republicans from the Middle West, led by La Follette, forced a debate and an examination of the bill. They discovered Aldrich and his followers had created a false impression about rates being cut. A number of articles Americans neither wanted nor needed had been placed on a free or reduced list, while there was a retention of high rates on essential items such as raw wool and woolen cloth. The bill contained a number of "jokers," and "Mr. Dooley" pointed this out when he said the Aldrich amendments had left curling stones, false teeth, canary bird seed, hog bristles, silkworm eggs, stilts, skeletons, and leeches on the free list. "Th' new Tariff Bill," he observed, "puts these familyar commodyties within th' reach iv all." Known now as the Payne-Aldrich Tariff, the bill passed both houses of Congress, and Taft signed it on 5 August 1909.

Taft was not happy about the tariff because the rates had not been reduced more substantially. But he signed it because he believed it was "really a good bill" and one he could justify "as a revision substantially downward." He also did not wish to fight the conservative leadership in his party on the matter, and he feared a veto would divide the Republican party.

The Payne-Aldrich Tariff disappointed progressive Republicans. The press was also hostile to it, partly because rates on wood for newsprint had not been materially reduced. Taft, worried about the unfavorable treatment of the tariff, decided to say something about it. He believed the public deserved a better explanation than what the press gave it. And conservative Republicans, alarmed by insurgency in their party in the West, had asked the president for help. On a speaking tour Taft made in the fall of 1909 he spoke at Winona, Minnesota, where he defended the Payne-Aldrich Tariff and declared: "I would say without hesitation that this is the best tariff bill that the Republican party has ever passed, and therefore, the best tariff bill that has been passed at all...." Taft was referring to some technical and administrative features of the law, making it an improvement over previous tariffs. But the press lifted the statement out of context as evidence of Taft being in league with the corporations and of going back on his promise to reduce the tariff. As the Des Moines (Iowa) *News* exclaimed, "Shades of Theodore Roosevelt! May ghosts of animals he has killed in Africa ever haunt him for having foisted on the country this man Taft."

Having failed to obtain the tariff reduction he wanted, Taft tried by diplomatic means to establish a system of reciprocity with Canada. In July 1910 Congress approved and Taft signed an agreement with Canada providing for free trade in grain, vegetables, and certain dairy products, and for reciprocal reductions of tariffs on flour, meats, and manufactured goods. But now Taft began to learn how troublesome the tariff question could be. Farmers who in 1909 had denounced the Payne-Aldrich Tariff because its rates were too high, attacked the Canadian reciprocity agreement because the rates were too low. However,

Canada rather than the United States finally rejected reciprocity. The project became involved in Canadian politics. The Liberals in Canada had worked out the reciprocity agreement, but the Conservatives opposed it on the grounds it would exploit Canada and eventually bring about the annexation of the Dominion to the United States. Thus, Canadians were alarmed when Champ Clark defended reciprocity in the House with the argument, "I hope to see the day when the American flag will float over every square foot of the British North American possessions clear to the North Pole." The reciprocity issue caused the Canadian Parliament to be dissolved and, in the new election, the Liberals and the reciprocity agreement were defeated.

Taft also ran into trouble with the progressive Republicans in the Ballinger-Pinchot controversy. Taft had not retained James R. Garfield, secretary of the interior under Roosevelt, but had replaced him in the cabinet with Richard A. Ballinger who had been commissioner of the Land Office under Garfield. This irritated Roosevelt, because Garfield agreed with the conservation policies of Roosevelt and Pinchot, and because Roosevelt believed Taft had promised to keep Garfield in the cabinet. Ballinger, a lawyer like Taft, reopened to public entry some water power sites in Montana and Wyoming and some coal lands in Alaska, because he regarded Roosevelt's action in setting aside these areas as illegal. Louis Glavis, one of Ballinger's subordinates, and Pinchot, chief of the Forestry Service, vigorously and publicly protested this decision. They charged Ballinger with being in league with greedy corporate interests seeking to gain control of the country's mineral reserves and water power sites and with criminal conspiracy in a deal to turn over valuable public resources to private interests.

After an investigation of the charges, Taft decided Ballinger had acted correctly. Then the president dismissed Glavis, and later on he removed Pinchot. Though Taft was a friend of conservation and continued and extended Roosevelt's policies on timber, coal, and oil lands, his dismissal of Pinchot, one of the most popular leaders of the conservationists, persuaded many that the president was against conservation, and widened the split between himself and the progressive Republicans who supported Pinchot. Moreover, Pinchot was one of Roosevelt's close friends, and his removal contributed to the widening breach between Taft and his predecessor.

Taft and his attorney general, George C. Wickersham, continued and intensified Roosevelt's antitrust policy. Taft proposed a federal incorporation law for firms engaged in interstate commerce, a corporation commission, and a means to end the watering of stock, but Congress refused to act on any of these measures. Taft had no desire to destroy the trusts. His policy was, as he stated, to investigate "all the industrial companies with respect to which there is any reasonable ground for suspicion that they have been organized for a purpose, and are conducting business on a plan which is in violation of the antitrust law." Thus Taft, like Roosevelt, maintained that size alone did not violate the law; it was only when large concentrations of capital, legal in themselves, were used for unjust purposes that they were subject to indictments. It was for the purpose of distinguishing between good and bad trusts that Taft recommended federal incorporation, with some supervision and considerable publicity. He reasoned that law-abiding corporations would voluntarily seek the benefits of federal incorporation, and those refusing to do so would come under suspicion and be prosecuted. Taft overlooked the fact that the profits of even some of the good trusts were so large that they would object to publicity. So business opposed the plan.

The Taft administration instituted ninety antitrust suits—more than twice as many as Roosevelt—and secured forty-three indictments. The president moved against such industrial giants as the General Electric Company, National Cash Register Company, United Shoe Machinery Company, United States Steel, International Harvester Company, the American Sugar Refining Company, and the Corn Products Refining Company. His two most important cases, against United States Steel and International Harvester, ended in failure. In his two most significant victories, over the Standard Oil Company of New Jersey and the American Tobacco Company in 1911, action on the cases had been started by Roosevelt.

Taft also secured new railroad legislation, the Mann-Elkins Act of 1910. This extended the Interstate Commerce Commission's authority over cable, telephone, and telegraph companies. It gave the commission power to suspend new general rate increases for ten months until they had been examined for their reasonableness. The commission could act on its own initiative without waiting for a complaint from a shipper. The measure outlawed the long- and short-haul abuse and created a Commerce Court to review the commission's decisions. However, because of the court's unpopularity and a scandal involving one of its judges it was abolished in 1912. La Follette unsuccessfully attempted to secure authority for the commission to make a study of the physical valuation of the railroads to provide a basis for fixing rates representing a reasonable return on actual investment. But this did not come until the Physical Valuation Act of 1913.

There were other reform achievements of the Taft years. Although he could not persuade Congress to restrict the use of the injunction in labor disputes, he was able to secure some reforms for labor. On his recommendation Congress created the Bureau of Mines to regulate safety in the mines. Other measures in behalf of labor regulated safety on railroads, abolished the production of white phosporous matches, established a Children's Bureau in the federal government, created a separate Department of Labor, fixed the eight-hour day for workers on government contracts, prohibited the transportation of women across state lines for immoral purposes, and enacted a federal Employers' Liability Law.

Other important legislative developments of the Taft years included: a law requiring publication of the names of persons contributing to campaign funds in federal elections, the amounts given, and a detailed account of the expenditures of the candidates and the purposes of these outlays (1910); the establishment of the postal savings system (1910) and of the parcel post system (1912); the Sixteenth Amendment (income tax) and Seventeenth Amendment (direct election of United States senators) to the federal Constitution; the admission of Arizona and New Mexico as states (1912); the placing of all assistant postmasters under civil service; the giving of territorial status to Alaska; and Taft's veto (February 1913) of an act of Congress imposing the literacy test on foreign immigrants entering the country.

Thus Taft's record for progressive measures and reform achievements is a good one. If he had been a more colorful personality and possessed some of Roosevelt's showmanship, he might have received more credit for advancing the reform movement.

Many blacks had opposed Taft in the campaign of 1908 because he had been chosen by Roosevelt whose handling of the Brownsville riot in 1906 had angered them. Booker T. Washington urged his race to support Taft, however, and when Bryan attempted to exploit the Brownsville affair, Washington asserted that "the bulk of the negro people. . . are more and more inclined to reach the decision that even though the President did go against their wishes in dismissing the soldiers at Brownsville. . . the intelligent portion of the race does not believe that it is fair or wise to condemn such good friends as Roosevelt and Taft." Largely through the efforts of Washington and Charles W.

Anderson, another black moderate, and the reputation of Roosevelt and the Republican party among blacks, Taft was able to overcome some of the ill effects of the Brownsville affair.

Nevertheless, a more assertive black group led by William Monroe Trotter and William E. B. Du Bois actively opposed Taft's election. They revolted against Washington's moderate position on Negro rights and formed their own movement at Niagara Falls, Canada, in June 1905, where they adopted a platform demanding political and economic equality for blacks. Known as the Niagara Movement they met the following year at Harpers Ferry, West Virginia, the place of John Brown's raid and stated, "We will not be satisfied to take one jot or tittle less than our full manhood rights...and until we get these rights we will never cease to protest and assail the ears of America." Late in 1907 the Niagara Movement organized the National Independent Political League to fight Taft, and after his victory, Du Bois comforted himself with the belief that "more Negroes had voted against Mr. Taft than ever before voted against a Republican candidate."

In its 1908 platform the Republican party claimed it had been for more than fifty years "the consistent friend of the American Negro," and had given him "freedom and citizenship." The platform demanded "equal justice for all men, without regard to race and color"; called "once more, and without reservation, for the enforcement in letter and spirit of the Thirteenth, Fourteenth, and Fifteenth amendments"; and condemned all devices to disfranchise the black as "unfair, unamerican, and repugnant to the Supreme Law of the land." During the campaign, however, Taft remained silent on the black question. But in an address to a meeting of the North Carolina Society in New York City about a month after his election, Taft stated that the federal government would intervene if the southern states did not abide by the electoral requirements established by the state legislatures. In his inaugural address, Taft again said he would use the force of the federal government to secure the black's voting rights if the South attempted to avoid the law. But seemingly to placate white southerners, he added, "Therefore, the Chief Executive, in recognizing the Negro race by appointments, must exercise a careful discretion that thereby to do it more harm than good." White southerners interpreted these remarks to mean Taft would not appoint any more blacks in the South and that he would dismiss some of those appointed by Roosevelt.

Like Roosevelt, Taft made no effort to enforce the Fourteenth and Fifteenth Amendments. Also like his predecessor, Taft toured the

South where he stressed the theme that the southern white was the best friend of the black. Despite the 1908 plank and Taft's subsequent statements, he gave the assurance there was no inconsistency between black disfranchisement and the Fifteenth Amendment. During Roosevelt's and Taft's presidencies, lynchings continued to be one of the great shames of the United States. From 1901 through 1910 there were 846 lynchings in the country, 754 were of blacks, and 91.1 percent of them took place in the South including Missouri, Kentucky, and Oklahoma. Neither major party in this period made a specific statement about lynching, and neither Roosevelt nor Taft nor Congress took any action to prevent the lynching of blacks. Senator Ben Tillman of South Carolina expressed an extreme white southern position when he said "to hell with Constitution," if it interfered with the lynching of rapists.

One of Taft's most trying difficulties was congressional insurgency in his own party. A group of western progressive Republicans revolted against the conservative leadership of Cannon and Aldrich. The leaders of this insurgency were George W. Norris of Nebraska in the House and La Follette and Wiliam E. Borah of Idaho in the Senate. Other well-known insurgents in the House were Edmond Madison of Kansas, John M. Nelson of Wisconsin, Victor Murdock of Kansas, Miles Poindexter of Washington, and Charles A. Lindbergh of Minnesota; and in the Senate, Albert B. Cummins and Jonathan P. Dolliver of Iowa, Joseph L. Bristow of Kansas, Moses E. Clapp of Minnesota, and Albert J. Beveridge of Indiana. The insurgents came from normally Republican states, but ones that were principally associated with agriculture. They were individualistic, rebellious, and vain and found it difficult to follow the party leadership in Congress. They liked being cast in the role of insurgents and "Gladiators of the Senate," as they were sometimes called.

The Republican insurgency in the House was largely directed toward limiting the powers of Speaker "Uncle Joe" Cannon. Cannon objected to "all babble for reform" and thus was regarded by the insurgents as an archreactionary and standpatter. Moreover, Cannon had great power, probably the greatest ever held by an American legislator, and he used it to promote conservative policies and to block progressive ones. Cannon appointed a majority of the members of all committees, including the important Rules Committee, and their chairmen. In this way, he was able to reward the loyal and discipline the rebellious. As chairman of the Rules Committee, Cannon decided what legislation would, and would not, be presented for consideration on the floor. He also determined the procedure in the House and controlled its debates. Thus, Cannon's position was one of extraordinary importance, and the progressive Republicans were anxious to reduce his authority.

The progressives resented the apparent close cooperation between Taft and Cannon and Aldrich. Roosevelt, an expert in group diplomacy in politics, had never appeared to be in either the conservative or progressive camp and had prevented any serious break in Republican ranks while he was president. But Taft, unlike Roosevelt, was unable to harmonize both groups and to subordinate them to his leadership. Personally, Taft disliked Cannon because he used profanity, played poker, and drank, and he objected to the Speaker's extreme conservatism. The president had misgivings about both Aldrich and Cannon and sometimes called them "wicked partners." He considered the possibility of removing Cannon as Speaker, but found him "so strongly entrenched...that it was impossible." Moreover, Roosevelt advised Taft not to fight Cannon.

The insurgents, with the support of the Democrats, were able in the spring of 1910 to exclude the Speaker from the Rules Committee, thereby breaking some of the iron grip Cannon held on the House. In 1911, with the Democrats in control of the House following the 1910 election, further limitations were placed on the Speaker's power by denying him the right to make committee assignments. Taft privately approved of these changes, but because he had not encouraged the insurgents in any way, they and the country concluded that the president was on Cannon's side.

In addition to insurgency, the old friendship between Roosevelt and Taft was broken. Roosevelt believed Taft had not only abandoned his policies but had allowed the Old Guard to maneuver him into a position making insurgency inevitable. In Roosevelt's eyes this was unpardonable, and he condemned Taft not for being a conservative, but for failing to keep "the party in substantial unity."

In the summer of 1910 Roosevelt made a speaking tour of the West, at the request of Republican leaders, in behalf of the party campaign that year. He tried not to side with one or the other of the two Republican factions, but as he spoke his ideas began to place him on the side of the progressives. At Osawatomie, Kansas, he voiced the creed of the New Nationalism when he advocated publicity for corporate affairs, government control over corporate capitalization, government supervision of corporations controlling the necessities of life, income and inheritance taxes, tariff revision, workmen's compensation laws, child labor laws, the direct primary, publication of campaign contributions before election time, and a ban upon the use of corporate funds for political purposes. He had earlier championed the cause of the initiative, referendum, and recall. Roosevelt asserted the New Nationalism "puts the national need before sectional and personal advantage," and subjects property to the public welfare. "Every man holds his property subject to the general right of community to regulate its use to whatever degree the public welfare may require it," he declared. Roosevelt's speech stirred the West, but it jarred conservative opinion, alienated the Old Guard, and antagonized even many moderate conservatives who had hitherto thought well of him. The New York *Evening Post* described Roosevelt's position as "not only the most extreme utterance that he himself ever made previously, but [that of] the most radical man in public life in our time.

The 1910 election was a Republican rout. The Democrats gained control of the House and picked up enough seats in the Senate to give them, when combined with those of the insurgents, control of that body. The Democrats elected twenty-six state governors, including one in Taft's own state and in such staunchly Republican states as Maine, Massachusetts, New York, New Jersey, and Indiana.

After the Republican defeat in 1910, the insurgent Republicans decided to break completely with Taft. Their aim was not to organize a new party but to capture control of the Republican party and nominate a candidate for president who supported their principles. In December 1910 they publicly defined these principles as "the promotion of popular government and progressive legislation," and went on to say in their declaration that government and legislation of this type "has been thwarted and...strangled by the special interests, which control caucuses, delegates, conventions, and party organizations." In January 1911 at La Follette's home in Washington, they organized the National Republican Progressive League. Senator Jonathan Bourne of Oregon was elected president of the league, but La Follette was the real leader. The league criticized the Taft administration for failing to secure satisfactory legislation on the tariff, trusts, banking, and conservation. And in its program to take government out of the hands of the privileged few and restore it to the people, the league advocated direct election of United States senators, direct primaries, presidential primaries, and the initiative, referendum, and recall.

In the light of what Roosevelt had said in the 1910 campaign, the insurgents asked him to join the league. Roosevelt refused, although he was not unfriendly toward them. On the assumption Roosevelt would not seek another term, La Follette launched his campaign to defeat Taft for the nomination, receiving financial assistance from a group of liberal millionaires such as Medill McCormick of Chicago, Joseph Fels of Philadelphia, and Rudolph Spreckels of San Francisco. If La Follette could obtain Roosevelt's backing, he had a good chance for the nomination. La Follette maintained he had a definite promise of support from Roosevelt, but there is no proof of this. This much is certain: at first Roosevelt gave La Follette informal encouragement, but he never endorsed La Follette's candidacy and, ultimately, weakened it by refusing to disavow his own availability.

A number of progressives had wanted Roosevelt all along and had sought a pretext to cancel their pledge of support to La Follette. This opportunity came on 21 February 1912, when La Follette, tired and ill, suffered a temporary nervous collapse while delivering a major speech. Many of his followers abandoned him with the excuse he was too ill to push the progressive fight, and they asked Roosevelt to lead them. A month earlier, Roosevelt had sent Frank Knox, later to be secretary of the navy under Franklin D. Roosevelt, to obtain the signatures of seven progressive Republican governors from Kansas, Michigan, Missouri, Nebraska, New Hampshire, West Virginia, and Wyoming to a letter—written by Roosevelt himself—asking him to run against Taft. On 12 February the letter appeared; on 21 February in a reply to a reporter's question, Roosevelt declared, "my hat is in the ring, the fight is on and I am stripped to the buff." Three days later in reply to the seven governors he wrote: "I will accept the nomination for President if it is tendered to me, and I will adhere to this decision until the convention has expressed its preference." Roosevelt now assumed the leadership of the progressive Republicans and challenged Taft. La Follette, now very bitter toward Roosevelt, believed he had been used as a stalking horse to measure and drum up progressive sentiment for putting Roosevelt in the field at the right time. La Follette regarded this as treachery to himself and the Progressive movement.

Though La Follette's cause collapsed, he stayed in the fight, and a three-way bitter struggle developed for the Republican nomination. Presidential primaries came into prominence, and on the basis of the primary vote, Roosevelt appeared as the overwhelming favorite. Out of

388 delegates elected to the national convention in 13 states using the presidential primary, Roosevelt received 281 to Taft's 71 and La Follette's 36. But the Taft people controlled the national convention at Chicago and won 235 of the 254 contested delegates' seats. On the night proceeding the opening of the convention, Roosevelt addressed a mass meeting. It was a moving speech, especially the closing words, quoted widely at the time and ever since: "We fight in honorable fashion for the good of mankind; fearless of the future, unheeding of our individual fates, with unflinching hearts and undimmed eyes; we stand at Armageddon, and we battle for the Lord." But Taft was renominated on the first ballot with 561 votes to 107 for Roosevelt, 41 for La Follette, 17 for Cummins, and 2 for Huges. Taft's margin of victory, appearing to be wide, was really a narrow one, because 344 Roosevelt delegates refused to vote, and 6 delegates were absent. Some historians believe at least 50 Roosevelt delegates were unfairly deprived of their seats in the fight over contested delegates, and had Roosevelt won these seats he might have gained the nomination. James Sherman was again chosen as Taft's running mate. He died before election day and Nicholas Murray Butler, president of Columbia University, replaced him.

The Republicans, aware of the reform sentiment in the country, advocated in their platform maximum hour laws for women and children, workmen's compensation laws, reforms in legal procedures, revision of the currency system, and parcel post. The platform still favored a protective tariff but admitted some rates were too high. It asked for a clarification of the antitrust laws and for a federal trade commission without specifying its function. The platform also called for an investigation of the high cost of living, easier credit facilities for farmers, the prohibition of corporation contributions to campaign funds, and publicity for all contributions.

Roosevelt accused the Republican national committee and Taft of fraud and charged the convention with overriding "the legally expressed will of the people" and of substituting "a dishonest for an honest majority." Immediately following Taft's nomination, the Roosevelt delegates and a large following met in another building and nominated Roosevelt. But he advised them to go home, sound out public sentiment, and then if they found evidence of popular support, they could call another convention and name a progressive upon a progressive platform.

With a Republican split assured, Democratic hopes went up. The leading contenders were the Speaker of the House, Champ Clark of

Missouri, Governor Judson Harmon of Ohio, Congressman Oscar W. Underwood of Alabama, and Governor Woodrow Wilson of New Jersey. Clark led on the early ballots and had a majority on the second day of voting, but he lacked the necessary two-thirds vote, a formidable obstacle for many Democratic aspirants ever since the party adopted this rule in 1836. When Tammany boss Charles F. Murphy switched the New York delegation on the tenth ballot from Harmon to Clark, Bryan shifted his support from Clark to Wilson on the fourteenth ballot. And while this has been regarded as being important if not essential in securing the nomination for Wilson, Arthur S. Link, the leading Wilson scholar in the country, maintains Bryan's action "was of no great help to the Wilson leaders." They worked not on Bryan men, "most of whom were fanatically loyal to Clark," but on the boss-controlled and Underwood delegates. Finally, on the forty-second ballot Roger Sullivan, the Chicago Democratic boss, put the Illinois delegation in Wilson's column, and the Underwood men changed to Wilson on the forty-sixth ballot, thus giving the nomination to the New Jersey governor. "What had seemed impossible only a few days before was now a reality," writes Link, "one of the miracles of modern American politics." Governor Thomas R. Marshall of Indiana received the nomination for vice-president.

Bryan still played an influential role in the Democratic party and dominated the writing of the platform, a Progressive document. It called for a downward revision of the tariff, a decentralized banking system free from control of eastern bankers, and legislation to "make it impossible for a private monopoly to exist in the United States." It also favored presidential preference primaries, a single term for the president, prohibition of corporation contributions to campaign funds, and exemption of labor unions from application of the Sherman Antitrust Act.

Now Roosevelt and his supporters decided to organize the new Progressive party. Its symbol was the "Bull Moose," adopted from Roosevelt's statement that he felt as "fit as a Bull Moose." The convention, meeting in Chicago in August, was marked by the presence of women delegates and by its religious atmosphere. "John Brown's Body" and "Onward Christian Soldiers" were sung, and social worker Jane Addams of Hull House delivered one of the speeches. Roosevelt made a "Confession of Faith" and denounced both old parties as "husks, with no real soul within either... boss-ridden and privilege-controlled, each a jumble of incongruous elements, and neither daring to speak out wisely and fearlessly on what should be the vital issues of the day." Roosevelt and Hiram Johnson of California were the nominees. The platform, the high-water mark of progressivism up to then, called for direct primaries, direct election of senators, initiative, referendum, and recall, woman's suffrage, limitation of campaign expenditures, a faster way to amend the Constitution, prohibition of child labor, the eight-hour day, a "living wage," social insurance, a federal trade commission, and a tariff commission.

The 1912 campaign represented the first meaningful division in American politics since 1896. The two extremes were occupied by Taft and Eugene V. Debs, the Socialist candidate. The Republican platform had progressive planks but, to the voters, Taft represented the Old Guard. The only speech Taft made was his acceptance speech, and late in July he wrote, "I think I might as well give up so far as being a candidate is concerned. There are so many people in the country who don't like me." Debs and the Socialist party campaigned on the platform of gradual nationalization of the nation's resources and industries.

The principal fight was between Roosevelt and Wilson. Both believed the most important problem for government was its relationship to business. Both favored using the power of government to protect the ordinary citizen. But they had different viewpoints on how to deal with this matter. Roosevelt's program, the New Nationalism, called for an expansion of federal power and participation in social and economic affairs. He contended the trusts were both necessary and inevitable. What was now needed was not new legislation and prosecution aimed at breaking up the large corporations, but federal regulation of them by means of a governmental commission to protect the consumers and to give smaller producers economic opportunities. In addition, Roosevelt's campaign envisaged the modern concept of the welfare state. As the campaign progressed, Roosevelt more and more stressed the social justice side of his program, calling for a minimum wage for women, a federal child labor law, a federal workmen's compensation act, federal intervention in labor disputes, and expanded federal health and conservation programs.

Wilson's program, the New Freedom, rejected the theory of public control of big business as advocated by Roosevelt and many other progressives. He had been a more recent convert to progressivism than Roosevelt and was still largely influenced by nineteenth-century laissez-faire concepts and the Democratic belief in states' rights. He was closer to the Jeffersonian tradition and hoped to see the progressive goals attained as largely as possible through state action. He believed the power of the federal government should be used only to destroy special privileges blocking individual development and to restore competition. Thus, he advocated a strengthening of the antitrust legislation to maintain and restore competition in private industry. "I stand, as the party behind me stands," he told an Indiana audience in 1912, "for regulated competition of a sort that will put the weak upon an equality with the strong." Also during the campaign, Wilson denounced Roosevelt's social welfare program as bureaucratic statism and paternalism. "The history of liberty," Wilson said, "is the history of the limitation of governmental power....If America is not to have free enterprise then she can have freedom of no sort."

Wilson with 6.3 million popular votes, or just under 42 percent of the total, carried 40 states and amassed 435 electoral votes. Roosevelt, with 4.1 million popular votes, more than 27 percent, won only 6 states and 88 electoral votes. Taft polled 3.5 million votes, slightly more than 23 percent, carried only 2 states (Utah and Vermont), and received 8 electoral votes. Debs secured 897,011 votes, about 6 percent of the total, and more than double his vote in 1908. The Democrats won control of both houses of Congress.

Though Roosevelt fought hard in 1912 and stirred many Americans, his Bull Moose campaign failed for several reasons. Wilson appeared progressive enough and ran on a progressive platform, making it difficult for Roosevelt to woo many progressive Democrats from their party. Since the Progressive party was not formed until August 1912, there was not enough time to develop a precinct organization for the party in the country and probably not enough time to conduct the campaign. Then there was Roosevelt's policy in the South. He rejected the idea of attempting to build a party there on black strength and instead sought to organize a lily-white Progressive party. Roosevelt maintained the only man who could help the black in the South was his white neighbor, and therefore, he wanted the Progressive party in this section led by white men. This policy angered northern blacks and also southern whites who believed Roosevelt still straddled the Negro issue. Hurting Roosevelt further in the South was the high tariff plank in the progressive platform. The attempt to appeal to rising manufacturing interests in the South on this issue was offset by progressive

platform demands for social justice, which repelled southern businessmen. Finally, one must remember that no party has ever won the presidency on its first time out.

Further Reading

A number of the readings for Chapters 8 and 9 will also be useful for this
chapter.

Anderson, Donald E. *William Howard Taft.* 1973.

Bryan, William Jennings. *A Tale of Two Conventions.* 1912.

Coletta, Paolo E. *The Presidency of William Howard Taft.* 1973.

Davidson, John W., ed. *A Crossroad of Freedom, The 1912 Campaign
Speeches of Woodrow Wilson.* 1956.

Hechler, Kenneth W. *Insurgency: Personalities and Politics of the Taft Era.*
1940.

Holt, James. *Congressional Insurgents and the Party System, 1909-1916.* 1967.

Link, Arthur S. *Wilson: The Road to the White House.* 1947.

Manners, William. *TR and Will.* 1969.

Pringle, Henry F. *Life and Time of William Howard Taft.* 2 vols., 1939.

Roosevelt, Theodore. *The New Nationalism.* 1910.

Wilson, Woodrow. *The New Freedom.* 1913.

Wilensky, Norman M. *Conservatives in the Progressive Era: The Taft Republicans of 1912.* 1965.

11

Woodrow Wilson and the New Freedom

Woodrow Wilson (1856–1924) was born in Staunton, Virginia, and spent most of his childhood and youth in Georgia and South Carolina. He was profoundly influenced by his experiences in the South, saying on one occasion, "The only place in the country, the only place in the world where nothing has to be explained to me is the South." The son of a Presbyterian minister and reared in a church emphasizing the rule of law and the moral code in politics, Wilson was also deeply affected by his religious faith. "My life would not be worth living if it were not for the driving power of religion," he said, "for faith, pure, and simple, I have seen all my life the arguments against it without having been moved by them." Educated at Davidson College and Princeton University, he studied law at the University of Virginia and practiced law for a year in Atlanta. Then he turned to graduate work at Johns Hopkins University where in 1886 he won his Ph.D. in history. His dissertation, *Congressional Government,* became his most famous and popular book. It was a critique of Congress, and his thesis was that American political leadership was ineffective because of the separation of executive and legislative powers.

From 1885 to 1902 he taught at Bryn Mawr, Wesleyan, and Princeton, and he soon became an eminent lecturer and writer. In 1902 he was made president of Princeton, where he brought about significant educational changes but had trouble with the faculty, trustees, students, and alumni.

While he was acquiring a national reputation as an educational leader, Wilson emerged as a spokesman for Democratic conservatism. He was hostile toward organized labor describing himself as a "fierce partisan of the Open Shop and of everything that makes for individual liberty." He maintained that organized labor was just as much an enemy to freedom of opportunity as were the capitalists. He was intolerant of agrarian radicalism and called the Populists "crude and ignorant." He criticized trust busting on the ground it destroyed "individual liberty." He labeled Roosevelt a "radical" and his program a "hostile one." He thought Bryan's ideas should be "knocked once and for all into a cocked hat," and he asked the Democratic party to stand again for the "conservative principles it once represented." Wilson was not so critical of the business community as he was of the Populists and trade unions. He believed trade was still the carrier of ideas and progress. In 1902 he told the Chicago Commercial Club that "Every great man of business has got somewhere. . . a touch of the idealist in him." Wilson was a late convert to progressivism, and as he told a Nashville audience in 1912 he was no radical who "pulls up roots to see if the thing is growing." Wilson added, "The true radical goes down to the roots to see that the soil is wholesome and that the tap-root is getting the pure nutriment that ought to come from the soil. That is the kind of radicalism I believe in; recultivation, thence reformation of the whole process."

Wilson's conservative views appealed to George Harvey, president of the publishing house of Harper and Brothers and a J. P. Morgan associate. Harvey sold Wilson to eastern conservative Democratic leaders and persuaded the Democratic bosses in New Jersey to run Wilson for governor in 1910. In his campaign he promised to fight special privilege, and as governor he carried out his pledges with a direct primary law, a corrupt practices act, an employers' liability law, tax equalization laws, and regulation of public utilities. In two years Wilson cleaned up one of the most boss-ridden states in the country and won recognition as a champion of reform to rank with Roosevelt and La Follette.

Many progressives who had suspected Wilson in 1910 now gave him their support. And Wilson's speeches became more progressive. Touring the West in 1911 he advocated the initiative, referendum, and recall. In a series of speeches between the spring of 1911 and the presidential campaign of 1912, Wilson set forth political ideas different from those he had espoused earlier. He maintained that the machinery of political control must be in the hands of the people. The government must give more service to the people—not merely protect them against monopoly. He promised to drive all beneficiaries of governmental policy into the open and to demand why they enjoyed governmental assistance. This was a progressive creed and a new creed for Wilson. He now found it necessary to break with his original political sponsors. Harvey's public support had become a liability in the West rather than an asset. In 1911 Wilson told Harvey as much and asked him to stop advocating his nomination for president; ever after, Harvey was Wilson's bitter opponent.

The breach with Harvey was balanced by an understanding with Bryan whose support was important. Edward M. House of Texas replaced Harvey as one of Wilson's trusted advisers. Unlike Harvey, House was sympathetic toward the Populists. He was a quiet man of refinement and wealth who wanted to push up from Texas politics to the national scene. Wilson and House met for the first time in 1911, and they became close friends. Wilson relied on House for political advice and took his suggestion to cut loose from Harvey and to woo the western faction of the Democratic party, especially Bryan.

When Wilson entered the White House, he had definite ideas about the presidency. He favored a strong president who would lead both his party and the government. He felt the entire responsibility of government should be with the president, and to meet that responsibility, strong control must rest in his hands. His concept of the office was English rather than American. Wilson's studies of comparative government led him to admire and respect the British system of a responsible ministry, a system he considered superior to the American system of checks and balances. Wilson believed the chief defect of the American system of government was the separation of powers and the constant struggle between the president and Congress. He hoped to overcome this flaw by acting as a prime minister to whom all Democrats would be loyal. Therefore, his duties as president embraced personal leadership of the party, the formulation of its legislative program, and the right of appeal to the voters for support in crises. Wilson also sought to surmount the rivalry between the chief executive and Congress by working closely with his party leaders in Congress, both conservative and progressive.

Wilson lacked the dramatic showmanship of Roosevelt, but he possessed many qualities of equal benefits to him—a distinctive appearance, expressive voice and fine eloquence. Another great asset he had was his ability to learn quickly. For example, he was very deficient in international matters when he became president, but he quickly remedied this. He also had the ability to phrase inspired and challenging slogans such as "to make the world safe for democracy," "peace without victory," and others. On one occasion he said: "What the country needs above everything else is a body of laws which will look after the men who are on the make rather than men already made."

Wilson was also headstrong, tenacious, and stubborn, and at times he was tactless, as some think he was in the fight over the League of Nations. But some scholars believe Wilson's party leadership was surpassed only by Jefferson's. The evidence they use for their conclusion was his ability to keep together the dissident elements in the Democratic party while keeping the Republicans out of power until after the election of 1918. Aiding Wilson was his success in associating his program with democracy and the outlawing of war. It was difficult to oppose such a program. As he once said, "I would rather lose in a cause that will some day win, than win in a cause that will some day lose."

As set forth in his campaign speeches of 1912, Wilson's New Freedom program proposed to lower the tariff and eliminate the special protection and favoritism that American industry had enjoyed since the Civil War, to have the national banks cooperate with one another and to free them from alleged Wall Street control, and to destroy monopoly in business by restoring the conditions necessary for free competition. Wilson intended to do the latter by specifying what were unfair trade practices, strengthening the Sherman Antitrust Act, and having the courts enforce the act. Thus as originally conceived the New Freedom program was a limited program. There was nothing planned specifically for farmers or workers. They would benefit from reduced tariff rates and from a restoration of competition in banking and business. But Wilson's original program occupied him for only a short time, he then moved to a more advanced program similar to the ambitious one Roosevelt had outlined in his New Nationalism. This significant change occurred because Wilson realized that his original program was inadequate to deal with the concentration of economic and industrial power in the country and because certain political forces moved him beyond his original purposes.

In his first inaugural address Wilson asserted the Democratic party had a mandate from the voters to secure political and economic reforms. He declared the country would use the Democratic party "to interpret a change in its own plans and point of view." He promised a "reinterpretation of democracy" and "to square every process of our national life again with the standards we so proudly set up at the beginning. . . . Our work is a work of restoration," he maintained. "This is not a day of triumph; it is a day of dedication. Here muster not the forces of party, but the forces of humanity. Men's hearts wait upon us. . . . I summon all honest men, all patriotic, all forward-looking men, to my side. God helping me, I will not fail them, if they will but counsel and sustain me!" More specifically Wilson promised tariff reduction, banking and currency reform, and additional trust legislation. In less than a year and a half he achieved all these objectives. It was a remarkable accomplishment and was made possible for several reasons. Wilson's intelligent and vigorous leadership had much to do with it, but so did the favorable situation Wilson had in Congress, enabling him to demonstrate this leadership. The Democrats not only had a large majority (73) in the House between 1913 and 1915, but a considerable number of the Democratic members were new and inexperienced (more than one-third of the Democrats in the House had been elected for the first time in 1912) and Wilson dominated them. In addition, the old line Democratic leaders such as Oscar Underwood and Henry D. Clayton of Alabama in the House and the conservative Democratic leaders in the Senate such as Furnifold M. Simmons of North Carolina and John M. Bankhead of Alabama were willing to cooperate with the president. And many of the Democrats in the Senate such as Joseph T. Robinson of Arkansas, Henry F. Ashhurst of New Mexico, and Thomas J. Walsh of Montana were progressives and wanted to make a good record too.

Throughout the Progressive era the Democrats, in their party platforms, attacked the protective tariff and called for a tariff for revenue purposes only. They emphasized a familiar theme when they described protective tariffs as "trust breeding measures." The Democrats wanted articles competing with trust-controlled products to be placed on the free list and a "material reduction" in the tariff on necessities. They also favored a policy of basing tariff revisions on "the intelligent research of a nonpartisan commission." On inauguration day, Wilson called Congress into special session on 8 April to revise the tariff. He appeared before the joint session to deliver his tariff message—the first president to address Congress in person since Jefferson abandoned the practice. On the following day he went to Capitol Hill to hold the first of many conferences with Democratic leaders. Wilson asked for lower tariffs; a bill sponsored by Representative Oscar Underwood of Alabama to cut the Payne-Aldrich Tariff of 1909 passed the House 281 to 139 and went to the Senate 8 May. Here it met the usual hostility of business interests. It seemed this bill would suffer the same fate as earlier efforts at tariff reform—a conservative Senate changing House measures into high protective tariffs.

Wilson, however, displayed unusual leadership. He resorted to a novel step that, since his day, has been commonly used by the president; he appealed directly to the people for support. On 26 May he denounced the lobbyists seeking to defeat the bill—the "great bodies of astute men who seek to create an artificial opinion and to overcome the interests of the public for their private good." This tactic led Senator La Follette and other progressives to conduct an inquiry into lobbying, and this investigation in turn forced senators to reveal personal holdings possibly affected by tariff legislation. The publicity ended almost all Democratic opposition, and the bill passed the Senate on 9 September with a vote of 44 to 37. On 3 October Wilson signed the measure now known as the Underwood-Simmons Tariff.

The new tariff was neither a free trade measure nor one solely for revenue. There was some protection. Reductions were made on 985 articles, increases were made in 86 items (mostly chemicals), and 307 were left unchanged. The average rate of duty of 36.8 percent under the Payne-Aldrich Tariff was lowered to 26.7 percent. The reductions covered largely those commodities on which protection had already served its purpose or where American goods dominated the world market. But it was a reform measure, because it was the lowest tariff since the Civil War and was at approximately the same level as the Walker Tariff of 1846. The most important reforms put wool and sugar on the free list. These had been the bulwarks of Republican tariffs. Wool went on the free list immediately. Sugar was scheduled to go on in 1916, but in that year Congress changed its mind. Another sweeping reform put nearly all the products made by the trusts, such as iron and steel products and agricultural machinery, on the free list. In addition, most raw materials, clothing, food, shoes, and other such items were either placed on the free list or given little protection.

The new tariff included an income tax to compensate for the expected loss of governmental revenue. It provided a tax of 1 percent on all net incomes over $3,000, or in the case of married men, $4,000. On incomes above $20,000 there was a graduated surtax beginning at 1 percent and going up to 6 percent on incomes over $500,000. The 1 percent tax on corporate profits above $5,000 levied in 1909 was retained.

Wilson was converted to the idea of a tariff commission, and Congress created one in September 1916. It got under way the following year under the chairmanship of Professor F. W. Taussig of Harvard. The commission had only a modest duty—to study the tariff situation and to make its services available to the president and Congress.

Banking and currency reform came next on Wilson's program. Both conservatives and progressives recognized the need for banking reform. The Currency Act of 1900 had established gold as the monetary basis of the country, but a number of serious problems remained. The National Bank Act of 1863 was still the basis of the nation's banking policy. By the first decade of the twentieth century, informed men of all parties recognized the inadequacy of this system in a great urban and industrial country. The country had an inelastic currency because under the act of 1863 the currency issues were based upon the bonded indebtedness of the United States and were therefore inflexible. Furthermore, the national banking structure had no machinery for mobilizing banking reserves.

The panics of 1873, 1893, and 1907 demonstrated the inadequacy of the banking structure, and in 1908 Congress passed the Aldrich-Vreeland Act. This measure permitted the national banks to issue emergency currency against securities and bonds. The act also created the National Monetary Commission to make a study of the banking and monetary problem. In 1912, under the chairmanship of Senator Aldrich, the commission issued a forty-volume report recommending the establishment of a great central bank with branches run by private bankers free of any real governmental control. In February 1913 the Pujo Committee, appointed by Congress to look into the concentration of control in money and credit, reported that the partners of three banking groups of New York City—J. P. Morgan and Company, National City Bank (James Stillman and William Rockefeller), and First National Bank of New York (George F. Baker)—held 341 directorships in 112 corporations whose combined capitalization amounted to over $22 billion. The total realized income of the country in 1910 was about $30 billion. Many Americans could readily agree with the committee's conclusion that there was a "great and rapidly growing concentration of the control of money and credit in the hands of these few men." While the Democrats had denounced the Aldrich banking proposal in their 1912 platform, they disagreed over what to do. The progressive element, led by Secretary of State Bryan, wanted a reserve system and a currency supply owned and controlled by the government and cited the revelations of the Pujo Committee to support its position. Conservative Democrats such as Congressman Carter Glass of Virginia favored a decentralized reserve system, disassociated from Wall Street, but owned and controlled by private bankers.

Wilson tried to steer a middle course between the demands of these two groups. Glass, the chairman of the House Banking and Currency Committee, drafted a bill setting up a system of as many as twenty reserve banks under private control and without central direction. Except for a central bank it resembled the Aldrich plan and received the tentative support of Wilson. But Wilson did insist on a central government board where bankers would have minority representation. The original Glass bill aroused the wrath of the Bryan Democrats, and Senator Robert L. Owen of Oklahoma, chairman of the Senate Banking and Currency Committee, drafted a countermeasure providing for a reserve and currency system owned and controlled entirely by the government. The agrarian leaders in the House opposed the Glass measure because it provided no way to destroy the money trust or give credit to farmers.

All this surprised and disturbed Wilson, and, of greater importance, it threatened to destroy his role as a leader. So he acted quickly and decisively. Louis D. Brandeis, whose opinions on economic matters he highly respected, told the president the progressives were right in their demands and converted him to the idea of denying representation to the bankers on the proposed Federal Reserve Board and of making the Federal Reserve Currency the obligation of the United States. Under Bryan's urgings, Wilson allowed the agrarians to amend the Glass bill to provide short-term credit facilities for farmers. However, private banking interests would own and largely control the Federal Reserve banks. While Wilson worked out a compromise satisfactory to all elements in the Democratic party, the bankers denounced the amended Glass bill as socialistic and confiscatory. But the Glass bill passed the House in September 1913, and the Senate on December 19; Wilson signed it four days later.

The Owen-Glass or Federal Reserve Act of 1913 divided the country into twelve districts, each containing a metropolitan center and a Federal Reserve bank. Every national bank in the country had to join the Federal Reserve System and contribute 6 percent of its capital to the district Federal Reserve bank. State banks and trust companies could join on the same terms as national banks. The twelve Federal Reserve banks were not to do business with individuals but only with member banks. The act also created a new currency—Federal Reserve notes—issued by the Federal Reserve banks to member banks and secured by commercial and agricultural paper and a 40 percent gold reserve. Managing the entire system was a Federal Reserve Board of Governors at Washington, consisting of the secretary of the treasury, the comptroller of the currency, and six other persons appointed by the president.

The Federal Reserve Act was a reform measure for several reasons. It provided a flexible currency to expand or contract in volume in direct relation to business needs. It provided a way to mobilize the major part of the banking reserves of a region or of the entire country whenever necessary. It ended the concentration of credit resources in a few financial centers. Finally, it afforded the farmer some short-term credit facilities. One serious shortcoming of the act was its failure to heed the recommendation of the Pujo Committee to regulate the stock market or to separate commercial from investment banking. These reforms had to wait until the New Deal period.

In less than a month after Wilson signed the Federal Reserve Act, he appeared before Congress on 20 January 1914 to ask for the third part in his program—new antitrust legislation. In these years Democratic platforms called private monopolies "indefensible and intolerable" and accused them of destroying competition, controlling prices, and robbing both producer and consumer. Wilson, in asking Congress for additional antitrust legislation, restated his belief in competition and contended the government had an obligation to "make men in a small way of business as free to succeed as men in a big way." Unlike Roosevelt, Wilson did not make the distinction between good and bad trusts, for he regarded any form of industrial concentration as unhealthy since it stifled competition. He believed the only way to handle the trusts was "to kill monopoly in the seed." Yet he was not opposed to mere size, for as he said, "I am for big business and I am against the trusts. Any man who can survive by his brains, any man who can put the other out of business by making the thing cheaper to the consumer at the same time that he is increasing its intrinsic value and quality, I take my hat off to." Wilson asked Congress for a "more explicit legislative definition of the policy and meaning of the existing antitrust law," and for measures to prohibit interlocking directorates in large corporations, to bring the issue of railroad securities under the control of the Interstate Commerce Commission, and to establish a Federal Trade Commission to assist and to regulate business.

The writing of the Federal Reserve Act was a turning point in Wilson's progressivism. It marked the end of the New Freedom program as it was conceived in the 1912 campaign and brought the progressives to a leading position in Wilson's administration. The writing of the antitrust legislation moved Wilson to an even more advanced progressive position and marked an even sharper break with his original reform program. And, as in the case of the Federal Reserve Act, Wilson's hand was largely forced in the antitrust laws.

The advanced progressives wanted an independent trade commission with authority to supervise business activities and to halt unfair trade practices. But Wilson originally favored a more limited intervention by the government. He believed all that was necessary was to replace the vague and general language of the Sherman Act with exact definitions of unfair trade practices or illegal restraints of trade and, as before, to leave the enforcement of the antitrust laws to the courts. Wilson's original antitrust program was embodied in two measures, the Clayton bill and the Covington interstate trade commission bill. The Clayton bill listed and forbade a series of unfair trade practices and prohibited interlocking directorates. The Covington bill established an interstate trade commission to supersede the Bureau of Corporations. But, like the bureau, the new commission would have no independent regulatory power and would act only as a fact-finding agency for the government.

These two measures provoked so much opposition that for a while it appeared there might be no antitrust legislation at all. The American Federation of Labor was unhappy because the Clayton bill did not provide immunity from antitrust prosecution for labor unions. The advanced progressives denounced it as a futile attempt to enumerate every conceivable restraint of trade. Southern and western agrarians criticized it for its failure to destroy the concentration of finance and industry in the hands of the few and because they regarded it as a betrayal of Democratic pledges.

Wilson was upset by these attacks and especially by the controversy with labor leaders and their supporters in Congress. Labor wanted complete immunity from the antitrust laws, but Wilson was unwilling to go that far. The most he would agree to was a compromise limiting the issuance of injunctions in labor disputes and stating that neither labor nor farm unions should be regarded as illegal combinations in restraint of trade when they used lawful means to secure legitimate ends. Although this was not satisfactory to labor leaders they had to accept the compromise when Wilson refused to go any farther.

In the dispute over the other antitrust provisions Wilson again turned to Brandeis for advice. The Boston lawyer converted the president to the idea of creating a strong federal commission with sufficient authority to prevent restraints of trade. The Brandeis proposal, embodied in a bill introduced by Congressman Raymond B. Stevens of New Hampshire, was similar to the type of governmental regulation that Roosevelt had advocated and Wilson had attacked in 1912. But since there seemed to be no other way out of the impasse, Wilson supported the new measure, made it the cornerstone of his antitrust program, and signed it on 26 September 1914. The Federal Trade Commission Act created a commission of five members, to be appointed by the president with the approval of the Senate for a seven-year term, to replace the Bureau of Corporations. This commission was empowered to "prevent persons, partnerships, or corporations, except banks and common carriers...from using unfair methods of competition in Commerce." To do this, the commission could investigate alleged violations of the antitrust laws and issue "cease and desist" orders enforceable through the courts against corporations found guilty of unfair competitive methods. In addition, the commission could examine "the organization, business, conduct, practices, and management of any corporation engaged in commerce, excepting banks and common carriers." The latter were already under the supervision of the Federal Reserve Board and Interstate Commerce Commission, respectively.

Meanwhile, having put his faith in regulation through the Federal Trade Commission, Wilson lost interest in the Clayton bill. Its stern provisions were seriously weakened by amendments in the Senate, and it had most of its teeth drawn by the time the president signed it on 15 October.

The Clayton Act was actually a series of acts in the twenty-six sections relating to railroads, banks, labor unions, and farmers' organizations. It amended the Sherman Act and attempted to avoid its generalizations by specifying those activities constituting restraint of trade. It prohibited a number of business practices: price discrimination if such discrimination should lead to monopoly, exclusive selling or leasing contracts (so-called tying contracts putting purchaser or dealer under promise not to handle products of a competitor manufacturer), and interlocking directorates.

The Clayton Act had several important provisions for labor. The measure declared, "The labor of human beings is not a commodity or article of commerce." Neither labor unions nor farmers' organizations were to be considered illegal combinations, per se, in restraint of trade. The right of labor to strike, picket peaceably, and to boycott an employer were made legal. Injunctions in labor disputes were prohibited except when necessary "to prevent irreparable injury to property." And in all cases of contempt, except when committed in the presence of the court, trial by jury was to be granted. These provisions pleased organized labor, and Samuel Gompers, president of the American Federation of Labor, called them labor's "Magna Carta." But in practice the labor provisions were not as favorable to labor as was expected. They did not free labor from the restraints of the antitrust laws, and court decisions in the twenties on the act's provisions greatly reduced their seeming benefits.

While the antitrust legislation pleased the progressives, it caused much unhappiness among businessmen. The younger J. P. Morgan, in describing conditions under the Wilson administration, declared: "The general situation here is perfectly unspeakable. . . . A greater set of perfectly incompetent and apparently crooked people has never, so far as I know, run, or, attempted to run, any first class country. The Mexicans are far better off, because their various bosses only murder and rape, but our bosses ruin the country and make life intolerable for a much larger number of people."

Like his predecessors in the presidency during the Progressive era, Wilson did little about the black problem in the United States. In fact the worst blot on Wilson's administration was his policy in this area. He permitted Secretary of the Treasury William G. McAdoo and Postmaster General Albert S. Burleson to put into effect a policy of segregating and downgrading blacks in their departments. During the campaign of 1912 Wilson appealed for black support when he wrote to one of their leaders: "I want to assure them through you that should I become President. . . they may count upon me for absolute fair dealing and for everything by which I could assist in advancing the interests of their race in the United States." But at a cabinet meeting on 11 April 1913 Burleson proposed the segregation of all blacks in the federal services. There was no opposition in the cabinet to Burleson's suggestion. Wilson issued no executive order on the matter, but throughout the rest of the spring of 1913 Burleson and McAdoo introduced the practice of segregation in the Post Office Department, the Bureau of the Census, the Bureau of Engraving and Printing, and the Washington City Post Office, in offices, shops, rest rooms, and restaurants. Employees who objected were discharged. The practice of segregation in federal bureaus was not limited to Washington. Post Office and Treasury officials in the South demoted and discharged black civil servants. "There are no Government positions for Negroes in the South," the collector of internal revenue at Atlanta declared. "A Negro's place is in the cornfield."

Wilson appointed few blacks even to the posts that they had traditionally occupied. And the president approved the discriminatory practices of his subordinates. When Oswald Garrison Villard, publisher of the New York *Evening Post* and a founder of the National Association for the Advancement of Colored People, protested against discrimination in federal departments, Wilson told him that he approved segregation because it would eliminate "the friction or rather the discontent and uneasiness which has prevailed in many departments." Wilson was convinced that his administration was acting only for the good of blacks. The concentration of blacks in one department, he believed, insured their possession of office and insulated them against discrimination.

There followed a storm of protest from blacks and their supporters against the discriminatory practices of the administration. They pointed out the glaring inconsistency between the theoretical democracy of the New Freedom and the social inequality imposed on the blacks. "Is the 'New Freedom' to be accepted as preaching political doctrines whose truths are no longer truths when they meet the color line?" asked the New York *Nation*. In August 1913 the officials of the National Association for the Advancement of Colored People (NAACP) sent Wilson an open letter calling "fallacious" his assertion that blacks could hold their political jobs with less fear in segregated departments. "Shall ten millions of our citizens say that their civic liberties and rights are not safe in your hands?" wrote Moorfield Storey for the executive board. "To ask the question is to answer it. They desire a 'New Freedom' too, Mr. President, yet they include in that term nothing else than the rights guaranteed them by the Constitution." Wilson's discrimination policies occurred at a time when the radical leadership of the NAACP was contesting with the moderation and gradualism of Booker T. Washington. Both groups opposed segregation in the federal government. "I have recently spent several days in Washington, and I have never seen the colored people so discouraged and bitter as they are at the present time," Washington wrote to Villard.

While Wilson was surprised and upset by these protests, he continued to believe that segregation was in the blacks' interests. He made his position clear in a letter to the editor of the Boston *Congregationalist* when he wrote, "I would say that I do approve of the segregation that is being attempted in several of the departments." Wilson never openly terminated the discriminatory practices, but the outcry from blacks and northern liberals brought a partial reversal of the segregation policy by late 1913.

In the spring of 1913 Villard suggested to the president that he form a National Race Commission, headed by Jane Addams, to undertake "a nonpartisan, scientific study of the Negro with particular reference to his economic situation." Wilson at first appeared "wholly sympathetic" to the proposal but wanted to see how Congress felt about it. However, he decided against the idea of a commission on political grounds. Personally Wilson welcomed the proposal, but he found himself in a delicate political situation. He was "absolutely blocked by the sentiment of Senators; not only Senators from the South...but Senators from various parts of the country." Wilson believed, as he told Villard in a letter, "that by the slow pressure of arguments and persuasion the situation may be changed and a great many things done eventually which now seem impossible. But they cannot be done, either now or at any future time, if a bitter agitation is inaugurated and carried to its natural ends." Wilson was distressed over the whole black question, and he told Villard in a personal meeting, "I say it with shame and humiliation, with shame and humiliation, but I have thought about this thing for twenty years and I see no way out. It will take a very big man to solve this thing."

Although the writing of the antitrust legislation moved Wilson to an advanced progressive position, until early 1914 he seemed determined to stick to his limited reform program and was successful in opposing the advanced progressive campaign to commit the federal government to a positive program of social and economic legislation. There was disagreement between Wilson and the agrarian, labor, and social justice reformers over the role of the federal government. The advanced progressives supported Theodore Roosevelt's position of 1912 that the federal government should take steps to aid underprivileged groups. But Wilson opposed this idea on the ground it would be special legislation for special interests. He proposed to adhere to the New Freedom doctrine of "special privileges to none." Such divergent views caused a fight within progressive ranks.

Wilson believed so firmly in the limited reform program he had outlined in 1912 that for a whole session of Congress he blocked or was unwilling to support much of the advanced progressive legislation. He initially opposed the idea of short-term rural credits ultimately embodied in the Federal Reserve Act. In the spring of 1914 he prevented a long-term rural credits bill from becoming law and resisted the AFL's attempt to secure immunity for labor unions from application of the antitrust law to their illegal strike activities. He also refused to back a child labor law in 1914 and a woman's suffrage amendment. And, as we have seen, he permitted his secretary of the treasury and postmaster general to introduce segregation of black and white employees in their departments in 1913.

In fact Wilson believed that with the antitrust legislation he had fulfilled his domestic reform program. In his Annual Message to Congress in December 1914 he said that his legislative program was now complete with regard to the regulation of business. In a public letter to Secretary McAdoo a few weeks earlier, the president pointed out that everything had been done to clear away special privilege and to put all

classes on an equal footing. The Republican system of special privileges had been destroyed, he wrote, and the antagonism between the
public and business had ended. In the future businessmen would adapt
themselves to the changed conditions, and the country would enter a
new era of "cooperation, of new understanding, of common purpose."

Thus Wilson maintained that the Progressive movement was over
and there was a reaction against progressive policies by Wilson and his
advisers in the spring of 1914. Relations between the progressives and
Wilson began to cool, and the president set out to win the friendship
of businessmen and to reduce the tension between them and his administration.

For instance, the president accommodated his antitrust program
largely to the desires of the business community. True, the Federal
Trade Commission did some vigorous work. Between March 1915 and
June 1921 it received 2,416 "applications for complaints," served 788
"formal complaints," and issued 379 "cause and desist" orders against
specified unfair practices. Yet Wilson did not appoint aggressive administrators to the commission. Moreover, while the commission was
designed to regulate business, Wilson hoped it would act like a coun-
selor and friend to business. "It was no large part of Wilson's purpose
that the Federal Trade Commission should be primarily a policeman
to wield a club over the head of the business community," wrote W. C.
Redfield, Wilson's secretary of commerce. "Rather the reverse was
true and the restraining powers of the Commission were thought a necessary adjunct which he hoped and expected to be of minor rather
than major use."

In addition, the Wilson administration adopted a new policy to
handle alleged combinations in restraint of trade. Attorney General
James C. McReynolds, with Wilson's approval, announced that any
corporation that had doubts about the legality of its size could seek
the advice and assistance of the Justice Department. And several did,
especially the American Telephone and Telegraph Company and the
New Haven Railroad. Wilson also welcomed bankers and businessmen
to the White House, and he let it be known in eastern business circles
that he was not an enemy of big business that had become big legally.

But while Wilson may have thought that this domestic reform
program had ended in 1914, he eventually changed his mind. The Progressive party of 1912 began to break up after 1914, and a hope for

Democratic success in 1916 seemed to hinge on winning over Bull Moose adherents. Furthermore, there were well-organized movements in favor of a federal system of long-term rural credits and in behalf of social justice. Then, too, the Republicans began to close ranks for 1916. Roosevelt abandoned the Progressive party and rejoined the Republicans for the purpose of defeating Wilson. If Roosevelt succeeded in bringing most progressives back to Republican ranks with him, a Democratic defeat was likely in 1916. A possible way for victory was for Wilson to come out for progressive projects such as rural credits, child labor laws, and other social and economic legislation that in the past he had either opposed or failed to support.

Wilson naturally wanted the Democrats to stay in power and this seemed possible by adopting the program of the advanced progressives and the concepts of the New Nationalism. Confronted by this political expediency and having new ideas as a result of his own experience in the presidency, Wilson threw his support behind this advanced progressive legislation. He expanded the federal legislative program regarding labor. He signed the La Follette Seamen's Act of 1915, which increased the safety requirements on American ships and freed merchant seamen of bondage to labor contracts. The Adamson Act of 1916 established an eight-hour day for workers on all interstate railways, and the Federal Workmen's Compensation Act of 1916 extended this form of accident insurance to civil service employees. The Keating-Owen Act of 1916 sought to outlaw child labor by prohibiting the interstate shipment of goods made by firms employing children under fourteen. However, in 1918 the Supreme Court in the case of *Hammer* v. *Dagenhart* declared the law unconstitutional on the grounds that the purpose of the act was not to regulate commerce, but to regulate child labor, a power reserved to the states. Undaunted, Congress in 1919 attempted to regulate child labor by placing a 10 percent tax on net incomes of industries and mines employing children. But this measure, too, was to no avail. The Supreme Court in 1922 in the case of *Bailey* v. *Drexel Furniture Company* rejected it.

The American farmer also benefited from additional legislation during the latter part of Wilson's first term. The Smith-Lever Act of 1914 authorized the federal government to match, dollar for dollar, the contributions of those states choosing to cooperate in a program of agricultural extension. The Smith-Hughes Act of 1917 appropriated funds, also on a dollar-matching basis, for vocational and agricultural education in schools below college level. The Federal Farm Loan Act of 1916 established a group of institutions similiar to the Federal Reserve Banks. It created a Federal Farm Loan Board and twelve regional farm loan banks. These banks could make loans to cooperative farm loan associations on the security of farm lands, buildings, and improvements, up to the value of 70 percent of these assets. Loans were on a long-term basis with interest not to exceed 6 percent and with profits to be distributed to the members of the subscribing farm loan associations. Finally, the Warehouse Act of 1916 authorized licensed warehouse operators to issue receipts against farm products deposited with them. Farmers could then use these warehouse receipts as negotiable paper. This plan embodied the essential features of the subtreasury proposal of the Populists in 1892.

Wilson also yielded to the mounting demands for an effective tariff commission to remove the tariff issue from politics, and in 1916 he sponsored and secured the passage of a law creating an independent tariff commission. Wilson also publicly reversed the traditional Democratic position on the tariff and came out for rational protection.

Therefore, by 1916 the Democratic Congress had enacted into law nearly every important plank of the Progressive party's platform of 1912. Wilson had abandoned his original New Freedom program and had accepted the concepts of the advanced progressives and Theodore Roosevelt's New Nationalism. It was an amazing performance and remarkable transformation, and Arthur Link maintains that by election time in 1916 Wilson had become "almost a new political creature." This change in Wilson and his program is the key to the understanding of his presidency.

Further Reading

Again, some of the readings of the immediately preceding chapters will be useful for this chapter.

Baker, Ray Stannard, and William E. Dodd, eds. *The Public Papers of Woodrow Wilson.* 6 vols., 1925-1927.

Billington, Monroe L. *Thomas P. Gore: The Blind Senator from Oklahoma.* 1967.

Blum, John M. *Joe Tumulty and the Wilson Era.* 1951.

_____. *Woodrow Wilson and the Politics of Morality.* 1956.

Coben, Stanley. *A. Mitchell Palmer: Politician.* 1963.

Coletta, Paolo E. *William Jennings Bryan: Progressive Politician and Moral Statesman, 1909–1915.* 1969.

Cramer, C. H. *Newton D. Baker, A Biography.* 1961.

Cronon, E. David. *The Political Thought of Woodrow Wilson.* 1965.

Diamond, William. *The Economic Thought of Woodrow Wilson.* 1943.

Freidel, Frank. *Franklin D. Roosevelt: The Apprenticeship.* 1952.

Garraty, John A. *Woodrow Wilson.* 1956.

Heckscher, August, ed. *The Politics of Woodrow Wilson.* 1956.

Latham, Earl, ed. *The Philosophy and Politics of Woodrow Wilson.* 1958.

Link, Arthur S. *Wilson: The New Freedom.* 1956.

Walworth, Arthur. *Woodrow Wilson.* 2 vols., 1958.

12

The United States as a World Power, 1899–1916

American foreign policy during the Progressive era was, for the most part, aggressive, nationalistic, and expansionistic. It involved the United States in two major conflicts—the Spanish-American War and World War I—and led to the nation's intervention in the Far East, Latin America, and Europe and to domination of the Caribbean. This nationalistic spirit in foreign affairs was in contrast with the progressive domestic programs of Roosevelt, Taft, and Wilson, and there are several reasons for it. For one thing, the United States had developed a sense of national superiority after its easy victory over Spain in 1898. For another the rise of Japan and Germany to the ranks of the great powers in the last quarter of the nineteeth century also produced feelings of nationalism in these two countries. All this resulted in the building of large navies, an armament race, an expansion of colonial empires, and power politics on the international scene.

The United States emerged from the Spanish-American War possessing the Philippines, Puerto Rico, and the Hawaiian Islands, and with responsibilities in Cuba. The acquisition of these islands in the Caribbean and Pacific compelled the United States to establish a colonial policy and to change its foreign policy. Both of these tasks were difficult and complex—far more so than the expansionists had thought in 1898. One problem was to reconcile the interests of the colonies and the United States. Another problem was the reluctance on the part of Americans to make sacrifices to defend their newly acquired interests.

When the Philippines were annexed, the Senate adopted the McEnery Resolution stating the islands would not be retained permanently. But two complications arose. One was an American commission report that the Philippines were not ready for self-government. The other was a revolt of the Filipinos from 1899 to 1901 under Aguinaldo, who desired independence and not simply a transfer of sovereignty to the United States. Ironically, the war fought to liberate the Cubans was now ending in an effort to conquer the Filipinos. The United States sent 70,000 troops to the islands and used harsh methods before it could put down the uprising.

While Americans forgot in the Philippines some of the professed ideals they had fought for in Cuba, they did revive them once the revolt was over. The United States built schools, hospitals, and roads, and purchased land from religious orders to sell on easy terms to small farmers. Public works were constructed and a currency system was established. The Organic Act of 1902 created a government for the Philippines that lasted until 1916. While the act reflected the belief that Filipinos were not yet ready for home rule, it indicated that the United States was prepared to give them an opportunity to learn. The measure set up an executive comprised of governor general and a commission appointed by the president, a legislature, and a court system. Presidents Roosevelt and Taft regarded the Philippines almost as their personal trust. They secured large appropriations for the islands and were determined that the foundations for self-government should be laid. By 1913, when Taft left the White House, four of the nine members of the commission, 71 percent of the classified employees in the civil service, 92 percent of the teachers, and all the governors of the Christian provinces were Filipinos. But the Filipinos still demanded independence, something the Jones Act of 1916 promised them as soon as they had "a stable government," but which they did not realize and proclaim until 1946.

The Spanish-American War affected American policy in Latin America in two important ways. In the first place, it set the stage for American predominance in the Caribbean, especially in the Canal Zone. Second, it made the primary concerns and chief objectives of American policy in this area from 1898 to 1916: (1) the consolidation of our new position in the Caribbean and Central America, (2) the building and control of an isthmian canal, and (3) securing the protection of both approaches from the United States to the canal, and the establishment of American naval supremacy in the Caribbean. The rest of the world acquiesced in American predominance in the Western Hemisphere. They accepted Roosevelt's interpretation of the Monroe Doctrine. England assented to the Hay-Pauncefote Treaty in connection with the Panama Canal, reduced its permanent garrisons in the West Indies, and took its principal naval forces out of the area. From that time on the United States was the dominant power in the Caribbean.

American policy in Cuba and in the Panama Canal incident illustrates both the origin and extent of our predominance in the Caribbean and the change that occurred in our policy in this area. It was a significant departure both in overseas responsibilities and policies of the United States.

The Spanish-American War had not liberated Cuba. The island remained under American rule from 1899 to 1902, with General Leonard Wood as governor. American occupation forces attempted to institute a new way of life for Cubans. The administrative machinery and the financial system were overhauled and reorganized. Schools on the American model were established. Considerable physical rehabilitation was undertaken; roads, railroads, bridges, and hospitals were constructed. And most important of all, yellow fever—Cuba's most dreaded disease—was conquered by the brilliant work of Major Walter Reed of the Army Medical Corps.

In the treaty of Paris, Spain had given up "all claim of sovereignty over in title to Cuba." As for our part, we had agreed during the period of occupation to "assume and discharge the obligations that may under international law result from the fact of its occupation, for the protection of life and property." The United States had never recognized the insurgent government in Cuba. But in the war resolution against Spain in 1898 the Teller Amendment had stated "That the United States hereby disclaims any disposition or intention to exercise sovereignty, jurisdiction, or control over said Island except for the pacification thereof, and asserts its determination, when that is accomplished, to leave the government in control of the Island to its people." Senator Teller stated he had sponsored the resolution to make it impossible for any European government to say, "when we go out to make battle for the liberty and freedom of Cuban patriots, that we are doing it for the purpose of aggrandizement for ourselves or the increasing of our territorial holdings." Teller wanted this point made clear in regard to Cuba, "whatever," he added, "we may do as to some other islands."

Despite the Teller Amendment, President McKinley in his annual message to Congress in December 1899 remarked that the United States "assumed before the world a grave responsibility for the future good government of Cuba." "The new Cuba," he said, ". . . . must needs be bound to us by ties of singular intimacy and strength if its enduring welfare is to be assumed." Thus, when the Cubans drafted their new constitution, they had to add to it the Platt Amendment, attached by Senator Orville H. Platt of Connecticut to an army appropriation bill of 1901. The most important parts of the Platt Amendment were: (1) the "Government of Cuba shall never enter into any treaty or other compact with any foreign power. . . which will impair. . . . the independence of Cuba, nor in any manner authorize. . . any foreign power. . . to obtain by colonization or for military or naval purposes- . . . control over any portion of the said Island"; (2) Cuba shall not "assume or contract any public debt to pay the interest upon which- . . . the ordinary revenues. . . shall be inadequate"; (3) Cuba agrees "that the United States may exercise the right to intervene for the preservation of Cuban independence, the maintenance of a government adequate for the protection of life, property, and individual liberty"; (4) Cuba will continue the sanitation program; and (5) Cuba will lease or sell coaling stations and naval bases to the United States to aid in Cuba's defense.

Cuba objected to the right of American intervention and to the naval stations and at first turned down the Platt Amendment. But several things changed her mind. It realized the Platt Amendment was an indispensable condition for the end of American military rule in Cuba. In several conferences with Secretary of War Elihu Root, Cuba was assured that intervention as set forth in the Platt Amendment was "not synonymous with intermeddling or interference with the affairs of the Cuban government" but would take place only in the event of foreign threat or domestic trouble. Other than this, Cuba would be left in entire control of its own affairs. Root argued that this article was "the Monroe Doctrine but with international force. Because of it, European nations will not dispute the intervention of the United States in defense of the independence of Cuba."

The Platt Amendment became part of Cuba's constitution and was put into treaty form in May 1903. General Wood believed the Platt

Amendment would mean the annexation of Cuba. So did many Cubans. But this was not the case. American public opinion moved away from annexation to trusteeship of Cuban independence, especially after World War I. The Platt Amendment remained in effect until 1934, when all of the 1903 treaty, save the naval base article, was repealed. Under that provision, the United States Navy has continued to have the use of Guantanamo Bay on the south coast near Santiago as a naval station.

The United States exercised its right of intervention in Cuba from time to time to maintain a stable government on the island. Our most notable intervention in Cuba occurred in 1906–1909 when the Cuban government broke down, but the United States intervened so frequently in later years that it appeared to violate Root's promise that the article on intervention would not result in "intermeddling or interference."

Since the Spanish-American War had given the United States an empire in both the Caribbean and the Pacific, an isthmian canal seemed to be more essential than ever before. The battleship *Oregon's* 71-day trip of 14,000 miles from San Francisco to the Atlantic coast during the war raised the question again of why there was no canal to shorten the sea voyage between the two coasts. Thus, most Americans recognized the need for an isthmian canal. But several matters blocked American action. They were the Clayton-Bulwer Treaty of 1850 with Great Britain, the concession for building a canal held by a French company, and the Treaty of 1846 between the United States and Granada (later Colombia).

Since the Clayton-Bulwer Treaty gave the British equal rights with the Americans in any canal to be constructed, the first step was to win British consent to a change in the treaty. Great Britain at first demurred. But the British, near the turn of the century, found themselves deeply involved in the Boer War in South Africa and under heavy diplomatic attack from the major European nations; hence they were unwilling to alienate American friendship. Besides, Congress seemed determined to go ahead with the canal, treaty or no treaty. So the British agreed to the Hay-Pauncefote Treaty of 18 November 1901. This pact gave the United States a free hand to build the canal and the "exclusive management and policing of it." In return, the United States promised to keep the canal "open to the vessels of commerce and war of all nations...on terms of entire equality." Thus, the first obstacle was removed.

The next move was to decide the canal route. Two possible routes were available, one through the Panama region of Colombia and the other through Nicaragua. In Panama a French company had gone bankrupt in attempting to dig a canal. The new Panama Canal Company had acquired the properties of the bankrupt French company and had its concession extended to 1904. The company had placed a value of $190 million on its property, rights, and previous work. Three commissions in 1895, 1897, and 1901 had recommended the Nicaraguan route. When the House of Representatives in 1902 authorized the construction of a canal through Nicaragua, the Panama Company offered to sell out for $40 million and set up a powerful lobby to promote the Panama route. Philippe Bunau-Varilla, chief engineer of the original French company, and Nelson W. Cromwell, a New York attorney, put pressure on the Senate to convince it of the superiority of the Panama route. After much maneuvering and debate, the Panama route won. In June 1902 Congress provided for the purchase of the French property for not more than $40 million and for the acquisition from Colombia of the necessary rights to Panama. Should the president fail within a reasonable time in negotiations either with the French company or with Colombia, he was authorized to build a canal through Nicaragua.

It remained now only to acquire the land. The Hay-Herran Treaty with Colombia was negotiated and signed in January 1903. The United States was to receive a canal zone six miles wide across the Isthmus in return for a cash payment of $10 million and an annual rental of $250,000 beginning nine years after the ratification of the treaty. The United States Senate approved the treaty, but the Colombian Senate rejected it in August 1903 by a vote of 24 to 0. Many believed Colombia was holding out until 1904, when it and not the French concessionaires would receive the $40 million supposed to go to the New Panama Canal Company. President Roosevelt, highly incensed, called the Colombians "bandits" and said their refusal to approve the treaty was a situation "exactly as if a road agent had tried to hold up a man." "The blackmailers of Bogota," Roosevelt declared, must not be allowed "permanently to bar one of the future highways of civilization." The Indianapolis *Sentinel* outlined the course that would be followed when it observed in August 1903: "The simplest plan of coercing Colombia would be inciting a revolution in Panama...and supporting the insurrectionary government."

Roosevelt was determined to have the canal site, and at first wrote an angry message to Congress demanding the United States take the canal zone by force. Then he changed his mind and never sent the message. It was not necessary because events at Panama now moved rapidly to the advantage of the United States. The people of Panama feared if the United States did not build the canal on their soil soon, it would turn to Nicaragua instead. The French company was anxious to close the deal since it did not want to lose $40 million. Thus Bunau-Varilla and others worked to foment a revolution in Panama against Colombia, but only after they received the impression that the United States government would prevent Colombia from suppressing it. The revolution in Panama was successful because of the cooperation of the United States Navy. On 30 October 1903 the commander of the USS *Nashville* was directed that in case of rebellion he should seize the Panama railroad and "prevent the landing of any armed force with hostile intent, whether government or insurgent" within fifty miles of Panama. On 2 November the *Nashville* dropped anchor at Colon. Its presence there prevented the Colombian troops, sent to Colon earlier, from moving across the Isthmus into the revolutionary area at Panama and putting down the uprising of 3 November. The revolution succeeded without violence.

On 6 November the United States recognized the independence of the Republic of Panama. Bunau-Varilla, the first minister of Panama to the United States, and Secretary Hay negotiated a new canal treaty, signed on 18 November. The Hay-Bunau-Varilla Treaty guaranteed the independence of Panama and gave the United States in perpetuity "the use, occupation, and control of a strip of land ten miles wide for the construction of a canal." The United States could exercise sovereign power over this strip and adjacent waters and fortify the area at will. Panama received an initial payment of $10 million and an annual sum of $250,000 beginning nine years after the ratification of the treaty.

Roosevelt was severely criticized for his Panama policy, but he defended it vigorously. "No one connected with this government," he said, "had any part in preparing, inciting or encouraging the late revolution of the Isthmus of Panama." All canal negotiations, he asserted, were conducted "by the highest, finest, and nicest standards of public and governmental ethics." He upheld the right of the *Nashville* to prevent Colombian troops from crossing the Isthmus to put down the revolt on the grounds that the United States in the Treaty of 1846 had pledged itself to maintain "free transit" across the Isthmus.

But the whole matter—the circumstances of the revolt, the blocking of Colombian attempts to suppress it, the unusual haste in recognition, and the favorable treaty—caused considerable resentment in Colombia and a division at home. The New York *Times* said it was "the path of scandal, disgrace, and dishonor," but most Republican newspapers supported Roosevelt, and so did a large number of independent and Democratic papers. For the rest of his life Roosevelt defended his policy in Panama and took pride in it. In his *Autobiography* he called it "By far the most important action in foreign affairs." And in a public address in 1911, after leaving the presidency, Roosevelt remarked, "If I had followed traditional conservative methods, I would have submitted a dignified state paper of 200 pages to Congress and the debate on it would have been going on yet; but I took the Canal Zone and let Congress debate; and while the debate goes on the Canal does so."

Historians today are critical of Roosevelt's actions in Panama and believe they were unnecessary and unjustified either by treaty or precedent. The incident antagonized public opinion in Latin America, and all Latin American countries condemned the Panama action. Colombia refused to recognize the independence of Panama and demanded arbitration of the controversy. Secretaries of State Elihu Root, under Roosevelt, and Philander Knox, under Taft, made a number of unsuccessful efforts to conciliate Colombia. In 1914 President Wilson's secretary of state, William Jennings Bryan, negotiated a treaty with Colombia providing for payment to her of $25 million in cash, giving her preferential rights in the use of the canal, and expressing "sincere regret that anything should have occurred to mar the relations of cordial friendship" between the two countries. Colombia, in turn, was to recognize the independence of Panama. Roosevelt denounced the treaty as "a crime against the United States and an attack on its honor," and his friends in the Senate prevented its approval. In 1921 after Roosevelt's death, the Harding administration negotiated a somewhat similar treaty deleting the "sincere regret" clause. This treaty the Senate accepted.

President Roosevelt appointed a canal commission to make plans for the construction of the canal. The decision was to build a lock canal instead of a sea-level ditch. When proposals of private contractors failed to meet government approval, the construction work was placed in the hands of the United States Army's Corps of Engineers with Colonel George W. Goethals as the chief engineer and chairman of the

Isthmian Canal Commission. At first sanitation loomed as a greater problem than excavation, but the splendid work of Colonel William C. Gorgas, an army medical officer who had cleaned up Havana a few years before, made the Isthmus a fit place to live. On 15 August 1914 the first ocean steamer passed through the completed Panama Canal. The United States spent $275 million to build the canal and an additional $113 million to equip it with military and naval defense.

Once the United States secured the right to build the canal, it had to find a means to insure its defense. While the surrounding Latin American countries were too weak to menace it, their very weakness could make them targets for any European power having designs upon the canal. Since the United States regarded the canal as vital to its national defense, it could not allow any European power to gain a foothold in the Caribbean. The result was a new aggressive policy for the United States in the Caribbean, aimed at preventing any country from gaining an excuse to intervene in the region.

Presidents Roosevelt, Taft, and Wilson were all aware of the dangers to the canal from European intervention in Central America and the Caribbean, and their Latin American policy was designed to maintain and expand American influence in this area. This policy had already begun with the establishment of a protectorate over Cuba and the negotiation of the canal treaties. Historian Samuel F. Bemis declared that this policy "rapidly built up a structure of comparatively benevolent imperialism and tutelage in the Caribbean and Central America."

This policy became known variously as the Caribbean or the Panama policy of the United States. There were several different ways to implement it and to further it. One was to make use of the Monroe Doctrine as Roosevelt and Lodge were to do. Another way was to buy up small islands in the Caribbean belonging to a small power to prevent their becoming a part of the empire of a larger naval power. This was also in line with the nontransfer principle of the Monroe Doctrine proclaimed in 1869. The United States acted on this basis when it bought the Danish West Indies in 1917. Still another way was to intervene and establish protectorates such as the United States had done in Cuba and Panama and such as it was to do in the Dominican Republic under Roosevelt and in Haiti under Wilson. This later method was described by the popular writers of Roosevelt's day as the "big stick" approach. The United States followed this latter policy until New Deal days when it and the Platt Amendment were repudiated. The net effect of this policy was frequent and prolonged intervention in Latin American affairs, especially from 1903 to 1921. The United States put money into shaky Latin American governments. It used the Monroe Doctrine in a way its originators had not anticipated, and it employed troops to set up stable governments in the Caribbean.

In pursuing this new Latin American policy the United States steadily advanced its economic and political authority in the Caribbean and therefore was accused of being motivated by economic reasons. But actually the United States adopted the new policy primarily for political and strategic reasons. In all the countries where the United States intervened frequently during this period—Panama, Santo Domingo, Haiti, Nicaragua—there was the least American capital or foreign capital of any kind, and these were the least promising areas for economic development. American intervention in the Caribbean arose for several reasons. One was to protect the Canal Zone and thereby protect the United States. This meant policing disorderly countries, establishing naval bases, controlling alternate canal routes on the Isthmus, and excluding foreign influence. Another reason was the aggressive nationalism that had played such a large role in getting the United States into the war with Spain and that made America feel and act like a great power. In addition, there was a genuine desire on the part of the United States to cure the chronic affliction of armed revolution in most of Central America and the Caribbean by the substitution of orderly democratic processes.

Between 1901 and 1907 the United States established a system of protectorates in the Caribbean—over Cuba, Panama, the Dominican Republic, Nicaragua, and Haiti. Special relations between the United States and these countries were defined in treaty form, although no two treaties were alike. Only to Panama did the United States actually promise protection—"The United States guarantees and will maintain the independence of Panama." Other treaties, especially those with Cuba and Haiti, obligated these countries not to lose their independence or to give any of their territory to a third party. These two treaties permitted the United States to intervene to maintain independence or orderly governments. Treaties with Cuba, Haiti, and the Dominican Republic either placed restrictions upon or allowed the United States to have supervision over those nations' financial policies. The treaties with Cuba and Nicaragua gave the United States exclusive canal rights (guaranteeing an alternate route) through Nicaragua.

The political and financial instability of the smaller Caribbean countries also posed a serious problem for the United States. Since a large part of the national debt of these countries, in the form of government bond issues, was held by Europeans, the United States was concerned about European intervention. The attempt of European powers in 1902 to collect a debt from Venezuela by force of arms caused much apprehension in Latin America, and was regarded as an example of what might happen if the financial affairs of the Caribbean were ignored. European countries might move in to protect their interests if the United States did not guarantee their protection. This possibility led to a major change in the Monroe Doctrine.

In 1904 the Dominican Republic found itself unable to pay its debts ($32,280,000)—two thirds of which it owed to European nationals. There was the possibility of several European countries using force to collect those debts. Fearing that European intervention might lead to annexation, the United States through Secretary of War Root declared: "What we will not permit the great Powers of Europe to do, we will not permit any American Republic to make it necessary for the great Powers of Europe to do." President Roosevelt later expanded this concept in his annual message to Congress in December 1904 when he said:

If a nation...keeps order, pays its obligations, it need fear no interference from the United States. Chronic wrong doing...may in America, or elsewhere, ultimately require intervention by some civilized nation, and in the Western Hemisphere the adherence of the United States to the Monroe Doctrine may force the United States, however reluctantly, in flagrant cases of such wrong doing or impotence to the exercise of an international police power.

The statement, known as the "Roosevelt Corollary" of the Monroe Doctrine, was a declaration of the first importance. It proclaimed to the world that the United States might intervene in the Western Hemisphere to prevent intervention there by European powers. Roosevelt applied the corollary to the Dominican Republic because of its inability to pay its debts. In 1905 the Dominican Republic agreed to having an American official collect its customs and to apportion them according to a fixed ratio between current expenses and payment of debt. Although the United States Senate failed to approve this arrangement, Roosevelt continued its enforcement by executive agreement until 1907, when a treaty containing substantially the same terms won approval.

In 1912 the Monroe Doctrine was again expanded, this time by the Lodge Corollary. In 1911 a Japanese fishing company had sought to lease a large area of land from Mexico in Magdalena Bay. The State Department indicated disapproval of this action, and the Japanese gave up the project. In 1912 the United States Senate adopted a resolution introduced by Henry Cabot Lodge stating the United States would look with "grave concern" on the acquisition by a foreign corporation of "any harbor or other place in the American continents...so situated that the occupation thereof for naval or military purposes might threaten the communication or the safety of the United States."

The policies exemplified by the Roosevelt and Lodge corollaries were followed by the Taft administration under the name of "Dollar Diplomacy." The methods were different but the objectives remained much the same. The basic goal of American policy in Latin America was still the defense of the canal. President Taft proposed to eliminate rival nations from intervening in the Caribbean by having American capital replace European investments in this area. This was aimed at removing all and any pretext for European intervention and thereby assuring the continued safety of the canal. For example, in 1909, when British bond holders wanted to collect their debts in Honduras, President Taft asked American financiers to assume the Honduran debt. In 1910 the president persuaded New York bankers to take over the assets of the National Bank of Haiti. And when a revolution occurred in Nicaragua, Taft refused to recognize the new government until it accepted large credits extended by American bankers for liquidation of its debts to the British. When Nicaragua refused, it was persuaded by a visit of an American warship, and in 1911 an American took over the collection of its customs.

When Wilson became president, the public expected a change in foreign policy in Latin America. Wilson verbally denounced Dollar Diplomacy, and he abolished it temporarily in the Far East. He repudiated imperialism, and in a speech in Mobile in October 1913 he declared the United States would "never again seek one additional foot of territory by conquest." He also avowed that United States policy in Latin America would no longer be concerned with the "pursuit of material interest" but would seek to promote "human rights" and "national integrity." By denouncing the use of force in Latin America, Wilson sounded as though he intended to reverse America's basic policy there. Actually, Wilson continued the Roosevelt-Taft policy of intervention throughout the Caribbean. The Lansing Memorandum of 24 November 1915 stated the United States would "not tolerate control over or interference with the political or financial affairs of these republics by any European power or its national." This warning expressed Wilson's basic policy in the Caribbean. Probably the reason for the discrepancy between Wilson's words and practice was the outbreak of World War I in 1914. The fear of a German victory made the control of the Caribbean of even greater concern to the United States.

In 1913 the Wilson administration negotiated a treaty with Nicaragua (occupied by American marines), giving the United States exclusive rights to construct a canal and to lease sites for naval bases on both the Atlantic and Pacific coasts of Nicaragua. In 1915 Wilson sent marines to put down a revolution in Haiti and to establish an American protectorate. They stayed until 1934. In 1916 the United States occupied the Dominican Republic over the opposition of the local government and kept American marines there until 1924. In 1917 the Wilson administration purchased the Virgin Islands from Denmark. Wilson intervened in Cuba, and from 1917 to 1922 the island was again under American control. By the time of World War I, the United States had acquired dominance in the Caribbean. American armed forces were in control of four nominally independent republics: Nicaragua, Haiti, the Dominican Republic, and Cuba.

But Wilson's most serious diplomatic problem in Latin America was Mexico. From 1876 to 1911, Porfirio Diaz ruled Mexico as a dictator. In addition to creating political stability, Diaz had encouraged the investment of foreign capital. By 1910 Americans had poured about a billion dollars into a variety of Mexican enterprises. They controlled approximately 78 percent of the mines, 72 percent of the smelters, and 58 percent of the oil production. Most of the rest of the capital in Mexican industries was European, much of it British. In 1910 native resentment against foreign exploiters, the Catholic Church, and large land holders who supported Diaz exploded in a revolution. It was ultimately to lead to far-reaching changes in Mexican society. In May 1911 a coalition of insurgents, led by the liberal idealist Francisco Madero, overthrew Diaz and elected Madero president. Diaz fled Mexico.

President Taft recognized the Madero government, which attempted to establish a constitutional democracy. But Madero was unable to keep order. Counterrevolutionaries representing the feudal elements in Mexico and the foreign investors were supported by Henry Lane Wilson, American ambassador to Mexico. Under the leadership of General Victoriano Huerta they seized the government in February 1913, threw Madero in jail, and murdered him a few days later. Ambassador Wilson publicly congratulated Huerta on his coup and urged the

United States government to recognize the new government as the major European powers had already done.

When Woodrow Wilson became president, Mexico was again plunged into civil war, for though Huerta had control of most of the country, opposition movements were led by Pancho Villa and the Indian peasant chieftain, Emiliano Zapata. Shocked by the assassination of Madero, Wilson's administration—almost alone among the Western powers—refused to recognize Huerta. He opposed "that scoundrel Huerta" and his "despotism" in Mexico, and he regarded Huerta as an enemy of the "submerged eighty-five percent of the people of that Republic who are now struggling toward liberty." American businessmen with heavy investments in Mexico urged Wilson to change his policy. Wilson refused on the ground the Mexican government did not rest on law and the consent of the governed. On 11 March 1913 at Mobile, Alabama, he publicly announced his opposition to Huerta when he declared, "We can have no sympathy with those who seize the power of government to advance their own personal interest or ambition." The president recalled Ambassador Wilson and sent John Lind to Mexico City as his special envoy to try to persuade Huerta to withdraw and allow a free election. When this mission failed, Wilson adopted a policy of "watchful waiting," hoping Huerta would fall from power. The president did, however, interfere in the Mexican conflict when he permitted Huerta's opponents to purchase munitions in the United States while placing an embargo on munitions for Huerta.

Wilson eventually intervened in Mexico. On 9 April 1914 several American sailors, who had gone ashore at Tampico to buy gasoline, were arrested and taken to local military headquarters. The commanding officer promptly released them with apologies. But Admiral T. H. Mayo, commander of the American Naval Forces, decided to make an issue of the incident. He demanded a formal apology, punishment for the officer involved, and a public ceremony whereby Mexico would "hoist the American flag in a prominent position and salute it with twenty-one guns." Huerta complied with the first two demands and also expressed a willingness to order a salute, provided the Americans responded with a twenty-one gun salute to Mexico. Mayo refused and was supported by the State Department. Wilson regarded Huerta's reply as an insult, and on 20 April he asked Congress for authority to use military forces to secure redress.

Before Congress acted, news reached Washington from Admiral Mayo that a German steamer filled with arms and ammunition for

Huerta was about to dock at Vera Cruz. Without waiting for the consent of Congress, Wilson ordered Mayo to "take Vera Cruz at once." On 21 April a detachment of Marines occupied the port city. On the same day, the House of Representatives by a vote of 323 to 19 gave the president the necessary authority to use the armed forces. The Senate concurred the next day 72 to 13.

Many believed the seizure of Vera Cruz was the prelude to war over what a Chicago editor called a "question of etiquette." At this point, Argentina, Brazil, and Chile urged mediation. Wilson accepted their offer. Mediators and principals met at Niagara Falls in May 1914. The result was inconclusive, but the embargo against Huerta finally forced him from office in July 1914. In August Venustiano Carranza became president, and Wilson accorded him recognition.

When the United States acquired insular possessions, the old problem of Congress' power over the territories, debated so much in the 1840s and 1850s, was raised again. Since the Constitution contained no express provision concerning the acquisition and government of new provinces, Congress faced some new legal questions.

In the treaty of cession with Spain, "the civil rights and the political status of the native inhabitants of a territory . . . ceded to the United States" were left to the determination of Congress. This raised a number of far-reaching questions. Could Congress do whatever it wanted to do without extending the liberties guaranteed by the Constitution to its island possessions? Or did the Constitution restrict Congress in the government of the islands, as if they were physically and politically a part of the United States, and particularly did the limitations in behalf of private rights, freedom of the press, trial by jury, and the like embodied in the first ten amendments control the power of Congress? Or to put it in the form of the popular query, "Does the Constitution follow the flag?"

The strict constitutionalist maintained Congress was limited everywhere, even in the territories, by the amendments providing for the protection of personal and property rights. The practical politicians, however, stated the Constitution and the laws of the United States did not of their own force apply in the territories of the United States and could not until Congress had expressly applied them. Congress assumed from the outset it was free from constitutional limitations. For example, in the Foraker Act it established a tariff on imports to the United States from Puerto Rico equivalent to 15 percent of the regular

Dingley Tariff. If Puerto Rico was a part of the United States, then these duties on her goods were clearly unconstitutional.

The question came before the Supreme Court in the insular cases of 1901. In *Downes* v. *Bidwell* (1901), the Court upheld the Foraker Act regarding the collection of duties on Puerto Rican goods on the ground that Puerto Rico was "not a part of the United States within the revenue clauses of the Constitution." This decision led "Mr. Dooley" to comment, "No matter whether the Constitution follows the flag or not, th' Supreme Court follows th' illiction returns."

In another case, the Court decided that in the period between annexation and the time of the passage of the Organic Act (1900), making Hawaii a territory, the inhabitants could not claim right of trial by jury. The Court went on to say that "rights alleged to be violated...are not fundamental in their nature." This logic meant that the Bill of Rights was divided into two parts: "a fundamental" part and a "formal" part. According to this viewpoint, only the fundamental part restricted Congress in governing possessions, and the Court would decide as specific cases arose which parts of the Constitution were fundamental and which were formal.

While intervention in Latin American affairs constituted an important change in American foreign policy, a more significant departure and an enlarged role in world affairs for the United States began to take place in its involvement in Far Eastern matters through the Open Door policy. As we have seen, the narrow concept of the Open Door when it was enunciated in 1899 was expanded in 1900 to include the preservation of the territorial integrity of China.

Despite the broadening of the Open Door, the United States seemed more concerned about American economic interests in China than the territorial integrity of China. In a letter to President Roosevelt in May 1902 Hay remarked: "We are not in any attitude of hostility toward Russia and Manchuria. On the contrary, we recognize her exceptional position in northern China. What we have been working for two years to accomplish, if assurances are to count for anything, is that no matter what happens eventually in northern China and Manchuria, the United States shall not be placed in any worse position than while the country was under the unquestioned dominion of China."

The maintenance of the Open Door depended upon an equilibrium of power in the Far East, and this was possible while Japan and

Russia contended for top position in this area. Because of difficulties Japan had with Russia in attempting to work out a solution in Korea and Manchuria, it attacked Russia in February 1904 and then declared war afterward, just as it had done to China in 1894 and was to do to the United States in 1941.

The main objective of the Russo-Japanese War was control of Korea and China. Both belligerents were traditional friends of the United States, but American sympathies were on the side of Japan. By this date Russia had lost many friends in the United States because of her Siberian exiles, her persecution of Jews, and her expansionism in the Far East. Moreover, Japanese propaganda had been effective in making Americans believe they had to strike first because Russia had bullied them.

While the Japanese scored a number of victories and the war seemed to end within a year and a half with success for Japan, both countries were near exhaustion by the summer of 1905. Japan had used so much manpower and financial resources to win that she faced collapse. Had the Russians been able to keep going they might have worn down Japan and gained a victory. But Russia had internal difficulties. In addition the Moroccan crisis, concerning French efforts to establish a protectorate over that country, was nearing a head, and France was urging her ally Russia to quit before she had spent herself.

In May 1905 Japan asked President Roosevelt to act as mediator. While the president was not enthusiastic about this role, he thought it would serve the interests of the United States and end the war. Above all, he wanted to maintain the balance of power between Japan and Russia in the Far East to preserve the Open Door. At a peace conference at Portsmouth, New Hampshire, from 10 August to 5 September 1905 the Japanese, among other things, demanded a large money indemnity and the Russian island of Sakhalin. Largely because of Roosevelt's pressure, the Japanese dropped their monetary demands, and Russia consented to cession of one-half of Sakhalin. Both Russia and Japan agreed to take all their troops, except railroad guards, from Manchuria and to return this province to China, except for the Liaotung Peninsula. The Portsmouth Treaty was regarded as a personal triumph for Roosevelt, who received the Nobel Peace Prize in 1906 for his efforts.

Japan, by the treaty, emerged as the dominant power in the Far East, and this development did not strengthen the Open Door. While Japan gained advantages at Portsmouth because of the friendly mediation of Roosevelt, the treaty marks the beginning of a period of strained relations between the two countries. Japan was resentful because it failed to secure all of Sakhalin and an indemnity, and, furthermore, because it regarded the Open Door as blocking its expansion in the Far East.

While Roosevelt had favored Japan during the war, he recognized she might cause trouble to American possessions in the Far East, especially the Philippines. Roosevelt also worried about Japan swinging away from an Anglo-American orbit to an alliance with Russia. To forestall these developments Roosevelt did two things. In the first place, he agreed to help make peace at Portsmouth. Second, he secured the Taft-Katsura Agreement of July 1905 to avert the possible intentions Japan might have toward the Philippines. Secretary of War Taft, ostensibly on a mission to Manila, had gone to negotiate in Tokyo—without the knowledge of the American ambassador—an agreement with Prime Minister Katsura whereby the United States approved Japan's "suzerainty over" Korea in return for Japan's disavowal of any aggressive designs on the Philippines.

This agreement actually violated the Open Door since the United States gave Japan a free hand in Korea. Roosevelt recognized that the United States could not prevent Japan from taking over Korea, so he decided to accept this situation and secure something in return—the disclaimer on the part of Japan to take the Philippines. Very shortly after this Japan informed the United States that it was taking full charge of Korea's foreign relations. The United States complied with this by withdrawing its legation in Korea and consenting to deal with Japan concerning Korea. In 1910 when Japan changed its protectorate over Korea to complete sovereignty, the United States did not protest. Elihu Root had been secretary of state in the acceptance of the Japanese proposal concerning Korea in 1905, and he wrote to his biographer in 1930, "Many people are still angry because we did not keep Japan from taking Korea. There was nothing we could do except fight Japan; Congress wouldn't have declared war and the people would have turned out the Congress that had. All we might have done was to make threats which we could not carry out."

The Japanese resented not only the Portsmouth Treaty but also the San Francisco School Board decision in 1906 requiring the city's ninety-three Japanese school children to attend a separate school. This action deeply wounded Japan's national pride. Some of her newspapers demanded war, and the government sent a strong protest. President Roosevelt was furious at the "infernal fools" in California, but the American federal system gave him no jurisdiction over the California public schools. Only after bringing heavy pressure to bear on local authorities did Roosevelt succeed in having the action reversed. In return, he promised to put an end to the unwanted immigration of Japanese. After some negotiation, the Japanese accepted the Gentlemen's Agreement of 1907-1908, whereby the Japanese government promised to issue no more passports to Japanese laborers who wished to come to the United States and the American government promised to pass no official exclusion act against the Japanese.

Roosevelt, however, feared the Japanese might regard his attempt to mollify them as a sign of weakness. He told a friend, "they should realize that I am not afraid of them and that the United States will no more submit to bullying than it will bully." Thus he decided to send the American fleet, now the second largest in the world, around the world to make a show of strength. The Japanese received the fleet warmly, and the voyage was a success. The war talk between the United States and Japan died down, and in November 1908 both countries signed the Root-Takahira Agreement whereby they agreed to maintain the status quo in the Pacific area, to respect each other's territorial possessions in that region, to uphold the Open Door in China, and to support by pacific means the "independence and integrity of China...." It was hoped this agreement would sustain the peace between the United States and Japan for a long time to come.

During World War I, however, a number of incidents renewed the tension between Japan and the United States. Japan entered the war on the side of the Allies in August 1914 and proceeded to seize the German holdings in Shantung, China. Now Europe's distress became Japan's advantage in the Far East. Japan capitalized on the struggle in Europe to make demands upon China that she might have hesitated to make under other circumstances. In January 1915 she presented her Twenty-One Demands to China. Had China accepted these in their entirety she might have become a protectorate of Japan. The demands created the strong impression Japan was preparing to close the Open Door, and they alarmed public opinion in the United States.

The European powers could offer no support to China, but the United States sent a warning in May 1915, signed by Secretary of State Bryan, and known as Bryan's Non-Recognition Note. It stated the United States would not recognize any agreement or understanding between Japan and China impairing the treaty rights of the United States in China, "or the international policy relative to China, commonly known as the open door policy."

Though Bryan's Non-Recognition Doctrine made it clear to Japan that the United States would continue to express its views in regard to Chinese-Japanese relations, the Open Door was further weakened by the Lansing-Ishii agreement of November 1917 between the United States and Japan. The agreement endorsed the principle that "territorial propinquity creates special relations between countries," and "consequently...the United States recognized that Japan has special interests in China, particularly in the part to which her possessions are contiguous." Nevertheless, the document continued, "the territorial sovereignty of China remains unimpaired," and the United States accepted Japan's assurances that it had no "desire to discriminate against the trade of other nations or to disregard the commercial rights heretofore granted by China in treaties with other powers." Then the two governments mutually disclaimed "any purpose to infringe in any way the independence or territorial integrity of China," and promised to adhere to "the so-called 'open door' or equal opportunity for commerce and industry in China."

Severely criticized for having given to Japan a free hand in China in return for recognition of an Open Door already acknowledged by Japan, Lansing attempted to rebut this by pointing out that by "special interest" he meant economic interests. He also maintained that circumstances compelled him to make the concessions (the possibility of Japan deserting the Allies), and he did try to limit them and even undo them at Versailles. Yet, in the eyes of diplomacy, Lansing had made a political commitment to Japan, because in diplomatic language "special interest" had a political as well as an economic connotation.

American diplomacy in the Progressive period involved more than the problems of colonial administration, intervention in Latin American affairs, and efforts to maintain the Open Door in China and peace in the Far East. The United States also sought to promote world peace and continued to support the doctrine of arbitration for settling international disputes.

The growing interest of the United States in general world affairs was shown in the efforts of both Roosevelt and Taft, in negotiating agreements with other nations, to submit to the Permanent Court of Arbitration at the Hague all cases coming within the scope of arbitration. Hay, Roosevelt's first Secretary of State had negotiated fourteen arbitration treaties, mainly with Great Britain, France, and Germany, by December 1904. However, they all excluded from arbitration questions affecting the vital interests, national honor, and independence of the contracting countries and thus the treaties were rather limited instruments. Whenever there was to be arbitration, however, there was to be a special agreement defining the matter in dispute, the nature and authority of the tribunal, and the like. The Senate, in acting on Hay's arbitration treaties, provided that the special agreement in every case must, like a treaty, receive Senate approval. This action angered Roosevelt, and he withdrew the treaties from further consideration. Following the Second Hague Conference of 1907, Secretary of State Root negotiated twenty-five arbitration treaties during the remainder of Roosevelt's second term with all the leading powers except Germany. These treaties were in the form that the Senate had prescribed and therefore were approved.

Taft and his secretary of state, Philander Knox, went further than Roosevelt and negotiated treaties with France and Great Britain that provided for submission to arbitration all questions that might cause war. But there was considerable criticism of the treaties on the ground they involved our national honor and vital interests. When the Senate weakened the treaties by exempting from arbitration questions concerning immigration, state debts, and the Monroe Doctrine, Taft withdrew them from further consideration.

Roosevelt also departed from traditional American policy of non-involvement in Europe in the Moroccan crisis. The German Kaiser, opposed to France's efforts to establish a protectorate over Morocco, demanded an international conference on Morocco at a time when France's ally, Russia, was bogged down in a war with Japan. France, with the backing of Britain, refused, and there was danger of a European war over the issue. Then the Kaiser appealed to Roosevelt for support. Although he was reluctant to intervene, Roosevelt, aware that war might come, pressured Britain and France to attend a conference.

The conference met at Algeciras, Spain, early in 1906. The American delegation supported France and Britain on the crucial issues, and thus the Kaiser was unsuccessful in his bid for a foothold in Morocco. Though the General Act of Algeciras, signed 7 April 1906, made reference to the independence of Morocco and to the principle of commercial freedom, it actually allowed France to extend its control over this North African country.

Roosevelt's action was criticized by some as a break with our traditional policy of noninvolvement in European affairs. The president, however, was pleased by his intervention and believed the conference had prevented war. So did his friend, Henry Cabot Lodge, who wrote: "We are the strongest moral force—also physical—now extant, and the peace of the world rests largely with us. So far you have saved the situation."

For most of the post–Civil War generation, the United States had not been very active in world diplomacy. She wanted to enjoy her isolation. But, as we have seen, all this changed as America acquired an overseas empire and emerged as a major power. By the time the First World War broke out in Europe in the summer of 1914, the United States had considerably enlarged its role in international affairs and had assumed greater responsibilities for helping to maintain peace. The Great War provided a severe test of Americans' stamina in carrying the new burdens they had assumed. Under the idealist leadership of President Wilson, whose administration witnessed the culmination of America's modern domestic reform era, the nation would step forth in the name of reform to face the international challenge that the war posed.

Further Reading

A number of readings for Chapter 7 will also be useful for this chapter.

Anderson, David L. *Imperialism and Idealism: American Diplomats in China, 1861–1898.* 1985.

Bailey, Thomas A. *Theodore Roosevelt and the Japanese-American Crises.* 1934.

Beale, Howard K. *Theodore Roosevelt and the Rise of America to World Power.* 1956.

Bemis, Samuel F. *The Latin American Policy of the United States.* 1943.

Berbusse, Edward J. *The United States in Puerto Rico, 1898–1900.* 1960.

Braisted, W. R. *The United States Navy in the Pacific, 1897–1909.* 1958.

Calcott, Wilfred H. *The Caribbean Policy of the United States, 1890–1920.* 1942.

Calhoun, Frederick S. *Power and Principle: Armed Intervention in Wilsonian Foreign Policy.* 1986.

Calvert, Peter. *The Mexican Revolution, 1910–1914: The Diplomacy of Anglo-American Conflict.* 1968.

Clendenen, Clarence C. *The United States and Pancho Villa.* 1960.

Cline, Howard F. *The United States and Mexico.* 1953.

Curry, Roy Watson. *Woodrow Wilson and Far Eastern Policy, 1913–1921.* 1957.

Dulles, Foster R. *America's Rise to World Power.* 1955.

Esthus, Raymond. *Theodore Roosevelt and the International Rivalries.* 1970.

Fairbank, John K. *The United States and China.* 1958.

Gilderhus, Mark T. *Pan American Visions: Woodrow Wilson in the Western Hemisphere, 1913–1921.* 1986.

Healy, David F. *The United States in Cuba, 1898–1902.* 1963.

Iriye, Akira. *Pacific Estrangement: Japanese and American Expansion, 1897–1911.* 1972.

Kennan, George F. *American Diplomacy.* 1951.

McCullough, David. *Path Between the Seas: The Creation of the Panama Canal, 1870–1914.* 1977.

Munro, Dana C. *Intervention and Dollar Diplomacy in the Caribbean, 1900–1921.* 1964.

New, Charles E. *An Uncertain Friendship: Theodore Roosevelt and Japan, 1906–1909.* 1967.

Quirk, Robert. *An Affair of Honor: Woodrow Wilson and the Occupation of Vera Cruz.* 1962.

Pérez, Louis A. *Cuba Under the Platt Amendment, 1902–1934.* 1986.

Perkins, Dexter. *The Monroe Doctrine, 1867–1907.* 1937.

Pratt, Julius W. *America's Colonial Experiment.* 1950.

———. *Challenge and Rejection, 1900–1921.* 1967.

Scholes, Walter V. and Marie V. Scholes. *The Foreign Policies of the Taft Administration.* 1970.

Stanley, P. W. *A Nation in the Making: The Philippines and the United States, 1899–1921.* 1975.

Vevier, Charles. *The United States and China, 1906–1913.* 1955.

13

America's Road to War: 1914–1917

Though the United States government and its informed citizens were presumably aware of increasing tensions among the European powers in the latter part of the nineteenth century and the first part of the twentieth century, the outbreak of World War I in the summer of 1914 probably surprised both the government and the American public. When President Woodrow Wilson had addressed Congress in December 1913, he expressed the general feeling of tranquility in the country when he said, "many happy manifestations multiply around us of a growing cordiality...among the nations, foreshadowing an age of settled peace and good will."

This optimism was ill founded. Ever since the Franco-Prussian War of 1871, strains among the great powers of Europe had been increasing. It was evident in economic rivalry, armament races, and international alliances among them. Over the years a series of crises had repeatedly threatened to involve Europe in a general war and, in 1914, it was divided into two hostile sides: (1) the Triple Alliance of Germany, Austria-Hungary, and Italy and (2) the Triple Entente of France, Russia, and Great Britain.

Many volumes have been written to explain the causes of World War I, and each coalition has attempted to place the responsibility for it upon its opponent. So there has been an endless debate about it. Surely the intense rivalry and suspicion prevailing among the European powers was an underlying cause. The direct and precipitating cause, however, was the assassination on 28 June 1914 of the Archduke Franz Ferdinand, heir to the Austro-Hungarian throne, by a Serb in Sarajevo in Bosnia. Nationalistic Bosnian Serbs opposed the archduke's plan to bring Serbia into the dual monarchy of Austria-Hungary.

The Austrian government, believing the murder had been encouraged by Serbian officials, sent to Serbia on July 23 a set of demands to be met within forty-eight hours. If Serbia accepted them, it would have ended her independence. Depending on her ally, Russia, Serbia refused compliance. On July 28, Austria, backed by her ally, Germany, declared war. At this point, the whole network of European alliances swung into action.

Russia mobilized her armed forces to forestall Austria's extension of power into the Slavic World. Germany hurriedly declared war on Russia on August 1, and on Russia's ally, France, on August 3, thereby hoping to defeat France before Russian forces came into the field. Though bound by treaty to respect Belgium's neutrality, German armies moved through Belgium to engage and destroy the French army at once. Germany's plan failed because of the resistance of the Belgians and the French. Great Britain was also pledged to protect Belgium.

Until the German invasion, Britain was uncommitted. Then on August 4, Britain declared war on Germany. So the First World War began. Bulgaria and Turkey joined Austria and Germany to form the Central Powers. Japan, Italy, Rumania, and Greece joined Russia, France, and Britain to make the Allies. Norway, Sweden, Denmark, Holland, Portugal, Spain, and Switzerland remained neutral.*

Before this titanic and monstrous war would end four years later tens of millions of men would be armed and fighting. No one will ever know how many died from it, but some historians believe that they numbered at least 30 million, including civilian deaths. Four empires were destroyed—the Austro-Hungarian, as well as the empires of the Germans, the Ottomans, and the Russian Czars. An entire way of life, encompassing tens of millions of people and reaching over great parts of the earth's surface, lay in ruins. "In many ways," writes historian Robert Kelley, "the greatest tragedy of the twentieth century is the First World War."

---

*Italian interests were opposed to Austria-Hungary's, and Italy finally entered the war on the Allied side.

It is this war the United States entered in April 1917. Much has been said and written about why the United States decided to do this. The official explanation came in President Woodrow Wilson's war message when he said, "We enter the war only where we are clearly forced into it, because there are no other means of defending our rights." Thus the earliest and the official view was that the war was forced upon the United States by Germany. The first historians to write about intervention supported Wilson's position. But dissent and disillusionment with this belief set in when the hope for a peace without victory was not realized in the Treaty of Versailles at the end of the war, and they continued to grow especially when a new war appeared in the making in the 1930s. In addition, new sources became available for historians to examine. So different explanations for intervention appeared, such as: (1) American intervention resulted from the heavy economic interest the United States had in an Allied victory over Germany, (2) American involvement came from the pressure of American public opinion built up by effective British propaganda in this country, (3) Wilson's idealistic search for a better world led him to follow a bogus neutrality that compelled Germany to use the submarine and involve us in the war, and (4) after Germany had defeated France in 1940 and threatened England, some wrote that Wilson intervened in 1917 to assure America's security in the face of a militaristic Germany seemingly on the way to the domination of Europe and to maintain Anglo-American control of the Atlantic sea lanes.

When the war broke out, most Americans believed their country had no particular stake in its outcome and were relieved to be far away from the conflict. It might cause some inconvenience in trade and travel but nothing more than that. A few did regard the war as a significant contest between Anglo-Saxon liberty and German militarism. But to most Americans, irrespective of their sympathies, the war was a European affair. "Our isolated position and freedom from entangling alliances," commented the *Literary Digest,*" inspire our press with cheering assurance that we are in no peril of being drawn into the European quarrel."

In April 1937, twenty years after the United States had entered the First World War and with another war on the horizon, the Gallup Poll asked Americans whether the decision to intervene in 1917 had been a mistake. Sixty-four percent of those polled thought it had been a mistake. After World War II began in Europe the question was asked three more times in November 1939, December 1940, and April 1941. The percentage of those who thought it had been a mistake dropped to 59 in 1939 and to 39 in both 1940 and 1941.*

President Wilson assumed full personal control of American policy during the European war. He wrote most of the important diplomatic notes and bypassed the State Department using his own private agents. During the period of American neutrality from 1914 to 1917, Wilson followed two somewhat contradictory main policies: (1) the United States must remain the great neutral during the war and must be the exponent of "peace without victory," and (2) the Allies must not be allowed to lose the war. Wilson himself expressed few personal views as to the merits of the war and appeared indifferent to the claims of either side. On one occasion in 1916 he said the United States was not concerned with the "causes and objects of the war." Later in the same year he told both groups of belligerents that they had virtually the same aims in the war as they had stated them in general terms to their own people and to the world. This surprised and dismayed many Englishmen that the President should think they were fighting for the same things in the war as the Germans. But even as late as February 1917, only two months before the United States entered the war and after Germany's decision to resume submarine warfare had become known to Wilson, the president was asked at a Cabinet meeting which side he wished to see victorious. Without hesitation he reportedly replied "he didn't wish to see either side win—for both had been equally indifferent to the rights of neutrals—though Germany had been brutal in taking life and England only in taking property." This was according to Franklin H. Lane, Wilson's Secretary of the Interior, who recorded this Cabinet episode.

Even after the United States joined the conflict, Wilson continued to believe that the primary interest of England in the war was commercial and imperialistic, a view that was painful to the English. Apparently Wilson did not change his views about the causes and objects of the war, and neither did he accept at face value any special merit of righteousness that either England, France, or Germany might have had.

One should remember that Wilson, like the majority of Americans then, opposed the use of force to achieve national objectives, and he was reluctant to use even the threat of force in diplomacy. The historian Charles Tansill, who was very critical of Wilson's decision to go to

---

*Public Opinion Quarterly, V (Fall, 1941), 476-477

war, wrote nevertheless about him, "In the long list of American Chief Executives there is no one who was a more sincere pacifist than the one who led us into war in April, 1917."

On 4 August 1914, when the major European powers were at war, Wilson issued a proclamation of neutrality—a policy not seriously tested since the Napoleonic Wars a century earlier. Two weeks later he appealed to Americans to be "neutral in fact as well as in name," to be "impartial in thought as in action." From then until April 1917, when Wilson asked Congress to declare war on Germany, he tried to maintain a neutral position although, according to many of his critics, his interpretations of neutrality favored the Allies.

For Americans to be impartial and neutral was almost impossible. This is a very important matter to keep in mind as we work our way through the period of neutrality. The majority of Americans spoke English. Literature, laws, customs, and institutions bound Americans to England. American friendship for France, more sentimental in character, dated back to French aid in the American Revolution. Furthermore, there were strong economic ties between the United States and the Allies. Friendship for the Allies was balanced by fear and suspicion of Germany. Americans thought of Germany as being ruthless and militaristic. The United States and Germany were rivals in a number of fields, and both had emerged as great powers at about the same time.

It was also difficult for the Wilson administration to be impartial. The president had warm personal feelings for the English. His model statesmen were English, and he admired the English form of government. Moreover, he was surrounded by pro-Allied advisers, especially after Secretary of State William Jennings Bryan resigned his post in 1915. While Bryan was in the Cabinet he was as evenhanded as anyone could be. But Robert Lansing, who succeeded him, Walter Hines Page, American ambassador to England, and Colonel Edward M. House, Wilson's most trusted adviser on foreign affairs, were ardently pro-Allied. Time and again Page took the sting out of American notes of protest to the English government for violations of American neutrality on the high seas by telling the British foreign office the notes were sent to placate public opinion at home and were not to be taken seriously. In Washington, House was telling the British ambassador much the same thing about the notes. Clearly the Allies in this respect had a position of vantage in the United States. As House wrote to Page in October 1914, "I cannot see how there can be any serious trouble between England and America, with all of us feeling as we do."

In the period of neutrality Americans were deluged with propaganda from both belligerents. The British cut the cables between Berlin and New York, and war news came to the United States largely through London where it was given a British slant. The Germans, however, were able to put their case before the American public. Information came through the mails and the dispatches of American news correspondents. Germany's chief disadvantage in this battle of words was how to explain its violation of Belgium's neutrality, which it had solemnly sworn to respect. Count von Bernstorff, German ambassador to the United States, conceded, "The Belgian question was the one which interested Americans most and which was most effective in working up American opinion against us."

Before 1915, not many thoughtful Americans accepted at face value the atrocity charges against Germany, because American newspapermen on the Belgian and French front were denying them. Then on 13 May 1915, the Bryce Commission, headed by the distinguished Englishman James Bryce and comprised of leading men, put out a *Report* accusing Germany of using a policy of deliberate cruelty in Belgium. Issued by such a prominent commission and following by only six days the sinking of the British liner *Lusitania* without warning by German submarines with the death of more than 1,200 noncombatants, including 128 Americans, the *Report* led many Americans to reconsider the atrocity charges against the Germans.

As in the Napoleonic Wars, both warring sides interfered with American rights as a neutral on the high seas. Each belligerent attempted to cut off trade with its enemies, thus raising an old question of contraband (ordinarily materials destined directly for the use of military forces) and blockade and a new question of the immunity of commercial vessels, their crews, and passengers from submarine attacks. Each belligerent denounced the other's conduct as illegal. Wilson found both to be at fault.

Britain controlled the seas, and its interference with neutral trade with the Central Powers created the first difficulties for the United States. By March 1915, Britain had mined the North Sea, imposed a naval blockade on Germany and neutral Europe, and seized American ships carrying even noncontraband goods (food, raw materials, and goods destined for use only by civilians) to European neutrals. The British opened American mail pouches and confiscated packages to neutral countries, claiming they were eventually going to the enemy. Britain also blacklisted American firms suspected of trading with the

Central Powers. Americans were angry. Wilson himself said he was "about at the end of my patience with Great Britain and the Allies. This blacklist business is the last straw...Can we longer endure their intolerable course?"

Thus the first difficulties for the United States over neutral rights were with Great Britain. The question was whether the United States should accept the British practices on the high seas. At first Wilson wanted to insist upon full respect for American commercial rights, but he finally resorted to a series of firm but friendly protest notes to serve as a basis for later adjudication. Though some of these notes were strongly worded they never were so strong as those sent to Germany.

Wilson's recognition of British maritime control just about ended American trade with Germany and Austria, which fell from $169.2 million in 1914 to a mere $1.1 million in 1916. In the same period American trade with the Allies rose from $828.8 million to $3.2 billion. The United States became a warehouse from which all kinds of materials flowed to the Allies. American sympathy now turned into sentiment for open aid to the Allies. In 1914, the United States suffered from a recession, but by 1915 enormous Allied war orders had taken up the economic slack in the country. Yet through their heavy purchases the Allies had exhausted their credit balances in the United States, and the question arose of extending them private loans. In peacetime American bankers would have given the necessary credit.

Loans to belligerents were, however, another matter. Bryan opposed loans to belligerents on the basis they were "inconsistent with the true spirit of neutrality." At first Wilson agreed with Bryan. But it soon became evident that the Allies would have to curtail their purchases or secure large loans in the United States. Businessmen put pressure on Wilson to change his mind. The *Financial Annalist* expressed the sentiments of many Americans about trade with the Allies when it pointed out, "We need it for the profits it will bring." Williams Gibbs McAdoo, secretary of the treasury and Wilson's son-in-law, thought Bryan's ban on loans threatened United States prosperity. To preserve this prosperity "we must do everything we can to assist our customers to pay," McAdoo wrote to the president in August 1915. "To maintain our prosperity we must finance it. Otherwise it may stop and that would be disastrous."

Recognizing the importance of the Allied trade, Wilson and Bryan himself began to retreat from the Bryan ban on loans. Soon the United States became the source of credit as well as of war materials for the Allies. By the time the United States entered the war the Allies had borrowed $2.25 billion. The larger part of this credit paid for Allied purchases and thus never left the United States. In contrast, American loans to Germany amounted to only $27 million. Thomas Lamont of the House of Morgan, which handled a number of the Allied loans, said later, "Those were the days when American citizens were being urged to be neutral in action, in word, and even in thought. But our firm had never for one moment been neutral; we didn't know how to be. From the very start we did everything we could to contribute to the cause of the Allies."

Loans and the Allied trade they financed kept the country prosperous until it entered the war. By then it had a large economic stake in an Allied victory. In the 1930s a United States Senate committee headed by Senator Gerald Nye, an isolationist Republican from North Dakota, charged the United States with going to war in 1917 to protect bankers' loans and munition makers profits. The evidence did not support this accusation. Nevertheless, the presence of strong economic ties with the Allies, and the absence of such ties with Germany, made it easier to break with Germany when the time came.

The close links of sympathy and trade between the United States and the Allies greatly concerned and handicapped Germany, also needful of trade with America. Germany urged Wilson to place an embargo on the shipment of arms contending that since they went only to the Allies this traffic was an unneutral act. Some senators, including William J. Stone, Democrat of Missouri and chairman of the Senate Foreign Relations Committee, agreed with Germany on this.

But Wilson opposed an embargo. He maintained an embargo itself was an unneutral act because it gave an advantage to one opponent. American policy had always been to keep its markets open to belligerents and neutrals alike. Germany's inability to obtain arms from the United States, Wilson argued, was the result of British control of the seas and not of American policy.

Germany's most effective weapon against Allied sea power was the submarine. Her decision to conduct a submarine campaign against merchant shipping confronted the United States with another difficult problem. So long as Germany used traditional military operations, there was little likelihood of conflict with the United States. No American interests were in reach of German land forces. But when Germany employed the submarine to challenge British supremacy on the sea, it became necessary for Wilson to reexamine his neutrality policy. If he continued to accept the British blockade, he would impair relations with Germany. If he acquiesced in German submarine warfare, he would impair relations with the Allies. He had reached the point where it seemed impossible to be impartial, because almost any decision appeared to give an advantage to one side or the other.

On 4 February 1915, Germany announced a submarine blockade of the British Isles. All enemy vessels in a broad war zone would be destroyed without warning. Neutral vessels could proceed through these waters at their own risk. Germany disclaimed responsibility for the loss of life among passengers or crews of vessels sunk by submarines, and warned it might not be possible for the submarine to make a distinction between neutral and enemy ships. Germany appealed to Americans for understanding. She contended it was necessary to retaliate against the British food blockade, and she said if the British would lift their food blockade she would lift her submarine blockade.

This turned out to be neither a serious nor a sincere proposal. Germany was not able to impose an effective blockade on the British Isles and was using a paper blockade to try to force the British to relax their controls, not only on food but also on other materials. In spite of Germany's bluff, the British agreed to allow food to enter Germany provided she would give up the use of submarines against merchant shipping. Germany, really not short of food, pressed the British to permit raw materials to pass through their blockade. But the British refused, because this concession would have destroyed the effectiveness of their blockade.

After Britain refused, Germany launched a campaign of unrestricted submarine warfare against unarmed Allied merchant and passenger vessels in the North Atlantic. As the submarine had been invented after the last general codification of international law in 1865, there were no provisions governing its use as a weapon. The only applicable laws were those of surface raiders. These required attacking warships to warn merchant vessels before sinking them and to provide for the safety of the passengers, crews, and papers. Obviously the submarine could not comply with these regulations. If it surfaced to search or to give warning to a merchantman, it ran the risk of being rammed or else sunk by the deck guns of the larger vessel. This danger was not theoretical. Once Germany started to use submarines, Britain fitted merchant ships with armaments and issued orders for them to sink submarines on sight. Thus, a submarine captain had little choice but to hit and run, disregarding whether or not he had accidentally struck a neutral vessel and doomed its passengers. Submarine warfare would have to be illegal to be effective, and Germany meant it to be effective.

How did Wilson respond to this new threat and danger on the high seas? In a note of 10 February 1915, only six days after Germany had announced her submarine policy, Wilson warned Germany that the United States would hold her to a "strict accountability" for American loss of life and property. As Allied ships were being sunk in 1915, it was clearly dangerous for Americans to travel or work on belligerent ships. It was also clear that unless neutrals kept their citizens and property off Allied ships, they were certain to become involved in quarrels with Germany. German officials in the United States issued warnings to Americans traveling on Allied ships, but Americans ignored the warnings. Bryan asked Wilson to allow Americans to travel on belligerent ships only at their own risk, but the president insisted upon protecting them on such ships. This was a dangerous game, and it had much to do with our entry into the war. Wilson also insisted upon submarines following the rules of surface raiders. His position on these two important neutral rights was probably determined by his pro-Allied sympathies and by his belief that submarine warfare threatened, as he put it, "the fundamental rights of humanity. . . ." for "the loss of life is irreparable." Wilson, however, had the support of all his advisers except Bryan on these two points.

Neutrals, such as Americans, regularly traveled as passengers on British ships. The question was what to do about it. To present-day Americans, the answer would probably be to prohibit neutrals from traveling in war zones and to keep neutral vessels away from them. This is what the United States did when World War II broke out. But during World War I, Wilson was not prepared to accept such a substantial change, and a demeaning one in his view, of the traditional customs of international travel. He talked constantly of protecting American neutral rights all the way.

On 28 April 1915, an American ship (*Cushing*) was attacked by a German submarine. On 1 May 1915, an American tanker (*Gulfflight*) was torpedoed with loss of its captain and two crew members. Then on 7 May 1915, a German submarine sank, without warning, the unarmed British liner, the *Lusitania*, off the southern coast of Ireland with the loss of nearly 1,200 passengers, including 128 Americans. The appalling toll of lives among women and children shocked and angered Americans.

The Germans committed a colossal blunder when they sank the *Lusitania*. Some American newspapers called it "slaughter" and "wholesale murder." Colonel House predicted the United States would be "at war with Germany within a month." Page wrote from London, "We live in hope that America will come in...." Bryan was nearly alone when he protested that England was "using our citizens to protect her ammunition."

Theodore Roosevelt described the sinking as an "act of piracy" and demanded war. "The torpedo that sank the *Lusitania*," declared *The Nation*, "also sank Germany in the opinion of mankind." But few Americans wanted war, and Wilson led the moderate forces. Three days after the tragedy he said in a public address, "There is such a thing as a man being too proud to fight. There is such a thing as a nation being so right that it does not need to convince others by force it is right." Wilson confined himself to three sharply worded protests to Germany. The second one was so strong that Bryan, still wanting to curtail American travel abroad, resigned as secretary of state rather than sign it. Wilson replaced him with Robert Lansing. Many notes passed between the two countries until in February 1916, Germany agreed to pay an indemnity for the loss of American lives.

In Germany's view the *Lusitania* was legitimately sunk, because the ship was carrying concealed armament, but the United States rejected this position. Two modern American historians Thomas Bailey and Paul Ryan in a deeply researched account of the affair demonstrated that the *Lusitania* was unarmed, carried no troops nor high explosives, and was sunk by one German submarine, firing one torpedo, which exploded the ship's boilers. The book destroyed allegations that Germany plotted to sink the *Lusitania* or that Winston Churchill as first lord of the Admiralty ordered its destruction to bring the United States into the war as an ally. The meeting of the ship and the submarine was entirely fortuitous.

Germany could not accept Wilson's position on the use of submarines, because this would have destroyed their effectiveness. While Germany would not change her original plans she did tell the American government it was "very far indeed from the intention of the German Government...to destroy neutral lives and neutral property." However, the refusal of either Germany or the United States to back down from their positions on the use of the submarine produced a series of further incidents on the high seas, increasing the tension between the two countries.

There were more German sinkings and more American protests. Then in June 1915, while arguing with Washington, Germany issued secret orders to submarine commanders to spare the larger passenger vessels. Yet on August 19, a U-boat sank the British liner *Arabic* with the loss of two American lives. To avoid a fresh crisis, Germany revealed the secret orders on September 1 and pledged "liners will not be sunk without warning and without the safety of the lives of the noncombatants, provided that the liners do not try to escape or offer resistance." The *Arabic* pledge maintained peace between the United States and Germany and was considered a diplomatic achievement for Wilson.

But sinkings continued, and matters again came to a head on 28 March 1916 when an unarmed French ship, the *Sussex*, was sunk and several Americans on board were seriously injured. Wilson considered the attack a violation of Germany's assurances and, appearing before a joint session of Congress on April 19, he stated that unless Germany immediately abandoned her "present methods of submarine warfare against passenger and freight carrying vessels the Government of the United States can have no choice but to sever diplomatic relations," a more serious step at that time than it would be now. In response the German government on 4 May 1916 gave the *Sussex* pledge. She promised to sink no more merchant vessels without warning provided the United States compelled Britain to abandon her allegedly illegal practices concerning neutral trade.

Wilson now placed himself at the head of a movement in the country for military preparedness. During the *Lusitania* controversy he authorized the Army and the Navy to strengthen the national defenses, and in his annual message to Congress in December 1915, he emphasized these proposals. Early in 1916 he toured the country to speak for preparedness, and, on June 14, he led a preparedness parade down Pennsylvania Avenue in Washington. Congress responded. On 3 June 1916, it enacted the National Defense Act, increasing the size of the standing army and the National Guard. On August 29, the Naval Appropriations Act authorized the construction of battleships, cruisers, destroyers, and submarines to create "incomparably the greatest Navy in the world." Congress also created a Council of National Defense and a United States Shipping Board to acquire and operate a fleet of merchantmen.

In the midst of these controversies with Germany and preparations for war there was a presidential election in 1916. The Progressive party seemingly launched under favorable circumstances in 1912 began to fall apart after the election of Wilson and had largely disappeared from the political scene by 1916. Wilson's domestic New Freedom program taking over many of the concepts and ideas of Roosevelt's New Nationlism had cut deeply into the voting strength of the Progressive party. Then, too, the European war diverted much attention from domestic matters, and this further weakened Progressive enthusiasm. Moreover, Roosevelt himself showed little interest in the Progressive party after 1914. Following the Congressional elections of that year when the Progressives lost more than half of their seats in the House, Roosevelt said the two party way of thinking was too strong in the country and the spirit of reform was too weak.

It should be remembered that Wilson was a minority president with only 41.8 percent of the popular vote in the 1912 election. His election then had been possible because of the split in the Republican party and the subsequent organization of the Progressive party. If the Progressives returned to the Republican party, Wilson could have a difficult time being reelected. In an effort to win the Progressives over to the Democratic party he had, as we have seen, supported an advanced legislative program between 1914 and 1916.

The Republicans also sought to win back the Progressives. The Old Guard Republicans controlled the party machinery, but they were prepared to welcome back the Progressives provided Roosevelt was not the party's nominee for president. However, it was clear the Republicans would have to nominate a candidate with Progressive sentiments if the two wings of the party were to be reunited. Thus, some Republican leaders urged Roosevelt's nomination. But Roosevelt had antagonized many German-Americans, whose votes were needed to defeat Wilson, with his anti-German remarks. Also a number of conservative Republican leaders could not forgive Roosevelt for breaking up and deserting the party in 1912.

The Republican and Progressives parties held their separate conventions at the same time in June 1916. The hope among their supporters was for both parties to nominate the same candidate and adopt the same platform. The Republicans nominated for president Supreme Court Justice Charles E. Hughes, sometimes called a "Wilson with whiskers." On the high court Hughes had avoided making statements about neutrality and preparedness and thus seemingly had not alienated those voters opposed to Wilson. He had ingratiated himself with the Progressives for prosecuting the insurance companies as a lawyer and for being a reform governor of New York.

The Republican platform denounced Wilson's foreign policy as one of "shifty expedients" and "phrase-making" and promised an "honest neutrality" and the protection of American citizens at home and abroad. The platform had a strong national defense plank, criticized Democratic policies toward business, and favored woman suffrage by state action.

The Progressives adopted a platform similar to that of the Republicans whom they hoped would nominate Roosevelt. When this did not happen, the Progressives named Roosevelt for president and John M. Parker of Louisiana for vice president. But Roosevelt declined the nomination and declared his support for Hughes. The Progressive National Committee, by a vote of 32 to 15, then endorsed Hughes and disbanded. Parker, however, backed Wilson.

The Democrats renominated Wilson by acclamation and, in their platform, praised his accomplishments and defended his policies abroad and at home. They strongly emphasized peace at their convention and came up with an effective slogan about Wilson for the campaign, "He kept us out of the war." Wilson had a more realistic view about this when he said privately, "I can't keep the country out of war. . . . Any little German lieutenant can put us into war at any time by some calculated outrage."

Hughes attempted to maintain during the campaign the equivocal position he had held on the Supreme Court, and the Democrats labeled him Charles "Evasive" Hughes. While he severely criticized the president's policies, he offered only vague alternatives. Damaging Hughes were Roosevelt's tirades against Wilson's neutrality, which persuaded many voters that the Republican party was a war party. Wilson seized on this and accused the Republican party of being a war party and charged that Hughes's election would mean almost certain war with Germany.

The Presidential vote was so close that the result remained in doubt for several days. The first returns indicated a Hughes victory since he had carried all the large eastern states and the pivotal midwestern states of Illinois, Indiana, and Michigan. But when all the returns were in Wilson had won not only the "Solid South" but most of the states west of the Mississippi to defeat Hughes by 277 to 254 in electoral votes and by 9,129,606 to 8,538,221 in popular votes. But he was still a minority president with only 49.3 percent of the popular vote.

Following his reelection, Wilson attempted to negotiate peace. On 18 December 1916, he sent a note to all belligerent governments to "state their views as to the terms on which the war might be concluded." He next conducted negotiations with the British and German ambassadors in Washington. Wilson then appeared before the Senate on 22 January 1917 and set forth his own concept of a just and lasting peace. "It must be a peace without victory," he said, for a peace imposed by the victor upon the vanquished "would be accepted in humiliation, under duress, at an intolerable sacrifice, and would leave a sting, a resentment, a bitter memory upon which terms of peace would rest, not permanently, but only as upon quicksand. Only a peace between equals can last." He went on to outline his idea of a just peace: equality of rights for nations, general acceptance of the principle of self government, the right of every "great people" to have an outlet to the seas, the freedom of the seas in law and fact, the limitation of armaments, and the freedom of all nations from entangling alliances.

The British answered first to Wilson's appeal to state their terms for ending the war. They would agree to a meeting of an early peace conference if the Germans replied favorably to Wilson. This was a change of position for the British who had previously opposed any suggestion of mediation. If Germany accepted Wilson's leadership in this peace effort, he was prepared to move the Allies to the conference table. As he told House late in January 1917, "If Germany really wants peace she can get it, and get it soon, if she will but confide in me and let me have a chance."

Germany's war fortunes at the time were at a high point and, only a week before Wilson made his appeal, she had offered to enter a peace conference. American and German policies seemed to converge at this time. But German-American cooperation in a peace campaign never materialized, because Germany finally made it clear she desired victory and domination and not negotiations. By the end of 1916, Germany had such a favorable military situation and believed she had such an effective submarine campaign that she could give up the idea of a compromise peace. Thus the German government informed the president it did not desire his presence at a peace conference. Then on 31 January 1917, Germany gave Wilson her peace terms. In the East she wanted a Poland under German control and the annexation of Lithuania. In the West, Germany sought an indemnity from Britain and France, the annexation of parts of France and Belgium, the reconstruction of Belgium as a German satellite, and the annexation of much of the Belgian Congo.

Germany, meanwhile, had decided to resume unrestricted submarine warfare, hoping to destroy enough of Britain's shipping to force her to sue for peace. The German navy had guaranteed its government to reduce Britain to starvation after the renewed submarine warfare began. Germany was now so confident of winning that fear of American intervention had little effect on her policy. Germany announced that beginning 1 February 1917, her submarines would sink on sight all ships, belligerent or neutral, found in specified war zones around the British Isles and the Mediterranean. The German navy would, however, allow one American ship to sail weekly between New York and Falmouth, England, provided the ship was clearly marked with red and white stripes and carried no contraband. Germany, thus, revoked the *Sussex* pledge, charging the United States had failed to stop Britain's illegal practices on the high seas. Wilson responded by breaking off diplomatic relations with Germany in a speech to Congress on February 3 and by warning Germany of sterner action if she sank American ships.

Wilson still hoped to avoid war. He still hoped Germany would not carry out its threats against American commerce. The days passed, and American ships remained in port, because shippers did not want to risk their goods with submarines. Goods piled up in warehouses and on wharves. The president was asked to provide convoys for merchant ships or to provide them with naval guns and crews. At first Wilson refused these demands and asserted the country was not willing to risk war.

Then on 25 February 1917, the president received a dispatch from London that outraged him. It was a copy of a message from the German Foreign Secretary Alfred Zimmermann to the German minister to Mexico von Eckhardt. It authorized him in the event of war between the United States and Germany to offer a wartime alliance to Mexico and to support her in an effort to recover her lost territory of the Mexican War in New Mexico, Texas, and Arizona. Mexico was to invite Japan to join the alliance. The British intercepted the Zimmermann note and read it, since they had broken the German code, and gave it to the Americans. When Wilson saw the message, he was shocked and exclaimed "Good Lord" several times.

The next day Wilson asked Congress for authority to arm merchant ships and to employ other measures to protect American commerce on the high seas. Few congressmen opposed arming the ships, but the "other measures" part of the request met overwhelming opposition. To prod Congress into action, the president on March 1 released the Zimmermann note to the public. A great surge of anger swept the country, and the armed ship bill passed the House, but some senators, led by Robert La Follette, Republican from Wisconsin, and George Norris, Republican from Nebraska, still opposed the measure and killed it by filibustering it until Congress adjourned later in the month. Wilson, however, was not deterred. On March 12, he announced he had found the necessary authority in a law enacted in 1797, and thus the merchant ships were armed.

On that same day the first American ship was sunk by the Germans. During the next three weeks, five more American ships went down with the loss of twenty-five American lives. The demand for war, hitherto largely confined to the East, now spread to the South and the West. Wilson now had to decide what to do about the new German challenge. He could acquiesce in what the Germans were doing, meet it head on, or rely more on armed neutrality.

Involved here was America's prestige and national honor. By resisting Germany's submarine warfare from the outset, Wilson was insisting upon respect for the power and rights of the United States. In each incident between the United States and Germany, American prestige was more deeply committed. If Wilson backed down in the face of this new German challenge, it might appear the United States could not command the respect she was entitled to as a great power. Also, there was the combined weight of official and public opinion driving Wilson to war. By the end of March 1917, every important member of the administration wanted Wilson to come around to the idea that there was already a state of war with Germany. Late in March, after news of the sinking of three more American ships had reached the president, Lansing conferred with him and later wrote, "I argued that war was inevitable, that I had felt so for months, and that the sooner we openly admitted the fact, so much stronger our position would be with our own people and before the world."

The Zimmermann note and the sinking of American ships increased the demand of Americans for war. Meanwhile another restraint against entering the war on the side of the Allies had been removed as a result of the March 1917 revolution in Russia. At its outset this revolution replaced an autocratic czar with a provisional republican government. This enabled Wilson to declare the major Allied governments were democratic, as Russia was then one of the Allies. It also made it easier to describe the war against the Central Powers as a war against autocracy, and it created the impression the United States was the only democracy not fighting for democracy.

Wilson had to make the final decision, and it was an agonizing one for him. For much of March 1917, he lived in what one of his biographers called his "valley of decision." For more than a week at this time he remained in his room receiving few visitors. As historian Charles Tansill, one of Wilson's leading critics, put it, "Surrounded by advisers who were eager for war, rebuffed by diplomats who had no thought of peace, President Wilson strove desperately to find some compromise which would not only put an end to the war then raging but would serve as a basis for a new world order." Frank Cobb, editor of the New York *World,* had an interview with Wilson during this decisive period. As Cobb recalled, "I'd never seen him so worn down. He looked as if he hadn't slept and he said he hadn't. . . . For nights, he said, he had been lying awake going over the whole situation. . . . He said he couldn't see any alternative, that he had tried every way he knew to avoid war. . . . if there were any possibility of avoiding war he wanted to try it. 'What else can I do?' he asked? 'Is there anything else I can do. If there is any alternative, for God's sake, let's take it,' he exclaimed."

After seeing the president, Lansing, on March 19, sent him a memorandum urging him to declare war arguing that the longer "we delay in declaring against military absolutism which menaces the rule of liberty and justice in the world, so much the less will be our influence in the days when Germany will need a merciful and unselfish foe." The next day at a Cabinet meeting Wilson asked those in attendance, without revealing his own position, what the United States should do. With only a little discussion the Cabinet favored a declaration of war against Germany. After the meeting, Wilson asked Lansing and Postmaster General Albert Burleson how long it would take to draft the necessary legislation for a declaration of war. When they told him April 2 would be the earliest possible date, Wilson called the newly elected Congress into special session on April 2 because of "grave questions of national policy."

On the wet evening of April 2, Wilson appeared before a joint session of Congress and crowded galleries with distinguished guests to

read his war message and to ask for a declaration of war against Germany. He reviewed the history of the submarine controversy and maintained the United States was not going to fight to avenge the loss of property but only to prevent "the wanton and wholesale destruction of the lives of noncombatants." We shall fight, Wilson declared, "for the ultimate peace of the world and for the liberation of its peoples-
. . . . The world must be made safe for democracy." Everything else had been tried, and now the only recourse was war, for as Wilson stated, "We enter the war only where we are clearly forced into it, because there are no other means of defending our rights."

When Wilson returned to the White House that night, with the applause of Congress and of the galleries still ringing in his ears, he told one of his aides, Joseph P. Tumulty, "Think what it was they were applauding. . . . My message to-day was a message of death for our young men. How strange it seems to applaud that."

Two days later, on April 4, the Senate passed the war resolution by a vote of 82 to 6, with La Follette, Norris, and Stone leading the opposition. Norris and La Follette spoke against the war resolution in long angry speeches. They accused the munitions makers, the stockbrokers, and bond holders of drumming up the war sentiment. "We are going to war upon the command of gold," exclaimed Norris. "We are about to put the dollar sign on the American flag." Three Republicans and three Democrats opposed the war measure in the Senate, and nearly all of the six were considered to be Progressives.

On the morning of April 6, Good Friday, the House approved the war measure 373 to 50. Here the opposition consisted of thirty-two Republicans, sixteen Democrats, one Socialist, and one Independent. Of these one came from the Northwest, nine from the South, and six from the Pacific Coast and Nevada. The other thirty-four were from the Middle West, with most of them from Wisconsin, South Dakota, and Illinois. Jeannette Rankin of Montana, the only woman in Congress and the first woman to be elected to Congress, voted against the war resolution in the House as she was to vote against it again in 1941 for World War II. On the afternoon of the same day, President Wilson signed the declaration of war, and the United States was at war.

Why did Wilson decide to go to war? There is no simple explanation for such a complex decision. The submarine issue played a leading role. Wilson entered the war only after Germany had renewed unrestricted submarine warfare. When Germany made it clear by overt acts that she would pursue this policy, Wilson had to make up his mind whether to risk war for neutral rights or to give them up. As defense of these rights had been the central part of his neutrality policy he could not easily abandon them.

Another important influence in Wilson's decision was that as he saw the United States lean closer to war, he began to think of ways of making the war beneficial and thus justifiable. His Fourteen Points, the idea of a League of Nations, and the concepts of "a war to end war" and "making the world safe for democracy" came to loom large in Wilson's mind. The overthrow of the czar in Russia and some liberalizing moves in Germany gave Wilson to believe that the time to bring about the changes he sought in the world was near. Wilson looked ahead to the end of the war with the hope of making a new world order where there would be no room for war. If war for the United States were going to come why not make it a war for democracy. Whether this decision was admirable or reprehensible continues to be debated. But the fact remains that idealism did profoundly influence Wilson's decision. So Wilson made the war a crusade, and his idealism led him to believe his goals could be achieved.

Further Reading

Bailey, Thomas A., and P. B. Ryan. *The Lusitania Disaster.* 1975.

Birnbaum, Karl E. *Peace Moves and U-Boat Warfare.* 1958.

Chatfield, Charles. *For Peace and Justice: Pacifism in America, 1914–1921.* 1971.

Coogan, John W. *The End of Neutrality: The United States, Britain, and Maritime Rights, 1899–1915.* 1981.

Cooper, John M., Jr. *The Vanity of Power: American Isolation and the First World War, 1914–1917.* 1969.

Devlin, Patrick. *Too Proud to Fight: Woodrow Wilson's Neutrality.* 1975.

Gregory, Ross. *The Origins of American Intervention in the First World War.* 1971.

_____. *Walter Hines Page: Ambassador to the Court of St. James.* 1970.

Hagedorn, Hermann. *The Bugle That Woke America.* 1940.

Lansing, Robert. *War Memoirs of Robert Lansing.* 1935.

Link, Arthur S. *Wilson: Confusion and Crises, 1915–1916.* 1964.

_____. *Wilson the Diplomatist.* 1957.

_____. *Wilson: The Struggle for Neutrality, 1914–1915.* 1960.

_____. *Woodrow Wilson: War, Revolution, and Peace.* 1979.

May, Ernest. *The World War and American Isolation, 1914–1917.* 1959.

Millis, Walter. *The Road to War.* 1935.

Peterson, H. C. *Propaganda for War.* 1939.

Smith, Daniel M. *The Great Departure: The United States and World War I, 1914–1920.* 1965.

Tansill, Charles C. *America Goes to War.* 1938.

14

America in World War I

Americans went to war in a mood of idealism. The war they entered was not only one to make the world safe for democracy but also a war to end war. Few Americans knew what the struggle was about. Wilson was largely responsible for this public ignorance. He did not educate the public about the war. Instead he used ringing phrases in saying, "we shall fight for the things which we have always carried nearest our hearts."

With such emotional overtones resounding in their ears, Americans began to mobilize. At first they believed their participation in the war would be limited to naval and financial aid. But by the spring of 1917, the Allied position was precarious. After the failure of a large French offensive defeatism grew in the French Army, and a number of French divisions mutinied. On the Western front the Allies were barely holding their own. The Russian Bolsheviks, after their revolution in 1917, wanted their government to withdraw from the war, and on the southern front the Italians were soon to suffer a staggering defeat at Caporetto. Worst of all the new German submarine campaign seemed to be having more success as 1917 went on. Germany's limited submarine activity of 1916 had destroyed about 300,000 tons of Allied shipping each month. In February and March 1917, the Germans were destroying approximately 570,000 tons of Allied shipping each month, and in April they sank 881,000 tons. About one ship in four trying to enter or leave England was sunk, and the Germans were torpedoing ships twice as rapidly as the Allies could build them. In April 1917, England reportedly had on hand only enough grain to last six or eight weeks. Admiral John Rushworth Jellicoe, the first sea lord of the British Admiralty, told the American liaison admiral in London, William S. Sims, "It is impossible for us to go on, if losses like this continue. . . . The Germans . . . will win unless we can stop these losses—and stop them soon."

The American government recognized this predicament and moved into action. The American navy was ready. Although German submarines continued to sink considerable Allied tonnage—more than 600,000 tons in both May and June 1917—American intervention began to turn the tide. United States destroyers hunted down submarines and helped to convoy troopships and merchant ships. Allied shipping losses started to decline and were down to 289,000 tons by November. After April 1918, British losses stayed below 200,000 tons a month. By a shuttle method the American navy convoyed nearly 90,000 vessels through the danger zone and lost only one half of 1 percent of them. To curtail submarine activity further, the American navy laid a mine barrage between the coasts of Scotland and Norway in the North Sea. The war ended before the project was completed, but by June 1918, this area for all practical purposes was closed to submarines. The American navy, now one of the most important in the world, numbered more than 2,000 vessels of all classes and 533,000 officers and men at the end of the war.

Raising, equipping, training, and transporting an American army took some time. On 19 May 1917, Congress enacted a Selective Service Act requiring all men between the ages of twenty-one and thirty-one, later extended to eighteen to forty-five, to register for military service. Eventually 24,234,021 men were registered, 6,300,000 were found to be eligible, and 2,810,296 were drafted into the army. At the outset of the war, some 378,000 men were in the army, navy, and national guard units. By November 1918, the draft and a large number of volunteers had brought the total number of American men and women under arms to 4,800,000.

Major General John J. Pershing, who had recently commanded an American military expedition in Mexico in pursuit of Pancho Villa, was appointed commander of the American Expeditionary Force to Europe. Allied military leaders wanted American troops to be integrated into their forces and to be placed under Allied commanders.

But Pershing would have none of this and thus maintained the identity and integrity of the American forces.

The total cost of the war for the American people from April 1917 to 1920, including economic aid to the Allies, was about $33.5 billion. Nearly a third of this total represented loans to the Allies and was used primarily for making purchases in this country; the remainder the United States spent waging the war. One third of the total cost was raised by taxes, and the balance was charged to future generations through war bond sales. Determining how much should be borrowed and how much should come from taxes provoked sharp differences of opinions in Congress. Conservatives did not wish to increase income taxes much to pay the war costs, while Progressives favored very high rates for income, inheritance, and excess profits taxes. The Revenue Acts of 1917 and 1918 reflected some of these divergent views and also the need to meet the mounting expenditures for the war. In both measures from three-fourths to four-fifths of the economic burden of the war was placed on large individual and corporate incomes and on inheritances and excess profits. Excise taxes were levied on a variety of items such as transportation, amusements, liquor, tobacco, and luxuries.

As for borrowing money for the war costs, Congress insisted upon individuals and not banks holding the national debt. So the war bonds were sold directly to small buyers as well as to large investors. Local civic groups promoted sales; newspapers gave generous support; actors and leading sports figures added their endorsements; and reluctant buyers were called slackers or German sympathizers. Each of the Liberty loan drives was oversubscribed.

In 1916, Congress created the Council of National Defense to supervise the wartime agencies then reorganizing the country's economy for war. The Emergency Fleet Corporation was busy attempting to build ships faster than the submarines could sink them. The Food Administration under Herbert Hoover had charge of food supplies. Hoover preached the "gospel of the clean plate," persuaded Americans to accept "wheatless" and "meatless" days, and urged all who could to plant war gardens. A Fuel Administration managed coal and oil supplies and a Railroad Administration took over the railroads without removing them from private ownership and operated them as a single system.

The most powerful of these agencies was the War Industries Board. Directed by Bernard Baruch, a Wall Street broker, it had almost dictatorial power over the American economy. It determined the materials manufacturers could use and what must be saved, and it decided the new products they could make. It set priorities, standardized products, and, with the president's approval, fixed prices.

Through these agencies the American government exercised greater power than it ever had before. These agencies were responsible to the president alone, and their directors met with him weekly to form a kind of war Cabinet. Congress granted sweeping powers to the president. The Overman Act of May 1918, allowed him, until six months after the war, "to utilize, coordinate, or consolidate any executive or administrative commissions, bureaus, agencies, offices or officers at will." The war boards largely replaced the usual civil authorities, and they might have come to exercise even greater power had the war lasted longer.

Wilson also sought to mobilize American public opinion as well as American resources. "Once lead this people into war, and they'll forget there ever was such a thing as tolerance," the president had told a newspaper editor just before the United States entered the conflict. "To fight you must be brutal and ruthless, and the spirit of ruthless brutality will enter into the very fiber of our national life, infecting Congress, the courts, the policeman on the beat, the man in the street."

To a large degree, Wilson's doleful prophecy became true. Ironically this happened because his administration helped to make it so. Only seven days after he signed the war declaration, Wilson created the Committee on Public Information, headed by George Creel, a progressive journalist from Denver, to generate public enthusiasm for the war effort. Such an agency was necessary, Wilson believed, because Americans were at the outset divided over the decision to intervene in the war. Millions of Americans such as Socialists, radicals, German and Irish-Americans, and many Progressives still believed the president had not followed a neutral policy in dealing with the belligerents and had allowed his unneutrality to drag the United States into the war. To convert this hostile opinion Creel went to work on the biggest advertising campaign in American history to that time. Assisting him were volunteer organizations such as the National Security League and Committees of Public Safety in every state.

The Creel Committee set up a system of voluntary press censorship. It supplied thousands of columns of newspaper material each week. Papers cooperated with the Committee both in withholding material it disapproved and in publishing the news stories the Committee issued. The Committee also set out to make Americans war conscious and, before hostilities ended, Creel had employed 150,000 lecturers, writers, artists, actors, and scholars in a huge propaganda campaign. There was no radio in 1917–1918, but 75,000 volunteers served as "Four Minute Men." They appeared on stages and in motion picture houses in more than 5,000 towns and delivered over 750,000 speeches before audiences numbering around 300 million.

Creel's Committee and the speakers it mobilized presented an official line about the war to the American public. American participation in the war was portrayed as a crusade to further the cause of freedom and democracy everywhere in the world, a theme that Wilson also repeated in his speeches in these years. As for Germany, these propagandists maintained she had started the war and had set out to dominate Europe and even the Western Hemisphere.

The Creel Committee's propaganda efforts came at a time when Americans were already upset by rumors of espionage and sabotage from the fancied or real fears of the Russian Bolshevik Revolution spreading to the United States. The propaganda of the Creel Committee and the efforts of such volunteer organizations as the National Security League and the National Protective Association resulted in a war madness never before seen in this country. Spy scares frightened Americans, and patriotic organizations sprang up to catch enemy agents and domestic traitors. In many communities citizens became self-appointed guardians of their neighbors' patriotism. People were often almost forced to subscribe to Liberty loans. The slogan was: "Fight or buy bonds"; and anyone who did not do so was subject to ostracism, physical violence, loss of employment, or official investigation.

The frenzy was mainly directed against German-Americans, German things, and the anti-war radicals and the progressives. Anyone with a German, Irish, or Scandinavian name became suspect and was restricted in his or her right of free expression. Each state had a Committee of Public Safety, with branches in every county and city. As historians who have studied public opinion and the war have pointed out, these Committees acted like vigilante groups against German-Americans especially in Montana, Minnesota, and Wisconsin. Senator La Follette, who had voted against the declaration of war, was burned in effigy in Madison and was publicly censured by most of the faculty at the University of Wisconsin. The Minnesota Public Safety Committee even demanded that the United States Senate expel him.

American war hysteria was also turned against all things German. Many states prohibited the teaching of German in the schools and the holding of church services in German. German books were burned. Symphony orchestras were forbidden to play German music masterpieces. Sauerkraut became "liberty cabbage" and German measles, "liberty measles." The crowning blow came, according to historian Arthur S. Link, "when Cincinnati ruled free pretzels off free lunch counters in saloons."

Federal and local officials encouraged groups containing large numbers of foreign-born persons to hold "loyalty meetings" where patriotic speeches were made and patriotic resolutions were adopted by a unanimous vote. In some communities, placards exhorted the people to speak only the "American language." In Oregon, one of the leading progressive states in the country, the legislature, a year after the Armistice in 1918, made it unlawful for any person, firm, corporation, or association of persons to print, publish, circulate, exhibit, sell, or offer for sale any paper, treatise, pamphlet, or circular in a language other than English unless the prints included translations. Editors of foreign language newspapers were at times arrested, the editions of such papers were confiscated and destroyed, and firms advertising in them were boycotted.

The Socialist party was the only important political organization in the country to oppose the war effort. "The country has been violently, needlessly, and criminally involved in war," asserted Morris Hillquit, a well-known Socialist. The extent of the anti-war sentiment in the country was indicated by the strong support the Socialist party received in the 1917 municipal elections. Socialist candidates for mayor polled 22 percent of the popular vote in New York, 25 percent in Buffalo, 44 percent in Dayton, Ohio, and nearly 34 percent in Chicago.

When a government is at war it seeks to protect itself from whom it regards as enemies from within as well as from without. In his war message Wilson warned, "If there should be disloyalty it will be dealt with with a firm hand of stern repression." In an effort to deal with the question of loyalty during the war, Congress enacted three measures—the Espionage Act (15 June 1917), the Trading-with-the-Enemy Act (6 October 1917), and the Sedition Act (6 May 1918). The Espionage Act provided for imprisonment up to twenty years or a fine up to $10,000, or both, for anyone divulging information about national defense or interfering with the draft. A section of the act empowered the postmaster general to deny the use of the mails to any matter he construed as advocating treason, insurrection, or forcible resistance to the laws of the United States. The Trading-with-the-Enemy Act was to prevent information useful to the enemy from entering or leaving the country. Mail, incoming and outgoing, was subject to censorship. Foreign language newspapers were required to furnish an English translation of their columns to the postmaster general, and periodicals issued in any language but English were subject to the postmaster general's control.

The Sedition Act, seeking to control free speech, was the most stringent of these three measures. It prohibited "the saying or doing anything with intent to obstruct the sale of United States bonds except by way of bona fide and not disloyal advice." How to determine the kind of advice given was a problem. The act also prohibited the use of disloyal, profane, scurrilous, or abusive language about the form of government, constitution, flag, or the uniform of the military of the United States, or any language intended to obstruct the war effort in any way. This legislation revived the worst features of the Alien and Sedition Acts of 1798.

Probably at no other period in American history was public opinion and free speech so regimented and restricted. What happened was a serious blot on the Wilson presidency, especially since it was considered to be the high-water mark of the Progressive Movement until then. All three of the acts already mentioned gave Postmaster General Albert S. Burleson of Texas considerable powers of censorship, which he used extensively. He put periodicals out of business by suspending objectionable issues and then by declaring the publication was no longer a periodical entitled to second class mailing privileges because it had not been continuously offered for mailing. Burleson excluded from the mail the leading Socialist publications, German-language publications, and anti-British and pro-Irish periodicals. He banned an issue of the single tax organ, *The Public,* because it wanted more revenue to be raised by taxes, and he also temporarily closed the mail to the *Saturday Evening Post* and the New York *Times.*

The law enforcement agencies enforced the new laws as vigorously as Burleson. Frank Cobb of the New York *World* reported Wilson as saying that once the United States entered the war, conformity would be the only virtue, and anyone who did not comply would have to pay the price. During World War I, approximately 4,000 conscientious objectors to the war were recorded, most of whom went into noncombatant military service; 500 were court-martialed and imprisoned, 17 were sentenced to death but never executed, and 142 were given life terms but released by 1921. World War I prisoners of conscience best known today included civil libertarian Roger Baldwin and Socialist leader Eugene V. Debs.

According to a noted authority on freedom of speech in the United States, Zechariah Chafee, Jr., who investigated these World War I verdicts, "It became criminal to advocate heavier taxation instead of bond issues, to state that conscription was unconstitutional though the Supreme Court had not yet held it valid, to say that the sinking of merchant ships was legal, to urge that a referendum should have preceded our declaration of war, to say that war was contrary to the teachings of Christ. Men have been punished for criticizing the Red Cross and the Y.M.C.A." Vague statements criticizing the war or the administration were held to have a "bad tendency" or to constitute "intent" to bring about insubordination in the military forces.

A movie producer, Robert Goldstein, received a ten-year prison sentence for his film *The Spirit of '76,* showing the British were responsible for the massacre of civilians in the Wyoming Valley in Pennsylvania during the American Revolution, because it allegedly stirred animosity against Britain, an associate of the United States in the war. In *Pierce* v. *United States* (1920) the Supreme Court made it a false statement of fact to differ with Wilson's war message and the congressional war resolution concerning the causes of American entry into the war. This case involved a Socialist pamphlet attacking conscription and the war. Though it was not shown there was any attempt to interfere with the draft, the Court held that the pamphlet might well "have a tendency to cause insubordination, disloyalty, and refusal of duty in the military and naval forces of the United States."

The most celebrated cases during the war were the convictions of Eugene Debs of Indiana, the leader of the Socialist party, and of Victor Berger of Wisconsin, a prominent Socialist in the country. Debs urged a Socialist convention in Ohio in June 1918 to "resist militarism wherever found." He was quickly brought to trial for stirring up disloyalty among Americans and for encouraging resistance to the United States. He was convicted and sentenced to ten years in federal prison. The Supreme Court upheld the conviction. Debs issued a statement through the Socialist periodical, the *Liberator,* saying the "cabal of begowned corporation lawyers at Washington have decided better than they knew. They have added a million fresh recruits to the ranks of Bolshevism in the United States."

Debs was still in federal prison when he ran for president on the Socialist ticket in 1920, and he polled nearly a million popular votes. Shortly before Wilson left office in March 1921, the Justice Department recommended Debs's sentence be commuted. Wilson refused, because he maintained Debs had attempted to undermine the Selective Service Act and if Debs were now pardoned it might result in disdain for law in future wars. Debs was finally pardoned by President Warren G. Harding in 1921.

Berger, from Milwaukee and the first Socialist member of Congress (1911–1913), was indicted under the Sedition Act in February 1918. While he was awaiting trial he was elected to Congress. In January 1919, Berger was convicted and sentenced to a twenty-year prison term for sedition, a decision reversed by the Supreme Court in 1921. The House of Representatives then, with only one dissenting vote, would not allow Berger to take his seat in Congress. The American Legion wanted Berger deported. Late in 1919, Berger was again elected to Congress, and again the House refused to let him take his seat. At the same time the New York state legislature was denying seats to five Socialists elected to that body.

Members of Congress were not interfered with in their rights of free speech and neither was Theodore Roosevelt. While Roosevelt severely attacked Wilson and his policies the administration let him alone, because he was too popular in the country and he was too patriotic to be considered pro-German.

In this period of hysteria and madness, the courts were no refuge for war dissenters. In the case of *Schenck* v. *United States* (1919), involving an appeal from Schenck's conviction in a lower federal court of a charge of distributing antidraft pamphlets to the military, Justice Oliver Wendell Holmes, speaking for an unanimous Supreme Court, upheld the constitutionality of the Espionage Act. The right of free speech, he said, had never been an absolute one, at any time, in peace or in war. When a country was at war, Holmes contended, "many things that might be said in time of peace are a hindrance to its [war] effort," and "no court could regard them as protected by any constitutional right." Yet Holmes limited the application of the Espionage Act when he added, "The question in every case is whether the words used are in such circumstances and are of such a nature as to create a clear and present danger that they will bring about the substantive evils Congress has a right to prevent. It is a question of proximity and degree." This was an important new constitutional doctrine justifying a curtailment of free speech on the basis of a "clear and present danger."

In *Abrams* v. *United States,* in 1919 after the war was over, the Supreme Court by a vote of seven to two upheld the Sedition Act. In this case the Court sustained the conviction of a group charged with violating the law by publishing pamphlets attacking the Wilson administration's decision to send a military force to Russia in 1918 to prevent the capture of military supplies by the Germans and to safeguard an escape route for a sizable Czech army fleeing eastward from the Bolsheviks. The majority opinion of the Court confirmed the conviction and the law on the ground the pamphlets excited "at the supreme crisis of the war, disaffection, sedition, riots, and...revolution" and maintained the First Amendment could not protect that right.

Justices Holmes and Louis D. Brandeis, whom Wilson had appointed to the Court, dissented in this case in one of the great and moving defenses of free speech. They argued for a narrow interpretation of the "clear and present danger" doctrine, pointing out if the Sedition Act were construed to prohibit all criticism of the government and its officials then we would be returning to the Sedition Act of 1798, long regarded as unconstitutional. "Now nobody can suppose," Holmes said, "that the surreptitious publishing of a silly leaflet by an unknown man, without more, would present any immediate danger that its opinions would hinder the success of the government arms or have any appreciable tendency to do so."

Then Holmes concluded with an eloquent defense of free speech. "But when men have realized that time has upset many fighting faiths, they may come to believe even more than they believe the very foundations of their own conduct that the ultimate good desired is better reached by free trade in ideas, that the best test of truth is the power of the thought to get itself accepted in the competition of the market, and that truth is the only ground upon which their wishes safely can be carried out. That, at any rate," he continued, "is the theory of our Constitution. It is an experiment, as all life is an experiment. Every year, if not every day, we have to wage our salvation upon some prophecy based upon imperfect knowledge. While that experiment is part of our system I think we should be eternally vigilant against attempts to check the aggression of opinions that we loathe and believe to be fraught with death, unless they so imminently threaten interference with the lawful and pressing purposes of the law that an immediate check is required to save the country."

The foreign-born in the United States were singled out in wartime legislation, making deportable any alien who advocated the overthrow of the American government by force or violence or who were members of, or affiliated with, any organization advocating the use of violence. Thousands of aliens were arrested and were tried by the Department of Labor where they were denied a jury and were compelled to testify against themselves, a violation of that protection in the Fifth Amendment. Attorney General A. Mitchell Palmer, with political ambitions of his own for the presidential race in 1920, was behind these raids, but Louis F. Post, acting secretary of Labor, was not swept away by the hysteria and acted with care and deliberation before making decisions. Some of the press criticized Post for moving too slowly against aliens, and some members of Congress thought he sympathized with radicalism and that he should be removed from office. Post later defended his policy in a book called by Senator Thomas J. Walsh of Montana "a ringing indictment of both the American government and the American people—the former for acts of heartless oppression...and the latter for the indifference with which the most hideous injustices perpetrated by high officials in perfect contempt of constitutional guarantees were regarded." But other Americans had a different view. Near the end of 1919, when the Army transport *Buford* left New York harbor with 249 deportees, among whom Emma Goldman and Alexander Berkman were the best known, some newspapers labeled it the "Soviet Ark," and a Boston paper believed "with its cargo of undesirables," it may prove to be "as epoch-making as the immortal voyage of Columbus."

Even the meaning of the word pacifist changed under the pressure for patriotic conformity during World War I. Having had the connotation of one who advocated international cooperation for peace, it narrowed to mean one who would not support even a "war to end war." According to Charles Chatfield, a leading historian of the American peace movement of these years, "Pacifists were linked with draft dodgers, socialists, and communists, portrayed in hues from yellow to red; and in the lobby of 70 Fifth Avenue [New York City], where some of their groups were housed, was rudely inscribed the taunt, 'Treason's Twilight Zone.'" The word pacifist thus came to have a double meaning, and a number of peace advocates in 1917–1918 hastened to explain that "those who are now called 'pacifists' here do not include all or most who were called 'pacifists' before the war." After the war when it was again respectable to be against war, the word was sometimes used in its original and broader sense. Of course there were always those pacifists who refused to sanction any war and who were motivated by obedience to religious injunctions against killing and against complying with the military. Their churches—Quaker, Mennonite, Brethren, Disciples of Christ, and Jehovah's Witnesses—supplied most of the conscientious objectors in World War I as they had done in the Civil War and were to do in World War II.

When World War I came in 1914, it absorbed many of the world peace movements. American peace leaders at first expressed abhorrence and dismay. But as leading peace advocates from all groups came to the defense of one belligerent power or another, the established peace societies vacillated or actually supported the Allied cause. When Congress declared war on Germany the American Peace Society, a peace movement of long standing since 1828, appeared to equate pacifist with patriot. It held that the world had passed beyond any reconciliation except by force of arms. The Society had changed from its stand against all war to a different emphasis when its paper, the *Advocate of Peace,* incredibly asserted in May 1917, "We must help in the bayoneting of a normally decent German soldier in order to free him from a tyranny which he at present accepts as his chosen form of government. We must aid in the starvation and emaciation of a German baby in order that he, or at least his more sturdy little playmate, may grow up to inherit a different sort of government from that for which his father died."

This change of emphasis also took place with the old line peace movement which also supported the war to end war. For example, the Carnegie Endowment for Peace, founded by Andrew Carnegie in 1910 with an endowment of $10 million, and the most important peace society in the country, favored the Allied cause from the outset of the war in 1914. With the American declaration of war, the trustees of the Carnegie Endowment issued a unanimous resolution saying "the most effectual means of promoting a durable international peace is to prosecute the war against the Imperial German Government to a final victory for democracy." The organization gave its Washington office to the government's official propaganda agency, the Creel Committee, and placed on its own stationery in red ink, "Peace through Victory."

The American peace movement during the time the United States was in World War I was divided between those who supported the war and those who opposed it. The internationalists within the movement supported American participation in the war, because they hoped a postwar world order of democracy and reform would emerge. Organizations such as the Carnegie Endowment and the League to Enforce Peace, founded in 1915, and peace leaders such as Harry Emerson Fosdick and James T. Shotwell believed people could change conditions and bring about a stable world order, based on cooperation rather than force, through the creation of world agencies. In supporting the war they attributed to the war values they had previously sought: the search for international equity, law, and order. Then there were the pacifists who resolutely opposed war. From their opposition would come in the postwar years new pacifist organizations such as the Women's International League for Peace and Freedom, the American Friends Service Committee, and the War Resisters League. Led by noted pacifists A. J. Muste, John Nevin Sayre, Norman Thomas, and Jane Addams, these organizations came to understand that lasting peace was contingent upon domestic social reform.

But these pacifists, unlike the internationalists, did not support Wilson's war to end war. They concluded that World War I was a result of the European state system and that American national interests were best served by staying out. According to the pacifists, the war was caused by European rivalries, in long-standing misunderstanding, suspicion, fear, and diplomatic and commercial struggles to which all nations contributed. While pacifists did make a distinction between the base motives of the belligerent governments and the lofty idealism of all the peoples who fought, as did Wilson, they could not support Wilson's idealistic war on behalf of the Allies. For the pacifists the war was a strictly nationalistic European conflict with which the United States had no business.

According to Chatfield, who has studied the American pacifists during World War I, the memory of this war was an important consideration in the responses of Americans to foreign affairs in the twenties and thirties. It was a formative influence upon the pacifists who used the war to popularize their view that wars are always futile and irrelevant to fundamental social issues and that the United States could stand aside from a European state system based on force of arms.

As already noted, German submarines sank Allied ships at an alarming rate, and it was not until the summer of 1918 that the British and American navies turned the tide. German armies subdued the Balkans and scored decisive victories on the Russian front. In November 1917, the Russian Bolsheviks overthrew the provisional democratic government of Kerensky and declared themselves ready for peace. Lenin and Trotsky wanted to consolidate the gains of their Communist revolution. In March 1918, Russia signed the Treaty of Brest-Litovsk with Germany and withdrew from the war. Rumania also signed a treaty with the Central Powers in the same month. Germany's eastern army was now free for action on her western front. Germany hoped to strike the Allies a knockout blow before the United States could give them effective assistance.

In the spring of 1918, as the Germans were preparing a great offensive, the American expeditionary force in France numbered about 300,000 men, but more were arriving every day. General Pershing's command added 1,750,000 Americans between March and October, and by the end of the war over two million men and more than five million tons of supplies had been transported to Europe.

The Germans launched their offensive in late March 1918. A few weeks later they were menacing Paris and the English channel ports. They confidently expected victory. At this point American military forces played a decisive role in checking German attacks. American troops, called upon to help stop the German thrust toward Paris, went into action at the end of May. They forced the German army back across the Marne River and in June cleared Belleau Wood of enemy forces. In July the Germans made a last great effort to reach Paris, but they were repulsed in the crucial Second Battle of the Marne in which the Americans played a prominent part. The Allies, with American help, now took the initiative and put the Germans on the defensive.

The Allies still had nearly four months of hard fighting. The principle contribution of the Americans was a series of victories in the area north of Verdun in France. Pershing now commanded a separate American army that captured the German fortress of Saint-Mihiel and fought battles in the Argonne Forest. The American offensive was part of an Allied coordinated drive that sent the Central Powers reeling. By mid-August 1918, the German high command realized that victory was impossible and awaited only some minor success as an occasion for proposing peace. But this did not happen. While the German army was pushed back, Germany's allies were succumbing one by one. Bulgaria surrendered September 29, Turkey a month later, and Austria in early November. An Austrian proposal on September 16 for a peace conference was rejected by Wilson, speaking for the Allies. With the end in sight Germany took steps to reconstruct its government. Parliamentary government was installed, Prince Max of Baden, a liberal antimilitarist, became the new chancellor, and Socialists were brought into the Cabinet. General Ludendorff, one of Germany's supreme military commanders, demanded at the end of September that the German government obtain an armistice. On October 3, Prince Max appealed to President Wilson for an armistice based on terms he had previously set forth in his Fourteen Points.

A few months before the United States entered the war, President Wilson had described in brief and general terms the kind of peace he believed the American people would support. In his "Peace Without Victory" speech to the Senate on 22 January 1917, he outlined a settlement of the war, giving self-determination to subject nationalities, guaranteeing freedom of the seas, preventing postwar indemnities or annexations, and creating a postwar League of Nations to maintain the peace. Such a program had already been put forth by western European intellectuals and humanitarians seeking a way to prevent future wars. For much of 1917, Wilson's attention had been absorbed with the mobilization of the American war effort. Before the end of the year, though, Wilson concluded that a more explicit statement of war aims was desirable. Such an announcement might please liberal opinion in the United States and England and commit the Allied governments to a peace of justice rather than a peace of vengeance. It might also satisfy the Bolshevik leaders in Russia and dissuade them from making a separate peace with Germany.

When the Bolshevik leaders seized power in November 1917, by overthrowing the provisional Kerensky government, they issued an appeal to all belligerents to make peace on the basis of universal self-determination and without annexations or indemnities. Only Germany and her allies responded favorably to this proposal, offering the prospects of a separate Russian-German peace already mentioned. Colonel House, in Europe, tried to persuade the Allied leaders to match the Russians in an idealistic declaration of war aims, thereby hoping to induce the Russians to stay with the alliance until the end of the war. When the French and Italian premiers refused to give up their nationalistic war aims, Wilson decided to make a unilateral statement of the war aims of the United States. This he did in his important Fourteen Points address to a joint session of Congress on 8 January 1918.

The purpose of the American war aims, said Wilson, was "that the world be made fit and safe to live in; and particularly that it be made safe for every peace loving nation." This was to be accomplished by the president's Fourteen Points which comprised "open covenants of peace openly arrived at," freedom of the seas "alike in peace and war," removal of economic barriers, limitations of armaments, an "absolutely impartial adjustment of all colonial claims," evacuation and restoration of territory in Belgium and France invaded by the Central Powers, readjustment of the boundaries of Italy, the Balkan states, and Turkey on lines of nationality, an independent Poland with access to the sea, autonomy for the peoples of Austria-Hungary, and the creation of "A general association of nations...affording mutual guarantees of political independence and territorial integrity to great and small states alike."

Some of Wilson's address was aimed particularly at Russia, now engaged in peace negotiations with Germany. In the introductory part of his speech, the president referred to these negotiations and assured the Russian people of the deep sympathy of the American people. "It is our heartfelt desire and hope," he declared "that some way may be opened whereby we may be privileged to assist the people of Russia to attain their utmost hope of liberty and ordered peace." Point six of the Fourteen Points called for the evacuation of all occupied Russian territory and a sincere welcome of Russia "into the society of free nations under institutions of her own choosing.... The treatment accorded Russia by her sister nations in the months to come," the president continued, "will be the acid test of their good will, of their comprehension of her needs as distinguished from their own interests, and of their intelligent and unselfish sympathy."

Wilson's address had no effect on the Russian-German peace negotiations. Neither did a speech of February 11 when he specifically endorsed the Russian peace program of "no annexations, no contributions, no punitive indemnities," nor a special message of friendship to the Russian people a month later. Russia and Germany had signed an armistice in December 1917 and then proceeded to negotiate a peace signed on 3 March 1918 in the Treaty of Brest-Litovsk. Russia accepted the harsh German terms of giving up her claims to Finland, the Baltic provinces, Lithuania, Russian Poland, and the Ukraine. The treaty, however, allowed the Bolsheviks to withdraw Russia from the war and to concentrate on consolidating their revolution in their country.

When Prince Max of Germany, in early October 1918, appealed to Wilson for an armistice based on his Fourteen Points, the president took it upon himself to act as spokesman for the Allied powers. Over the next few weeks Wilson and the German government discussed questions and conditions that Wilson wanted from the Germans before the Allies would enter into peace negotiations. Wilson insisted upon full acceptance of his terms, the complete evacuation of Allied territory, and the cessation of Germany's illegal practices on sea (submarine warfare) and land. On October 20, Prince Max informed Wilson that Germany accepted the president's conditions.

Satisfied with Germany's responses to his terms Wilson, on October 23, told the German government that he would place the American-German correspondence before the Allies and discuss with them the question of an armistice. He also told the Germans that their government, to conduct the negotiations, should represent the people, not "the military masters and the monarchial autocrats" of Germany. This was understood in Germany as requiring the abdication of Kaiser William II. Pressure for the kaiser's abdication began to build up in Germany. Sailors mutined at Kiel, and councils of workers and soldiers were formed in various cities. The Socialists threatened to withdraw from the newly formed Cabinet unless the kaiser abdicated. There was also the beginnings of a general strike in Germany led by Socialists and syndicalists. Prince Max told the kaiser, "Abdication is a dreadful thing, but a government without the socialists would be a worse danger for the country." William II abdicated on November 9 and fled to Holland where, despite demands to try him as a war criminal, he lived quietly until 1941. On the same day there was organized a provisional German People's Government, headed by the Socialist deputy Friedrich Ebert.

While these events were taking place, the Allies were discussing the terms of an armistice. In these talks the Allied and American differences over peace terms came to the surface. Wilson sent Colonel House to a conference of the Allies in Paris to win approval of the Fourteen Points, but the European Allies did not want to assent to some of them. Only after a long argument and a threat that the United States might make a separate peace with Germany did House win acceptance of the Fourteen Points by Britain, France, and Italy. But the acquiescence was qualified by two reservations. On Wilson's second point, "freedom of the seas," the Allies reserved freedom of decision. And the other one was that the Germans should be told that they would be required to pay reparations for civilian damages by their aggression.

Wilson gave his approval to these two exceptions. The reply of the Allies, including the reservations, was sent to the Germans on November 5, and they were informed that Marshal Ferdinand Foch, chief of the Allied Supreme Command, was ready to receive their representatives to arrange an armistice. German delegates met Foch and a British naval representative in Foch's headquarters in a railroad car in Compiègne Forest on November 8. To prevent a destructive invasion of Germany, the German government accepted Foch's terms, which included evacuation of all Allied territory and of the German lands west of the Rhine and the surrender of the German fleet, of heavy military equipment, and of large numbers of locomotives and freight cars. At 5 A.M., on 11 November 1918, the German commissioners signed the armistice to become effective six hours later. World War I was over.

It was a costly war. One study estimated the financial cost of the war to all belligerents at $337 billion. The United States lost 50,510 men in battle. Another 62,760 Americans died of diseases, and 182,674 were wounded. Other nations had greater losses—in Russia, 1.7 million men died in battle, Germany, 1.8 million, France, 1.3 million, and Great Britain, 947,000.

The end of the war was supposed to usher in a new era of peace. "A New World was born yesterday," read a fashionable New York City store ad on 12 November 1918, the day following the armistice. It was to be "a world brighter, happier, better than men had ever known before." President Wilson was just as optimistic about the future. "Everything for which America fought has been accomplished," he said. "It will now be our fortunate duty to assist by example, by sober, friendly counsel, and by material aid in the establishment of just democracy throughout the world." And so it went as Americans felt relief and joy with the end of the war. "Every city village and hamlet," the *New York Times* reported, "expressed its emotion at the victorious ending of the war." Not many Americans would have agreed or understood what some European newspapers, however, were saying at the time: "the Allies ought not to crowd Germany to the wall so hard that she may be unable to establish herself under a democratic government." Nor would many have given thought to the fact that it was just an armistice and not an end to war.

Further Reading

Some readings in Chapter 13 are also useful for this chapter.

Barbeau, A. E., and Florette Henri. *The Unknown Soldiers: Black American Troops in World War I.* 1974.

Chafee, Zechariah, Jr. *Free Speech in the United States.* 1941.

Coffman, Edward M. *The War to End Wars: The American Military Experience in World War I.* 1968.

DeWeerd, H. A. *President Wilson Fights His War.* 1968.

Ferrell, Robert H. *Woodrow Wilson and World War I, 1917-1921.* 1985.

Frothingham, Thomas G. *The Naval History of the World War.* 3 vols., 1924-1926.

Gilbert, Charles. *American Financing of World War I.* 1970.

Harbord, James G. *The American Army in France, 1917-1919.* 1936.

Kennan, George F. *Soviet-American Relations, 1917-1920.* 2 vols., 1956, 1958.

Kennedy, David M. *Over Here: The First World War and American Society.* 1980.

Lawrence, Joseph Douglas. *Fighting Soldier: The AEF in 1918.* 1985.

Livermore, Seward. *Politics Is Adjourned: Woodrow Wilson and the War Congress, 1916-1918.* 1966.

Luebke, Frederick C. *Bonds of Loyalty: German-Americans and World War I.* 1974.

Mock, J. R., and C. Larson. *Words that Won the War.* 1939.

Morison, Elting F. *Admiral Sims and the Modern Navy.* 1942.

Murphy, Paul L. *The Meaning of Freedom of Speech: First Amendment Freedoms from Wilson to FDR.* 1972.

Murray, Robert K. *Red Scare: A Study of National Hysteria, 1919-1921.* 1955.

Parsons, Edward B. *Wilsonian Diplomacy.* 1978.

Paxson, Frederick L. *American Democracy and the World War.* 3 vols., 1936-1948.

Pershing, John J. *My Experiences in the World War.* 2 vols., 1931.

Peterson, H. C., and G. C. Fite. *Opponents of War, 1917-1918.* 1957.

Safford, Jeffrey. *Wilsonian Maritime Diplomacy.* 1978.

Scheiber, H. N. *The Wilson Administration and Civil Liberties, 1917-1921.* 1960.

Unterberger, Betty M. *America's Siberian Expedition, 1918-1920.* 1956.

Vandiver, Frank E. *Black Jack: The Life and Times of John J. Pershing.* 2 vols.; 1977.

Weigley, Russell F. *The American Way of War: A History of United States Military Strategy and Policy.* 1973.

15

Wilson and the Versailles Treaty

To try to win a different kind of peace from the one he believed was on the mind of the Allied leaders, President Wilson, in other speeches in 1918 expanded on the Fourteen Points. On February 11, he set forth the "Four Principles," in which he stated "that peoples and provinces are not to be bartered about from sovereignty to sovereignty as if they were made chattels and pawns in a game," and " that all well-defined aspirations should be accorded the utmost satisfaction that can be accorded them without introducing new or perpetuating old elements of discord and antagonism." When Wilson gave a Fourth of July address at Mount Vernon he listed the "Four Ends" as the objective of the United States and the Allies, and all of these, he asserted, could be put into a single sentence, "What we seek is the reign of law, based upon the consent of the government and sustained by the organized opinion of mankind." And on September 27, when the president spoke at the Metropolitan Opera House in New York City on the occasion of the launching of the Fourth Liberty Loan, he added the "Five Particulars," where he said, "The impartial justice meted out must involve no discrimination between those to whom we wish to be just and those to whom we do not wish to be just."

So Wilson had his Fourteen Points, Four Principles, Four Ends, and Five Particulars in setting forth his ideas of what constituted a just peace. The Fourteen Points appeared as a master stroke in reassuring the Allied peoples there was idealism in the Allied war aims. People everywhere, weary of the sacrifices and horrors of war, greeted the Fourteen Points with enthusiasm and renewed hope. Wilson was hailed as a great moral leader. Unfortunately, however, the Allied governments paid the Fourteen Points only lip service. Britain would not even endorse the idea of freedom of the seas in principle, and Georges Clemenceau, Premier of France, observed, "I do not understand this principle of the Freedom of the Seas. War would not be war if there was freedom of the seas." While Wilson's Points were idealistic enough to wage a program of psychological warfare, many considered them too visionary to fashion a peace. "He [Wilson] could have preached a sermon on any one of them," wrote John Maynard Keynes, prominent English economist, "or have addressed a stately prayer to the Almighty for their fulfillment, but he could not frame their concrete applications to the actual state of Europe."

While the Allied leaders were pleased with the Fourteen Points as counterpropaganda, they were unhappy about Wilson's efforts to solve European problems and to interfere with their war aims. At home Republican critics of the president led by former President Theodore Roosevelt and Henry Cabot Lodge of Massachusetts, a prominent member of the Senate, attacked the Fourteen Points and what they considered to be weak peace terms. Until Wilson had proposed an association of nations to enforce future world peace, Lodge and Roosevelt had thought the idea was an excellent one. Lodge in 1915 had said, "The great nations must be so united as to be able to say to any single country, you must not go to war, and they can only say that effectively when the country desiring war knows the force...is irresistible." But when Wilson advocated a league of nations, Lodge changed his mind and warned that such an organization "might plunge us into war at any moment at the bidding of other nations." As for peace, Lodge demanded unconditional surrender. Roosevelt, who regarded Wilson as a weakling and a fraud, also wanted a tough peace. "Let us dictate peace by the hammering guns," he insisted, "and not chat about peace to the accompaniment of clicking typewriters."

These Republican leaders believed the country was normally Republican and that the Democrats were in power only because of factional disputes among Republicans. The Republicans not only denounced Wilson's war aims, but they attempted to show voters they were united and that their split of 1912 was healed. Roosevelt and Taft appeared together in public, and there were other manifestations of unity. Concerned about these political developments, Democratic congressmen up for reelection in 1918 asked the president for help.

Wilson feared a Republican Congress would wreck his peace program. He was informed of the large amounts of money the Republicans were spending to win the 1918 elections. This concern led him to make a serious political mistake. He could have asked the voters to return Senators and Representatives, of whatever party, who would support his war and peace program. Instead he sought the election of a Democratic Congress, so that he would not be hampered in his peace negotiations. With reluctance Wilson appealed to the voters through the newspapers on October 24, near the end of the congressional campaigns: "If you have approved of my leadership and wish me to continue to be your unembarrassed spokesman in affairs at home and abroad, I earnestly beg that you will express yourself unmistakeably to that effect by returning a Democratic majority to both the Senate, and the House of Representatives. The leaders of the minority in the present Congress have been unquestionably pro-war, but they have been anti-administration," Wilson continued. "The return of a Republican majority to either House of the Congress would. . . certainly be interpreted on the other side of the water as a repudiation of my leadership."

Wilson, determined to attend the peace conference himself, wanted a vote of confidence when he should have known that such a vote was just about impossible in the American political system. True, President McKinley had issued a similar call for a Republican Congress and had been successful. But it was unnecessary and unwise for Wilson. His appeal invoked a partisan issue. During the war the public had little opportunity to discern the differences between the two major parties as both supported the American war effort. But Wilson's call for a Democratic Congress alienated many Republicans who had supported his war policy and revived partisan politics that had been largely adjourned since intervention in April 1917.

Wilson's blunder along with a number of domestic grievances at the time allowed the Republicans to win majorities in both houses of Congress (237–190 in the House and 49–47 in the Senate) in the 1918 elections and to gain control of the congressional committees, especially the Foreign Relations Committee in the Senate where any peace treaty would have to be considered. The vote was a shattering blow to Wilson's prestige. In view of what he had said in his appeal to the voters, he appeared to have been repudiated by his own people and, therefore, unable to speak for them at the peace conference. When Wilson went to France in December 1918 as head of the American peace delegation, Theodore Roosevelt publicly said, "Our Allies and our enemies and Mr. Wilson himself should all understand that Mr. Wilson has no authority whatever to speak for the American people at this time. His leadership has just been emphatically repudiated by them. . . . Mr. Wilson and his fourteen points and his four supplementary points and his five complementary points and all his utterances every which way have ceased to have any shadow of right to be accepted as expressive of the will of the American people. . . ."

Republicans might have been mollified if some of their leaders had been asked to join the peace delegation. This would have made it a bipartisan group which could have claimed to represent the United States. It might also have made it easier for Wilson in the Senate during the fight over the treaty. His serious setback in the elections underscored the necessity for conciliating the Republicans and the Senate and for educating the public. But Wilson was unable or unwilling to recognize the significance of the Republican electoral victory. Instead he made some disparaging remarks about the Senate, and he believed American public opinion was behind him.

Wilson decided to attend the peace conference himself, a decision that provided considerable criticism. No president had ever before gone to Europe during his term of office, and at the time many believed the president should not leave the country.* Then when Wilson announced the members of the peace delegation there was also more criticism. Wilson not only failed to put a leading Republican on the peace commission, but did not choose any member of the Senate either. It was another serious and obvious blunder on his part.

The commissioners, in addition to the president, were Secretary of State Lansing, Colonel House, General Tasker H. Bliss, a member of the Supreme War Council, and Henry White, an experienced diplomat. All were capable people, but not one of them had the kind of political influence that would be useful in seeing the treaty through the Senate. Though Bliss and White were Republicans they were not politically important Republicans.

President McKinley, a wiser politician than Wilson, had named three senators, two Republicans and a Democrat, as members of the Commission to make peace with Spain in 1898. Thus he flattered the

---

*Theodore Roosevelt was the first president to go abroad when he went to Panama to see the Panama Canal.

ego of the Senate and assured bipartisan support for the treaty in that body. But Wilson defied an important precedent and took no senator to Paris. His failure to make a bid for Republican support was a serious mistake, because the Senate that would pass upon the treaty would be controlled by a Republican majority. Under these circumstances Wilson would have been wise to include at least one prominent Republican on his peace commission. Lodge, who would become chairman of the Senate Committee on Foreign Relations when the new Congress would convene in March 1919, would have been, for this reason, the logical choice if Wilson chose any senators at all. But if Wilson found Lodge objectionable there were other prominent Republicans such as Elihu Root, former President William H. Taft, and Charles Evans Hughes who sympathized generally with the president's program for a peace settlement and a league of nations.

Wilson also failed to realize the departure in American foreign policy that the peace settlement could mean for the ordinary American. He also neglected to build support among American voters by informing them clearly of his purpose. Moreover, he was overconfident about his influence with the European Allied leaders he would meet at the peace conference. He believed they did not represent their people and that he could therefore appeal over their heads to their own people as he had done on occasions at home over the heads of Congress to American voters. However, the Allied leaders believed that it was Wilson who had been repudiated in the recent congressional elections, and that he did not represent the American people. If Lloyd George of Britain or Georges Clemenceau of France or Vittorio Orlando of Italy had lost such an election as Wilson did, they would have had to resign their premiership. So in their eyes Wilson's loss of the election weakened his bargaining power.

There were no transatlantic planes in 1918, and Wilson and the peace delegation sailed on 4 December 1918 on the liner, the George Washington, and arrived at Brest, France, on December 13. Since the peace conference did not begin for a month (12 January 1919) Wilson used this waiting period to visit Paris, London, and Rome where he received a jubilant welcome,* and ordinary people hoped he would be able to bring about a perfect peace settlement. On his way to Europe Wilson had been asked about his plans for a league of nations. "I am

---

*Imagine a modern American president having this much time for a visit.

going to insist that the league be brought out as part and parcel of the treaty itself," he replied. "A league I believe will of necessity become an integral part of such a treaty as I trust we shall work out." The great welcome from the peoples of Europe convinced the president that the league must precede, not follow, the peace.

Three main obstacles stood in the way of making a just and lasting peace. One was the secret treaties the Allied governments had made for the division of German and Austro-Hungarian territory and colonies at the end of the war. Russia had been promised Constantinople and the Dardanelle Straits; France, Alsace-Lorraine, the Saar Valley, and an independent Rhineland; Italy, Trentino, southern Tyrol, some Adriatic ports, Dodecanese Islands, and a protectorate over Albania; Britain, to have spheres of influence in Persia and Mesopotamia, a protectorate over Egypt, and the major share of Germany's colonies in Africa and in the Pacific; and Japan was to receive Germany's colonies in the northern Pacific. The only country in the war not having territorial aspirations was the United States.

Thus there were inconsistencies between the war aims of these treaties and those the Allies publicly espoused, especially those of Wilson and his Fourteen Points. Wilson was aware of this, because he knew the terms of some of the secret treaties. When the United States entered the war, some of the Allies sent missions to Washington to discuss war aims, among other matters. The British delegation discussed the secret treaties with Wilson and showed him copies of some of them, but he made no criticisms and did not ask the Allies to give up their territorial objectives. When the Bolsheviks took over Russia they released to the world information from the czar's archives about the secret treaties to dispel the notion that the Allies were fighting solely for the cause of democracy. So Wilson must have known about the secret treaties, but he either dismissed them as so much propaganda or else he hoped to persuade the Allies to give up their designs. Whatever the reason the fact is that Wilson never confronted the Allies about the secret treaties, and he went to Paris handicapped by them.

Another obstacle was France's desire for revenge. France wanted to destroy Germany's economic power and to take from her all her territory outside of Europe. France wanted to seize just about all of Germany's iron, coal, and transport so as to eliminate her as a world power. The matter of reparations was also an obstacle. The Allied leaders meant to make Germany pay the entire costs of the war.

According to Charles Seymour, who accompanied Wilson and the American peace delegation in a minor capacity as a young man and who later became a prominent historian of American diplomacy and president of Yale University, the president thought there were two great difficulties blocking his success at the peace conference. One was that the Allied leaders would interpret the Fourteen Points in terms of national self-interest. The other was the demands that small countries like Poland, Rumania, Serbia, and Greece would make for territory. Seymour contends that Wilson failed to understand accurately his difficulties and did not strive for a general preliminary treaty that would have included the general lines of a territorial settlement and the disarming of the Central Powers. Wilson had thought about this in November 1918, but he did not push for it when he arrived in France. Seymour believes such a treaty would have increased his prestige and strength instead of diminishing it and causing him trouble at the Conference and in the Senate.

The Paris Peace Conference, comprised of the representatives of the thirty-two "allied and associated powers," including the four British dominions and India, met from January to June 1919. Neither the defeated nations nor the neutrals had been invited to send delegates, nor had the Bolshevik (or Soviet) government of Russia. None of the countries represented at the Conference had yet recognized that government, and some believed that the Soviet leaders in making a separate peace with Germany had forfeited any right to be represented at the peace conference.

Wilson and Lloyd George, however, believed that the Russian people should be represented at a conference that was to remake the map of Europe. But since Russia was still in a civil war between "Reds" and "Whites," there was no government or party that could speak for the Russian people as a whole. Thus, at Wilson's suggestion, the Conference leaders proposed that all warring groups in Russia agree to a cease fire and to send representatives to an island in the Sea of Marmara, located between Europe and Asia, to confer with one another and with spokesmen for the Allies and the United States. This plan broke down when the leading "White" leaders, with the encouragement of France, refused to cooperate. Later an American secret mission to Russia, approved by Lloyd George and headed by William C. Bullitt, brought back a conciliatory offer from Lenin. But news of the mission leaked to the press, and there was so much opposition to it in some quarters that Lloyd George repudiated it, and Wilson refused even to see Bullitt when he returned to Paris.

So the Soviet Union was not represented at the Peace Conference. But as Julius W. Pratt, one of the top historians of American diplomacy, has pointed out, "The threat of Bolshevism, however, was always present, like Banquo's ghost at the feast, and influenced in various ways the decisions of the Allied statesmen."*

Since the vanquished nations were excluded from the Peace Conference it was clear that the Allies intended to impose a peace treaty upon Germany and her associates despite Wilson's earlier "Peace Without Victory" program. The plenary sessions of the Conference were too large and unwieldy to accomplish much, and a council of four made up of the three leading Allied prime ministers or premiers, Lloyd George of Britain, Clemenceau of France, Orlando of Italy, and President Wilson, representing the "Big Four" powers, assumed executive control of the Conference and settled all matters of consequence. These men, frequently in a room even without secretaries, made the fundamental decisions of the Conference. Wilson, because he was the only chief of state present and represented the wealthiest power, stood out as the chief figure among them.

Wilson was committed to the Fourteen Points, but the Allied leaders felt bound by the secret treaties and other considerations. Lloyd George, for example, came to the Conference with not only the pledges of the secret treaties but with the glib promises he had made in a hot British election campaign of 1918. During that election there had been cries and slogans of "Hang the Kaiser," and "Make Germany pay to the last pfennig." George Creel relates that Lloyd George came to Paris in a joking mood remarking, "Heaven only knows what I would have had to promise them if the campaign had lasted a week longer." Clemenceau's power of decision was limited by the French passion for revenge for the Franco-Prussian War (1870-1871) defeat and for security against a repetition of the German invasion of 1914; and Orlando's decision was limited by the popular Italian hysteria over Adriatic possessions, which was stirred by such strong nationalists as Gabriele D'Annunzio.

Wilson believed the League of Nations might save the whole situation. This is why he strove so hard to preserve the League. But the Al-

---

*Julius W. Pratt, Vincent P. De Santis, Joseph M. Siracusa, *A History of United States Foreign Policy,* 4th. ed., 1980, p. 252.

lies, desiring security, vengeance, and the spoils of war above all else, were loath to accept the Fourteen Points. In the beginning Wilson gained two important victories at the Conference. One was the adoption by a plenary session of the Conference in mid-February of the Covenant of the League of Nations after ten hard meetings of the commission, headed by Wilson, to draft the Covenant and the decision to make it an integral part of the final peace treaty. The other was Wilson's persuading the Allies to accept a compromise between the secret treaties and the Fourteen Points. Wilson stubbornly opposed the parceling out of the territorial spoils as had been agreed to in these treaties. He managed to have the Allies accept an arrangement whereby they would not receive the conquered territory outright, but only as trustees or mandates of the League of Nations. According to Thomas A. Bailey, a leading historian of American diplomacy, "This half-loaf solution, as applied to certain under-developed countries, proved to be little more than the old pre-war imperialism, thinly disguised."

After these initial successes Wilson had to return to the United States to make decisions on bills passed by Congress and to take care of other presidential business. Here he learned he was going to have to convince fellow Americans of the necessity for the League of Nations as he had the delegates at the Peace Conference. This was especially the case in the Senate where any treaty had to be approved. In this body Senator Lodge, largely out of personal and political reasons, was rallying his Republican followers to oppose the League and thus the treaty. They were joined by a dozen or so isolationists, mostly Republicans, known as "irreconcilables" or "bitter enders," and led by Senator William E. Borah of Idaho and Senator Hiram W. Johnson of California.

At Colonel House's suggestion, Wilson invited the members of the Senate Foreign Relations and the House Foreign Affairs Committees (some members declined) to discuss the League Covenant over dinner at the White House on February 26. Wilson defended his League project, but he was not able to persuade any of those who opposed it. Then in early March 1919, a few hours before Congress adjourned, Senator Lodge read in the Senate a statement signed by thirty-seven Republican senators or senators-elect, declaring that "the constitution of the league of nations in the form now proposed-
...should not be accepted by the United States"; that peace with Germany should be made as soon as possible "and that the proposal for a

league of nations to insure the permanent peace of the world should then be taken up for careful and serious consideration."

This "Round Robin," signed by more senators than were needed to block a treaty, announced to the world that the Senate would not accept the League of Nations in its present form. It was also a serious message to the president who, instead of being conciliatory, was defiant in a New York speech just before going back to Paris, when he said the League would be inseparably tied to the treaty. In such a union of League and treaty, the Senate could not reject the League without killing the entire treaty, and Wilson was confident it would not do this.

However, both Democratic and Republican friends of the League, including former President Taft and President Abbott Lawrence Lowell of Harvard, warned Wilson that without some changes the League would never receive Senate approval. When Wilson returned to Paris he reconvened the League of Nations Commission and asked that the Covenant be amended with the following changes to insure Senate approval: (1) recognition of the rights of members to withdraw from the League, (2) exemption of domestic questions (such as tariff and immigration) from League jurisdiction, (3) a statement that no member would be required, against its will, to accept a mandate over a former enemy colony, and (4) a declaration safeguarding the Monroe Doctrine.

On two of these changes—the right of withdrawal and the Monroe Doctrine—Wilson met considerable opposition, especially from the French who argued that such changes would weaken the protection from the League. The Allies also asked for something in return for agreeing to the changes. France wanted an international general staff to direct action against new aggressions. Britain asked the United States to give up its ambitious naval building program. Italy insisted on having Fiume, a city and port on the Adriatic. Japan renewed a proposal, made and discarded earlier, for a recognition of racial equality in the Preamble of the Covenant. After many days of debate and deadlock, Wilson obtained the desired amendments without accepting the changes in the Covenant proposed by others. But he did pay in concessions in other matters for the acquiescence of the Allies in his efforts to placate the Senate, and his position at the Conference was weakened. The amended Covenant was approved at a plenary session of the Conference on April 28.

In Wilson's mind the making of the League of Nations was the most significant part of the peace settlement. To have the Covenant adopted, incorporated in the peace treaties, and accepted by the Allies was so important to Wilson that he was willing to pay for it by making concessions in other matters—concessions that in many cases contradicted the Fourteen Points. But it would be a mistake to conclude that Wilson yielded on everything except the League. "The surprising fact is not that he compromised on some points," wrote Julius W. Pratt, "but that he saved as much of his program as he did."

Wilson did obtain assurances that hereafter international engagements would be "open covenants" as provided in his Fourteen Points, but he was not able to have any steps taken to implement the points on "freedom of the seas" and the removal of economic barriers. On the matter of the limitation of armaments the League Covenant recognized the necessity for their reduction and the League Council was charged with formulating plans for such reduction. But the League members did not have to accept such plans, and in fact no armaments were limited except those of the enemy countries.

On the important matter of an "absolutely impartial adjustment of colonial claims," there was a compromise in applying this principle to the former German colonies in Africa and the Pacific, all of which had been conquered during the war, and to the non-Turkish parts of the Ottoman Empire, which had been occupied by the Allied armies. A system of mandates was devised whereby these former colonies and territories, which were not considered ready for self-government, were placed under the responsibility of other nations acting on behalf of the League and making annual reports to the League about them.

Wilson had hoped to see the mandates assigned to small neutral countries such as those of Scandinavia and Switzerland. But they were given to the victorious Allied powers—Britain, France, Belgium, and Japan—and in a way that closely corresponded to the provisions of the secret treaties. Of course, these different powers handled their mandates in different ways.

Japan received the mandate for the former German islands in the North Pacific—the Marshalls, Carolines, and Marianas, but not to German rights to China's Shantung peninsula.* Wilson opposed the Japanese claims to Shantung, because to turn over 30 million Chinese to Japanese rule would be an intolerable violation of the rights of self-determination, one of Wilson's cherished ideals. China, of course

---

*In time Japan illegally fortified these islands and used them as bases against the United States in World War II.

wanted the return of all German rights and property in Shantung. Japan put pressure on Wilson by threatening to walk out if she did not receive Shantung. Wilson finally yielded and accepted a compromise that allowed Japan to keep Germany's economic holdings in Shantung but that pledged Japan to "hand back the Shantung Peninsula in full sovereignty to China," later on. China rejected this compromise and refused on that account to sign the treaty.*

Half of Wilson's Fourteen Points (6–13) were concerned mainly with the restoration of territory occupied by the enemy and the redrawing of national boundaries along lines of nationality or self-determination. In the peace settlement of these matters there were both achievements and failures. Alsace-Lorraine was restored to France. The new states of Poland, Czechoslovakia, and Yugoslavia were created from the breakup of Austria-Hungary and from Polish territory taken from Germany and Russia. Germany ceded to Denmark, Belgium, and Czechoslovakia small areas inhabited principally by people of those nationalities. Austria and Hungary were separated and Transylvania was taken from Hungary and added to Rumania. These changes in the European map were made in response to nationalism and were in accord with the Fourteen Points.

So were the decisions by Wilson not to give in to the Italian demands for Fiume and the French demands for German territory west of the Rhine. While the city of Fiume on the Adriatic had a population more than half Italian, the inland country was Slavic, and it was an outlet to the sea for both Yugoslavia and Austria. The secret treaties had not given Fiume to Italy, but she now wanted Fiume and the non-Italian portions of the Dalmatian coast to give her naval control of the Adriatic. To turn over Fiume to Italy was a violation of self-determination, and Wilson stubbornly refused to do this. When the Italian delegates persevered in their demands, the president resorted to a tactic he had successfully used at home when he issued an appeal on 23 April 1919 over their heads to the Italian people themselves.

Wilson's maneuvers failed, because Orlando and his associates left the Conference and returned to Italy where they were enthusiastically acclaimed by the Italian people and given a vote of confidence by the Italian parliament. Even so Wilson would not yield, and the question of Fiume was not settled at the Conferences. It was left to Italy and Yugoslavia to solve. For a while they treated it as a "free state,"

---

*China became a member of the League of Nations by signing the treaty with Austria.

and then in 1924, they divided it between themselves, Fiume proper going to Italy and the adjacent Port Baros to Yugoslavia.

As for France, she demanded that the Rhineland (German territory west of the Rhine where several million Germans lived) be separated from Germany and become a buffer state, and that the coal-rich Saar Valley, inhabited almost entirely by Germans, be annexed to France. Both demands were a violation of self-determination and Wilson opposed them. France, however, justified these demands on grounds of security, reparations for French coal mines flooded by the German armies, and the fact that France had exercised temporary sovereignty over the Saar a century earlier. During this impasse with the French in early April 1919, Wilson became ill with influenza and a high temperature. He also had exhausted his patience with the French and made preparations for his return to the United States.

Wilson's departure, which probably would have wrecked the Conference, was averted by a compromise in the French deadlock. France received title to the Saar coal mines, but the Saar territory would remain under the League of Nations for fifteen years. At the end of that period the Saar population would vote on whether it should rejoin Germany, be annexed to France, or continue under international control. In 1935, the Saar people voted overwhelmingly to rejoin Germany.

The Rhineland, although remaining under German sovereignty, was demilitarized as was a strip of land fifty kilometers wide east of the Rhine. For additional security for France, an understandable French concern, Wilson agreed to a treaty whereby the United States and Britain promised to come to the aid of France if she should again be attacked by Germany. The American treaty was sent to the Senate, but it was never reported out of committee.

"For France, which still bore the marks of the Hunnish invader, the outcome was supremely disillusioning," wrote historian Thomas A. Bailey. "Deprived of both the Rhineland and a feeling of security, she was forced to drink the bitter dregs of betrayal."

But Wilson did not fight on every question of self-determination as he had on Fiume and the Rhineland. He allowed, for example, the Italians to have the strategic Brenner Pass even though this meant the surrender by Austria of territory and peoples. With his consent, Austria, with its seven million Germans, was forbidden to unite with Germany. There were other violations of self-determination. "Yet, by and large," contends Julius W. Pratt, "self-determination won at Paris." According to Bailey, "Many more millions of minority groups were released from alien domination than were consigned to alien domination. The result was the closest approximation that modern Europe has ever had to an ethnographic map coinciding with a political map."

The Versailles Treaty was completed on 29 May 1919 and was signed by Germany on June 28 in the Hall of Mirrors at Versailles where the victorious Prussians in the Franco-Prussian War had in 1871 proclaimed the establishment of the German Empire. The majority of the 440 articles of the treaty were technical and noncontroversial. The first 26 comprised the Covenant of the League of Nations. The League consisted of two bodies: an Assembly, where all the members were represented, and a Council of nine members, five of whom—the United States, Britain, France, Italy, and Japan—were permanent members. In addition, a World Court would sit at the Hague, near the North Sea in Holland, to arbitrate international disputes, and the League was to create a number of commissions to foster international cooperation in a variety of fields.

Under the terms of the treaty, Germany had to agree to the war guilt clause (Article 231) of the treaty by which Germany and her allies had to accept responsibility "for causing all loss and damage" that the Allies had suffered "as a consequence of the war imposed upon them by the aggression of Germany and her allies." Thus the sole responsibility for starting the war in 1914 was imposed upon Germany and her allies. The men who wrote the treaty may have believed this, but the Germans who had to accept this view under duress did not believe it, and it has not been supported by history.

The reparations matter was also a serious failure for Wilson at Paris. In an address on 18 February 1918, he had said there should be "no contributions, no punitive damages." This statement seemed to check any attempt to levy the cost of the war upon Germany, but the Allied leaders, especially the British in the 1918 election campaign, had promised to do just that. While Wilson objected to the "war costs" he was persuaded by the British argument that pensions and separation allowances paid to allied soldiers and their dependents should be regarded as "damages done to the civilian population" and that Germany should pay for these as well as for claims to other losses.

So a huge reparations bill was imposed on Germany and was placed upon her at a time when her resources for it had been substantially reduced. These resources included her colonies, most of her merchant marine, German-owned property in Allied countries, the coal of the Saar, the iron ore of Lorraine, and much of her industrial and agricultural capacity. Altogether she lost about one-tenth of her population and about one-eight of her territory. The Allies were unable to agree on a reparations figure, and a Reparations Commission in 1921 set it at $33 billion, thirty-three times the indemnity that Germany had imposed on France in 1871. Although Germany only actually paid about one-tenth of this amount (the remainder was forgiven by the Allies during the Great Depression), the enormous bill fixed on her left many Germans and many Western liberals with the feeling of having been double-crossed.

The terms of the treaty were harsher than those Wilson had initially proposed. But while he believed it was "a very severe settlement with Germany" he maintained "there is nothing in it that she did not earn." Just before leaving Paris he was asked at a press conference: "Mr. President, do you feel that you achieved here the peace that you expected to make?" "I think," replied Wilson, "that we have made a better peace than I should have expected when I came here to Paris."

Wilson pinned his hopes for a just peace on the League of Nations, which he believed would correct whatever injustices there were in the Versailles settlement. The heart of the Covenant, as Wilson insisted, was Article Ten. It pledged all members of the League to respect and preserve the independence of all members against "external aggression." In cases of any such aggression or in the case of any threat or danger of such aggression, it read, "the Council shall advise upon the means by which this obligation shall be fulfilled." Here was the idea of collective security that Wilson was unwilling to compromise on with opponents of the League and that we have had in the United Nations since the end of World War II.

Probably no document written in the twentieth century has generated greater or more enduring controversy than the Treaty of Versailles. Critics, contemporary and historical, have censured it for different reasons. Some have condemned it as too harsh and as a "Carthaginian Peace" of vengeance. Others have denounced it as too mild. It compared favorably with Germany's treaty of Brest-Litovsk with Russia in March 1918, whereby Russia had to give up all claims to the Ukraine and the Causasus as well as to Poland, Finland, and the Baltic states. Had Germany defeated the Allies she might have demanded more of them than they did of her, and there would not have been the hope of the League of Nations.

Wilson had said, "Only a peace between equals can last," and he desired a peace without victory. But as historian Richard Hofstadter has observed, "What he really wanted was not simply a 'peace without victory' but a victory to be followed by an unvictorious peace."* Wilson wanted the Allies and Germany to come to the conference table as victors and vanquished and to sit down as negotiators. This was not possible. When one really reads the treaty and considers the diverse aims of all those who made the peace, the treaty is probably what it had to be. Hence Arthur Link has asked, "What kind of a peace treaty would have been written if Wilson had not been at Paris?" As the spokesman of the only disinterested nation at the Conference, Link wrote, "Wilson emerged from the fiery trial with the greatest stature precisely because he was able to accomplish so much in spite of stupendous obstacles."*

When Wilson formally submitted the treaty to the United States Senate on 10 July 1919, it appeared that public sentiment favored approval. A *Literary Digest* poll reported 718 newspapers in the country supported American membership in the League, 481 conditionally approved it, and 181 opposed it. Thirty-two of the forty-eight state legislatures and thirty governors endorsed it. Just about all the Democrats in the Senate favored the treaty as it was. The small group of isolationists in the Senate, known as "irreconcilables" and mentioned earlier, flatly opposed the treaty. They wanted no American participation in a league of any kind, because they believed the United States should not become involved in European affairs. The remainder of the senators, called the "reservationists," favored the treaty with some changes.

The treaty and league question became involved in domestic American politics and in the approaching presidential election of 1920. There developed a lineup of opposition to the president and to the treaty—senators who had been snubbed and who resented Wilson's wartime powers, Republican leaders who wanted to win in 1920, isolationists who opposed the idea of the United States having to make any advance political commitment abroad as envisioned in Article 10 of the League, parents who believed their sons would have to fight in all

---

*Richard Hofstadter, *The American Political Tradition and the Men Who Made It* (1959 Ed.), p. 272.
*Arthur S. Link and William B. Catton, *American Epoch, A History of the United States Since 1900* Vol. I. 1900-1945, Fifth Ed., 1980, p. 218.

parts of the world in an international military force under the League, those Americans who thought Wilson had made a mistake in going to war, and those who thought Germany should have been militarily invaded and occupied rather than merely surrendering.

The treaty also had alienated some of the groups who had been among the staunchest supporters of the Democratic party—Irish-Americans who resented the failure of Ireland to obtain the right of self-determination at the Peace Conference, German-Americans who regarded the treaty as being too hard on Germany, and Italian-Americans who held Wilson responsible for Italy's failure to secure Fiume.

This anti-Wilson feeling, strong along the Atlantic Coast and in the industrial centers of the Middle West, had been intensified by the president's apparent disregard of Congress. Many businessmen, for example, argued that the treaty must be bad, because it was Wilson's work, and the League must be worst of all, since it was his pet scheme. "One heard daily in the clubs and on the golf courses of New England and the Middle Atlantic States the remark: 'I know little about the treaty, but I know Wilson, and I know he must be wrong,'" wrote Charles Seymour.*

Despite the initial apparent public sentiment in favor of the treaty, its opponents gained so much momentum in the months following its submission to the Senate that Wilson decided to take his case to the country as he had done in other matters. Like President Andrew Johnson before him he set out on 3 September 1919 on a "swing around the circle." His tour took him through the Old Northwest, the Upper Mississippi Valley, the Rocky Mountain Region, and the Pacific Coast. During the next three weeks he traveled 8,000 miles, delivered thirty-seven speeches, and addressed many groups from the rear platform of his train. His audiences, at first apathetic, especially in the Middle West where there was much opposition to the treaty, became more enthusiastic as we he went farther West. He roused much popular enthusiasm with his appeal that a League was essential to prevent further aggressions in Europe and the necessity for another intervention by the United States.

Wilson had been in good health since the peace conference, and his western trip strained him to the utmost. After a long pleading speech for the League at Pueblo, Colorado, on September 25, on his

---

*Charles Seymour, *Woodrow Wilson and the World War,* 1921, p. 332.

return, he nearly collapsed from physical and nervous exhaustion. On his physician's advice, he cancelled the remaining speeches and went back to Washington. On October 2, Wilson suffered a stroke paralyzing the left side of his face and body and keeping him in bed for much of the time for the next six months. He never fully recovered, although his mind was clear and alert. For at least the first month, Wilson was probably incapacitated within the meaning of the Constitution. He considered no legislation and made no appointments. Neither Congress nor the public nor the Cabinet was fully informed of the president's condition. For seven and a half months he did not meet his Cabinet. Who actually ran the American government during this time is still somewhat of a mystery. For quite some time the Democratic leaders in Congress could see the ailing president usually only through his wife who decided what things should be given to Wilson. It was during the time of the president's illness that the treaty was defeated in the Senate.

In the meantime the Senate Foreign Relations Committee under Senator Lodge had completed hearings on the treaty, and on September 10 its majority report proposed forty-five amendments and four reservations that would have significantly changed the League. But administration Democrats and some Republicans, who considered these changes too drastic, joined together to vote down the committee's plan. Then Lodge changed his tactics, and on November 6 he proposed fourteen reservations, which became known as the Lodge reservations. On these the Republicans held together almost solidly and had the assistance of some Democratic votes on some of the reservations.

The success of Lodge's tactics to defeat the treaty by indirection after failing to amend it rested on his assumption that Wilson would not allow the Democrats to accept a treaty with any reservations, and especially those proposed by Lodge. When Senator James Watson of Indiana suggested that the president might accept the reservations, Lodge replied, "But, my dear James, you do not take into consideration the hatred Woodrow Wilson has for me personally. Never under any set of circumstances in the world could he be induced to accept a treaty with the Lodge reservations appended to it." He was, of course, tragically right. "Wilson, hating Lodge, saw red at the mere suggestion of the Lodge reservation," wrote Bailey, a recognized authority on the treaty fight. "He was quite willing to accept somewhat similar reservations sponsored by his faithful Democratic followers, but he insisted that the Lodge reservations 'emasculated' the entire pact." Yet, all the enmity was not on Wilson's side. Lodge had also a personal hostility toward Wilson and thought he was the worst president of the United States, with the exception of Buchanan. In this appalling spectacle of mutual hatred, two highly educated and literate men, with Ph.D.s from leading universities in the country and holding two of the top political positions in the nation, acted irresponsibly and more like school boys with petty jealousies to defeat the treaty and the league.

The Lodge reservations thus became the focal point in the struggle in the Senate over the treaty. Most of these reserved powers to the United States that under the Covenant could hardly have been denied her, and they provided that the United States could take no action in important matters without the consent of Congress. They declared, for example, that the United States could not accept a league territorial mandate without the consent of Congress, that the league could not consider domestic affairs of the United States, that the Monroe Doctrine was "wholly outside the jurisdiction of the League of Nations and entirely unaffected by the Versailles Treaty," that the Reparations Commission of the league would have no right to interfere with trade between the United States and Germany, without the consent of Congress, and that Congress had the right to provide by law for the appointment of an American representative to the league and to appropriate funds for the American share of league expenses.

The most important of these reservations was the second one, which stated that the United States assumed no obligations under Article X of the Covenant to preserve the territorial integrity or political independence of any other country, to interfere in controversies between nations, or to use its armed forces to uphold any article of the treaty, unless Congress by joint resolutions so provided. This reservation was especially obnoxious to Wilson who believed it impaired the obligations of the United States under the league and rejected his idea of collective security. But it was simply a statement of fact—for under the Constitution only Congress has the power to declare war. That right, however, has been set aside since the end of World War II by four presidents—Truman in the Korean War, and Kennedy, Johnson, and Nixon in the Vietnam War. The Senate approved the Lodge reservations, including the controversial second, after an acrimonious debate. It was now up to the ailing Wilson and the Senate Democrats as to what to do.

The Republicans were ready to approve the treaty with the Lodge reservations but the Democrats, under instructions from Wilson, would not go along. The president, from his sickbed, told the Senate Democrats that approval would mean not ratification but "nullification of the treaty." "I trust," he added, "that all true friends of the treaty will refuse to support the Lodge reservations."

On 19 November 1919, the Senate voted on the resolution to approve the treaty with the Lodge reservations. All but four of the Democrats joined the Republican irreconcilables to defeat the treaty with the reservations by a vote of 39 to 55, with two-thirds of the Senators present necessary for concurrence. A second vote showed a slight shift, 41 to 50. The Senate then refused to reconsider with the reservations of Senator Gilbert M. Hitchcock of Nebraska, Democratic leader in the Senate, and finally voted down, 38 to 53, a Democratic resolution to approve the treaty without reservations. It was apparent from these votes that neither with the Lodge reservations nor without any could the treaty win even a majority of the Senate, let alone the required two-thirds.

The Senate then adjourned, and the treaty question was put off until the spring of 1920. In the interval an increasing number of people, here and abroad, concluded it was better to have a treaty with reservations than no treaty at all. Former Secretary of State William J. Bryan urged the adoption of the treaty with reservations, and probably most Democratic senators privately agreed. The French and British leaders asked the president to compromise and even publicly stated the Allies would accept the Lodge reservations without requiring a reopening of negotiations. A number of organizations in the United States pressed Lodge and Wilson to settle their differences. But it was clear from the first votes that if Wilson wanted Senate approval of the treaty, he would have to compromise largely on Lodge's terms. This Wilson steadfastly refused to do. He firmly believed the reservations would weaken the league's authority, and he just as firmly believed that an overwhelming majority of Americans desired approval of the treaty without the reservations. In a letter he sent to Democrats at their Jackson Day dinner in Washington on 20 January 1920, he said that the United States must take the treaty "without changes that alter its meaning, or leave it"; that if the Senate refused to approve it, then the presidential election of 1920 should be made "a great and solemn referendum" in which the voters would decide the issue. "It was one of the greatest tactical errors of Wilson's public career," Arthur Link has written. Before this Wilson had avoided any show of partisanship in the treaty fight. "By making ratification a partisan issue, he made it inevitable that most Republicans in the Senate would follow their majority leader," added Link. "Moreover, public opinion now turned decisively against the President, who had put himself in the position of being the chief obstacle to a solution."

Under considerable pressure from home and abroad for favorable action on the treaty, the Senate in March 1920 relented and agreed to reconsider the matter. Again Wilson ordered the Democratic senators to reject any treaty with reservations. By this decision he ruled out compromise and missed his last opportunity for an alliance with some of the reservationists, and thereby gave Lodge a victory. To the very end, Wilson persisted that the choice lay between the treaty as he had sent it to Senate and a treaty with the Lodge reservations. The vote showed that Wilson was wrong. The actual alternatives were the treaty with the reservations or no treaty at all.

When the final vote came on the treaty on 19 March 1920, 21 Democrats broke with the president and joined 28 Republicans to vote for the treaty with reservations to give the treaty a majority vote of 49 to 35. But the treaty failed by 7 votes to secure the necessary two-thirds. Twenty-three Democrats and 12 Republicans (the irreconcilables who wanted no league and thus no treaty under any circumstance) voted against it. It was ironic that the Wilson Democrats and the irreconcilables joined hands to defeat the treaty. Even if the treaty with the reservations had been approved by the Senate it is doubtful whether Wilson would have ratified it, because he did intimate that he would refuse to proclaim it if the Senate adopted it with the reservations. So the treaty was dead, and the Senate, on Lodge's motion, returned it to the president.

Defeat of the treaty meant the United States was still legally at war with Germany and Austria. On 15 May 1920, Congress adopted a joint resolution repealing the war resolutions of 1917 and reserving to the United States all rights under the Versailles Treaty. Wilson vetoed this resolution on the ground it "would place an ineffable stain upon the gallantry and honor of the United States." So legally the war did not end for the United States until 2 July 1921 when Congress passed another joint resolution declaring the end of hostilities, which President Harding signed.

Who was responsible for the American rejection of both the treaty and the league? This question is still debated. Wilson and Lodge are largely responsible. Both were inflexible and unyielding in their demands and unwilling to compromise in "this costly failure of American statesmanship." Their personal feud and passionate hatred for one another played the major role in this high drama. Lodge's estimate of Wilson was that "Mr. Wilson in dealing with every great question thought first of himself," because he "was devoured by the desire for power." Wilson equally loathed Lodge telling Senator James Watson, "Accept a treaty with Lodge's reservations? Never, never. I'll never consent to adopt any policy with which that impossible man is so prominently identified." Traditional isolationists and, in particular, the irreconcilables must also share some of the responsibility. They wanted no league of any sort, and their description of it as a "treacherous un-American scheme" to send "our boys to fight throughout the world" probably frightened and misled Americans about what they might have to do as a member of the league.

Wilson lived on quietly for several years in Washington after leaving the presidency. Not long before his death, a crowd gathered before his home on Armistice Day, in November 1923. He came out to thank them and then suddenly spoke again with all his fervor: "Just one word more; I cannot refrain from saying it. I am not one of those who have the least anxiety about the triumph of the principles I have stood for. I have seen fools resist Providence before, and I have seen their destruction.... That we shall prevail is as sure as that God reigns."

Further Reading

Bailey, Thomas A. *Woodrow Wilson and the Great Betrayal.* 1945.
_____. *Woodrow Wilson and the Lost Peace.* 1944.
Baker, R. S. *Woodrow Wilson and World Settlement.* 3 vols., 1922.
Birdsall, Paul. *Versailles Twenty Years After.* 1941.
Czernin, Ferdinand. *Versailles, 1919.* 1964.
Fleming, Denna F. *The United States and the League of Nations.* 1932.
Floto, Inga. *Colonel House at Paris.* 1980.
Garraty, John A. *Henry Cabot Lodge.* 1953.
Gelfand, Lawrence E. *The Inquiry: American Preparations for Peace, 1917-1919.* 1963.
Hoover, Herbert. *The Ordeal of Woodrow Wilson.* 1958.
Kennan, George F. *Russia Leaves the War.* 1956.
Levin, N. Gordon, Jr. *Woodrow Wilson and World Politics: America's Response to War and Revolution.* 1968.
Mamatey, Victor S. *The United States and East Central Europe, 1914-1918.* 1957.

Mayer, Arno J. *Politics and Diplomacy in Peacemaking: Containment and Counterrevolution at Versailles, 1918-1919.* 1967.

Nicholson, Harold. *Peacemaking, 1919.* 1933.

Rudin, Harry R. *Armistice, 1918.* 1944.

Schwabe, Klaus. *Woodrow Wilson, Revolutionary Germany and Peacemaking, 1918-1919.* 1985.

Stone, Ralph A. *The Irreconcilables: The Fight Against the League of Nations.* 1970.

Stromberg, Roland N. *Collective Security and American Foreign Policy.* 1963.

Thompson, John M. *Russia, Bolshevism, and the Versailles Peace.* 1966.

Tillman, Seth P. *Anglo-American Relations at the Paris Peace Conference of 1919.* 1961.

Walworth, Arthur. *America's Moment: 1918.* 1977.

Index

The Shaping of Modern America, 1877-1920,
Second Edition, was copyedited by Martha
Kreger and proofread by Andrew Davidson.
The index was compiled by Schroeder Edito-
rial Services. Production manager was Judith
Almendáriz. The book was typeset by Point
West, Inc., and the first run was printed and
bound by Edwards Brothers, Inc.

Cover design by Roger Eggers and Judith
Almendáriz.